IT HAPPENS
EVERY SPRING

It Happens Every Spring

DIMAGGIO, MAYS, THE SPLENDID SPLINTER, & A LIFETIME AT THE BALLPARK

IRA BERKOW

TRIUMPH
BOOKS

Library of Congress Cataloging in Publication Data available upon request.

The following pieces in this book first appeared in various publications, and herewith appreciation for permission where needed:

Essays in the following books: "The Extraordinary Life and Times of Ping Bodie," *Reaching for the Stars: A Celebration of Italian Americans in Major League Baseball.* "Ralph Branca," *Extraordinary Lives* (an American Express anniversary publication). "The Shooting of Eddie Waitkus," *Baseball's Natural: The Story of Eddie Waitkus.* "What Would Koufax Have Said?" *Chasing Dreams: Baseball and Becoming American* (from the National Museum of American Jewish History). "A Boy, A Man, A Ball Park," *Wrigley Field: An Oral and Narrative History of the Home of the Chicago Cubs.* "Red Smith: The Shakespeare of the Press Box," *Red Smith on Baseball: The Game's Greatest Writer on the Game's Greatest Years.* "They Served Ice Cream Every Friday," *The Jerome Holtzman Baseball Reader.* "Jim Bouton and the Author," *To the Hoop: The Seasons of a Basketball Life.*

The following first appeared in print or in online magazines: "The President Appears at a Ball Game," NBCSportsUniversal.com. "Can the Cubs Really Be for Real This Time?" and "Yes, For Real They Were," National Sports Media Association. "McGwire and Sosa," The World of Fine Wines. "Bruce Gardner," Inside Sports. "Jim Woods," Chicago Magazine. "Painting with Words," Creative Non-fiction.

All other column and feature stories in this collection that were written between 1967 and 1977 appeared first in the Newspaper Enterprise Association syndication; all other column and feature stories here that were written from 1981 to 2006 appeared first in *The New York Times.*

All columns and feature stories prior to 1981 are reissued with permission of Newspaper Enterprise Association. All columns and feature stories after 1981 are reissued with permission of The New York Times Co.

This book is available in quantity at special discounts for your group or organization. For further information, contact:

Triumph Books LLC
814 North Franklin Street
Chicago, Illinois 60610
(312) 337-0747
www.triumphbooks.com

Printed in U.S.A.
ISBN: 978-1-62937-318-8
Design by Prologue Publishing Services, LLC
Page production by Patricia Frey

For Dolly

Contents

Introduction

BY A HAPPY AND, as it turned out, remarkable coincidence, I happened to be a guest in a private suite at the Nationals Park in Washington, D.C., on a warm evening on June 20, 2010, and had come to observe the latest big-league pitching phenom, young Stephen Strasburg, when who should walk into the box but a tall, thin black man wearing an engaging toothy smile and a White Sox cap—he's from Chicago and the Sox are the opponents this night. The tall, thin black man happens to be the president of the United States, Barack Obama.

What transpires over the next two and a half hours—with unfettered and cordial conversational access virtually unheard of with the person who is sometimes referred to as "the most powerful man in the world"—became an essay I wrote for NBCSportsworld.com, and is the lead of the baseball pieces included in this book, some of which subscribe generally to what has come to be called "long form" while others include shorter-length pieces such as those I wrote in my *New York Times* "Sports of the Times" columns. For the most part, the contents of this book are a compendium of stories, from George Steinbrenner to Mickey Mantle to Casey Stengel to Jackie Robinson to Tom Seaver to Yogi Berra to Sandy Koufax—often with personal interviews with each—to less famous but in my view no less historical and no less compelling baseball figures, such as in the piece titled "The Extraordinary Life and Times of Ping Bodie." Bodie was an outfielder for nine seasons in the big leagues and a daffy inspiration for a major character in Ring Lardner's enduring and hilarious baseball stories.

In the best of all possible baseball worlds, I envision the author and the reader taking a long journey together, say cross country by train or by car, and the conversation turns to baseball—the characters, the drama, the humor, the moments that remain indelible in a sportswriter's memory, going back, for me, essentially half a century.

Perhaps the companion, or one of the companions, on this trip is another sportswriter, or even a former ballplayer or manager, who has his own stories—and he or she definitely would, and would decidedly want to share in the recollections and, such is my experience, take pleasure in their telling. ("You were there the historic night Pete Rose singled and passed Ty Cobb on the all-time hit list? What was that like? What is Rose like?") But in this case, I'm reminded of the opening paragraph of a Dylan Thomas autobiographical tale called "Reminiscences of Childhood": "I like very much people telling me about their childhood, but they'll have to be quick or else I'll be telling them about mine."

"I was born…" Well, you get the picture. But what also resonated with me in that story was his description of a park in the "large Welsh town" that he grew up in: "And that park grew up with me; that small world widened as I learned its secrets and boundaries, as I discovered new refuges and ambushes in its woods and jungles; hidden homes and lairs for the multitudes of imagination, for cowboys and Indians, and the (big) terrible half-people who rode on nightmares through my bedroom…"

And such in some ways—not all, to be sure—were identifiable to me as I, as it were, born and raised in Chicago and a Cubs fan, spending considerable boyhood afternoons in Wrigley Field, as described in another of the essays in this book, "Wrigley Field: The Boy, the Man, and the Ballpark," actually lived to see a day that seemed so unlikely, a dream deferred, for much of my life. It was the day, rather the night of November 2, 2016, that the Cubs—striving and failing, striving and failing for 108 years to win a World Series, like a knickered reincarnation of the mythological Sisyphus, condemned for eternity to push a boulder up a hill only to have it forever fall back down—these same now faux-Sisyphean Cubs finally succeeded to ascend the mountain, weighted down with all their historic baggage, and won the World Series.

They outlasted the gritty Indians in a most dramatic, extra-inning Game 7, following a rain delay after the ninth inning that seemed to have been concocted by MGM in Tinseltown to keep the suspense tingling.

I had written a piece for a website early in the 2016 season with the headline: "Can the Cubs Really Be for Real This Time?" Following the season, I concluded with, "The Answer Is…" Both are included in this book.

Like most young fans, I grew up not with nightmares of the seductive North Side park—this one ivy-walled with a miraculously green field—but with glorious dreams of one day playing for the Cubs, as delineated in "The Shooting of Eddie Waitkus," as well as my pride in playing in early June of 1957 against Jim Woods in our senior year of high school, he at Lane Tech and me at Sullivan in the Chicago Public League, and *three weeks later*, following our graduation, the 17-year-old Woods—at six feet, 175 pounds, no bigger than me, but at a vastly different talent level—was signed by the Cubs (he pitched against us but was signed as a hard-hitting and hard-throwing third baseman) and immediately placed on the roster and was in the Cubs dugout—uniform No. 15, an actual big-leaguer!

As I grew older, and became a sportswriter I, like Dylan Thomas, began to learn some of the secrets of the ballfield, and a mentor, among many others, in this regard was none other than that fabled and cerebral Hall of Fame hurler Tom Seaver. In my piece on him here he sagely explains the mix of art and science from the mound. "I remember when I was a rookie with the Mets and facing Henry Aaron for the first time," said Seaver. "Henry was my idol because of his consistency. I threw him a slider down and away and got him to hit into a double play. I thought to myself, 'Gee, this is easy.' I threw him the same pitch the next time he came up, and he hit it into the left-field stands for a two-run homer. That taught me to start thinking more than I ever had before. And I found that the game continues to shift, and there are no absolutes. Each batter, each situation, each pitch I throw is dependent on so many variables."

As a writer I, to be sure, had my own learning experiences in the art of composition, and observation. I ran across a small book, *Painting as a Pastime*, by Winston Churchill, in which he writes that before he took up painting in middle age, he had never taken notice of the dramatic shadows on buildings at various times of day, primarily daybreak and dusk. This insight opened my own eyes to see more when writing about a sports event, as I hoped to do when, for example, describing an at-bat in what would be the last season in the 22-year career of the great Willie Mays, soon to be 42 years old. It was in a 1973 spring training game in St. Petersburg, Florida, and I noticed the shadow extended by his presence in the batter's box. On a 3-2 pitch, I wrote, "he and his shadow took a mighty swing at an outside-corner curveball. 'Whoo' went the crowd. But Mays' effort was fruitless. He struck out.

"Mays walked back to the bench: his shadow trailed behind. The shadow was longer than before. The sun was lower. It was later in the afternoon." It was metaphor that I had sought, and whether it succeeded or not, Willie didn't. He retired after that season, with an uncommonly low .211 batting average, nearly a hundred points below his career average (.302).

If, upon reading this book, you hear a train whistle and the muffled clickety-clack of the train on its tracks, it may only be your imagination as the stories proceed apace. Or, in fact, you might just be reading it on a train traveling cross-country.

I.

HEADLINERS

The President Appears at a Ballgame

July 28, 2015

ON THURSDAY, JUNE 17, 2010, I was having lunch in a restaurant near my home in Manhattan with Bill Marovitz, a friend from Chicago, where I was born and raised. Marovitz, of medium build and with a thick thatch of sandy hair, is a former Illinois state senator and possesses a broad smile that surely helped him get elected several times in his Gold Coast district of lakefront Chicago. Marovitz is friends with Jerry Reinsdorf, principal owner of the Chicago White Sox, and the Chicago Bulls. When Marovitz was in the state senate, in 1988, he co-sponsored a bill to keep the White Sox in Chicago rather than, as team ownership threatened, to have the franchise moved to Tampa–St. Petersburg unless it would get a tax break on building a new ballpark. Marovitz was the political face of the bill, appearing on television on numerous occasions and being quoted in newspapers with, "Let's keep the White Sox where they belong, in Chicago. What's it say about a city that can't keep a valuable franchise like this big-league ballclub?"

And Marovitz meant it. He is a fervent sports fan, especially when it comes to the White Sox. (He had even been known to attend a play in a downtown theater while listening to a Sox game with a transistor radio earpiece glued to his ear.) And the bill allowing the use of public funds passed, narrowly, enabling the White Sox to build and finance their present ballpark, U.S. Cellular Field, across 35th Street from old Comiskey Park (now a parking lot). The passing of that bill most surely had something to

3

do with Reinsdorf later smiling when Marovitz would come into his view. And they became very friendly.

"I'm going to D.C. tomorrow," Marovitz was now saying to me. "Strasburg is pitching against the White Sox tomorrow night and Jerry'll be there in a suite." Stephen Strasburg was the new pitching phenom for the Washington Nationals. "Why don't you join us? It'll be great."

"He invited you?" I said.

"Sure."

"I'd love to see Strasburg pitch, but if I'm going to sit in Reinsdorf's box, maybe you should ask him if it's okay. If it's not I still have my Lifetime Baseball Writer's card. I'll go down with you and sit in the press box. Been there before."

"No, I'll call Jerry. It'll be fine. I'll let him know you're coming with me."

In my 26 years as a sports columnist for *The New York Times* (retired in 2007), a writer for the paper wouldn't want to be caught dead—even worse, *alive*—in the suite or box of an owner of a team you were covering. It would have the odor of non-objectivity, of being bought off for a chance to hobnob with the swells, something that one could never be accused of while ensconced in the press box. A stringent policy against cozying up—or appearing to cozy up—to Movers and Shakers had been laid down for years by *Times* editors. I'd been gone from the paper for three years now, and, yes, career experiences are hard to shake, but I considered myself a free agent, and decided to take up Reinsdorf's—and Bill's—offer.

I had known Jerry Reinsdorf for 30 years, and had a good journalistic relationship with him. As for Strasburg, this would be only his third game in the major leagues. In the previous two games, starting both, he had struck out a total of 22 batters—a record start for a pitcher. Some baseball pundits were calling him the next Bob Feller or Bob Gibson, Hall of Fame fireballers. June 18 would be his second start in a home game. Like most baseball fans, Reinsdorf—who would be given a suite and adjoining box by the Nationals as is a league courtesy to a visiting team's owner—was surely eager to see the 21-year-old Strasburg pitch—and now the heralded rookie was going up against his team.

On the morning of June 18, Bill Marovitz and I met at Penn Station on Seventh Avenue and we took the Acela train to Washington, checking the newspapers for late news on the game and on Strasburg—and the weather. We had no need for rain.

As the train whizzed along through the New Jersey countryside and past towns that emerged however briefly outside the car window, I'm sure we talked about the previous two outings of Strasburg, the No. 1 pick in the major-league draft of 2009, who was a pitching marvel at San Diego State and in a brief minor-league career. In his major-league debut on June 8, 10 days before Bill and I boarded our train to Washington, Strasburg had struck out 14 Pittsburgh Pirates—including every batter in the starting lineup—only one strikeout short of the record for a rookie debut. His fastball was clocked as high as an astounding 100 mph. Strasburg's second outing five days earlier, against Cleveland, was only a bit less impressive, eight strikeouts in 5⅓ innings. His won-lost record was now 2–0. "He was," wrote *Sports Illustrated*, "the most hyped and closely watched pitching prospect in major-league history." Perhaps an exaggeration, but name one pitcher more hyped and more closely watched. As I recall, the conversation went something like this:

"Doc Gooden of the Mets?" said Bill.

"Not quite like this in his first games, I don't think," I said.

"Bob Feller?"

"No TV in his day. And he played for Cleveland, not a big national newspaper story, either."

"Christy Mathewson?"

"Hardly even *radio* in his time. And the telegraph wouldn't have done the trick. When was the Pony Express, anyway?"

And thus the train rattled on to D.C. Trenton came and went. So did Philadelphia and Wilmington.

"Do you think Obama might show up for the game?" Bill mused. "He's a great White Sox fan, and a great baseball fan."

"Great sports fan. He loves basketball, still plays. I have friends who played with him at the East Bank Club."

"I worked out there with him—in the weight room! When he was in the Illinois Senate."

"Well, in basketball, a friend who has played with him there said that they close off the court and if you guard him too closely the Secret Service guys run out and push you back."

"Hadn't heard that," said Marovitz, with a chuckle. "Funny thing, when Obama was asked to throw out the first ball at the All-Star Game in St. Louis last year, MLB wanted him to wear a Cardinals jacket. He refused."

"Refused?"

"Yeah, he insisted on wearing a White Sox jacket. And that's what he wore."

"I remember him wearing the jacket."

"He threw out the first pitch at the Nationals opener in April, and wore the Nationals jacket—but he wore his White Sox cap—he had hid it in his glove."

"Doesn't give up."

"But I'll bet he's as curious about Strasburg as everyone else," said Bill. "Hey, Reinsdorf's even coming in from Chicago for the game."

"So?"

"So if Obama's in town I'd bet he'd give it serious thought. Jerry told me that he invited him to the game but doesn't know if he'd come."

"But he is kinda busy these days—dealing with the world…"

"You never know," said Marovitz.

"That would be something," I said. Years later, I learned that Secret Service had checked out the stadium a week prior to the game just in case the President was able to make it.

Bill had known Obama for several years. Besides having worked out with him, he had also organized a fundraiser for him at the Park West concert hall in Chicago when Obama was running for the U.S. Senate from Illinois, in 2004, and elicited entertainers like Stevie Wonder and Robin Williams to perform. Marovitz acted as master of ceremonies for the event.

We rumbled out of a stop in Baltimore and very soon we were at Union Station, D.C. Bill and I made our way through the throngs, caught a cab to our hotel, dropped off our stuff, freshened up, and at around 4:30 caught the Metro subway Green Line to Nationals Park and the first pitch of the game, which would be with Strasburg on the mound in the top of the first inning, scheduled for 7:05.

As we emerged from the train station, it was still rather early for the game but we saw despite that that traffic was heavy around the park. It was a beautiful, balmy night. In the twilight of a clear sky, with only a hint of twinkling stars, the stadium lights glowed in the distance. Bill and I flowed into the mostly shirt-sleeve crowd of fans, some topped by cherry-red Nationals caps with the letter "W" scripted on the front and others with cameras looped about their necks. There was a palpable anticipation. I imagine it's that way with aficionados in Madrid streaming to the Plaza de Toros to see the new hot toreador, or, in medieval times in England, a crush of nobles and vassals in sight of the castle battlements to check out the latest, greatest jousting knight. We walked the long block along Half Street to our destination.

As we got closer, a bright red sign on the façade came into view: NATIONALS PARK. Beyond it, a portion of the blue-seat upper decks seemed beckoning. To the left was the center-field scoreboard, a kind of colossus. Bill and I turned left on N Street to the Will Call window, and picked up our tickets, the tops of which read NATSTOWN, and below that, under Row, it stated LINCOLN SUITE II. I still carried my Baseball Writer's card in my pocket just in case there was a problem, and I'd simply repair to the press box, if need be.

At the elevator to the luxury suites we ran into Jerry Reinsdorf, waiting to ascend. Reinsdorf seemed pleased to see us. "Great night for a game," he said greeting us, his voice gentle, though a bit raspy. His graying hair was combed in a boyish wavelet at the top of his high forehead, his eyes behind horn-rimmed glasses were direct. He carried a slight paunch. Reinsdorf had been a powerful voice among the owners, most notably in toppling then commissioner Fay Vincent and elevating Bud Selig to the post. Reinsdorf can be sentimental to his roots, which are in Flatbush, Brooklyn. Though he left Brooklyn to attend Northwestern University Law School and remained in

Chicago and amassed a fortune in real estate, he has hung on the walls of his Chicago office photographs of Flatbush's long-gone Ebbets Field. Reinsdorf also can be self-deprecating: some 20 years earlier we had gone to dinner in Chicago and went to his private club. I had insisted on paying, since the *Times* policy was to foot the bill at all times, if possible, but this was his private club and he would just sign the bill, so I'd have to take a rain check on buying him dinner. He hadn't made a reservation and asked the tuxedoed maître d' if he had a table. "Of course, sir," the man said, "right this way." "It's amazing," Reinsdorf whispered to me as we walked, "the influence you can have if you happen to know Michael Jordan." Reinsdorf, after all, was the owner of the basketball team in Chicago that Air Jordan played for.

Both Reinsdorf and Marovitz wore sport jackets with shirts open at the collars. I wore just a long-sleeve shirt, no jacket, and so was, for a sportswriter, even a former one, under-dressed, I felt, though not quite as rumpled as, say, *The Odd Couple*'s Oscar Madison.

At the door to the second-tier suite, we were met by two well-built men in business suits who were checking IDs, and with a list of names on clipboards. "Odd, they aren't your conventional ushers," I thought. "Is this how suites work?" Inside were hot plates with a variety of food and drinks and an assortment of people as well, including the mustachioed David Axelrod, the senior adviser to President Obama, and who was friendly with Reinsdorf and obviously now a guest of his. I had met Axelrod several months earlier, when my wife and I were invited to his office in the White House, following an exchange of emails. We had a Chicago political connection of sorts—he being a political consultant in the city and I was the son of a former Chicago precinct captain under the first Mayor Daley. We had a newspaper connection, as well, since he had been a political columnist for the *Chicago Tribune*. He was also a baseball fan, a season-ticket holder with the Cubs, but he also followed the White Sox and was a basketball fan, like his boss in the Oval Office. On a shelf in his office Axelrod proudly displayed a basketball signed by Bill Russell who rarely signed autographs, but did for Axelrod when the former Boston Celtic great had been honored at the White House. This autograph read simply, YO DAVID. BILL RUSSELL.

There was some small talk: I remember Axelrod asking Reinsdorf if the Bulls had a chance to land LeBron James, then a free agent from the Cleveland Cavaliers. Reinsdorf said that he and a few members of the Bulls had gone to Akron, LeBron's hometown, to try to lure him to Chicago. "I don't think we persuaded him," said Reinsdorf. I was about to say something when Axelrod put his hand on my arm. "Wait," he said, with a smile, "this might be breaking news!" Reinsdorf continued, "But I think he's going to stay with the Cavs." It turned out that Reinsdorf was only half right about LeBron—no Bulls and no Cavs, either; James, of course, signed with the Miami Heat.

It was getting close to game time. Most of us walked out from a door of the glass-enclosed suite and into the box. Ed Rendell, the former governor of Pennsylvania, and Janet Napolitano, then the Homeland Security Secretary, remained in the suite for much of the game, as I recall. Reinsdorf did as well—and almost never sat down while nervously rooting for his team.

Rendell, Reinsdorf, and Napolitano were talking about sports broadcasters. "All they do is talk about the obvious, work a few hours and then are off," said Reinsdorf, with a laugh.

"Gee, sounds like a great job," said Napolitano, "how can I get a job like that?"

Axelrod; a man named Eric Whitaker, a long-time friend of Axelrod's; Ken Williams, White Sox general manager; Marovitz and I took our seats, which were located on the third-base side of the field. All of us were surely guests of the owner, and baseball fans. For whatever reason, I thought nothing more of it. There were two rows of cushioned seats, 14 in each row. We all sat in the second row. Axelrod sat to my left and Marovitz to my right, at the left side of the row of seats, with several seats empty to the right. Just below us over the railing was the grandstand, now mostly filled with the baseball fans nestling into their seats—attendance would be listed at 40,325, nearly capacity—only soon to stand again for the national anthem (Jerry Krause, the former general manager of Reinsdorf's Bulls, once told me that if he were to write a book of his experiences, he'd title it *Ten Thousand National Anthems*).

Beyond those fans just below us was the lush green and clean tan of the ballfield, the stark white bases seemingly popping up like mushrooms on the base paths, the ballplayers trotting out to take their positions, and beyond that the bleachers and the hulking center-field scoreboard that nearly seemed out of place in this otherwise serene setting.

On the mound now taking his warmup tosses was the swiftly acclaimed rookie Strasburg, a strapping 6-foot-4 right-hander, throwing in a sweeping overhand motion, and looking quite cool as his pitches popped into the catcher's mitt. His red cap was tugged low, his red jersey top bore the number 37, his white knickers were tucked just below his knee and thus showed his long red stirrup socks. From my vantage point, I could also make out a clump, as it were, of facial hair clinging to his chin—perhaps a proud symbol of maturity for someone who was not considerably past voting age.

The White Sox, however, seemed not as altogether taken with Strasburg as was the local fandom, to say nothing of the rest of the country. Juan Pierre, Chicago's speedy leadoff batter, managed a slow roller to the first baseman, with Strasburg a little slow coming off the mound to cover first base for the toss. Base hit. Pierre was followed in the lineup by shortstop Omar Vizquel, who—a right-handed batter swinging late on a sizzling fastball—promptly lifted a bloop to right that wound up a double. Pierre stopped at third. Strasburg tugged again at his cap, kicked a little dirt around the mound in apparent slight frustration, and then got Alex Rios, next up, to ground out weakly to first, but Pierre scored. Vizquel made it to third, but went no farther as Strasburg struck out the next two batters. The crowd clamorously expressed its approval. However, despite no solid blows by Chicago, Strasburg's team was behind 1–0 before it even came to the plate. On first sight, though—and in the first inning—it certainly appeared that Stephen Strasburg had a million-dollar arm—actually, $2 million, which was his salary for the 2010 season.

It was around this time that there was a sudden murmur in our box and we looked up to see coming through the door and down the few steps a tall, light-skinned black man in a black-and-white White Sox cap, a white short-sleeve shirt, blue jeans, and white sneakers—followed by two young girls. It was the President of the United States and his daughters, 11-year-old Malia and nine-year-old Sasha.

The President was all smiles, and energetic, fairly bounding down the stairs, though not too bounding since he had a plastic cup of beer in his hand. It was as though, at least on this gentle night, and in only his 16th month as "The Leader of the Free World," *and* commander in chief, the burdens for the 48-year-old President—from Congressional obstacles for his economic programs to the Mideast to say nothing of crumbling bridges and rutted roads—seemed cast aside. He gave Bill a warm greeting, and shortly after, the President came to me.

"I'm Ira Berkow," I said. He shook my hand firmly and said, "I know who you are. You wrote a lot of Knick columns with the *Times*, and you wrote *Rockin' Steady* with Clyde."

"Yes," I replied.

"I bought the book when I was..." (He paused, as though searching his memory.) "I was 12 years old. I loved all the fashion stuff and how to catch flies with your bare hands."

I smiled. "Some memory," I said. Not only did he recall specifics in the book, he referred familiarly to my co-author, Walt Frazier, as "Clyde," the former star Knicks guard's basketball nickname. At the compliment, Obama smiled with all his bright white teeth—a smile that editorial cartoonists love to depict—adding an incandescence to the box.

"*Rockin' Steady* is being reissued in hardcover in October," I added. "I'll be happy to send you a copy."

"Why don't you and Clyde come to the White House and give me an autographed copy?"

"Oh, absolutely," I said.

I knew, of course, that he was a great basketball fan, and when he was 12 he was probably thinking of making the Punahou High School basketball team in a few years (he was sixth man on its Hawaiian state championship team), and *Rockin' Steady*, an off-beat coffee-table basketball instructional book, was popular, especially with fans of Clyde. Besides how to dribble and shoot, the book also highlighted Clyde's unusual, if not sometimes weird, wardrobe, along with diagrams of Clyde demonstrating his quick hands by catching flies both in the air and in a standing position. (I neglected to ask the President how his fly-catching was these days, though a year before he was shown killing a pesky fly in the Oval Office during a televised interview—he watched, waited, and then when the buzzing fly to landed on Obama's left hand he then swiftly, with cupped right hand, swatted down and it was curtains for the intruder—impressive, but not quite the same thing, alas, though maybe *Rockin' Steady* served as inspiration. Retrieving a napkin after the TV interview, Obama neatly picked up the deceased fly from the carpet.)

The President asked me what I thought of Game 7 of the NBA Finals, in which the Los Angeles Lakers defeated the Boston Celtics, played the night before. I said I thought it was exciting, if not artistic. He nodded, and then his attention was diverted to say hello to someone else, and moved on, though not too far, since it was a small box.

While the Presidential kids took a seat in the first row with two men not identified to me, I assumed they were Secret Service, Obama eventually took a seat to the right of Marovitz in the second row. Shortly before, I had overheard Bill asking Axelrod, "What should I call him? Barack or Mr. President?" He hadn't called him anything yet.

Since the two were sitting essentially inches from me, I leaned over, as a participant in the conversation.

Bill said, "Mr. President, the Mideast, and peace, that has to be a tough thing to deal with."

"I'm doing the best I can for peace over there. Not easy," said Obama. Indeed, one of his first actions in office was to send Sen. George Mitchell to Israel and Palestine. Mitchell had recently negotiated a peace in Northern Ireland and Obama hoped he could do some of the same there. "I want to ensure security for Israel, and have sovereignty for the Palestinians. But I keep running into roadblocks."

"Netanyahu?" said Bill, referring to the Israeli prime minister.

"To a certain extent," replied Obama. "Yes, it's frustrating."

Bill said, "So tell me, how do you handle all the critics, the criticism coming at you all the time?"

"Keep doing what you feel is right. What's in your heart."

Bill said, "You know, just a few short years ago we worked out together at the East Bank Club, and then I was in Arizona when you were making a speech, who would have thought it would end up like this, you President of the United States?"

Obama smiled that broad smile. "I would have," he said evenly.

We talked some baseball. Later Marovitz said, "He exhibited a knowledge about the White Sox that was as great as any ordinary fanatical fan. He was optimistic about the team. He's an optimistic guy."

Strasburg struck out another batter in the second inning, and it caught the President's attention. "He's the real deal, isn't he?" he said.

And we talked basketball. Bill raised a question about whether a superstar player like LeBron James can dictate strategy to his coach, as was rumored he had in Cleveland. "The best coaches run the show—Phil Jackson, Popovich, Sloan," said Obama. "They make certain that they, not the star player, decide the strategy. K.C. Jones told me a story of when he was coaching the Celtics in a playoff game. It was something like 91–91 with 10 seconds to go in the game and the Celtics called timeout. Larry Bird comes back to the team huddle and says, 'Give me the ball. I wanna take the last shot.' Jones says, 'You don't run this team. You don't tell me what plays to run. Go sit down!' Then Jones says to the other players, 'OK, here's what we're going to do. We inbound the ball to Bird and let him take the last shot.'"

Obama told it well and got a genuinely good laugh in response. At about this time Sen. Kent Conrad, a progressive Democrat from North Dakota, came by to greet Obama. The President bade him to take the empty seat to his right. I wasn't able to catch the conversation, though admittedly I tried (a reporter's blood continues through my veins, after all). I remembered that Obama grew more intense and spoke quietly with Conrad. While he periodically kept his eye on the ballgame, Obama also seemed to focus intently on what Conrad was saying.

A few years later, I had an opportunity to speak with Conrad, and asked him if he remembered the conversation with Obama.

"I certainly do," he said. "He seemed kind of down. He was taking heavy criticism for his economic policy. I thought he felt under siege. Wow, he's trying to pull the country from out of a ditch. I remember saying to him, 'There needs to be a narrative, remind people of what you inherited. This country was on the brink of depression. What was occurring before you took office.' Bush would have vetoed any chance for regulation of business practices. We had massive debt. The stew that was cooked there was hard to choke down. Republicans were against anything and everything he tried to do. I told him, 'Stick with your narrative. Gotta keep reminding people. Connect the dots.' He has a high level of natural intelligence, and he's no ideologue. He wants what's best for the country. But I think part of that problem is that because of his makeup he gets bored saying the same thing over and over—in this business you have to. You can't effectively get bored hearing yourself say the same thing over and over, and still lead. Those of us more pedestrian don't necessarily get bored that way."

"I was trying to buck him up," added Conrad. Strasburg had recorded a few more strikeouts during the conversation, and Conrad remembered Obama saying "Whoa, this guy can bring it!"

When Conrad got up to leave, he gave Obama a manly hug and heard him say, "Stay strong." Obama thanked him.

Annette Lerner, wife of the Nationals owner, Ted Lerner, had left her own box to chat briefly with the President. Then Stan Kasten, the president of the Nationals, and onetime president of the Atlanta Braves baseball and Atlanta Hawks basketball teams, dropped by to say hello to Obama. He asked Obama if he had called Phil Jackson to congratulate him on the NBA championship.

"I spoke to Phil," said Obama, "and I tried to reach Doc but couldn't get him." (He referred to Glenn (Doc) Rivers, coach of the Celtics, which came in second to Jackson's Lakers.) Kasten said, 'Let me try.'" (Rivers used to play for the Hawks and maintained a friendship with Kasten.)

"Hey, Glenn," said Kasten on his cell phone. "I have the President here, he wants to say hello." Kasten handed Obama the phone and Obama and Rivers chatted for a few minutes. "Okay," said Obama, signing off, "talk to you soon," and returned the phone to Kasten. (Kasten smiled and, when leaving, said quietly to me, "I can get Doc Rivers on the phone and the President of the United States can't?")

Periodically, Obama took out his BlackBerry and fiddled with it for messages. Axelrod now suggested that we change seats—he had wanted all of us to have some chance to sit next to the president for a chat. And now it was my turn.

I said to the President, "I saw film clips of you shooting a basketball. Looks like you have a nice shot."

"I have some game," he said, with pride.

"Growing up, did you model your game after anyone?" I asked.

"I liked Clyde a lot, but it was Lenny Wilkens. He was a lefty, too."

"I once did a magazine article on Lenny when he was coaching Seattle," I said. "Before going out there, I saw Clyde and asked if he had a question for Lenny. He said, 'Yes, I always knew he was going left, but I could never stop him. Ask him why."

"And what did he say?" asked the President, leaning forward in his seat.

"He said, 'Clyde always knew I was going left—but he never knew when."

"That's like me!" Obama said. "I can still go left against 25-year-olds. They know I'm going left, but don't know when!"

We laughed. I said, "I was talking one day to Jonathan Alter—" "He's a good guy," said Obama. "Yes, he is," I continued, "and we were talking about you and he said, 'Have you read Obama's book *Dreams From My Father*? I said I hadn't. He said it was terrific, beautifully written. He said that when he saw you after reading it, he told you, 'You're ruining it for the rest of us.' So I did read it and I agreed all around with Jonathan," I said.

Obama smiled. "Thank you," said Obama.

"Like a lot of people, though, I wondered if you had really written the book yourself," I said. "I had noticed in the acknowledgements that Ruth Fecych was one of your editors—"

"She's a really good editor," he said, "and I had been with another publisher but didn't get the manuscript in on time and had to go to her publisher—"

"Yes, she's a fine editor. She edited two of my books. And I called her and asked if Obama had really written that book himself. I believed I'd get a straight answer from her. And she said, 'Yes.' And I said, with a recollected mutter, 'Son of a bitch.'" (The essence, which I hoped he caught, was, again, "You're ruining it for the rest of us".) He laughed, I'm happy to report.

Malia came by and told her father that there were now desserts in the suite. "Daddy, do you want some cake?" she asked. "No," he replied, but noticed the rather large chocolate cookie she had. "Can I have a bite?" he asked. Malia handed the cookie to him. He took a generous bite out of it—about half the cookie—and returned it to its owner, who looked with some surprise at the cookie, but said nothing.

At the seventh-inning stretch we all stood up and sang, "Take Me Out to the Ballgame." The President seemed in good tenor voice. The fans nearby had turned more to the President in his box than to the field itself, and waved and shouted hellos and snapped photos with raised smartphones. Upon seeing the President, whose presence was never announced, those fans had to have been utterly surprised, if not totally shocked.

After seven innings, Strasburg was taken out of the game. He had thrown 85 pitches and the manager, Jim Riggleman, was trying to limit the wear and tear on a young pitcher's arm. But Strasburg had given the crowd its money's worth. He allowed just that one run in the first and then shut the White Sox down for the next six innings, striking out 10, to set a major-league record for a pitcher's first three career starts, with 32 Ks. His control was superb; he walked no one. At one point, he retired 15 batters in a row, and in the sixth he recorded two straight strikeouts, on 90-mph changeups for the third swinging strikes, and the last two outs of the inning. However, Washington could score just one run off the Sox's Gavin Floyd, and so Strasburg left the game at 1–1. He would receive a "no decision," neither a win nor a loss. With Strasburg gone, it seemed Obama rooted more openly for the White Sox, with an occasional whoop, "Let's go!" and a hand clap.

With the score still tied at the top of the ninth, Obama rose to leave, but first went down to the first row of the box and reached out to shake hands and make small talk and smile for photos with some of the nearby fans. I noticed that one of the Secret Service men standing in the aisle looked on, if not glowering, then eyeing the situation quite closely, like a hotel detective checking out a suspicious character possibly loitering in the lobby.

Reinsdorf, when he invited the President to the game at first got a No, then a Maybe, still wasn't sure he'd show up—until he did. The President told Reinsdorf at the game that he was not going to stay through nine innings, for the same reason he had come a little late for the start of the game. "He told me that he didn't want his motorcade to snarl traffic," said Reinsdorf, which, I'm sure, was appreciated by the non-Presidential motorists around the ballpark.

When Reinsdorf saw that Obama was preparing to leave, he went into the closet to get some presents (just in case he'd come to the game) for Obama's daughters. They were from Scott Reifert, the Sox's publicity director. Reifert's daughters and Sasha and Malia were friends from Chicago and Reinsdorf had placed the gifts in the suite closet prior to Obama's possible arrival. "Just as I reached in to get the presents," said Reinsdorf, "I saw a leather briefcase that hadn't been there before. I bent to move it out of the way when a very strong hand grabbed my arm and said, 'Don't touch that!' I guess it was 'the football' and the guy with that grip was Secret Service, or a plain-clothes military aide." As I learned "the football" carries with it nuclear information, including retaliatory options, and is always near the President's side, or, as in this case, just a few feet away hidden in a closet.

Obama said farewell to those in the box. When he came to me, I could think of nothing more to say than repeat Sen. Conrad's good-bye, "Stay strong." He looked me in the eye and offered a good handshake. And then he was gone.

The White Sox went on to win in 11 innings, 2–1. A news report the next day stated that the President left the park at 9:18 and his motorcade arrived back at the White House—which is down the road a piece on Pennsylvania Avenue from Nationals Park—at 9:31, having traversed from southeast

Washington to northwest Washington. The last out of the game was made at precisely 10:00, Nationals center fielder Nyjer Morgan grounding out to second base. My guess is that the President, with or without his Sox cap, watched the end of the game from the Lincoln bedroom, or thereabouts, and was pleased with its outcome.

Marovitz and I had planned to catch a cab back to our hotel, but thought we'd have trouble getting one in the crowd. "I imagine Jerry came in a limo," said Bill. "Do you think I should ask him for a ride back?"

"Why not?" I said. "That's the least he can do for us." (When as a young reporter I was once told by an old sportswriter, "When you freeload, bitch, you maintain dignity.")

Jerry said he came on the team bus and we were welcome to ride back with him and the players, and naturally we accepted. It wasn't the Presidential motorcade, but it was fine. And the end to a most remarkable night.

Dear Mickey: Messages and Prayers for an American Hero

June 25, 1995

DALLAS, TEXAS—The letters and get-well cards and telegrams flood into the hospital every day, filling up boxes that begin to cover a wall, disconcerting some of the staff with the sheer volume—"tens of thousands," by one estimate—and, in a way, painting a portrait of America, its hunger for a hero, its love of a self-described flawed sports star, its embrace of and identification with an American dream and the face of the American nightmare.

Most send their correspondence to "Mickey Mantle/Baylor University Medical Center/Dallas, Texas." One, though, wrote "Mikey," another "Mickey Mantle/Dallas, Tex.," another "Mickey Mantle—patient," as if to try to avoid possible confusion, and yet another mailed his postcard to, simply, "#7/Baylor Hospital/Dallas," as though the post-office sorters, and the whole world, for that matter, must know without a doubt who is identified that way. The digit being the former Yankee center fielder's uniform number. Hundreds of letters were also sent to Mickey Mantle's Restaurant on Central Park South in Manhattan.

Mantle, who is 63 years old, is now recovering from a liver transplant performed June 8, after a cancer had been removed and cirrhosis from a lifetime of alcohol abuse had been diagnosed. His outlook is good despite indications last week that his body is slightly rejecting his new liver. As a player, he is remembered not only for his switch-hitting, home-run-producing

19

exploits, but for the fact that he played with injuries and did so without complaint, until he retired as a ballplayer in 1968, at age 36, after 18 big-league seasons.

The letters come from men and women, boys and girls, professional people—from doctors and professors to lawyers and businessmen—and blue-collar workers, from every state in the union, and Canada and Mexico and around the world.

Ages range from "a senior citizen of 88" to a lass of nine who plays second base on a coach-pitch Little League team named the Red Birds in Canton, Texas, and wears No. 7, too.

The letters offer hope, inspiration, and, most of all, heartfelt gratitude for what the former baseball slugger, the legend, the image, has meant in their sometimes lonely, sometimes frustrated, sometimes tortured lives.

"I am a 21-year-old college student so I am too young to have ever seen you play," wrote Kyle Fletcher of Kennedale, Texas, "but your name has spanned the generations. It is also a fact that you overcame such physical adversity in your childhood in order to achieve your dreams. I was born with spina bifida. Doctors told me that I would never walk on my own. However, they were wrong and, although I will never be a great baseball player like you, it is through the example of men like you that I have found the courage to achieve my own personal goals. Not only do I now walk on my own with only the aid of plastic braces on my legs, but I also played high school basketball for three years. I will pray for you until you are back in good health. Forever your friend and loyal fan."

A middle-aged man from Ontario, Canada, wrote: "Every young lad should have a real-life hero to look up to, and maybe you don't really real-ize it, but you have single-handedly guided countless young people in life through your athletic prowess, but just as importantly, through your grit and determination. In my last year of baseball, when I was mired in a bat-ting slump and hitting just .111 and wanted to quit, my dad asked me if I thought that 'Mickey' would just quit. Well, I ended the season with a .591 average and an even greater respect for life and how to handle problems."

"When I was a small girl, my father's idea of a vacation was driving to Kansas City (we lived in Omaha) for a long weekend and watching you and the Yankees play K.C. on Friday night, a day game Saturday, and a double-header on Sunday, then drive home on Monday!" wrote Maureen Austin. "Eventually in high school I played fast-pitch softball. I played center or right field and hit home runs. My father was proud. He said the 'M' in my name was really Mickey. You were my mentor. I used to watch you hit and tried to do it just your way. Lately I've seen interviews and now find you a real nice person. We've never met but I feel like you're a friend who has been around for my lifetime."

"I loved baseball but I did not grow up to become a ballplayer, though I learned from watching you that I could overcome my shortcomings and excel if I just focused my mind and worked very hard," wrote Ken Frankovich, of northern California. "I became a timber faller, and whenever I had an extra-dangerous tree to fall, I had to dig down inside of me and find that courage that you had shown me years earlier.

"For 23 years that courage sustained me. Then four years ago a freak accident occurred and I got my back broken. While recovering, I was laying in the hospital torn by the pain and frustration and the worry of how I was going to feed my family.

"Then I remembered how effortlessly you made playing baseball better than anyone look, and I thought of all the times in my life I had pictured that swing of yours and the way you caught that impossible fly ball. I knew that I could make it and everything would work out. They sent me to junior college and I made almost straight As at the age of 47. I can get around without limping too much and things are O.K."

On the surface, Mantle had seemed the most uncomplicated of heroes, a boy from the sticks of Oklahoma who came to the big city with a straw suitcase, who had a big smile and a big swing, and took Joe DiMaggio's place in the Yankee lineup and in the hearts of millions. The fact that he was complex, or that his life became so, that he was a carouser and an alcoholic, that he was at times a surly man and a poor husband and sometimes an unreachable father to his four sons—and that he has openly admitted such—brings a sense of forgiveness by many.

"When I was a little boy growing up, I had only one real hero, and it was you," wrote Stephen Groo, of Churchton, Maryland. "I know that millions of others felt that way, and still do; but what I understand now, as a 42-year-old man with three kids, is that the hopes and dreams I placed at your feet were also a burden on your shoulders. I know that my hero was also a man, with pain, sorrows, and a deep longing for peace."

"Father's Day is right around the corner and, as a father, I have had to deal with children who once considered me a hero but now see me as a frail human and are, thus, disappointed," wrote Ken Allen, of Tustin, California. "I have a feeling you face the same thing as an 'American Hero.' Sure, you're human! And we fans of baseball have grown up to realize you don't fulfill our childhood memories any longer.

"I saw a replay of an interview where you said you felt bad about letting your fans down. Let me say, you don't need to beat up on yourself. We love you. You are part of us and we are part of you."

Some letter writers reveal other personal agonies to Mantle. "I really wish you could have been my dad," wrote a man from Brownwood, Texas, "'cause my dad put me down all my life, and still does, and it has worked on my mind."

Some people wrote recalling kindnesses that Mantle had extended to them, from talking to them in an elevator to buying them a baseball in a five-and-dime to the following: "We were traveling from L.A. to the East Coast and baby Whitney needed his milk bottle heated," wrote Marguerite Crist, of Ventura, California. "You and your precious wife, Merlyn, helped us in Joplin, Mo., and gave us a safe haven."

A 47-year-old man from Northbrook, Illinois, on his business stationery, wrote, "Last night I heard about your liver problems and felt devastated. I still have trouble explaining my feelings, which closely resemble how I felt when my father died of cancer in 1979. I would be willing to share my liver with you. I have no motivation other than to help someone who I care for very much: someone who has brought me tremendous enjoyment for many years; someone who I think about when my world starts to go down. I am quite serious about my offer, and my family supports me in this decision. I presume there is some type of compatibility testing I would have to undergo, which I would prefer to do in Chicago, if possible. If I qualify, I would be willing to remain anonymous and sign a document saying I would not 'sell' my story to anyone. I want you to know this is a sincere offer, and not motivated by greed."

Several others offered parts of their livers. Some simply sent, to comfort him, pictures of their children or grandchildren or dogs, or of themselves. Many sent religious books and poems. Some asked for autographs. An insurance salesman said that "if you're ever in Indianapolis, and bored, I'd love to buy you lunch." Someone sent best wishes and reminded him that if he's ever in Tallahassee, she happens to be a broker and could sell him "a nice piece of commercial real estate" (she naturally enclosed her card).

People who had had transplants of various sorts, and recovering alcoholics, sent words of encouragement and understanding. "I've been sober since Feb. 23, 1977," wrote a man from Nevada. "I, too, have traveled many of the same dark, lonely paths you have had to walk."

Not everyone, however, was sympathetic. "I do not feel sorry for Mickey Mantle!" wrote R.C., from Hickory, North Carolina. "If he possesses no more strength than this, then he deserves to have progressive liver cancer."

Such sentiments were in the vast minority. Family-like invitations to Mantle were many. A man in New Mexico suggested that as soon as Mantle was out of the hospital, he wished to have him and his family over for a barbecue. And Ed Meyers of Great Falls, Montana, who had a successful kidney transplant, wrote: "Don't give up and maybe someday we can go fishing together. Life can be good. I'm 53, my son's 32, my granddaughter is 7 on the 4th of July, food in the ice box, gas in my truck, friends around, God on my side, how blessed I am."

And another letter arrived recently from another fan, this one in Washington: "Dear Mickey: Hillary and I were so sorry to learn of your health problems. You hold a special place in the hearts of Americans across the country, and I hope that all of our thoughts and prayers will bring strength to you during this difficult time. Sincerely, (signed) Bill Clinton."

Mantle, with his family at his bedside, has begun to walk with help, has started physical therapy, and is undergoing chemotherapy. The prognosis is guarded but promising despite the latest development. "My father has been amazed at the reaction to him, and grateful," said Danny Mantle. "But Dad has never really understood why there has always been such a fuss about him. He never saw himself as an idol or a hero of any sort. He saw himself only as a baseball player who tried to do the best he could."

Mickey Mantle:
"A Day to Remember"

August 14, 1995

ON THIS WARM, SUNNY, gently breezy and otherwise perfect baseball afternoon yesterday, the American flag in left-center field of Yankee Stadium stirred at half-staff.

The game between the Yankees and Cleveland wouldn't start for another 15 minutes, but the scoreboard in center field listed a batter for the Yankees: No. 7.

The Yankees no longer have a player who wears No. 7, and never will again. The number is retired. And the batter's box was empty. But in the mind's eye of many of the 45,866 fans who spun through the turnstiles on this summer day, some of whom had heard the news broadcast that morning and decided to come to the stadium to pay tribute, the presence of No. 7, who hadn't played a game for the Yankees in 27 years, was deeply felt.

"We ask you now to rise," came the sonorous voice of Bob Sheppard over the public-address system. "Today is a sad day for the Yankee family and Yankee fans. Today we have lost one of our own, and one of the greatest players in the history of baseball.

"Please join now for a few moments of silent prayer as we all remember Mickey Mantle."

The DiamondVision screen in right-center showed the back of Mantle's No. 7 pinstriped Yankee uniform, and across it were the words, WITH

Us FOREVER. Everyone in the park stood, including all the Indians and Yankees, who were at the edge of their dugouts, caps in hand, heads bowed.

Earlier, Mel Allen, who had been the Yankee broadcaster through much of Mantle's career, recalled how, in spring training of 1951, the general manager of the team, George Weiss, wanted to send the blond, 19-year-old kid from Oklahoma back to the minors for more seasoning. Casey Stengel, the manager, argued against it. "He hits balls over buildings," said Stengel.

And the kid would stay, to become, in his 18-year major-league career, something even beyond simply a swift Hall of Fame center fielder and the most powerful switch-hitter baseball had ever known. He developed into one of America's icons, one of its most beloved celebrities.

Those who knew him well, like Bobby Murcer, a current Yankee broadcaster, a fellow Oklahoman, and a teammate in Mantle's last seasons, sought to hold back tears when speaking of him, as did some fans in the ballpark during the tribute. "There was no more honest individual than Mickey Mantle," said Murcer.

And that honesty, that vulnerability, that openness to his frailties despite his larger-than-life persona, contributed surely to his popularity, even years after he had rapped the last of his 536 home runs.

He admitted his fears, his failures, his foolishness. On the DiamondVision, there were now film highlights of his career, of his prodigious swing and the touching way he ran gimpily around the bases after having suffered terrible knee injuries. But in later years he talked about how he could have played beyond age 36 if he had not "wasted" the talents God had given him. He confessed to being an alcoholic, a poor father and husband, and to a profligacy wrapped in self-absorption.

While some dreamed of having Mickey Mantle as their father, one of his four sons, Danny, told me recently: "I only began to know my dad when I was about 16. He was just never around much before that. And when I did see him, he was more like a buddy than a father." Mantle would take his sons drinking with him, and all four became alcoholics, too.

And while those who live through nostalgia would forever remember Mantle as Super Hero, he knew otherwise, one reason he "could never understand" the hold he had on America. When he admitted himself into the Betty Ford Center for his alcoholism, he was reduced, one night, according to a family friend, to taking his pillow and blanket in the room he shared with another man and sleeping in the bathtub to distance himself from the snoring of his roommate.

In the restaurant that bears his name on Central Park South, I introduced Mantle to Dr. Isaac Herschkopf. "He's a psychiatrist," I told Mantle. Instead of extending his hand in greeting, Mantle bent and presented his head. "Maybe you can do something with this, Doc," Mantle said.

He rarely took himself too seriously, and, while sometimes short-tempered, he could be funny, often at his own expense. After his recent liver transplant, Mantle said he was going to do all he could to make people aware of how important organ donations were. Would he offer his own organs? "Nobody'd want those things," he said wanly.

He understood, too, how his drinking had debilitated his body. In a news conference last month, looking pale and hardly able to stand, the once lusty slugger said that kids shouldn't look to him as a role model, not the way he had conducted his life off the field. It was honest, it was poignant, it was tragic.

On the DiamondVision at Yankee Stadium after the moments of silence, the crowd cheered a Mantle World Series home run, they cheered a great Mantle catch, they cheered him when he stood at a microphone on June 8, 1969, Mickey Mantle Day at Yankee Stadium, and recalled another ballplayer's "day." Mantle had said: "I didn't know how a man who knew he was going to die could stand here and say, 'I am the luckiest man on the face of the earth.' Now I know how Lou Gehrig felt.'"

A few years after he had retired from baseball I spoke to Mantle at the Yankees' spring training camp in Fort Lauderdale, Florida. He recalled the cheers of the crowd that sounded to him, he said, "like the roar of some animal."

He said he still missed it. "Yep," he said, "the old days were great while they lasted. They just didn't last long enough."

Yesterday at 2:10 AM Eastern time, Mickey Mantle, his body ravaged with cancer, died in his bed at age 63 in the Baylor University Medical Center in Dallas.

Several hours later, at Yankee Stadium, on a perfect baseball afternoon, the crowd again cheered for Mickey Mantle—the tone muted, appreciative, loving, sad.

The sound would echo into baseball history.

Casey Stengel: Ever the Perfesser

September 1, 1991

THE FIRST TIME I saw Casey Stengel in person was in a dugout before an old-timers' game at Shea Stadium, in July of 1968. He had come not to play but as a special guest, a former manager of the Amazin' Mets, as he called them. He was then 78, he said, though one record book disagreed, and stated he was 79. No matter, he looked ancient, like a wizened sage, who could say something profound, but then add a stage wink to remind you that there was humor at the end of the tunnel. Someone once described the late Senator Everett Dirksen of Illinois as having a stained-glass voice. If that were so, then Casey's voice was cracked stained-glass. And his syntax was cloudy but as compelling as rubbings from old churchyard tombstones.

When someone asked him about the lack of hitting in the major leagues then, he said, "They ask you, you ask yourself, I ask you, it's them good young pitchers between 18 and 24 that can throw the ball over the plate and don't kill the manager, isn't it?"

Stengel's white hair, still plentiful, was sun-tinged in spots, and a wave fell across the side of his face, which was wrinkled like a rutted road. His expressive white eyebrows shaded blue eyes that watered now and then, and he wiped his eyes with a handkerchief as large as a hand towel. His tasteful blue suit was specked with light brown, and looked almost natty on him. His hands and gnarled fingers had a kind of grace when making a point that one might expect from a symphony conductor.

And his legs. Of course, his warped old legs. He crossed them at the knee and one foot worked nervously under black executive socks. On his feet were black slippers—he had been suffering pain in the lower extremities. Before ever knowing very much about Casey Stengel, I knew about his legs. I remember reading Damon Runyon's account of old Casey Stengel—he was 33 (or 34), but seemed elderly even then—scoring an inside-the-park home run in the ninth inning of the first game of the 1923 World Series, to give his Giants a 5–4 win over the Yankees:

> "This is the way old 'Casey' Stengel ran yesterday afternoon, running his home run home…
>
> "His mouth wide open,
> "His warped old legs bending beneath him at every stride.
> "His arms flying back and forth like those of a man swimming with a crawl stroke.
> "His flanks heaving, his breath whistling, his head far back…"

Three thousand miles away in California, Edna Lawson, Stengel's fiancée, had proudly showed newspaper clippings of Casey's game-winning blow to her father.

"What do you think of my Casey?" she asked.

Her father shook his head. "I hope," he said, "that your Casey lives until the wedding."

He did, of course, and well beyond. ("For the bridegroom," Casey said when they wed, "it is the best catch he ever made in his career.")

With the other who gathered around Casey in the dugout, I listened, and laughed. But also on that first afternoon that I saw him, I realized something that I had never quite appreciated. The man made some of the most interesting, original, and thoughtful comments on baseball strategy and technique that I'd ever heard, and said it in the most entertaining fashion.

He spoke then, as he would on other occasions, about players he played with or against, from Babe Ruth to Walter Johnson, and about those he managed, from Van Lingle Mungo to Joe DiMaggio and Mickey Mantle, and those he managed against, from Dizzy Dean to Jackie Robinson. Stengel is in the Hall of Fame, having managed the Yankees to 10 pennants and seven World Series titles in 12 years. He managed great players in those years, from 1949 to 1960. But he also had managed some terrible teams, like the Brooklyn Dodgers in the mid-1930s, the Boston Bees (later named the Braves) in the late '30s and early '40s, and the expansion Mets of the early 1960s.

Warren Spahn, who pitched under Casey for the 1942 Braves and the 1965 Mets, said, "I played for Casey before and after he was a genius." Casey would be the first to agree that, as he said, "it was the players that made me what I am." For good or for bad. But he also was an outstanding handler of men, a brilliant teacher, as former players attest, and an inspiration to future outstanding managers who played for him, such as Billy Martin, Whitey Herzog, and Roger Craig.

In 1974 I had written and published—with Walt Frazier of the New York Knicks, then one of basketball's best and most creative players—a rather off-beat instructional book complete with photographs and illustrations titled, *Rockin' Steady: A Guide to Basketball and Cool.* I thought that it would be a terrific thing if I could do the same with Casey Stengel, and call it *Casey Stengel's Inimitable, Instructional, Historical Baseball Book.*

I knew Casey was coming into New York for the annual dinner of the New York chapter of the Baseball Writers' Association of America, and so made an appointment to see him in his hotel room. It was late January, 1974. I remember that we talked about numerous baseball subjects, and at one point, to demonstrate a particular play, he got up from his chair—he was now 84 years old, more or less—and with his bowed, lumpy legs chased down an imaginary ground ball that bounced under the coffee table.

I remember his telling me about one of the most prominent players of the day, who, the next season, would break Babe Ruth's record for career home runs: "Now this fellow in Atlanta is amazin'. He hits the ball the best for a man of his size. But I can't say he hits the ball better than Ruth. Ruth could hit the ball so far nobody could field it. And that's even with the medicinal improvements today. They come along now with the aluminum cup and it improves players who only used to wear a belt and it's better for catching ground balls."

We talked about language. He said, "Today I make speeches all over. People ask me, 'Casey, how can you speak so much when you don't talk English too good?' Well, I've been invited to Europe and I say, they don't speak English over there too good, either."

I got around to telling him about my proposed book in some detail, and I also showed him *Rockin' Steady*. He took the book in his old hands and turned the large-sized, glossy pages packed with color, with great care and interest. When he got to the end and closed the book, he said, "It's a perfection thing." I took that to mean he liked it. I was delighted.

"Will you do it then, Casey?" I asked.

"Let me think about it," he said. "I'll let you know."

His word was good. He did let me know, writing to me at my office—I was then the sports editor and sports columnist for Newspaper Enterprise Association. His letter arrived about two weeks after we had met. It was written in a firm but uneven hand on lined notebook paper. The letter was in blue ink, though the envelope was written in green ink. The envelope, which was personal stationery, announced at the top left:

Casey Stengel
1663 Grandview
Glendale, California 91201

The letter read exactly as follows:

Dear Ira:
Your conversations, and the fact you were the working Writer were inthused with the Ideas was Great but frankly do not care for the great amount of work for myself.
Sorry but am not interested. Have to many propositions otherwise for this coming season.
Fact cannot disclose my Future affairs.
Good luck,
(signed) Casey Stengel
N.Y. Mets & Hall of Famer

It wasn't quite the answer I was hoping for—though otherwise I loved the letter (still do, and of course have saved it). I thought perhaps I'd get a chance to talk with him again about the project, but he died before that could happen, later that following year.

The idea for that book, however, stayed with me. One morning in 1989 I was having breakfast with my friend Jim Kaplan, the highly respected baseball writer, author, and former *Sports Illustrated* staffer. I happened to mention the Stengel idea, and Jim loved it. He said he'd be willing to work on it with me. We agreed to keep it Casey's book, and keep it as close as possible to the idea that Casey had considered.

Though Casey said he "frankly" didn't "care for the great amount of work" for himself, we determined that he wouldn't have minded our doing it for him. Casey, to quote one of his favorite phrases, had "done splendid." Our hope was to capture some of that splendor.

Billy Martin: Something Was Cooking

July 3, 1983

THE CHEF WORE SPIKES. A pair of pork chops was sizzling on the skillet in the kitchenette and he swabbed them with a slab of butter. It was late afternoon of a recent weekday and this scene of tender domestic bliss in the manager's office in Yankee Stadium was unexpected.

The smell was enchanting, unlike the odor generally associated with a baseball locker room. And the chief of cuisine contending with the pork chops was Billy Martin, who is customarily seen in contention with umpires, sportswriters, some players, and assorted owners and barroom acquaintances.

This is the same Billy Martin who has three times been hired and twice fired as manager of the Yankees. Martin, who had been snacking on hard licorice candies from a paper bag, now considered the meat done to his satisfaction and plucked the two pieces with a fork, dropped them on a plate, and carried them from the kitchenette to his desk.

It seemed out of context. "Everyone's gotta eat," Martin explained, as a piece of pork chop disappeared under his gray-black mustache. Despite preparing himself such gastronomic delights, yond Billy retains a lean and hungry look. By his own admission he does not always tuck in early, and he invariably is embroiled in some kind of upheaval.

He is 55 years old. "The speed limit," he says. Yet he hardly seems to have slowed down since he first broke in with the Yankees in 1950 and was described in this newspaper as "the effervescent rookie from the Coast." As years went by, he would run a spectrum of description, from aggressive to pugnacious, from brilliant to paranoid.

About two weeks ago it appeared he was going to be dismissed once again by the Yankees' principal owner, George Steinbrenner. Martin berated a woman doing research for *The New York Times* and ejected her from the clubhouse. The *Times* reported that Martin used obscene language and otherwise verbally abused the woman, and stands by its account. Martin contended she had represented herself poorly in the clubhouse and that he wasn't notified beforehand that she would be there. He maintains he used crude language common to the clubhouse, and no more.

Although Steinbrenner would say that Martin used poor judgment—and that, because of past incidents, his credibility is somewhat shaky—both the principal owner and the American League, after an investigation, exonerated him.

Martin had played for seven major-league teams in 12 years and managed five major-league teams over 12 years—leading teams to five divisional titles, two pennants, and a World Series championship—and may hold some kind of record for most brawls and altercations and incidents off the field and on.

Now, just three months after the start of his third term as the Yankee field leader, he has already been suspended and fined for arguing with and kicking dirt on an umpire; been the focal point of a barroom scuffle; had two clashes with reporters in the Yankee clubhouse; broke a dugout urinal in a tantrum after a loss in Cleveland, and been accused of napping in his office when the team was taking batting practice and of chatting with a female friend beside the dugout while a game was in progress. And he was choked with emotion when his pitching coach and close friend, Art Fowler, was dismissed by Steinbrenner because Martin, said the owner, was ignoring the other coaches.

Meanwhile, the team started shakily, but has since been moving up in the standings, and some of the credit must go to Martin, who has employed such bold and imaginative moves as, in a recent game against Milwaukee, having Willie Randolph bunt for two successive, and successful, suicide-squeeze plays.

Yet, after all that has gone on this season, can baseball be fun anymore for Martin? "It was, up until about a week and a half ago," he said. He was finished with his meal—no vegetables, no drink—and sat back in the chair behind his desk. Behind him is a photograph of Casey Stengel, Martin's beloved mentor, who once described Martin the second baseman as a "hard-nosed, big-nosed kid." Martin would later have his nose bobbed.

"I thought I was being used by some of the newspapers to get at me, to get me fired, to sell papers—even the Pope was mad at me, I knocked him off the front page," said Martin, with hardly a smile. "But I felt it was like vultures hanging over a piece of meat."

On the afternoon of the incident with the female researcher, Martin had earlier learned of the dismissal of Fowler. According to observers, Martin was terribly upset. His thin face was drawn and lined, his eyes were tired.

"Art's been with me for 15 years," said Martin, "and he's one of the best pitching coaches there is. He doesn't overcoach, like a lot of 'em do. Not only that, but he's my bumper. He's my friend and companion. Here, look at this."

Martin turned and pulled out a sheet of paper from a drawer. "This is what Art wrote on the pitching schedule before he left," said Martin. There was a slight quiver in his voice.

The note read: DON'T QUIT—ART. I LOVE YOU. "I was so shaken up when I got to the clubhouse that I went to get a pill to relax me from the trainer, and that's when I saw that girl researcher who I had never seen before," he said.

Martin said he is aware of his reputation as a drinker, that he can't handle liquor, and that whenever there is an incident involving him off the field, the question of his drinking is invariably brought up. After all, some of his most celebrated battles have been at night spots, from the fight at the Copa in 1957, which got him traded from the Yankees, to his punching a marsh-mallow salesman in a bar in 1979, which got him discharged for the second time as manager of the Yankees.

"I don't need to drink," said Martin. "I can go six months in the off-season without having a drink. But then I can go and have a release of hunting and fishing, of going to some remote place where there's just mountains and streams and there's nobody around and I look out and think, 'Isn't this beautiful? Isn't this wonderful?'

"But during the season, with all the pressures, sure I drink, to block certain things out, to get a release. But I never drink before coming to the clubhouse. Sometimes I don't drink before 1:00 or 1:30 in the morning after a game. And I'm no bar-hop like I've been made out to be by some people. I'm like a lot of coaches and managers. I drink in the hotel bar. I live downtown in a hotel in Manhattan, and I drink there. I don't drink in my room, either. In Seattle, I drink in the hotel bar. In Detroit, it's the hotel bar. In Boston, it's the hotel bar, or J.C. Hillary's across the street, or Charley's. They let you alone in those places. In Chicago, it's the hotel bar. In Oakland, it's a little place in Danville, where nobody bothers me, five minutes from my house there." Martin, who grew up in Berkeley, lives in Oakland in the off-season.

"I seem to always be running into turkeys who want to show how tough they are. There's a gunslinger mentality, like the Wild West. 'Oh, Billy Martin, you think you're so tough. I can take you.' A lot of it has to do with my size, too, I think. You don't see anyone picking on Frank Howard."

Nor do people seem to pick on someone like Earl Weaver, who is shorter than both Howard and Martin. "Earl's got this outgoing personality," said Martin. "I want to be left alone. When he's in a bar, he zips on. I zips up. But drinking isn't a new thing, you know, especially among baseball people. Hey, if you took out all the guys in the Hall of Fame who drank, you'd have a pretty empty hall. Don't get me wrong, they were nice guys, they were great guys. But they weren't goody good shoes, either."

"Anyway," he added, "why does somebody always have to be drinking when he gets mad, why can't he just be mad?"

The questions of the effects and the amount of Martin's drinking may be debatable, but Martin has made some public statements when emotionally upset that would later be proved false.

When in 1978, for example, emotionally distraught over threats of being dismissed, he called Reggie Jackson "a born liar," and Steinbrenner a "convicted" one (a reference to the owner's having pleaded guilty to making illegal political contributions to the Nixon campaign in 1972), he had been drinking beforehand. Some observers believed he had had numerous drinks, but he says it was only a couple of Scotch-and-sodas. The following day he denied making the remark and said he was misquoted.

A day or so afterward, though, he admitted he had in fact said it, thus adding himself, of course, to the company of fabulists. "I was angry when I said it to begin with," Martin said now. "But later when I calmed down, I realized that it wasn't fair to George. I would like to have retracted it, though I didn't care about the other guy."

In the fight with the marshmallow salesman, Steinbrenner dismissed Martin because, Steinbrenner says, Martin had said at first that he didn't punch the man.

"I never said I didn't punch him," said Martin. "All I said was I wasn't going to comment on it right now." The fact, however, is that Martin issued a statement through Mickey Morabito, then the Yankees' publicity director, that as Martin walked through the hotel lobby he heard a noise. "I turned and saw the guy laying on the floor," the statement read. "A security guard said the guy fell and cut his lip."

Now, says Martin, "He was a big guy—can you imagine a guy like that telling people a little guy like me knocked him out?" Martin is 5-foot-11, 170 pounds. "I would have been embarrassed to tell anybody. I knocked him as cold as a cucumber."

The style of Martin on the field reflects this combativeness. "When I come into the clubhouse," he said, "I become a different person. I get wound up. Winning is so important, and I want to win so bad, something comes over me. I'm thinking more. I become quieter. Things come sharper into focus."

Once, Dave Winfield, the Yankee outfielder, asked a manager about his arguing with umpires. Was it for real, or was it for show? Winfield remembers the manager saying, "50-50."

"Not me," said Martin. "When I put on a uniform as a player or coach or manager, it's a coat of pride, a coat of armor. Like going onto a battleground, one so-called enemy against another enemy."

At one point this season, he was quoted as saying that he was "declaring war on umpires." "I didn't say that," said Martin. "What I said was, 'We're not going to take any garbage from umpires.' Something to that effect." Martin's combative behavior with umpires has become a model for some Little League coaches and parents. "That's wrong," said Martin. "I'm a professional, they're amateurs. For kids, the game should just be fun. I'm in it to win no matter what. I mean, if I had Benito Mussolini and Hitler and Hirohito on my team, and they could execute the double steal and hit sacrifice fly balls, they'd be in my lineup. And they were pretty terrible people.

"But the Little Leagues is different. Kids should be taught how to play, and then let alone so they can play and enjoy themselves. You see these kids striking out"—he stands up—"and they walk back to the bench dragging their bat like this"—he walks hang-dog. "It's the saddest sight in the world.

"You know, one day several years ago I went to watch my son Billy Joe play in the Little League. I'm sitting in the stands. And there's a boy at bat on the other team who ain't this big"—Martin puts his hand about knee high—"and his team is losing by about 10 runs and the first pitch is over his head. The umpire calls it a strike. I holler, 'Let the kid hit!' I don't think the adults should take the game away from the kids. Well, the next pitch is over his head again and again the umpire calls a strike. I holler, 'What's wrong with you, let him hit!' Then the umpire walks over to the stands—he doesn't know who I am—and says, 'One more word out of you, mister, and I'll forfeit the game to the other team.' I said, 'My son's on the other team.'"

Martin's anger can spill over at what seem to be odd moments. Last year, in the second year of a five-year contract as manager and general manager of the Oakland A's, Martin was having tax problems, and the Internal Revenue Service had threatened to put a lien on his salary. Martin says that the A's had made a verbal agreement for him to manage for an additional five years beyond the original contract, and he sought an advance on his sixth year's salary to help ease his financial problems. The A's refused. Martin, enraged after learning of Oakland's position, tore apart his office, including even the telephone.

He can also get beside himself after a loss. The most recent example came after a 9–0 defeat in Cleveland. Martin came up the ramp from the dugout and saw a cart filled with bats and hurled it at the wall.

"But wouldn't you know," said Martin, "I missed the wall and the cart hit a urinal and shattered it completely. I mean demolished it. I never did have very good aim."

This brought a recollection of when he and Mickey Mantle were rooming together with the Yankees in the mid-1950s: "It was a Sunday morning. We had ordered three half-minute eggs and they came in about a minute and a half. We couldn't eat them. What were we going to do with them? Well, I looked out the window and saw Vic Raschi, the pitcher, and another player all dressed up and looking for a cab. They were going to church. I said, 'Mickey, watch this. I'm going to scare Raschi.' He said, 'Don't do it, Billy, something always goes wrong.' I said, 'Nah, it'll be fun.' So I throw the egg and just as I do a cab pulls up. The egg hits the cab and splatters all over Raschi's suit.

"I said, 'Mickey, get all the furniture and pile it against the door.'" How did Raschi know it was Martin who threw the egg? "Who else would do something like that?" Martin said. Martin and Mantle remained good friends. It seemed that Martin—a good player but never a star—liked being with important people in baseball, starting with Joe DiMaggio.

"When I first came up, in 1950," said Martin, "Joe took a liking to me right away. Maybe because we were both Italian and came from the Bay area. Guys would kid me about hanging around with Joe. 'What does he see in you?' they asked. I said, 'Class, fellas, class.' Joe would laugh, and he said, 'You fresh little kid.'

"Joe was a wonderful guy, and I tried to copy everything he did. He used to undress by taking his pants off first. Well, I lockered next to him and now I took my pants off first, too. He asked the clubhouse man for a half cup of coffee. I ordered a half cup of coffee. He spit some of the coffee out through a gap in his teeth. I didn't have a gap, so I just spit it out between my lips." He laughed. "Mine got a little messy."

But he was a tough competitor, no one ever said he wasn't that. He says he grew up tough. His father left home when Billy was eight months old. He remembers the embarrassment of standing in line for food and clothes during the Depression. He remembers the fights in the parks on the way home from school. He was small and he was skinny.

"I've never forgotten where I came from, and I'm proud of the jump I made. A lot of guys back there are still back there, on street corners."

In 1959 he was hit with a pitch in the face and it broke seven bones in his cheek. He was out for the season. "When I came back, I was scared," he said. "There was an inner fear. I wasn't afraid in my heart and mind, but there was some inner thing that I never knew existed. I took batting practice wearing three warm-up jackets and had the pitchers hit me with pitches as hard as they could throw, so I could try to get over it. Just when I was succeeding—it was three years later—I was cut from the major leagues."

But in order to overcome such fears, or to gain a hold on his emotions, Martin said that he never felt the need to seek psychological counseling.

"All a psychiatrist knows is what you tell him." he said. "You know what direction you're going in. And you know what direction you want to go in. So what can a psychiatrist tell you that you don't already know?

"You gotta know that life is mountains and valleys. Up and downs. That's my strength. I know nothing is ever going to always go smooth. You know you need certain releases. Maybe people without releases have to go to psychiatrists. I go duck hunting. I go trout fishing and bass fishing. And you know something else, temper is a release. That's right. Look at Jesus, didn't he get angry and whip the moneychangers?"

Whip them, or overturn the tables in the temple? "What's the difference, he got his anger out." But wasn't Jesus better known for turning the other cheek? "So have I," Martin said. "But no one writes about that." Martin, who says he is a devout Catholic, and wears a small gold cross pinned to his Yankee cap above the NY insignia, moved from the Bible to the Civil War. He is a Civil War buff.

"And as for drinking as a release," he said, "I remember reading where General McClellan asked Lincoln to fire General Grant. He said Grant was drinking and smoking too much. Lincoln said, 'Find out what Grant's drinking and smoking and send it to the other generals because they ain't winning any battles—Grant's the only one winning any of 'em.'"

Martin got up now, clamped on his baseball cap and picked up a fielder's glove. "I'd better get out on the field and watch batting practice, or some people will think I'm not doing my job," he said, pursing his lips.

There were a number of photographs in his office. Some were magazine covers of Martin, some had him with former Yankees, and some were of his son and daughter—Billy Joe, now 18, and Kelly, 30—and a grandchild.

One photo on the wall was of Martin and an elderly woman in a kitchen. "That," said Martin, "is my mother." Martin is wearing glasses that are tipped on his nose. His eyes seem blurred and his face looks flushed and his mouth is agape in a rather painful expression.

What, he is asked, are you doing there? "Singing," he said, "I'm singing."

A Humbled Michael Jordan Learns New Truths

April 11, 1994

HOOVER, ALABAMA—Every morning when he wakes up, Michael Jordan was saying, he sees the face of his dead father, James. Every morning, as he did this morning when he rose from bed in his hotel room here, he has a conversation with his father, his greatest supporter, his regular companion, his dearest and most trusted friend.

"I talk to him more in the subconscious than actual words," said Jordan today, in front of his locker in the Birmingham Barons' Class AA clubhouse. "'Keep doing what you're doing,' he'd tell me," said Jordan. "'Keep trying to make it happen. You can't be afraid to fail. Don't give a damn about the media.' Then he'd say something funny—or recall something about when I was a boy, when we'd be in the backyard playing catch together like we did all the time.

"It takes your mind away from what's happening. Lifts the load a little bit."

The memory and the pain of his father's murder are still very much alive in Michael. It has been less than a year since James Jordan was murdered last July, at age 56 after having pulled his car to the side of the road one night to take a nap in North Carolina. The police say his killers were two young men who chose at random to rob him.

The days since then have often been wrenching for Jordan, who retired from his exalted state as the world's greatest basketball player and decided

43

to pursue a career as a baseball player. And while he still says his baseball experiment is fun, these days lately for Michael Jordan have not been strictly a fantasy camp. They have been difficult.

"For the last nine years," he said, "I lived in a situation where I had the world at my feet. Now I'm just another minor-leaguer in the clubhouse here trying to make it to the major leagues."

He is a 31-year-old rookie right fielder for the Barons of the respectable Southern League, considered a "prospects league," and his debut has been less than auspicious.

"It's been embarrassing, it's been frustrating—it can make you mad," he said. "I don't remember the last time I had all those feelings at once. And I've been working too hard at this to make myself look like a fool."

In his first two games for the Barons, Air Jordan had hit little more than air, striking out five times in seven tries, along with a pop-out and groundout.

There has been much speculation about why Michael Jordan would walk away from basketball to subject himself to this new game, one he hasn't played since he was 17 years old, and had played in high school and the Babe Ruth league.

"It began as my father's idea," said Jordan, in the season of 1990 when the Bulls were seeking their first National Basketball Association title. "We had seen Bo Jackson and Deion Sanders try two sports and my father had said that he felt I could have made it in baseball, too. He said, 'You've got the skills.' He thought I had proved everything I could in basketball, and that I might want to give baseball a shot. I told him, 'No, I haven't done everything. I haven't won a championship.' Then I won it, and we talked about baseball on occasion, and then we won two more championships. And then he was killed."

On the night last October when Jordan announced to Jerry Reinsdorf, the owner of both the White Sox and Bulls, that he was going to quit basketball, they were sitting in Reinsdorf's box watching the White Sox–Toronto playoff game. Eddie Einhorn, a partner of Reinsdorf on the White Sox, was home recuperating from an illness when he got a phone call from Reinsdorf that night. Reinsdorf told him what had happened and then added, "And guess what he wants to do next. Play baseball!"

In December, Jordan was hitting in the basement batting cage at Comiskey Park. This spring, Reinsdorf allowed him to play with the White Sox in Sarasota, Florida, and then permitted Jordan to try to realize his dream—and "the dream of my father, both our dreams"—by starting in Class AA ball.

"My father used to say that it's never too late to do anything you wanted to do," said Jordan. "And he said, 'You never know what you can accomplish until you try.'"

So Jordan is here trying, lifting the weights, shagging the fly balls, coming early to the park for extra batting practice, listening while another outfielder, Kerry Valrie, shows him how to throw from "the top," or over the head, and Jordan then practicing over and over by throwing an imaginary ball.

This morning, he sat among players who are as much as 12 years younger than he is. Black-and-silver uniforms hang in his locker with the No. 45, which he wore in high school, and not the No. 23 he made famous in Chicago. He had several bats stacked there, with the names of Steve Sax, Shawn Abner, and Sammy Sosa on them. He is still looking for a comfortable bat, the Michael Jordan model.

"It's been humbling," he said. And you could see that in his eyes. Gone is that confident sparkle they had at playoff time against Magic's Lakers, or Bird's Celtics, or Ewing's Knicks.

"I just lost confidence at the plate yesterday," he said about his three strikeouts on Saturday. "I didn't feel comfortable. I don't remember the last time I felt that way in an athletic situation. You come to realize that you're no better than the next guy in here."

The other day in Chicago, Einhorn offered a theory on Jordan's baseball pursuit.

"This is the most amateur form of psychology, but I wonder if Michael in some way is not trying to do penance for the murder of his father," said

Einhorn. "I wonder if he's not seeking to suffer—to be with his father in this way."

"Seems to be true, doesn't it?" said Jordan, removing his designer bib overalls and reaching to put on his Barons uniform. "I mean, I have been suffering with the way I've been hitting—or not hitting."

He smiled wanly. "But I don't really want to subject myself to suffering. I can't see putting myself through suffering. I'd like to think I'm a strong enough person to deal with the consequences and the realities. That's not my personality. If I could do that—the suffering—to get my father back, I'd do it. But there's no way."

His eyes grew moist at the thought. "He was always such a positive force in my life," said Jordan. "He used to talk about the time my Little League team was going for the World Series and we were playing in Georgia and there was an offer that if anyone hit a homer they'd get a free steak. I hadn't had a streak in quite a while, and my father said, 'If you hit a homer, I'll buy you another steak.' It was a big ballfield, and in the fourth inning I hit that sucker over the center-field fence with two on to tie the game, 3–3. We lost it anyway, 4–3, but I've never experienced anything in sports like hitting one out of the park."

He was reminded about the time his father, bald like Michael, was told that he has the same haircut as his son. "Same barber," said James Jordan. "That," said Michael, "was my father."

The effects of his father's death remain with Jordan in other ways. He has purchased a couple of guns that he keeps in his home in Highland Park, Illinois. He says he always looks out of the rearview mirror of his car and drives down streets he wouldn't normally take. "You never know, someone might be following you. I'm very aware of that. It's second nature now."

And his offer to lease a luxury bus for the Barons' road games had another motive beyond just giving his 6-foot-6-inch frame more leg room. "I don't want to have a bus break down at 1:00 at night in the South," he said. "You don't know who's going to be following you. I don't want to be caught in a predicament like that. I think about what happened to my dad."

The people in the organization see progress. "When I first saw him hitting in the winter," said Mike Lum, Chicago's minor-league batting instructor, "it was all upper body. He was dead from the waist down. I think that's been a big change." But Jordan still has not demonstrated power in a game, though in the Cubs–White Sox exhibition game in Wrigley Field last Thursday he hit a sharp double down the third-base line. "He's got to learn to hit before he hits with power," said Lum. "He's got to master the fundamentals."

Jordan has had so much advice that, he said, "I've got a headache." Before today's game, he said, "I was thinking too much. It's just got to flow."

He has played adequately in the field, catching all the flies hit to him and playing a carom off the WESTERN SUPERMARKETS sign in right field with grace and making a strong throw to second base that held the runner to a single. "My defense has kept me respectable," he said.

The players in the clubhouse, at first in awe of this personage, have come to treat him like a teammate. "And I can learn from his work ethic," said Mike Robertson, a three-year minor-league outfielder. "He's good to be around."

One fellow who wasn't so happy was Charles Poe, who was sent down to Class A to make room for Jordan. Poe had said that he resented Jordan's having taken his position.

"I talked to Charlie about that," said Jordan. "The coaches told me that he was going to be sent down anyway, that he wasn't ready for Double A. But I said to Charlie, 'Sometimes in life, things don't go your way. You just have to use that as energy to move forward. Never give up.'

"I don't think he really meant to come down on me. But he has to learn that as much as he loves the game—as much as I love the game—it's a business. Charlie's a good kid. He had a tough life, growing up in South Central Los Angeles.

"I told him, 'Charlie, you and I are in the same boat. We're hoping to make it to the big leagues. If it's meant to be, we will. I had some bad days in basketball, and things improved. We just got to hang in, no matter what.'"

Jordan said he had planned to play all season, all 142 games, make all the bus rides—some as many as 10 and 12 hours long—and then see what happens. As for the NBA, the only reminder is a sticker on his locker that someone had put up. It reads: BARKLEY FOR GOV.

Charles Barkley, an Alabama native, has spoken of his desire to run for governor of the state. "I told Charles," said Jordan, "that if that ever happened, you be like Huey Long in the movie *Blaze*, a total dictator. I told him to stick to TV commercials."

Jordan laughed, then grabbed a couple of bats and went out to the batting cage to try again, and again. After that, he trotted out to right field, a position his father's baseball hero, Roberto Clemente, played. Perhaps it is only coincidence.

Where Had Joe and Ted Gone?

July 17, 1991

MANY NEWSPAPERS AND NIGHTLY newscasts in this country will report the melancholy fact today that Joe DiMaggio failed to get a hit in three times at bat against the Indians in Municipal Stadium in Cleveland, thus ending his record streak of having hit in 56 straight games. Today, that is, plus 50 years.

I don't know if anyone will have to go and get looped to ease the pain when they hear the news, but they must understand that everything has to end sometime, though just yesterday, after No. 56, *The New York Times* reported: "If there was ever a time during his streak DiMaggio seemed unstoppable, it had to be after this game. In July, he was getting hits half the time on his first time at bat."

Day after day for the last 56 games we have followed DiMaggio's streak in a box in the sports sections ("July 14. Streak: Game 54. AB: 3, H 1.") He was only one-half of an aged, but legendary, entry, however; Ted Williams, pursuing the goal of a .400 batting average for that season of 1941, was the other.

All of this, this daily rendering of what happened in the lives of these two men 2,600 weeks ago as if it were only yesterday, and flush against the contemporary doings of today's Ewings and Cansecos, Goodens and Bavaros, Agassis and Ryans, seemed a quaint, if not altogether queer, undertaking.

Then one day, early on, mysteriously and abruptly, there was no box about them in the newspaper. About 100 phone calls came in to *The Times*: "Where did they go? What happened to Joe and Ted?"

49

The question was quickly cleared up. There simply had been no games scheduled. Who cares about a day off 50 years ago? When it comes to Joe and Ted, apparently, a lot of people do. And from then on, when there was an off day or a rainout, it was duly reported.

It's hard to imagine anyone much caring about such long-ago pursuits or streaks or records other than in baseball. The hold the game has on us still surpasses that of any other sport, and almost any other public activity. (Imagine: July 14, 1952. Day 24. Filibuster in the Senate.)

And baseball players seem to inspire a mythology that is grander and warmer than others in the public eye. There will be no attempt here to plumb the reason why; professional baseball noodlers have done that until we reel from it: it's because we played catch with our fathers, or didn't; it's because it was the oldest, or once the only, game in town; we forever retain the saccharine smell of baseball gum cards in our nostrils; baseball deals with people with normal pituitary glands, and so on.

Meanwhile, we return to those delicious summer days when no one had yet heard of Pearl Harbor, or McCarthyism, or Lee Harvey Oswald, or 3D, VCRs, Saddam Hussein, Egg McMuffins, Madonna, moon rocks, or the designated hitter.

DiMaggio achieving a record that still stands, and Williams attaining a batting average, .406, that hasn't been topped, signify a professionalism, a glory, an excellence that related to pure ability, dedication, passion, and, to be sure, luck.

The passage of half a century has seemed even to enhance these men and their accomplishments. More than 20 years ago, Paul Simon wrote a song that included these lyrics: "Where have you gone, Joe DiMaggio, a nation turns its lonely eyes to you."

DiMaggio once said: "I've never been able to figure out what the song means." Simon explained: "It has something to do with heroes. People who are all good and have no bad in them at all. That's the way I always saw Joe DiMaggio."

Graceful, purposeful, forever young and powerful. That's how most envision Joe DiMaggio.

A few years ago, in the locker room at Yankee Stadium, a man with thinning white hair, rheumy eyes, in his seventies, was putting on a baseball uniform. He worked his way into the spiked shoes. "Oh, god," Joe DiMaggio said, "these hurt like hell."

It had been years since he wore baseball shoes for baseball, and not for an old-timers' recital. He said he could feel all his old baseball injuries, and now couldn't throw a ball 15 feet. Then he buttoned up his famous old pinstriped shirt, No. 5.

Outside, along the railing, a group of kids who knew only the legend begged for his autograph. A middle-aged man elbowed his way in and sought a signature, too.

"What about the kids?" DiMaggio admonished gently.

"You've been my idol all my life," the man replied, "and I'm still a boy at heart."

And today, when DiMaggio's streak has finally ended at Game 57, the hearts of a lot of boys and girls, some middle-aged and older, have to hurt at least a little bit.

Ted Williams: "The Slugging Professor"

March 23, 1985

WINTER HAVEN, FLORIDA—In his open-air classroom here among the swaying palms and noisy bats, Prof. Theodore Samuel Williams was expounding on the virtues of getting your belly button out in front of the ball.

"It's that little magic move at the plate," he was saying recently, beside the batting cage on a field behind Chain O'Lakes Stadium. He wore a Red Sox uniform and a blue windbreaker with little red stockings embossed at the heart and stood on ripple-soled baseball shoes. It was late morning, cool but sunny as he spoke to a couple of young players. "Hips ahead of hands," he said in a deep, ardent baritone, "hips ahead of hands."

And the onetime Splendid Splinter—he is a Splinter no longer—demonstrated with an imaginary bat and an exaggerated thrust of his abdomen. "We're talking about optimum performance, and the optimum is to hit the ball into your pull field with authority. And getting your body into the ball before it reaches the plate—so you're not swinging with all arms—that's the classic swing. But a lot of batters just can't learn it, or won't."

Dr. Williams—and if he isn't a bona fide Ph.D. in slugging, who is?—is author of the authoritative textbook *The Science of Hitting*. He also is the last professor or hitter or anyone else to bat .400 in the major leagues (he hit .406 in 1941) and had a scholarly career average of .344. This spring, he is serving the Red Sox as batting instructor with minor-league players.

Ted Williams on hitting is Lindbergh on flying, Picasso on painting, and Little Richard on Tutti Frutti.

52

Professor Williams is now 67 years old and drives around the Red Sox complex in a golf cart, stopping now at this field, now at that. And though he says he's "running out of gas," it hardly seems so to the casual visitor, and there are many who come just to see him in the leathery flesh. He arrives before 9:00 AM at the training site and spends a long, full day under the Florida sun observing the young players.

He knows that there are as many theories on hitting as there are stars in the sky. "Like I've heard some where they tell a batter to keep his head down," he said. "No way you can open your body and carry through with your head down that way." He says that he may not be right for all the players, but he urges them to "listen—you can always throw away what you don't want, and keep what works for you." And, like the good teacher, he listens, too. An image returns of him in the clubhouse, sitting on a storage trunk and nodding in understanding while a minor-leaguer quietly talks to him.

In the batting cage now was the third baseman Steve Lyons, a 6-foot-3-inch, 190-pound left-handed batter who bears a physical resemblance to the young Ted Williams. Lyons, after four seasons in the minor leagues, has a chance to make the parent club.

Williams watched him swing. "He's improvin' good," said Williams, "improvin' good. Has good power and good contact."

Last season, Lyons' batting average jumped to .268 in Triple A ball, 22 points higher than the previous year in Double A. He credits some of that improvement to Williams.

"He's not quick to criticize or change you immediately," Lyons said. "He watches, and then when he talks, people listen. He tries to be positive in his approach. He'll say, 'You've got a good swing, but there's not enough action into the ball. Cock your bat back farther.'"

When Williams was young, he sought advice. Before his rookie year with the Red Sox in 1939, he met Rogers Hornsby and asked, "What do I have to do to be a good hitter?" Hornsby said, "Get a good ball to hit."

"That's not as easy as it sounds," said Williams. "If the pitcher throws a good pitch, low and outside or high and inside—in the strike zone but not in the batter's groove—you let it go with less than two strikes. With two strikes, you move up a little bit on the knob of the bat. But too many hitters aren't hitters from the head up, and never become as good as they can be."

Sometimes the best advice is no advice at all. "When I was comin' up," said Williams, "Lefty O'Doul said to me, 'Don't let anybody change you.' And when I saw Carl Yastrzemski, I thought pretty much the same thing. He had a big swing, and I thought he should cut down his swing just a little. But I never came right out and said it. I'd say, 'Gotta be quicker, a little quicker.' And I think it took him longer than it should've to get his average up. Look at his record. He batted under .300 his first two years in the big leagues. Then he hit .321. Same guy, same swing, same everything. But he got a little quicker, got a little quicker."

It was Paul Waner who told Williams about getting the belly button out in front of the ball.

"And I saw the best hitters doing it. Cronin did it, and Greenberg did it, and York and DiMaggio," he said. Of current-day players, Pete Rose and Rod Carew hit that way. "Reggie Jackson doesn't, but he's so strong that he can get away with that arm action. Now, Al Oliver isn't the classic hitter—a swishy, inside-out hitter—but he's gonna get 3,000 hits because he makes such good contact.

"Guys like Mantle and Mays—great, classic hitters—could have been even better if they had thought more at the plate. They struck out too much—and they'll tell you that, too. You got to concede a little to the pitcher, even the greatest hitters have to. Look at DiMaggio, he struck out only a half or a third as many times as he walked. It meant he was looking for his pitch—he was in control, not the pitcher."

Williams no longer teaches by example, and said that the last time he stood in the batter's box was in last year's old-timers' game in Fenway Park.

"I hit two little ground balls to the pitcher," he said. "I was so anxious up there, I couldn't wait for the ball, and hit them at the end of the bat."

Was he embarrassed? "Was I?" said the professor. "I didn't want to run to first base."

For Williams, a Joy
Found in the Debate

July 6, 2002

TED WILLIAMS WAS MANAGING the Washington Senators in the spring of 1969, and I was a dewy-eyed young sports reporter given the assignment of following up on a thought that was growing more widespread around the country. That is: is baseball doomed?

Why, even the media theorist Marshall McLuhan had said exactly that, that baseball wasn't a "hot" sport—too slow for modern times, and unsuited for television. It was at a time when defense was suffocating offense. Deadly dull, it was reasoned.

Ted Williams, with his team in spring training in Pompano Beach, Florida, was one of those I was to interview about whether baseball was on the verge of joining the pterodactyl in extinction.

I did not know, nor had I ever met, Williams, but of course I had followed his remarkable career. The first time I ever saw him, I was struck by him. I was a boy in the early 1950s, and he was a player with the Red Sox, and playing the Chicago White Sox, my hometown team, in Comiskey Park.

You couldn't take your eyes off him. And this was when he was on the on-deck circle. Crouched on one knee, waggling the bat, he studied the moves of the pitcher with such intensity, such ferocity, it resembled a tiger in the bushes about to pounce on his unsuspecting lunch. I don't remember

55

how Williams did in that game; it doesn't matter. What he brought to that moment matters.

All this came back to me when I learned that William had died yesterday, in Florida, at age 83, of cardiac arrest.

I had followed him in the box scores as a player, marveling at his batting feats. I was impressed with his military record in World War II and Korea—and his honesty. He had landed a burning plane during the Korean War, which exploded shortly after he fled it, and he had said, "Hell, yes, I was scared." Many said that Williams was a real-life hero. It was said that he was of the stature, and his voice sounded like, John Wayne. No, John Wayne sounded like Ted Williams. And John Wayne was a hero in celluloid. Williams was flesh and blood.

And so when I went back to the small locker room of the Senators in their training camp, and found my way into the modest manager's office, I found Williams, tugging out of his uniform—he was no longer, at 6-foot-3, the Splendid Splinter, and had gained some weight, sometimes wearing a jacket to hide the paunch.

I introduced myself, and told him the story I was working on. A small, elderly clubhouse man was handing Williams a towel. When he heard about "Is baseball doomed?" the clubhouse man began to berate me: "Do you know who you're talking to? This is Ted Williams. He's baseball. What nerve to come in here and ask him such a stupid question."

I said nothing, taken aback. I turned to Williams for a reply. I had read about his occasional temper outbursts.

"It's okay," he said to the clubhouse man. Then he turned to me. "When I come out of the shower, I'll answer your questions."

The thing about Williams that I learned was that he was as challenged by a good question as he was by a good fastball. He was thoughtful, direct, and candid. He liked an intellectual test, from figuring what Bob Feller's next pitch would be, to landing a salmon, to flying a plane, to a discussion that could lead to a dialectic. He loved a good argument.

When he emerged from the shower in Pompano, he did answer my questions. And the one answer I recall regarding my quest was: "Everything goes in cycles. Baseball will return to the popularity it has enjoyed in the past." He may have used several expletives to punctuate those brief sentences, for that was his style, and that was, as I perceived it, his grace. He made you feel comfortable in his presence.

Over the last three decades or so, I've had the pleasure of being in his company.

I once came across a newspaper story titled "Your Child's Creativity" that began: "What do Henry Ford, John F. Kennedy, and Ted Williams have in common?" The answer: the burning drive for achievement.

I asked Williams about that. "I can't speak for those other guys, but to succeed I believe it starts with enthusiasm," he said. "And certainly no one ever worked at hitting a baseball harder than I did."

The last time I saw him was two years ago, and at one point we talked about death. "I don't know what's going to happen, if anything, when I'm dead," he said. "I'll tell you this, though, I'm not afraid to die."

For many of us, Ted Williams never will.

Joe DiMaggio:
"And All that Cheering"

November 25, 1998

IN THE PRESS ROOM of Yankee Stadium not long ago I saw Joe DiMaggio sitting at a table with a few friends. Even in repose he looked elegant, still trim in his dark suit, hair graying and thin but neatly coiffed. I was reminded of a remark by Henry Kissinger when he sat near DiMaggio in the owner's box in Yankee Stadium. The Yankees had lost a playoff game and Kissinger, on the way out, had said, "Joe, put on a uniform—they can use you." In the mind's eye, Joe still could lope after a fly ball.

When I saw DiMaggio now I related to him an unfortunate incident that happened to him some 45 years ago and which he didn't know about.

I was a small boy growing up in Chicago in the 1950s, I told him, and aware of the DiMaggio legend, as was anyone else who followed baseball in America. I had written to the Yankees for a photograph of him, was sent a glossy head shot with him in his baseball cap, and nailed the picture to my bedroom wall. The unfortunate part, I told DiMaggio, was that I hammered the nail right through his forehead.

"You did?" he said, wincing.

"Looks like it's okay now," I said.

"Oh yeah," he said. "I heal fast."

Today, which marks DiMaggio's 84th birthday, one wonders if he can heal as he lies in a hospital in Hollywood, Florida, amid reports that he

58

has been battling lung cancer as well as pneumonia. He is fighting for his life. One wonders whether the man who once hit in 56 straight big-league games, a record that has stood for 57 years, can summon the energy and, perhaps, the requisite miracle to regain health.

Even before his admission to the hospital on October 12, DiMaggio's name was in the news, in an indirect fashion. The Yankees' sterling center fielder, Bernie Williams, the American League's leading hitter and Gold Glove fly-chaser, heir to DiMaggio and Mickey Mantle, and a free agent, has been in controversial negotiations with the Yankees. Williams is as distinguished a ballplayer, if not as iconic, as his famous predecessors.

It is difficult for fans to imagine that their athletic heroes are vulnerable to everything human. The youth of the ballplayer, or, sometimes, even the coach, is eternal, if only in photographs and film—DiMaggio in his baggy pinstripes is still rapping out hits in his familiar long stride and sweeping stroke of the bat—and in our memory.

Red Holzman can still be seen in that fashion in the huddle, instructing Bradley and Frazier, and Weeb Ewbank may be forever visualized discussing strategy with a mud-splattered Joe Namath on the sidelines. In that sense, Coach Holzman of the Knicks and Coach Ewbank of the Jets, who died recently, remain vital to us.

And Catfish Hunter, because of the Lou Gehrig's disease he has, may soon lose such control in his muscles that he will be unable to even grip a baseball. Such thoughts seem to fall off the radar screen of our comprehension.

And so it is with Joe D., that intensely proud man, that sometimes impatient and unforgiving man, who, the Yankee management knew, would be insulted if, at Old Timers' Day, he should not be the last announced.

On the day I apologized for pounding that nail into his head, I gave DiMaggio a photograph of him and Marilyn Monroe taken by Richard Sanborn, who is now a judicial magistrate living in Maryland. Sanborn had been a sergeant in the Army stationed in Tokyo in 1954 when DiMaggio and Monroe went on their honeymoon to Japan. I had done a column on DiMaggio and Sanborn sent it to me to give to DiMaggio, saying he had always wanted Joe to have it and didn't know how to get it to him. Would I do it? I did.

As most people know, bringing up his former wife to DiMaggio would end any conversation with him. It was too personal. But I handed DiMaggio the photograph. He thought it was great. "And this guy was just an amateur photographer?" DiMaggio said. "I've got to send him a note and thank him."

Shortly after, alone with DiMaggio, I said, "Marilyn looked beautiful in the picture." "She was beautiful," DiMaggio said, as though relating an insight.

I said, "Joe, there's a question I've always wanted to ask you, if you don't mind." He nodded, knitting his brow. "There's that great anecdote first written by Gay Talese," I went on, "about when you were in Japan and Marilyn was asked by the brass to entertain the troops in Korea. When she returned to your hotel room, you asked how it went and she said, 'Oh, Joe, you never heard such cheering!' And you said quietly, 'Yes I have.'

"Did it happen?"

"Yes," DiMaggio said, "it did."

Roberto Clemente's Legacy

February 1974

SAN JUAN, PUERTO RICO—Except for the threat that always lurks of a brief outburst of tropical rain, it was a glorious day.

Bright kites soared in the blue sky. On the green ballfield below, a high school band, all tasseled, high hatted, and white booted, practiced a merengue to the beat of a drum, the toot of a whistle, and the perky tinkle of a xylophone. In more serious matters, Little Leaguers warmed up by tossing and chasing baseballs and baseball caps.

And soon, the highlight of this sun-splashed February morning: Mrs. Vera Clemente was scheduled to throw out the first ball of the official opening of the new Roberto Clemente Little League in the old quarter of San Juan.

Members of the nine teams were assembling. One 11-year-old center fielder wearing a floppy Dodgers uniform carried a tube of Ben-Gay in his back pocket. He explained that the ointment made his throwing arm feel good.

Nearby, leaning against a palm tree as he slipped on spikes, was Angel Ramos, the brightly smiling umpire. "I grew up with Roberto in a barrio in California," he said. Carolina is a small town just west of San Juan. "I remember we were on a baseball team together. He was 13 years old, and he did not play much. We say it is 'eating bench.' This is very bad, to 'eat bench.' People fight when you say it to them. But one day Roberto was called to bat and he hit a double. From then on, it was 'Roberto, Roberto, Roberto.'"

The location of the ballfield in the Old San Juan is beside El Morro fortress, a 16th-century battlement that kept Corsairs from invading the island.

Today, the fortress holds back only the sparkling waves of the Atlantic Ocean.

It was into this ocean that Roberto Clemente's plane vanished shortly after takeoff, two years before, on New Year's Eve, 1972. Clemente was taking food and clothes he had collected to Nicaragua, where he had ones played winter ball, and which had just suffered a devastating earthquake.

For days after the plane fell, Vera Clemente walked the beaches searching for a sign of her husband.

Angel Ramos, the umpire, was asked if anything was ever found.

"*Nunca*," he said, "not even a shoe."

Why?

"The sharks," he said.

Angel Ramos told how a wreath had later been placed on the waters where the plane went under. "And the wrath disappears soon too," he said.

It was getting into midmorning, and Mrs. Clemente still had not arrived at the ballfield.

Most of the boys on the nine teams of the Roberto Clemente Little League of the Old San Juan knew the Pittsburgh Pirates Hall of Fame outfielder personally. He often organized baseball clinics where he taught them the finer points of the game.

What did they learn? Angel Ramos called over his young nephew Ricky, and asked him. "*Cogelo suave*," replied Ricky. The phrase is Spanish slang for "keep cool." Ricky adds, "He tells us always to get along with teammates, and when we lose, not to fight with someone. The most important thing is fun of competition."

Clemente had long been a popular figure on the island. He was more than just a countryman who brought pride because he had become a famous baseball player. "He grew up poor and he died trying to help the poor," said Ricky.

Before he died, Clemente was working to realize a dream of his, a sports city for Puerto Rican youth. It would house about 1,500 boys and girls who would get expert instruction not only in sports but also in crafts. "Roberto," said Angel Ramos, "felt such activities could help unite humanity."

As the Little Leaguers lined up along the foul lines for the opening ceremonies, one notices that no No. 21 was worn. "No one in Puerto Rico is allowed No. 21, Roberto's number," explained Angel Ramos. "It is out of national respect."

The ceremonies began without Mrs. Vera Clemente. Sponsors of the teams were introduced. Polite applause. The lady with sequined glasses who was translating the Little League rules from English into Spanish was introduced. A painting showing Roberto Clemente's strong, dark face on a baseball in heaven was given to Mrs. Clemente's stand-in, the secretary of the Clemente Sports City project. She bit her lip to hold back tears.

There had been no stir when it was announced that Vera Clemente would not come this day. It seemed that all understood. She had been under great strain. "Everywhere," explained Luis Mayoral, a Sports City official, "it is 'Roberto, Roberto, Roberto.'" He related how she must go to Pittsburgh to arrange exhibition games with major-league teams in San Juan. She goes to Cooperstown. She helps filmmakers on a Roberto picture, spends time with magazine writers and book authors, attends dinners to raise Sports City money, and sifts requests for appearances.

"She has long had the virus, maybe for three months," said Luis Mayoral. "But mostly it is the end of the year and the remembrances of Roberto. So Vera, she is in a depression during the holiday season. And she knows that she must spend more time with the children, Robertito, who is eight, Luisita, seven, and Enrique, four. For a long time they were like in a vacuum, especially Robertito, who understands best what happened.

"They only have one mommy and one daddy and they need a great deal of mommy now. She has done all this with the marvel of a champion—breathtaking. And I think the family has finally defeated this past year."

The band again struck up a merengue in the infield dust. Kites bobbed in the sky. The ocean rolled against the thick fortress. And a baseball game was about to begin in the new Roberto Clemente Little League in Old San Juan.

Satchel Paige: "New Generation Is Taking Over"

March 25, 1969

WEST PALM BEACH, FLORIDA—One flamingo-thin leg was wrapped around the other and two long leathery fingers cradled a cigarette in a V. Satchel Paige rocked back in his locker-room chair, curled his lower lip onto his anchovy mustache. He raised his eyebrows, nearly spilling a couple eyeballs over drooping horn-rimmed glasses. His forehead furrowed like Venetian blinds.

"I couldn't have taken it the way Jackie done," he said. "No siree. The first time someone called me a black S.O.B. I would quite naturally have been a little peeved. There woulda been a fuss, sure.

"They wanted some youth, someone who wouldn't go feudin'. Jackie had a top education, too. Me, I didn't have nothin' but the ninth grade and mother wit and 20 years throwin' a baseball all over the world every day for every one of them years."

So Satchel Paige was not the first black to break the color barrier in the major leagues. Jackie Robinson, in his 20s in 1947, was.

"Now you look at Jackie," said Paige, dangling his long, wide, flat baseball shoe, "and his hair's white and you'd think he was my great grandfather. And I'm 63."

Late last season the Atlanta Braves signed Paige, who started his professional baseball career in 1926 with the Chattanooga Black Lookouts, to a contract as a pitcher. He did not see game action. The Braves' move was

64

mainly a good-will gesture. Paige had needed 158 days to complete five major-league years, thus qualifying for the baseball pension.

The baseball strike hassle this winter resulted in, among other things, lowering the pension qualifying to four years. But the Braves have kept Paige as a coach.

In 1962 Paige wrote an autobiography entitled *Maybe I'll Pitch Forever*. It did not seem out of the realm of possibility then.

"Forever is a pretty good while," said Paige. "And I'm like a fire horse in olden days. I hear the bell and I run under the harness. I can still get anyone out for three or four innings. My onliest problem is the bunt on me, and my wind's short. If I'd pitch, I might bring back the old lost art of bunting, all by myself.

"People here are doubtin' my vision, too. My eyes do give me some troubles now and again. And maybe I'm just too old and gentle to pitch no more.

"Besides, here come another generation altogether. It's all changed over, saw it happen with my own natural eye. The colored man's accepted now like never before. But times are rough now, real rough. The world's in too big an uproar.

"Lotta things are bad, but some are good. I ain't heard the word 'nigger' in 10 years, and I been from one end of the United States to the other.

"And these white boys here. Look 'round. Not a one would ever dream about a lynchin' or pourin' gas on a colored man. That's why I don't like to talk much about problems that used to be. Just let dead dogs lie.

"I think about other things. Like maybe some day gettin' in the Hall of Fame. The whole world wants me in it. But I didn't play in the major leagues long enough—that's how it's wrote up, even though for years and years I was the world's greatest pitcher.

"I pitched in the Negro leagues and barnstormed against the best white hitters like Musial and Williams and DiMaggio and Pepper Martin and the Waners—Oh, Lord, I forget who else. Kept 'em all in the park, too.

"Maybe some day I'll fall into the Hall of Fame, like I done the pension. But I'm not sayin' they'd change the rules for me. Maybe some day before I die I could sorta sneak in. You know, for good conduct or somethin' like that."

Nolan Ryan's "Exalted Victims"

July 25, 1990

HARRY SPILMAN WAS AGITATED, and got Nolan Ryan on the phone. "Nolan, how come I'm not on the list?" he asked one day last summer to his neighbor in Alvin, Texas, and former opponent and teammate, Nolan Ryan. "What list?" asked Ryan. "The list of every guy you ever struck out in the major leagues," said Spilman. "There are 1,063 different players on it, and I'm not one. But you got me, too. One time."

"Gee, Harry," said Ryan, "I'm sorry. I'll see if I can get it fixed."

In the Texas Rangers' clubhouse, Ryan, who tonight against the Yankees will try for the 300th victory of his 24-year career, recently recalled this conversation with Spilman with a smile.

Though only 19 other pitchers have won 300 or more games in the big leagues, Ryan is still best known for his strikeouts; he holds numerous records in this category, including his career total of 5,202.

Spilman had indeed struck out against Ryan, in 1987, with the Giants.

He had also played with Ryan on the Astros in the early 1980s, and they became good friends.

The list was originally compiled last August by the Rangers' publicity office and was printed in full in *Sports Illustrated*, where Spilman saw it.

The error occurred because Jose Uribe was given one more strikeout against Ryan, seven, than he deserved. Spilman one day pinch hit for Uribe and struck out.

A correction was made for the Rangers' 1990 media guide. The list has since expanded to 2,009 different players whom Ryan has struck out, with 22 fresh victims this season.

For some, especially lesser-known players like Spilman (now an outfielder with the Tucson Toros of the Pacific Coast League), it seems a badge of honor, humorous or otherwise, to have whiffed against Ryan. And so naturally Harry wanted credit where credit was due.

Before Ryan's last outing, last Friday night against Detroit here—he would win his 299th game—a 21-year-old rookie third baseman named Travis Fryman anticipated facing him for the first time.

"It's kinda weird to think that I wasn't even born when Ryan was pitching up here," said Fryman. "But I've heard about him all my life. They say you're nobody until you've struck out against Nolan Ryan." He shrugged. "So maybe tonight I'll become somebody."

It is some list of somebodies. Included are 13 guys named Davis, 11 named Johnson, seven Browns and one Browne, seven Smiths, seven Joneses, seven Williamses, and six Martinezes. Ryan struck out 19 players who are in the Hall of Fame, from Henry Aaron (four times) to Carl Yastrzemski (seven); six father-son combinations, including the Bondses and the Griffeys, and 11 brother groupings, from the three Alous to a pair of Ripkens.

One family, the Alomars, is included in each of the last two categories. Ryan struck out Sandy Alomar Sr. with the Yankees, and his sons, Roberto, with San Diego, and Sandy Jr., with Cleveland.

"Roberto came up to me before the game the first time I pitched against him," Ryan recalled, "and he asked, 'Do you remember me?' I said, 'Sure.' He was a toddler around the Angels' clubhouse when his father was my teammate. I said, 'Glad to see you up here.' I think I struck him out the first time he batted."

When Ryan ran his eye over the strikeout list in the media guide recently, he said, "One of the surprises for me is Claudell Washington." Washington, now a Yankee, leads the list of Ryan victims, with 39 strikeouts. "I always regarded Claudell as a tough out. But our careers paralleled, and we were in the National and American Leagues at about the same times. So I saw him a lot."

Ryan's next most-frequent victims were Fred Patek and Jorge Orta, with 31 strikeouts each. "Both batted high in the order, so they came up a lot against me, and both were free swingers," explained Ryan. Tied for fourth was another surprise, Rod Carew, with 29 strikeouts.

"I may have struck Carew out," said Ryan, "but he hit over .300 off me. So when he made contact, he was his usual trouble."

Looking at the list of Hall of Famers he had fanned, Ryan said, "I was fortunate to catch some of them, like Ernie Banks and Eddie Mathews, at the end of their careers in the National League, and then guys like Killebrew and Kaline when they were finishing in the American."

Against Ryan last Friday night, young Travis Fryman batted twice, bouncing out to third and flying to left.

"Ryan's got that aura of intimidation," said Fryman, "and I was a little nervous facing him. But I didn't strike out." He smiled. "So I guess I'm still nobody."

He may yet have an opportunity, however, to one day add his name to the same list that includes Aaron and Yastrzemski, and Harry Spilman.

Tom Seaver: His Remarkable Art and Science

July 30, 1985

CHICAGO, ILLINOIS—Two items caught the attention of a visitor at Tom Seaver's locker stall in the White Sox clubhouse. This was on a late afternoon before a recent ballgame.

One of those items was *The New York Times* crossword puzzle that the veteran pitcher had begun before being interrupted: He had just completed 4 Down, "Spud feature," three letters (he penned in "eye") and 13 Across, "Bailey, Belli et al.," seven letters (he wrote "lawyers").

The other item was a White Sox cap hanging on a hook. It was a dark blue cap inscribed with dry perspiration stains, perhaps worn in his last outing a few days previously.

The two items in his locker, the crossword puzzle and the stained cap, indicate what has helped make Tom Seaver such a remarkable performer for nearly two decades. That is, cerebration and sweat.

"Pitching," Seaver says, "is still enjoyable, still rewarding. For me, it's the greatest combination of physical and mental skills."

Few operatives have broken down the components of the art and science of pitching as Seaver has, and few have given so mighty an effort for so long.

The picture from the stands of Seaver on the mound is virtually unchanged since his rookie year, 1967, and has remained that way through two pennant-winning seasons with the Mets, and two stints with the Mets and one each with the Reds and White Sox. It is a picture of this 6-foot-1-inch, 220-pound pitcher, a no-nonsense, scrutinizing look under the bill of his cap, and then that smooth, near-perfect windup and that high release and low follow-through, his right knee scraping the ground as he lets the ball fly.

Against Oakland last Tuesday, Seaver was seeking his 296th career victory in the major leagues, but instead got no decision. He departed in the seventh inning, with two runners on base and one out and the score tied. The White Sox eventually lost in 13 innings.

Even when yanked, Seaver managed to impress his manager, Tony La Russa.

"Some pitchers just don't want to come out of a game, but you'll always get a honest call from Seaver," said La Russa. "If he's got something left, he'll tell you. Otherwise, he'll say he's just out of gas."

So Seaver didn't finish in Oakland. But there will be other games, and it seems simply a matter of time, probably some day in August, when Seaver will come off the mound stuffing the baseball of his 300th victory into his back pocket.

He tried again for No. 296 yesterday but the Twins beat the White Sox, 4–3. Seaver took the loss, his sixth against seven victories.

Tom Seaver is 40 years old and remains one of the better pitchers in baseball, an extraordinary feat of consistency and effectiveness, considering that he has been one of the best pitchers in baseball for most of his 19 years in the major leagues. He is just five games short of 300 victories, a significant milestone. Only 16 pitchers in the history of the game have accomplished that, and only one of them is still active—Steve Carlton, with 314 victories.

Seaver's career earned-run average of 2.81—the ERA is often considered the best barometer to judge a pitcher—is fourth on the list of pitchers with more than 3,000 innings, behind Walter Johnson, Grover Alexander, and Whitey Ford.

Last season, he led his team in victories, with a 15–11 record, and his 236 innings pitched were nine innings short of leading in that category as well.

In a game that is garnished with statistics, one that is of paramount interest in depicting the longevity of Seaver: he averages about three and a half strikeouts a game now. Once, he averaged as many as nine. Five times he led the National League in strikeouts, and he is fifth on the career list of strikeout pitchers.

He has, then, gone from being primarily a power, or strikeout, pitcher, to a control, or finesse, pitcher.

He was sitting on the dugout bench in Comiskey Park. In the twilight, with the grass half in shadows, there was an intermittent crack of ball against bat from the batting cage, and an occasional spatter of Seaver's tobacco juice on the dugout floor. His face retains a youthful quality, and he still has an engaging, high-pitched laugh and still delights in banter. When, for example, a teammate, the catcher Marc Hill, came by and said "I'd like to ask you something when you have time," Seaver replied, "Okay, Booter,"—Booter is Hill's nickname—"but I don't think I'll have time." Hill gave a double-take and Seaver grinned. Maybe because of that boyish quality, it is still surprising to find him so broad-shouldered and deep-chested and thick-legged.

"I used to be able to just blow the ball past people, just rear back and physically overpower a hitter," said Seaver. "If one batter hit a triple off me with no outs, I used to be able to strike out the next three hitters with fastballs. But I can't do that anymore, not for one inning, not for one batter, and sometimes not even for one pitch."

It has been a few years now since he could consistently "blow pitches" by batters. His fastball is not what it was. Once, he could throw his fastball 97-plus miles an hour. Now, his fastball is usually in the high 80s. Recently one fastball against the Angels was clocked at 91 miles an hour.

"I've had to make a gradual transition and it became necessary to mix up the pitches more than ever. A back-door slider, a slider down and away, a hard curve, a flop curve, and different speeds on the fastball," he said. "The last four or five years I've developed a changeup, and I never had one, or needed one, before.

"The three most important points of pitching are movement, location, and velocity. Movement is whether the ball rises and dips, or breaks inside or out. Location is placing the ball at a particular spot. Velocity is speed. And of the three, velocity is the least important."

So the elements must mix properly, and, for Seaver, rarely do you pitch the same hitter—especially the good hitters—the same way twice. That, he said, is a lesson he learned a long time ago.

"I remember when I was a rookie with the Mets and facing Henry Aaron for the first time," said Seaver. "Henry was my idol because of his consistency. I threw him a slider down and away and got him to hit into a double play. I thought to myself, 'Gee, this is easy.' I threw him the same pitch the next time he came up, and he hit it into the left-field stands for a two-run homer.

"That taught me to start thinking more than I ever had before. And I found that the game continues to shift, and there are no absolutes. Each batter, each situation, each pitch I throw is dependent on so many variables. It's not just the number of outs and the score and how many runners on base, but what did I throw this batter the last time up, what have I thrown him the last pitch? Where is he standing in the box? What is he expecting?"

It is a matter of also keeping one's composure under precarious circumstances. Tony La Russa had recalled one of the first times Seaver pitched for him, last year when Seaver had joined the White Sox from the Mets. It was a game against Boston and the White Sox were leading, 5–3, in the fifth inning, but Boston was threatening. The Red Sox had runners on second and third with one out and Mike Easler and Tony Armas the next two batters.

"One of the things a pitcher must know is that there are usually four or five times in a game when the game hinges on the next batter," said Seaver. "You have to be able to recognize those instances—a lot of pitchers don't— and if you do, you have to be able to understand it mentally, decide what to do, and execute it physically.

"Now, I hadn't had a strikeout all game, and I knew that I needed one against Easler, because if he makes contact that could mean two runs and we're in trouble. And I might need a strikeout against Armas, too.

"With Easler, I needed to get two strikes on him, to set him up for the third. I knew I wasn't going to get those strikes on power fastballs. I wanted him to foul off two pitches.

"As I recall, my first pitch was a slider down and in, but in the strike zone, and he pulled it foul. Then I threw a curve low and away. It couldn't come inside and break over the plate because he'd rap that, so it had to be on the outside corner at the knee, and it was and he bit at it. The best he could do was foul it off, and that's what he did.

"Now I have two strikes on Easler. The next pitch I throw is a sinking fastball inside at the waist. I didn't throw it for a strike, but I wanted him to know that I could go inside on him, too. Just to give him more to think about, that he would have to defend inside as well as outside. And I thought that he was thinking that then I'd go back to a slider low and away. I didn't. I came in with a rising fastball high and in. And struck him out."

Next, with two out, Seaver got Armas to foul off two pitches, and then struck him out, too. Armas was called out on the third strike.

"The next time these two hitters come up," said Seaver, "I might pitch them completely different. I might even want them to hit the ball. It's a matter of what you've got to work with on a particular day. On that day, I was feeling especially strong and had the old-time confidence in the fastball."

And adjustments must be made on various pitches during the game. "I might be going along well with my slider for seven innings," he said, "and then I'm starting to get fatigued and I'm not quite able to roll it over as well as I had, and so I'd better realize this, and change to a curve, or to more off-speed pitches."

Seaver also noted that an experienced pitcher must be cognizant of how an umpire is calling a particular game. "Every umpire is different, and sometimes they're different on different days," he said. "You have to learn early in the game what this umpire's strike zone is today, and hope he's consistent.

"There was a game in old Jarry Park in Montreal that I'll never forget. I struck out Rusty Staub three times, and each time the third strike was a fastball about three inches outside. But I knew the umpire was calling the pitches that way. Rusty took a called third strike each time. Rusty wouldn't change, and he argued bitterly, and rightly so, each time. But I didn't argue."

Ironically, adaptability must also be balanced with uniformity. Though he has changed in some ways through his career, he has remained constant in others. Most important, he has not varied from the sound mechanics of his pitching motion.

"Look at the four older starting pitchers who continue to be effective—Nolan Ryan, Jerry Koosman, Steve Carlton, and Tom Seaver," said Seaver, who excluded Phil Niekro because the knuckleballer is a "freak pitcher." "Each us has a great deal of flexibility in the lower part of the body. We get a lot of push from the biggest muscles in the body—the thighs, the calves, and the rear end. That takes the strain off the smaller muscles in the shoulder and elbow and back."

And all this must be in proper harmony as he winds up and throws. When Seaver was knocked out in another game against the A's, he made no excuses. "I was lousy," he said. He believed that the problem was with the lower part of his body. "I was rushing it," he said, and the arm had to hurry to catch up. Thus, the location of his pitches was thrown off.

"You try to get into a positive groove, but you have to work to stay there," he said. "Sooner or later, you're going to fall out of it. You have to get back as quickly as you can. You're not a machine. We're all human beings."

And as a human, Seaver must keep healthy and strong, and does that by staying fit throughout the year, jogging, watching his diet, working with a trainer to maintain flexibility in his arm, and working with weights. "When I first came up to the major leagues, I walked into the Mets camp with a 10-pound dumbbell," he said. "A few of the veteran pitchers laughed at me because weightlifting was considered to stiffen the muscles," he said. "But it helps a lot if you do it in moderation, and most pitchers lift weights now."

It's work, says Seaver, but it's worth it. It's worth it, at this point, to the tune of about $700,000 a year. "The money is important, certainly," he says. "And it has provided security for my family. But I think right now, with this chance to win 300 games, and I know I don't have a lot of time left, I'd almost pitch for free.

"But there are times when you can get sick and tired of the travel, the road trips where we get into a town at 2:00 in the morning, the working seven days a week, the being away from your family. But I know I'm lucky, I know it's a great way to earn a living, and an excellent living. And I still feel good, I feel that I can pitch for five more years. I don't know if I can, or if I'd want to, but I feel like I could."

On off days, though, even together with his family—his wife, Nancy, and their two daughters, Sarah, 14, and Annie, nine—he still thinks of baseball, and sometimes plays it with them.

Last Thursday, an off day, the family went to the aquarium in Chicago, and then went out to Comiskey Park. He pitched to his daughters, while Nancy, he said, was the "designated shagger."

Seaver moved up from the mound and pitched from about 45 feet from the plate.

"Sarah hit me pretty good," he said, "and I knocked her down. She said, 'Daddy, don't do that again!'"

And Annie? "She needs more work on her hitting. But I think the bat was too big for her."

There was no indication that Seaver attempted to get her a smaller bat. Never give a hitter a break is a time-honored axiom among great pitchers like Seaver. Even if the hitter is nine years old, and even if she's your daughter.

Willie Will Be There

July 28, 1983

FANS ADORED WILLIE MAYS. That bright, boyish smile straight from the sandlots of Birmingham, Alabama. The perky greeting: "Say Hey!" The cap flying off as he rounded first and dug for second, leaving puffs of dirt in his wake. The whirling throws. The long-ball power in the clutch. Stopping for a game of stickball in the evening and, according to legend, walloping a pitch beyond two sewers.

"Willie Mays," someone once said, "was born for the game." No matter how many times you watched Willie Mays play, there was always something new and fresh and purely pleasurable about it, like a root beer float.

Yet there was more to Willie Mays. He could be overly sensitive, suspicious, cantankerous. When he came up to the Giants, at age 20, he was scared. It is not news that he went 1-for-26. Tearfully, he asked manager Leo Durocher to send him back to the minors. Durocher, as most schoolchildren know, wisely declined.

Some 20 years later, nearing the end of his glittering career, and just having passed two batting milestones, Mays was asked when he thought he might retire.

"How come you ask me a question like that?" he said, irked. "How come you don't say, 'Willie, congratulations on your 600th homer and your 3,000[th] hit.' Not many people ever hit that many."

Saturday afternoon at Shea Stadium is Old-Timers' Day, and No. 24, Willie Mays, will be introduced to the crowd along with many other players from the Mets' second and last National League pennant winner. The theme is the 10th anniversary of the 1973 championship season. It happens that this is also the 10th anniversary of the retirement of Willie Mays.

Mays says he will be there for sure, quashing doubt. Mays has been in the news on occasion since he left baseball as a player, and it has often involved some form of controversy. The latest was 12 days ago when he left the dug-out of the Cracker Jack Old-Timers' Game in Washington, D.C., after he had been introduced to ringing applause, and just before the game started. He learned he wouldn't be starting, and stalked off.

In an Old-Timers' Game at Yankee Stadium earlier this month, Mickey Mantle didn't show up for the first time since he retired. He said he couldn't make it because of personal problems. Some thought he was boycotting the event because he was banned from holding a job in baseball after he accepted a position in public relations with a gambling casino in Atlantic City.

Mays, too, took a similar job in Atlantic City, and he became a nonperson in baseball business circles. Although the baseball commissioner's office allows both Mays and Mantle to participate in old-timers' games, each has expressed unhappiness with the ruling. Mantle's absence from the Yankees' geezer set stirred a question that Mays might react in the same fashion.

"No," he said by telephone from his home in San Francisco, "I'm all set to be at Shea Stadium." Even at age 52, even having just awakened in the morning, Mays' high, lilting voice remains. There is still a boyish quality to it. If his voice were a play, it would be the basket catch.

He wanted to make clear that what happened in Washington was simply a misunderstanding. "The people who run it aren't baseball people," he said. "They're nice people, I'm sure, but they don't know too much about how to run a ballgame. But I've forgotten all about it.

"The other day I read where someone said I still hadn't grown up because I didn't stay for the game. Well, there's a saying that the older you get the wiser you become. I think that's true with me. If I was younger and told in that game that I was going to go in as a pinch runner, there'd probably have been a brawl. I'd have been plenty mad. But now I just walked away. Gee, I stayed in the clubhouse.

"I've still got a lot of pride in me. Maybe I don't hit like Willie Mays hit when he was 22 or 23 years old—who would when you get to be 52?—but I still love the game. There's still a lot of little boy in me.

"For me, playing baseball was so much fun, meeting all those people, hearing the cheers. You have no idea what it's like. You make a certain throw or catch and all those people are clapping and hollering for you. There's a feeling—it just comes over you, it washes over you for a few seconds, and then it's gone. But for those few seconds, you're on top of the world. You never forget it."

Near the end of his career, Mays may have been uncertain about his future and once said, quietly, "I'm glad the Mets will be able to take care of me when I'm finished."

After his playing days, Mays was a coach for the Mets for a short period, and there was some talk about his not showing up at the ballpark when he was supposed to. Nevertheless, he kept his job as a part-time coach until he went with the casino in 1980.

At the Cracker Jack game he was quoted to the effect that the commissioner's office had made a mistake in banning him because, he said, "I thought the game needed me."

"What I meant was," said Mays, "that the game needs a Mays, a Mantle, a Duke Snider, a Joe DiMaggio, to keep the game going, for those people who grew up with the game. In football, it's the same, they need Unitas and Marion Motley and O.J. Simpson."

Mays said that in his last three years in baseball he began to plan for his retirement. "I had to sit down and ask, 'What can Willie Mays do after he takes off the uniform?' There wasn't a lot I was qualified for, but everyone's qualified for something," he said.

"Well, I like people, and being in the major leagues for 22 years, they treated me so well. So I figured I'd try for public relations. Through some people I met in baseball I got a p.r. job with a food company in Boston. Been with 'em 12 years now. And I hooked up with a stockbroker company on

Wall Street, and then with the Bally hotel in Atlantic City. Keeps me busy, and there's only 30 days in a month.

"So I'm not mad at nobody. Sometimes not everything's great, but it wasn't always a good day on the ballfield, either. It's a combination of fun and work. Just like in baseball. All those hours and hours of practice. I needed it. I'm not a Superman, by any means."

Roger Maris: Bittersweet Memories

July 1970

GAINESVILLE, FLORIDA—Roger Maris holds a special place in American sports. He performed the unprecedented feat of hitting 61 home runs in a single big-league season and has never been forgiven for it.

To many persons in this quiet college town, Roger Maris is now just another beer salesman. But to many sports fans across the country, Maris is at best an enigma, at worst an object of scorn, and, in fact, an iconoclast of sorts.

He retired from baseball two years ago, at the relatively youthful age of 33, and became, with his brother Rudy, the full-time Budweiser beer distributor in Gainesville, Florida, and nearby Ocala. He weighs 225 pounds, about 20 pounds more than he did in 1961 when he broke the revered Babe Ruth's legendary record of 60 homers—which caused Maris as much pain as pleasure.

"If I ever had to have good memories about my baseball career," he said recently, "they probably had to be before 1961."

Few men have had to withstand the withering pressure of publicity that Maris did in 1961 and after, and few men were as ill suited to endure it.

"It would've been a helluva lot more fun to play the game under one mask, and then leave the park wearing another mask. Some guys loved the life of celebrity, like Pepi (Joe Pepitone). Some of 'em would have walked down Fifth Avenue in their Yankee uniforms if they could have. But all it brought me was headaches. You can't eat glamour."

Maris now seems content, relaxed, and happy. His hair is still cropped in a crewcut, his pale eyes are candid and kindly, his dark tie is unfashionably thin, his socks are unfashionably white, his belly is ample, and his neck and forearms are still as thick as a slugger's.

"I don't read the papers much," he said, "too busy. Rudy and I drive to the brewery in Jacksonville, we go into the taverns and supermarkets and other outlets to see how our Bud stock is, how it's placed on the shelves. I'm usually out of the house by 8:00 in the morning, and sometimes I don't get home until 1:00 in the morning.

"My customers don't talk baseball much. They used to. But now they'll ask how I think the Cardinals will do or something, but that's all. I never look at the standings. Not at all."

He was asked what he thought of the Yankees' recent winning surge.

"The Yankees?" he asked, smiling. "Did I ever play for the Yankees?" Then, seriously, he asked what division they're in. He did not know.

He has little fond recall for his seven years (1960–66) as a Yankee.

Although he says it is all in the past, "finished and done," his voice betrays a resentment to what he refers to as the "Yankee organization." For one thing, he felt the Yankees did not want him to break Babe Ruth's record. (For much of '61, Maris stayed just a couple of homers ahead of Mickey Mantle and both pursued the ghost of Babe Ruth.)

"They favored Mickey to break it," said Maris. "I was never the fair-haired boy over there. When I'd get hurt, they thought I could still play. When Mickey or Tom Tresh or someone got hurt, they'd let 'em rest.

"I'll never forget the 1965 season. I injured my right hand on about May 18. Ralph Houk, the general manager then, said I should keep trying to play. Finally, with about two weeks left in the season, I went up to his office and told I wanted permission to go home to take care of my hand, and I said if he didn't give me the okay, then I'd go anyway.

"Then he said to me, and I'll never forget it, Houk said, 'Rog, I might as well level with you, you need an operation on that.' Now what do you think?"

Maris also felt that many writers did not want him to break the record. "They tried to make me into the mold of Babe Ruth, and I didn't want to fit anyone's mold. I'm Roger Maris. And a lot of the older writers didn't think anyone should break Babe Ruth's record. Some of the younger writers felt they could make a reputation at my expense. So I was called surly. Yet I'd stay and answer their questions, sometimes the same questions as new writers came over to my locker, for two or three hours after a game. If I had that to do all over again, I wouldn't say a word until all the writers were there. Then I'd talk for 15 minutes, and quit."

The controversial and infamous asterisk was placed by then baseball commissioner Ford Frick alongside Roger Maris' name in the record book after the 1961 season. Maris had hit 61 homers in a 162-game schedule, Babe Ruth had hit 60 in a 154-game schedule.

"I didn't make the schedule," Maris said. "And do you know any other records that have been broken since the 162-game schedule that have an asterisk? I don't. Frick should have said that all records made during the new schedule would have an asterisk, and he should have said it before the season—if he should have said it at all. But he decided on the asterisk when I had about 50 homers and it looked like I'd break the record.

"But I understand—and this is only what sportswriters have told me— that when Frick was a New York sportswriter, he was a big drinking buddy of Babe Ruth's.

"But when they say 154 games, which 154 games are they talking about? The first 154, the middle 154, the last 154? If it's the first 154, then I'd still have tied Ruth, because I didn't hit my first homer until the 11th game. If it was the last 154 games or the middle 154, then I'd have broken the record anyway."

If he had to do it all over again, would he have wanted to break the record again?

"I was a professional baseball player," he said, "and when I was out on the field I gave everything I had. No one ever worked harder than me. Baseball was my life then. If there was a record in the way of my doing my best, then the record had to fall. So what's to regret? The fact is, no one ever had as good a season as I did in 1961."

Is there anything he would have done differently during his baseball career?

"Yes," he said. "I would have been more careful not to jeopardize my health. Every day, my body tells me I used to be a baseball player. I can't sleep on my stomach because my rib cage is so tender. It got that way because of how I'd bust up double plays. But that's the way I was taught to play baseball, in the minors, by Jo-Jo White.

"And my knees hurt if I just brush against them. That's from banging into outfield walls. And I still don't have any feel in the ring finger and little finger of my right hand, from when I broke my hand in '65."

Maris announced plans to retire from baseball after the 1966 season. Then the Yankees traded him to the St. Louis Cardinals. He played two more years for them. (It was Cardinal owner August Busch who helped establish Maris in his present business.)

"With the Yankees," said Maris, "I was booed for 81 games at home, and for 81 games on the road. You say it doesn't affect you, but it does, finally. All that stopped when I went to the National League. Oh, I got booed the first series at Shea Stadium against the Mets, but the booing stopped after then.

"I knew it would be different in St. Louis on Opening Day in '67. The team was paraded around the field in open convertibles. My name was announced and the people cheered. After those seven years in New York, I felt that, hell, there is some good left around here yet."

But no longer was he a long-ball pull-hitter, because of his injured hand. "I couldn't tell anyone because then the pitchers would know—and they found out soon enough. But I became a guy who tried to punch the ball over the third baseman's head.

"Finally, I couldn't stand to play anymore. I'd had my fill of it. The game itself was enjoyable, but the traveling was the big factor. It's not the kind of life for a family man…It's all in what you like."

Maris now has six children, ranging in age from four to 12.

Roger Jr., 11, and Kevin, nine, play in the local Little League. "I haven't encouraged them to play, and I haven't stopped them" he said. "They haven't asked for my help, and so I haven't done nothin' with either one. Better they play the way they want to."

Would he want to return to baseball as a coach or manager?

"I don't say I'd *never* want to, but right now I like it down here in this small town, and I'll let the other guys do it up there. It's fun to sit back and watch.

"You know, but I was happy my first year in New York, in 1960, before the writers stuck the poison pen up my tail. But now, when I think about the good times, I think that I was just as happy my first game in the big leagues, in 1957 with Cleveland, as I ever was.

"I remember we played the White Sox, and Billy Pierce was pitching against us. They beat us 2–1, I think. But I got most of our hits. I went 3-for-5. We only got five hits altogether.

"I remember that a couple days later I got my first major-league homer, up in Detroit. It was with the bases loaded. I don't think many guys can say that their first big-league homer was with the bases loaded. But don't print that, it might sound like bragging.

"But the 61 homers? I don't think much about that. It's in the past. And I'm too busy now, anyway. Maybe it'll become important to me when I'm 65 or 70. Maybe then I'll think about it, and enjoy it."

Rose Gets a Single to Break Cobb's Career Mark for Hits

September 12, 1985

CINCINNATI, OHIO—Ten miles from the sandlots where he began playing baseball as a boy, Pete Rose, now 44 years old and in his 23rd season in the major leagues, stepped to the plate tonight in the first inning at Riverfront Stadium. He came to bat on this warm, gentle evening with the chance to make baseball history.

The Reds' player-manager, the man who still plays with the joy of a boy, had a chance to break Ty Cobb's major-league career hit record, 4,191, which had stood since Cobb retired in 1928.

The sell-out crowd of 47,237 that packed the stadium hoping to see Rose do it now stood and cheered under a twilight blue sky beribboned with orange clouds.

Now he eased into his distinctive crouch from the left side of the plate, wrapping his white-gloved hands around the handle of his black bat. His red batting helmet gleamed in the lights. Everyone in the ballpark was standing. The chant "Pete! Pete!" went higher and higher. Flashbulbs popped.

On the mound was the right-hander Eric Show of the San Diego Padres. Rose took the first pitch for a ball, fouled off the next pitch, took another ball. Show wound up and Rose swung and hit a line drive to left-center.

The ball dropped in and the ballpark exploded. Fireworks being set off was one reason; the appreciative cries of the fans was another. Streamers and confetti floated onto the field.

Rose stood on first base and was quickly mobbed by everyone on the Reds' bench. The first-base coach, Tommy Helms, one of Rose's oldest friends on the team, hugged him first. Tony Perez, Rose's longtime teammate, then lifted him.

Marge Schott, the owner of the Reds, came out and hugged Rose and kissed him on the cheek. A red Corvette was driven in from behind the outfield fence, a present from Mrs. Schott to her record-holder.

Meanwhile, the Padres, some of whom had come over to congratulate Rose, meandered here and there on the field, chatting with the umpires and among themselves, waiting for play to resume. Show took a seat on the rubber.

Rose had removed his batting helmet and waved with his gloves to the crowd. Then he stepped back on first, seemed to take a breath, and turned to Helms, threw an arm around him and threw his head on his shoulder, crying.

The tough old ballplayer, his face as lined and rugged as a longshoreman's, was moved, perhaps even slightly embarrassed, by the tenderness shown him in the ballpark.

Then from the dugout came a uniformed young man. This one was wearing the same number as Rose, 14, and had the same name on the back of his white jersey. Petey Rose, a 15-year-old redhead and sometime bat boy for as long as he can remember, fell into his pop's arms at first base, and the pair of Roses embraced. There were tears in their eyes.

Most people in the park were familiar with the Rose story. He had grown up, the son of a bank cashier, in the area in Cincinnati along the Ohio River known as Anderson Ferry. He had gone to Western Hills High School here for five years—repeating the 10th grade. "It gave me a chance to learn more baseball," he said, with a laugh.

He was only about 5-foot-10 and 150 pounds when he graduated, in 1960—he is now a burly 5-foot-11 and 205—and the only scout who seemed to think he had talent enough to make the major leagues was his uncle, Buddy Bloebaum, who worked for the Reds.

Three years later he was starting at second base for the Reds, and got his first major-league hit on April 13, 1963, a triple off Bob Friend of the Pittsburgh Pirates.

Rose was at first called, derisively, "Charlie Hustle." Soon, it became a badge of distinction. He made believers out of many who at first had deprecatory thoughts about this brash young rookie who ran to first on walks, who slid headfirst into bases, who sometimes taunted the opposition and barreled into them when they were in the way.

But never was there malicious intent, and he came to be loved and appreciated by teammates and opponents for his intense desire to, as he said, "play the game the way it's supposed to be played."

He began the season needing 95 hits to break Cobb's record, and as he drew closer and closer, the nation seemed to be watching and listening and wondering when "the big knock," as he called it, would come.

Tonight, he finished in a most typical and satisfying fashion. He got two hits—he tripled in the seventh inning—and walked once and flied to left in four times at bat. It wasn't just the personal considerations that he holds dear. He cares about team accomplishments, he says his rings for World Series triumphs are his most cherished baseball possessions. And this night he scored the only two runs of the game, in the third and seventh innings, as the Reds won, 2–0.

After the game, in a celebration at home plate, Rose took a phone call from President Reagan that was relayed on the public address system.

The President congratulated him and said he had set "the most enduring record in sports history." He said Rose's record might be broken, but "your reputation and legacy will live for a long time."

"Thank you, Mr. President, for taking time from your busy schedule," said Rose. "And you missed a good ballgame."

Charlie Hustle's Second Chance

February 28, 1993

BOCA RATON, FLORIDA—In a modestly lighted corner of the Pete Rose Ballpark Cafe, the familiar-looking man with the broad face and direct eyes and slightly upturned lip sat in a booth and wrote his signature in blue pen on a stack of cards with his baseball picture.

It was early afternoon on a recent Sunday and Pete Rose handed the cards to the tourists and sundry locals who approached.

He wore a cream-colored cap that read HIT KING, a cream-colored jacket that said HIT KING on the left breast, and jogging pants of the same hue and with the same imprint, HIT KING. The legend is emblematic of Rose's major-league record for most career hits, 4,256, and emblematic, too, of one of his several businesses—the Hit King line of apparel—and would-be businesses under the heading Pete Rose Enterprises.

The clothes are on sale in the gift shop of the restaurant, along with numerous other baseball-related items, including an $8 baseball that, with the name Pete Rose scripted across it, sells for $38.

For more than two decades, Pete Rose hustled in a different way, wearing a different uniform—that of the Reds, or the Phillies, or the Expos, teams he played for in one of the most illustrious baseball careers of all time. He loved baseball with a passion that was obvious and uncommon, running out everything, pumping full bore around the bases. In All-Star Games. In playoff games. In the World Series.

The crowds cheered mightily and Rose, above all others, basked in the baseball spotlight. And he made millions of dollars at it. Then he became a manager, being paid $1 million a year, and still, in his fashion, hustling every step of the way.

It is a different world now, in the relative quiet of the Pete Rose Ballpark Cafe, and a different hustle, selling himself in a way he never quite had to before, as a Willie Loman of baseball memorabilia. But it is a world he made, through arrogance, perhaps, through stupidity, maybe, through an uncontrollable and destructive passion, possibly. The thrilling and rewarding world of baseball is no more for Pete Rose.

"Yes," he said, "they've taken something from me that I love."

A small boy, with his mother, approached Rose at the booth. "Do you know you're called Charlie Hustle?" the boy asked, barely looking up.

"Yeah, I do," Rose said gently.

"In Little League, I was called Charlie Hustle," the boy said.

"That means you're aggressive," said Rose, handing him an already signed card. "That's good."

Rose, who will be 52 in April, has been retired as an active player now for eight years, and out of baseball for three years, and out of prison for two years. He signed an agreement in August 1989 with Bart Giamatti, the commissioner of baseball, to accept being placed on baseball's permanently ineligible list. In 1990, Rose was sent to prison for five months for failing to file proper income-tax returns. Since then, as he has tried to straighten out his life, he has had no reported problems.

He says he has come to terms with his recent, troubled past. He still denies that he bet on baseball games, and maintains that the investigation by Major League Baseball into his gambling activities was unfair. Although he still bets on horse races, he denies that he does, or ever did, have a gambling problem.

Rose says that his time in prison was an embarrassment, an indignity, but that he believes he paid his debt to society. And he believes strongly that his was a Hall of Fame baseball career and he deserves at least the chance to be voted in.

But as he sat in his booth in this combination family-style restaurant and sports lounge, hawking T-shirts and signing autographs, Rose seemed every bit the outsider, looking in on a game that once was his life and now is his business. He can derive money, if not pleasure, from baseball.

To Rose, this is his comeback.

"John Q. Public has given me a second chance," he said. "And now I'm trying to build an empire. I want to be the most successful ex-player ever."

In the restaurant, a couple came by and the man told Rose they were from Cincinnati. "I remember when you broke in with the Reds, in 1963," the man said.

"You're older than you look," Rose said with a smile.

They ask him to sign a Pete Rose T-shirt that they had bought at the gift shop. "And try our Cincinnati chili; you'll like it," said Rose. "My brother Dave makes it."

This might be the only restaurant in the country that has not only a dress policy listed at the entrance (No FLIP FLOPS OR TANK TOPS AFTER 5:00 PM) but also an autograph policy: No MERCHANDISE MAY BE BROUGHT IN FROM THE OUTSIDE TO BE AUTOGRAPHED.

"If we didn't," said Rose, "I'd be signing balls and bats and gloves that everybody brings from home. It would never end."

If such items are purchased in the gift shop, though, that is a different story. While Rose does not own a part of the restaurant that bears his name, he does have a licensing contract for the numerous products sold at the gift shop. He said he signs as many as 500 autographs a day.

With this restaurant deal and with plans to open others, and a marketing program for Charlie Hustle's Dip and Sauces, and a soon-to-be-released energy drink, Power Plus ("I'm the publicity director for it for the whole world, yes sir!" said Rose), the Hit King line of apparel, and a sports radio talk show that he conducts every week night from a recently constructed radio booth in the restaurant, Rose appears to be on his way back financially.

Rose lost more than his image and prestige when he was banned from baseball and later sent to prison. He lost a lot of money, in both potential earnings and in debts. He had to pay $366,043 in back taxes and penalties to the Internal Revenue Service. He still resents some "so-called friends," he said, "who didn't help my wife when she needed money when I was in prison."

"But I'm getting back on my feet now," he added.

Whatever it is that has driven Rose, the boy of modest means who grew up as one of the "river rats" along the Ohio and then soared to stardom for the hometown Reds, he appears still to be driven.

Rose seems to work as hard at business as he did at baseball, which was probably another major-league record, to go along with, besides most hits, others like most games played, most at-bats, most singles, most total bases for a switch hitter, most seasons with 200 hits or more, and being the only player in major-league history to have played more than 500 games at five different positions (first base, second base, third base, left field, and right field).

"And I hold the record for playing in the most games on a winning team—1,952," Rose said. "That's 500 more games than Joe DiMaggio even played in.

"But you know, there are still a lot of people who think I went to prison for betting on baseball games. What people don't understand is that I wasn't even suspended from baseball for betting on baseball games. I was suspended for admitting that I bet on football games with bookmakers. The agreement I signed with the commissioner says, 'There will be no finding or denial that Pete Rose bet on baseball.' And then at the press conference, Giamatti answers a question saying he believes I bet on baseball. But they could never prove it."

Rose was now asked if in fact he bet on baseball games.

"No," he said. And he repeated his often-stated remark: "My only crime was picking the wrong friends."

"And did they conduct a fair investigation?" he went on. "No way, Jose."

The circumstantial evidence, however, seemed utterly convincing to many: a long and suspicious log of phone calls from the Reds' clubhouse to Paul Janszen, a friend at the time, who later contended that the calls related to Rose's betting on baseball games, and testimony from a bookmaker.

At the time Rose signed the five-page agreement cutting him off from baseball, Giamatti was asked in a news conference what it would take for Rose to be reinstated into organized baseball one day. Giamatti, the former president of Yale and a Renaissance scholar, who died a week later, on September 1, 1989, said Rose would have to "reconfigure" his life. The fact is that of the some two dozen players placed on the permanently ineligible list in history, including Shoeless Joe Jackson, none has ever been reinstated.

Rose has a good idea what Giamatti meant by "reconfigure."

"It meant that I should clean up my life, and do no more illegal gambling," he said. "It meant that I should be a good citizen, which I am. I have a nice family, with two young kids, a great wife; we're going to be moving into a big new house, I work, and I'm a damn good tax-paying citizen."

A man in the restaurant came by with a little girl to get a Pete Rose T-shirt autographed. They had purchased it in the gift shop. "Shake hands with a Hall of Famer," the man said to the girl. Pete Rose took the small hand in his thick one. When the two people departed, it was mentioned to Rose that he didn't correct the man.

"I may not be in the Hall of Fame," said Rose. "But I had a Hall of Fame career. I was in control of my career for 24 years as a player, I'm not in control of whether the sportswriters vote me in. All I wanted was a fair shot on the ballot."

The Hall of Fame executive board voted a stipulation that in effect was designed to keep Rose out of the Hall, saying that anyone on the permanently ineligible list was not eligible to be on the ballot. It drew protests from the Baseball Writers of America, who vote for the players for the Hall.

"I'd like to look any writer in the eye to explain to me why they didn't vote for me," said Rose. Then he mentioned an Ohio sportswriter who said that he would not have voted for Rose on the first ballot, but would have on the second. "Who is he to take it on himself to penalize me? Like I haven't been penalized enough."

When he was banned from baseball, Rose was advised to visit a psychiatrist, who determined that Rose in fact suffered from a gambling disorder, that he was a compulsive gambler. "I don't know what a 'compulsive gambler' is," said Rose. "If it's someone who bets beyond his means, then that isn't me."

He had said that he may have bet a few thousand at the track, but was making millions. "I think a guy who has a gambling problem can't go to bed with a dollar in his pocket unless he's got it on a bet," he said.

But shortly after his signed agreement with Giamatti, Rose admitted that he had a gambling problem. "That was a mistake," he said now.

Does he still bet? "Yes," he said, "but only legally, and only at the race track, and very seldom. I'm in the horse business. I own three race horses, and another is about to be born. When I go to the track, it's often to check out horses that I might be interested in. I don't even stay for all of nine or 10 races. I went to the Kentucky Derby last year and I'm going again this year.

"I go with the governor of Kentucky, Brereton C. Jones. He's a friend of mine. But I also go to the race track to relax. And then like when I was in Chicago with my wife and we went to the harness races, I still always come back with enough money to tip the cab driver."

He said he doesn't bet anymore on certain sports he once bet on, like football and basketball. It is true that while once he frequented the dog track regularly he has not been seen there by regulars in the last few years. And unlike in times past, there are few rumors around race tracks of his betting or winning and losing large sums of money.

When Rose talks about his life in prison, at the Marion (Illinois) Federal Penitentiary, he says that the worst thing was "the embarrassment." "Not just embarrassment for me," he said, "but for my family. They had to live with my being in prison. They visited me once a month. And the worst thing was when my boy, Tyler, would be leaving. He was six years old. They'd drive away past my window in the camp and he'd be hangin' out of the car window as long as he could, calling, 'Bye, Daddy, I love you.' That never, never got any easier for me to take."

Rose was eligible for reinstatement to baseball a year after the ban, but he has not yet applied for it. "Who'm I going to apply to?" said Rose. "The agreement said I had to apply to the commissioner. But there's no commissioner. I'll wait until they get a new commissioner, and then I'll decided what's the best way to go.

"I'm not bitter toward baseball. And I don't blame anybody."

He said this with some conviction, although the hurt, when he mentions Giamatti and Giamatti's successor, Fay Vincent, is obvious. "I gave a lot more to baseball than Giamatti—God rest his soul—or Fay Vincent," Rose said.

But he tries to retain perspective on the game he seems to have given his soul to, even, it is often believed, to the exclusion of his first family, his former wife, Karolyn, and his two other children, whom he says he now keeps in close touch with. They are Pete Jr., now a minor-league player in the Cleveland Indians system, and Fawn, who works with abused children in Columbus, Ohio.

"Everything I have in life is because of baseball," said Rose. "But I also deserve everything I got in baseball. Like someone said to me as if it's a surprise, 'They've kept the name Pete Rose Way on the street outside of Riverfront Stadium.' Well, why shouldn't they? I worked hard for it. And I'm probably still one of the game's greatest ambassadors.

"I love baseball. I always talk positively about it. I'm like a lot of older players who really come to appreciate the game. The guys playing today don't think they have to talk about it and the owners don't seem to know how to be good for it."

He said that he left Cincinnati only because of the weather and because his family—his wife, Carol, and his two children with her, Tyler, now eight, and Cara, three and a half—likes it in Florida. "I'm not in exile," he said.

But Rose does admit to another reason. "I didn't get bashed here in the press the way I did up north," he said.

Another man came by and told Rose he remembered the day he hit three home runs. Rose, not known as a home-run hitter, remembered it, too.

"It was in 1978, at Shea Stadium, on a Saturday, a Game of the Week," he recalled. "I had stayed out a little late the night before. Had a rough night partying in New York. And the first time up Nino Espinoza blew me away on three pitches. I had a slow bat and then for the first time in my career

I decided to choke up. And I hit three home runs, and off three different pitchers. I got two singles, too—went 5-for-6 that day."

At that point, the restaurant's manager, Rob Cooperman, appeared and asked Rose if he would say hello to a group celebrating a small boy's birthday. It was in an enclosed room, and colored balloons were bouncing on the two tables. "Ow, wow!" said one of the mothers. "Look who's here, Pete Rose!"

The birthday boy was at the head of one of the tables. "How old are you, 13?" Rose asked him. "No," said the boy, "seven."

"Is this your date?" he asked one of the girls? She blushed. "No," she said.

The kids and the parents laughed. Rose posed for photographs with the kids. He was clearly a great public-relations man, genuinely enjoying this, and maybe, knowing his penchant for statistics and goals, even going for some kind of all-time P.R. record.

"How's the chicken?" he asked one of the kids. The lad nodded.

"Well, happy birthday," said Rose. "Happy birthday." And then almost as an afterthought, he said to the birthday boy, "Are you a baseball player?"

"No, not yet," said the boy.

"Well, said Rose, "I'm not a ballplayer anymore, either."

And then, in his cream-colored Hit King cap, jacket, and pants, Charlie Hustle went out to continue doing what he has always done best. Hustle.

A Vote for Wilheim

December 8, 1984

THE YEAR WAS 1969, and Hoyt Wilhelm, a relief pitcher then with the California Angels, was in town for a series against the Yankees. It was late morning of a summer's day, and the renowned knuckleballer sat on the edge of a rumpled bed in his hotel room, one bare foot tucked under a dangling leg, the way he might have sat 40 years before while fishing in a creek near his home in Huntersville, North Carolina.

He was then the oldest player in baseball, at age 46, with a receding hairline. But he was still so effective with a knuckleball that no one—not the pitcher, not the hitter, and not the catcher—knew which way it would break.

"I remember once when I was with the White Sox, this rookie catcher said he didn't need no mask to warm me up," Wilhelm said in his easy drawl. "I didn't say a word, but the other players began yackin' at him like players will do.

"So a day or so later, I was goin' to throw batting practice, and who's warmin' me up but this rookie fella, without a mask. The second pitch I throw caught him as fair in the eye as if you'd a stuck it there. It was swollen before he hit the ground."

Wilhelm came to mind recently when his name was noticed on the ballot for the Baseball Hall of Fame, which has arrived in the mail.

He is now a minor-league pitching instructor for the Yankees, but for 21 years was perhaps one of the best pitchers in baseball, and surely one of the most extraordinary.

In last year's balloting for the Hall of Fame, 303 votes were needed for entry. Harmon Killebrew, Luis Aparicio, and Don Drysdale each received the necessary votes. Wilhelm fell 13 short. This will be his eighth year on the ballot, and the concern is that, with such fresh blood as Lou Brock, Catfish Hunter, and Elston Howard entering the eligibility ranks, Wilhelm might never muster the necessary votes within the 10-year limit.

One is reminded that Gil Hodges was close so often in the balloting but never quite got over the hump and into the Hall. It would be a gross injustice if this happened to Wilhelm. For pure grit and effectiveness, there could hardly be anyone better.

He was a rookie at age 29, when many players are winding up their careers. It was 1952, and he had spent seven years in the minor leagues, with time out to fight at the Battle of the Bulge in 1944, where he was awarded the Purple Heart.

In his first major-league season, as a reliever with the New York Giants, throwing in that effortless manner and sending the ball fluttering and dipping madly across the plate, he won 15 games and lost three. He led the National League in percentage that season, with .833, and in earned-run average, 2.43. No rookie had ever accomplished that distinctive double.

Wilhelm had been a starting pitcher for his entire minor-league career, but Leo Durocher, the Giant manager, needed a reliever and gave Wilhelm a chance at the top. Wilhelm overcame a concern that his floating knuckleball would allow base runners to steal with impunity. "The trick," he said, "is not to let them get on in the first place." And also to have a deceptive motion to first base.

For most of his long major-league career, Wilhelm was a relief pitcher. However, he did start numerous games, and in 1958, with Baltimore, he pitched a no-hitter against the Yankees. The next year he won nine straight starts and finished the season with 15 victories.

He played for nine major-league teams, and, each time he was let go, management had decided that he was simply too old. But, as Wilhelm has recalled, almost every time he was dropped he had led the team in earned-run average.

Someone else always took a chance on the old man, until 1972, when, one month short of his 49th birthday, and after having pitched in 16 games for the Los Angeles Dodgers that season, he was cut for the final time.

Now, John Picus Quinn, born, for some strange reason, John Quinn Picus and called "Jack," was 49 years old when he pitched in 14 games for the Cincinnati Reds in 1933. And Satchel Paige, born, it is assumed, sometime after the Battle of Hastings, was rather wintry when cranking it up for the St. Louis Browns in 1953. (According to the Baseball Encyclopedia, he was then 47 years old.) Beyond that, no major-leaguer has rivaled Hoyt Wilhelm, born James Hoyt Wilhelm, for playing regularly at such an advanced age.

Wilhelm still holds the major-league career records for most games pitched, 1,070; most innings pitched by a reliever, 1,870; most games finished, 651—a mighty figure, because he was frequently in games that were on the line and wasn't on the slab simply to mop up; and most victories in relief, 124. The save, which is now often a yardstick to measure a relief pitcher's effectiveness, was not an official statistic for the first 17 years of his career, or until 1969.

As for Wilhelm's career earned-run average, it was 2.52, and in six of seven years, from 1962 through 1968, it was, stunningly, under 2.00.

There are pitchers in the Hall of Fame, such as Stan Coveleski and Waite Hoyt, who did a considerable amount of relief pitching, but no one who was primarily a reliever has ever been selected.

The relief specialist, invaluable to a team, has been sorely mistreated by the sportswriters who finger deities for the Hall. There should be a place in the pantheon for one like Wilhelm.

And what was it that made him so successful?

"Well," Wilhelm said when he was with the Angels, "I never went into a game and got all flustered up. I try to take a close game and men on base in stride.

"I've always thought baseball was just a game—and I enjoy it. And ever since I was a boy and learned that knuckleball, I've thrown it with a lot of damned determination."

Drysdale Could Laugh at Himself

July 5, 1993

I SAW DON DRYSDALE for the last time two months ago at a formal baseball dinner at the Waldorf-Astoria. He was still looking very large at 6-foot-6, about 220 pounds, large enough, strong enough, young enough, even at age 56, that in the mind's eye I could see him back on the mound, alone under the stadium lights, as cool in his black tuxedo as he had ever been in his Dodger blue.

There he was, winding up, wheeling and coming in sidearm with his fearsome fastball that sizzled over a corner of the plate, when it wasn't rattling the beak of the batter's cap, or bouncing off his shoulder. "The trick against Drysdale," Orlando Cepeda once said, "is to hit him before he hits you."

That's how Drysdale performed in his 14-year major-league career, all with the Brooklyn and Los Angeles Dodgers, from 1956 through 1969—a career that led him into the Hall of Fame.

On Saturday, Donald Scott Drysdale was found dead of a heart attack in a Montreal hotel room. He was with the Dodgers, working as a broadcaster for their games with Vin Scully. Drysdale would have been 57 on July 23. The shock of his death reverberated through the sports community, and beyond. Beyond to his family, of course, and to his wife, Ann Meyers, and his four children. Meyers is in the Basketball Hall of Fame; they are possibly the only husband and wife to be in sports halls of fame.

Drysdale was not only an important baseball pitcher who ended up with a 209–167 won-lost record and a 2.95 earned-run average and six seasons of 200 or more strikeouts. He was the one who with Sandy Koufax held out in tandem for a fairer salary and thus helped open the doors to the salaries of today. But I also remember him as a man who could laugh at himself, a rare and wonderful trait.

A few years ago he told me this story: Drysdale started Game 1 for the Dodgers in the 1965 World Series against Minnesota. Koufax had originally been scheduled to pitch but the game fell on Yom Kippur, the Jewish high holiday, and Koufax sat out the game in deference to his religion. The Twins scored one run off Drysdale in the second inning and six runs off him in the third and there were still only two outs when Walter Alston came out of the dugout to remove Drysdale. As the manager approached the mound, Drysdale said: "I know, Skip. You're wishing I was a Jew."

Drysdale, the strapping blond kid out of Van Nuys, Calif., broke into the major leagues when he was 19 years old, after having pitched only 44 games in the minors.

He had a lot to learn, and Sal Maglie, who had been bought by the Dodgers from the Indians for pitching insurance, helped teach it to him. Maglie tutored Drysdale in the art of knocking down batters. Drydale said that Maglie instructed: "It's not the first one, it's the second one. The second one makes the hitter know you meant the first one."

And Drysdale developed a philosophy of his own: "My own little rule was two for one—if one of my teammates got knocked down, then I knocked down two of the other team. And if they knocked down two, I knocked down four. I had to protect my guys."

In 1965, Koufax was 26–8 and Drysdale 23–12, the best pitching duo in baseball. In contract negotiations the Dodgers had usually played one against the other. This time, the two pitchers decided to do something unique. They presented themselves during spring training of 1966 as an entry, asking for $1 million over three years, and holding out. They also hired an agent. This had never been done successfully before.

The Dodgers' owner, Walter O'Malley, grumbled. "I have never discussed a player contract with an agent," O'Malley said, "and I like to think I never will." But he did. And while the pitchers didn't get what they asked, each nearly doubled his salary, Koufax getting $130,000, Drysdale $115,000.

Marvin Miller, who became executive director of the Major League Players Association in April 1966, said the Koufax-Drysdale holdout set the stage for the free agency of players that came about 10 years later. "It was a kind of educational tool to the other players," Miller said. "It showed how banding together might get them something that individuals acting alone never had."

Drysdale once said that the three things people often associated him with were his record in 1968 of pitching a string of 58 scoreless innings (subsequently broken by Orel Hersheiser in 1988), of "my reputation for being mean, or the fact that I was durable and never missed a turn." For nine years in a row he pitched in 40 or more games, sometimes coming in in relief if he was asked to in a pennant drive.

The irony of his death is that he was so relatively young and, just two months ago, still seemed able to strike out the side, even in black tie.

Brooks Robinson: A Touch of Gold

December 23, 1982

BROOKS ROBINSON PLAYING THIRD base was, like a rainbow, routinely marvelous. He didn't always look beautiful, however. He had a wobbly, heavy-footed way of locomotion. Once, the former track star Jesse Owens tried to show him how to run better. "But he gave up," Robinson would recall. "He said I ran like a duck."

But Brooksie, as he was called by friends and fans, didn't play like a duck. In 23 seasons in the major leagues, all with the Baltimore Orioles, he set an armful of records for third basemen, including highest career fielding average (.971), most chances, most assists, and most putouts. He won the Gold Glove for fielding excellence 16 times.

He could also hit. He often did so in streaks, though Earl Weaver, the manager during his last 10 seasons at Baltimore, said that Robinson, from the seventh inning on and with the game on the line, was one of the best hitters ever.

Robinson finished with a career .267 average and 1,357 runs batted in. And his 268 home runs were, until Graig Nettles passed him, more than any other American League third baseman ever hit.

Robinson was in the news the other day because ballots for the Hall of Fame had been mailed to the voting members of the Baseball Writers Association of America, and Robinson, who retired five years ago, is eligible for the first time. A headline noted that B. ROBINSON TOPS HALL LIST.

Alphabetically, of course, he does not top the list. Dick Allen, Luis Aparicio, Jim Bunning, Lew Burdette, and Orlando Cepeda, all bona fide candidates, do that. But, of the 46 former players on the ballot, B. Robinson is considered to have the best chance of getting elected. He will head this voter's ballot to join his longtime teammate F. Robinson—Frank -who made it into the Hall last summer, in his first year of eligibility.

Perhaps B. Robinson's single most famous play was also the best example of his style. It occurred in the sixth inning of the first game of the 1970 World Series, Orioles versus Reds in Cincinnati's Riverfront Stadium. Robinson was at third for the Orioles, wearing swatches of charcoal under his eyes to protect against the sun, when Lee May hit a bouncer down the third-base line. Robinson hurried over and speared the ball after it had already gone past him.

"He was going toward the bullpen when he threw to first," recalled Clay Carroll, then a relief pitcher for the Reds. "His arm went one way, his body another, and his shoes another."

The ball arrived in Boog Powell's glove at first base on a bounce but got the batter, who had had sugarplum visions of a double. The play dashed a Cincinnati rally.

Robinson also hit the tiebreaking homer in that game to give the Orioles a 4–3 victory. He continued in each of the succeeding games—Baltimore won in five—to dominate the Series as no one man had since, it was said, Pepper Martin, also a third baseman, some 40 years before.

To a baseball fan, watching Robinson at third was pure joy. Here was a man working to the best of his ability and performing better than anyone else did, or perhaps ever would. Excellence is thrilling to see, whether in a Robinson or a Rembrandt or a plumber.

This fine artisan's tool, his glove, has preceded its owner to the Hall of Fame. In the World Series exhibit in Cooperstown is the Rawlings KBG-3H Pro Model that Robinson used in the 1970 Series.

Picking it up in the locker room before one of the Series games, a reporter was surprised at how old it seemed even then. The color was a tobacco-juice brown from heat, sweat, dust, line drives, and spit. It was cracking in the pocket and ripped inside from summer perspiration. The wool on the underside of the wrist flap was dark and shrunken.

Robinson had traded for the glove. Ballplayers often do that. He had got this one a couple of years before from Dave May, an outfielder who at the time was a teammate. "I picked it up and liked the feel of it," said Robinson.

Neither Robinson nor the glove was perfect, to be sure. In the final game of the 1970 Series, for example, he was angry at himself for not gobbling up a ground ball by Tommy Helms. It had ticked Robinson's glove. "I didn't get a jump on it," he said, "because I wasn't concentrating."

Unusual, because if he had a particular secret of success—beyond extraordinary reflexes and timing—it was his power of concentration at third base, a position that, because of the proximity to right-handed sluggers, is sometimes only a little less dangerous than being a member of a bomb squad.

That was while playing. Off the field, Robinson, now a television color commentator for the Orioles and involved in a consulting firm for players, was and is well known for his decency.

"I've never seen Brooksie hurt anyone's feelings, intentionally or unintentionally," said Weaver. "And I never saw him lose his temper. And I've only seen him get mad at one person, himself. I think he's a fella who knew how to handle success."

It seemed he could also handle rough times.

On July 6, 1976, Weaver performed what he would later call one of the hardest tasks of his managerial career. He told Robinson, then age 39, that a younger player, Doug DeCinces, would be starting in his place.

Weaver recalled, "All he said was, 'If you need me, I'll be here.'"

One year later, on August 21, 1977, the Orioles had to make room for Rick Dempsey's return from the injured list, and the man they dropped was Brooks Robinson, making him a coach. Some people felt that the Orioles had virtually ripped the uniform off his back. If Robinson felt that way, he never said a word about it.

On September 18, though, the Orioles had a "Thanks Brooks Day." A crowd of 51,798 streamed into Memorial Stadium to honor him. It was, up to that time, the largest regular-season crowd in Baltimore history.

For the game on the following day, the Orioles drew 3,325.

II.

JACKIE ROBINSON

Dixie Walker Remembers

December 10, 1981

FRED (DIXIE) WALKER IS not particularly eager to talk about the role he played when Jackie Robinson broke the color line in major-league baseball.

"You reach a stage," he said the other day over the telephone, "where you don't want no one to bother you." He spoke in a soft Southern drawl that was not unfriendly.

Walker is 71 years old and living in Birmingham, Alabama, not far from the town of Leeds, where he was born. Walker was the Dodgers' right fielder when, in the spring of 1947, the unwritten rule that blacks could not play in the major leagues was broken. For more than half a century, it had been strictly enforced in all professional team sports in America. Then Jackie Robinson was signed by Branch Rickey of the Brooklyn Dodgers. The resistance from some opponents—and teammates—was fierce and dramatic.

Of the many people in baseball who opposed the breaking of the color barrier, the name Fred (Dixie) Walker, a onetime National League batting champion, is often mentioned first.

A fine play currently on Broadway, *The First*, recalls that powerful moment in the history of what is often called our national pastime. It portrays a handful of Dodgers trying to force Rickey to change his mind.

Dixie Walker was one of the most popular players in Brooklyn. In the patois of the borough, he was known as "The People's Cherce." When it was announced in spring training of 1947 that black Jackie Robinson would be

109

a rookie with the Dodgers, Walker wrote a letter to Branch Rickey asking to be traded.

"I've been called the 'ringleader' to try to stop Jackie from playing with the Dodgers," Walker said. "I was no ringleader. I was supposed to have organized a meeting of some of the players to boycott Robinson. When it was announced that Robinson was to join the Dodgers, the team was playing an exhibition game in Panama. I was in Miami, meeting my family. We then took a boat to Havana, where the Dodger training camp was. I met the team plane there when it flew in from Panama. I heard a good deal of talk about Robinson. But I didn't know a thing about any insurrections, as it was later called. But I get a message that Mr. Rickey wants to see me. I went to the Hotel Nacional—or whatever it's called—and I sat down with Mr. Rickey in his room.

"He really reamed me out. I was so mad at him accusing me of being a ringleader that a few days later I wrote him this letter requesting to be traded. But I did not mention Jackie Robinson's name. I still have the letter. If you want, I'll read it to you. Just hold on."

A few minutes later he was back on the phone. He began to read: "'March the 26th, 1947. Dear Mr. Rickey: Recently the thought has occurred to me that a change of ballclubs would benefit both the Brooklyn ballclub and myself. Therefore I would like to be traded as soon as a deal can be arranged. My association with you, the people of Brooklyn, the press and radio has been very pleasant, and one I can truthfully say I am sorry has to end. For reasons I don't care to go in to, I feel my decision is best for all concerned. Very truly yours, Dixie Walker.' That's the letter.

"Well, Mr. Rickey was now in the States and I had one of his assistants deliver it to him. But when he got back he did his dead level best to say that my opposition to Robinson was the reason I wanted to be traded. Well, I had been with the club for nine years and I resented being the scapegoat."

Walker did admit that there were pressures on him from people in Alabama not to play with Robinson. "I didn't know if they would spit on me or not," Walker said. "And it was no secret that I was worried about my business. I had a hardware and sporting goods store back home."

Walker's anger toward Rickey subsided. "I told him to forget about the letter," Walker said. The relationship between Walker and Robinson was strained. Robinson, sensitive to the tension, avoided putting Walker into difficult positions; when Walker hit a home run when Robinson was on base, for example, Robinson discreetly did not shake his hand at home plate. Early in the season, Judge Samuel Leibowitz of Brooklyn, a friend of Robinson and Walker, tried to play peacemaker. He asked Walker to pose with Robinson for a newspaper photo. Walker refused. He was already receiving letters that called him "nigger lover."

Walker said he begun to respect Robinson when he saw how Robinson handled "all that guff." "God knows how many times he was thrown at, how many times he was hit," Walker said. "We all got thrown at, but some of the pitchers carried it to extremes with Jackie. But he showed backbone. I never saw anyone who could get that forearm up as fast to keep the pitch from hitting his head. The man could take care of himself."

Robinson had said that one of the most important moments in his baseball life was when Dixie Walker gave him a batting tip. "I remember it well," Walker said. "It was early in the first season. Jackie was having a problem at the plate. I saw something. And I went to him one morning when he was on the rubbing table and told him. It was just a suggestion. I think it worked."

The Dodgers won the pennant, and, at the end of the season, Robinson, who was named Rookie of the Year for his play as the team's first baseman, was given a day in Ebbets Field, the Dodgers' home park.

One of the players on the field to shake Robinson's hand was Dixie Walker.

"I grew up in the South," Walker said, "and in those days you grew up in a different manner than you do today. We thought that blacks didn't have ice water in their veins and so couldn't take the pressure of playing big-league baseball. Well, we know now that that's as big a farce as ever was. A person learns, and you begin to change with the times.

"I'll say one thing for Robinson, he was as outstanding an athlete as I ever saw. He had the instinct to always do the right thing on the field. He was a stemwinder of a ballplayer. But, you know, we never hit it off real well.

"I've gotten along with a lot of blacks since then—I managed 'em in the minor leagues and there's many I came to respect and like—but Jackie was a very antagonistic person in many ways, at least I felt he was. Maybe he had to be to survive. The curses, the threats on his life. I don't know if I could have gone through what he did. I doubt it. But we just didn't gee and haw, like they say down here.

"Over the years, though, Robinson and I would meet at Old-Timers' Day games and we sat and chatted some." He continued. "The other night I watched a television program and heard mention of a number of people who were important in the blacks gaining advantages in America. And the name of Jackie Robinson never came up. It surprised me. I mean, how soon people can forget."

Who's He?

WHO WAS JACKIE ROBINSON, and why is it that so many know so little about him?

In the January issue of *Sport* magazine, William L. Ladson asked 20 black players, "What does Jackie Robinson mean to you?"

The question came up because 40 years ago this month Robinson was named the National League's Most Valuable Player for 1949. He became the first black player to win the award.

This hardly begins to explain, of course, who Jackie Robinson was.

"Jackie Robinson?" said Phil Bradley of the Baltimore Orioles. "What year did he die? I wasn't old enough to remember him."

"I know he was the first black in baseball," said Barry Larkin of the Cincinnati Reds, "but if he were a shortstop I'm sure I would want to know more about him."

"When I was growing up," said Tim Raines of the Montreal Expos, "I really didn't know too much about baseball."

"I don't know anything about Jackie Robinson," said Ken Griffey Jr. of the Seattle Mariners.

Others, though, do. Mel Hall of the Yankees said that "Robinson is the reason why I'm here today. Robinson gave us equal opportunity." Lee Smith of the Boston Red Sox said, "If Jackie Robinson hadn't stuck his neck out for me, there would be no way I'd be making over $1 million."

And Dave Henderson of the Oakland A's said: "The success of Jackie Robinson is the reason why I wear his number. The man was a great player."

To a white boy growing up when Jackie Robinson was breaking into the major leagues with the Brooklyn Dodgers, it seems improbable that not everyone knows and understands and has been moved by the story of Robinson.

The boy remembers going to Wrigley Field in Chicago to see Robinson in the late 1940s, and being a part of the crowd not far from where the bulk of the black fans, proudly and anxiously, sat, in a section in the right-field grandstands.

And all of us were watching him, in his odd but poised and powerful pigeon-toed movements. And though certainly there were some who still wanted to see him fall on his face, the majority, it was felt, even Cub fans, rooted for him, openly or otherwise.

Jack Roosevelt Robinson was a marvelous player: a daring and brilliant base runner, a batter who could hit the long ball and drag a perfect bunt, and a fielder of such skill that, when he made a spectacular, diving catch at second base to save the Dodgers' pennant chances in the 14th inning against the Philadelphia Phillies in 1951, Red Smith wrote of him "stretched at full length in the insubstantial twilight, the unconquerable doing the impossible."

For the young boy, the story of Robinson was glorious, not unlike a fairy tale, of the ugly duckling who succeeds beyond anyone's fantasy, or a Biblical story, like that of Joseph and his coat of many colors, or David, against all odds, vanquishing Goliath.

The story unfolded as Branch Rickey, president of the Dodgers, clandestinely picked Robinson to break the color barrier, and informed him of the certain and terrible hurdles: he would be spat upon, thrown at, reviled, but that, at first, he must turn the other cheek. Until he was established, if he could make the grade. There were experts like Bob Feller who said he wouldn't be able to hit major-league pitching.

He did, of course, and was Rookie of the Year in 1947 and retired 10 years later with a batting average of .311. In 1962, he won election to the Baseball Hall of Fame, again, the first black chosen.

He seems now to be a historical national figure. There are public schools named for him. He was honored with his image on a United States stamp. He is discussed in textbooks. And yet some people don't know who he was, or what he meant.

Of course, there are college students who don't know when the Civil War was, or on which side Japan fought in World War II, or what Columbus and an ocean had in common.

Jackie Robinson was instrumental in opening for blacks the doors of baseball, and other sports, and in other areas, too, including the doors of many people's minds.

Not all, to be sure. And not enough. But many.

And it is important to remember that he didn't do it alone, that there were, for example, whites like Pee Wee Reese and Leo Durocher and Hank Greenberg and Rickey who were supportive.

The tragedy in the lack of knowledge of the story of Robinson—by the time he died in 1972 at age 53, Robinson was lamenting the lack of background of young people for black leaders such as Martin Luther King and Rosa Parks—is the rippling ignorance of some, particularly the young. But Robinson sympathized with their frustration "to get a piece of the action."

Some have, of course. In sports, meanwhile, we see some blacks being as coarse, as self-important, as stupid as some whites. This is one side of egalitarianism. But there are also other blacks manifesting, like other whites, the character, the humanitarianism, and the concern that was the legacy of Jackie Robinson.

Some, like Henry Aaron, keep the flame alive. "Before Jackie died, in the days when he was going blind," said Aaron, "we had long talks. I will never forget that he told me to keep talking about what makes me unhappy, to keep the pressure on. His courage and intelligence showed what the black man could be made of."

Yet the lesson of Robinson is not that he was only a hero for blacks. He was also a hero for mankind. He demonstrated the possibilities for those who—through great effort, and will, and hope, and determination, and the resistance to feel sorry for oneself and to blame others—can indeed triumph over enormous and vicious adversity, and realize one's dreams.

Jackie and Pee Wee

November 2, 2005

IT WAS SIMPLE ON its face, but as deeply layered as the gesture it memorialized.

Yesterday, a statue was unveiled in front of a Brooklyn ballfield, KeySpan Park, where the Mets' Class A Cyclones play. The statue was not of a general on a horse, or a poet in deep thought (with a pigeon on his head), but of two long-ago baseball players—Jackie Robinson and Pee Wee Reese of the Brooklyn Dodgers.

On this uncommonly warm, sun-filled fall morning, a crowd of a few hundred had gathered outside the entrance to the park, in front of the statue, which was under a yellow covering. A band of five, wearing "Brooklyn Symphony" sweatshirts, a nostalgic touch for the Dodger Sym-Phony, a group that once played in long-gone Ebbets Field, struck up several songs, including their classic "Three Blind Mice," which paid homage to umpires.

The monument was representative of a time in history, beyond baseball, that in the late 1940s reached to the deepest, the most tragic, and yet the most elevating moments of a nation in racial crisis. Robinson, a black man, was breaking the long-held racial barrier in the major leagues. Reese, from Louisville, Kentucky, had inherited a teammate whom many people did not want to see play major-league baseball.

Both Reese and Robinson are dead. Reese died in 1999, Robinson in 1972, but their widows attended the ceremony yesterday. Rachel Robinson and Dottie Reese were there with their children, as well as Mayor Michael

R. Bloomberg; two former Dodgers teammates of Reese and Robinson, Johnny Podres and Joe Pignatano; Jeff Wilpon, senior executive vice president of the Mets; and John Franco, the Brooklyn-born pitcher and a former Met.

The statue captures a significant moment that is much remembered, although the precise details surrounding it are hazy. With Robinson receiving death threats and heckling and taunts from the crowd in a ballpark on the road, Pee Wee Reese walked over to him on the infield at a point either before or during a game and offered a quiet but significant gesture of friendship and comradeship.

"My father had done his own soul searching," said Mark Reese, Pee Wee's son, "and he knew that some fans, teammates, and yes, some family members didn't want him to play with a black man.

"But," Mark Reese added, "my father listened to his heart, and not to the chorus."

He added that his father admired Robinson as a ballplayer and as a man. When a petition was passed around in spring training by some Dodger players saying they would refuse to play with Robinson, Reese declined to sign it. And when the moment came for him to demonstrate his concern for a teammate, in the most subtle but unmistakable fashion, he took it.

The statue shows the two players, with Reese's arm around Robinson's shoulder. There is no photograph of the moment. It is not totally certain if Reese, the shortstop, put his hand on Robinson's shoulder, or his arm around him, or just moved up close to him.

Robinson played first base in his rookie season, 1947, and second base the next year. The statue's first design had Robinson wearing a fielder's mitt. But if the incident took place in 1947, Robinson had to be wearing a first baseman's glove, so the sculptor, Will Behrends, changed the baseball ware. The incident probably happened in Crosley Field in Cincinnati, although another Dodgers teammate, Duke Snider, said he remembered it occurring in Boston.

"I remember Jackie talking about Pee Wee's gesture the day it happened," Rachel Robinson said yesterday. "It came as such a relief to him, that a teammate and the captain of the team would go out of his way in such a public fashion to express friendship."

In the biography *Jackie Robinson* by Arnold Rampersad, Robinson himself was quoted as recalling the incident this way: "Pee Wee kind of sensed the sort of helpless, dead feeling in me and came over and stood beside me for a while. He didn't say a word, but he looked over at the chaps who were yelling at me and just stared. He was standing by me, I could tell you that."

The hecklers ceased their attack. "I will never forget it," Robinson said.

"Pee Wee thought nothing of it," Dottie Reese said. "For him, it was a simple gesture of friendship. He had no idea that it would become so significant. He would be absolutely amazed." She added, "I just wish he were here today."

Indeed, Reese's gesture did not come from a save-the-world mentality. It was simply the act of a decent man doing the decent thing. In 1997, Reese told *The New York Times*: "Something in my gut reacted at the moment. Something about what? The unfairness of it? The injustice of it? I don't know."

Bloomberg said that Robinson, like Rosa Parks, who died October 24, was a civil rights hero.

"Jackie was a role model" who, said Bloomberg, went about his life and his athletic pursuits with "style, grace, and dignity," and "electrified a nation."

Marty Markowitz, the Brooklyn borough president, said, "When Pee Wee Reese threw his arm around Jackie Robinson's shoulder in this legendary gesture of support and friendship, they showed America and the world that racial discrimination is unacceptable and un-American."

Several of the speakers said they hoped the monument and the memory of that moment would be an inspiration to young people.

It was mentioned during yesterday's ceremony that the memorial came about because Stan Isaacs, a columnist for *Newsday*, had suggested on a radio show shortly after Reese's death the creation of a statue commemorating the moment. Jack Newfield wrote about the idea in the *New York Post*, and Rudolph W. Giuliani, the mayor at the time, picked up the momentum. Numerous donors followed suit.

With the speeches ended, the yellow covering was taken off and the statue revealed. There was applause, and some gasps at the startling likenesses of the ballplayers.

Then the Brooklyn Sym-phony broke into "Take Me Out to the Ballgame."

III.
_____

SPECIAL MOMENTS

Cal Ripken Jr.: At the Very End

October 6, 2001

IN THE BALTIMORE ORIOLES' clubhouse in Camden Yards the other day, Cal Ripken was asked if he would have preferred being a basketball player. Silly question, meant to be a little joke.

There was a pause. Ripken was actually mulling over the question. It is known that Ripken loves basketball. He has a full-court gym in his home in Reisterstown, Maryland, and, at 6-foot-5 inches and a rock-solid 220 pounds and with a closely shaved head that resembles the coiffure of Michael Jordan, is known to be a good player in the games in which he invites college and sometimes pro players to participate in the off-season.

"Well," he said, "I think I chose the right game for me."

If there is a record for greatest understatement, that observation would rank high. This weekend, the end of baseball's regular season, was the culmination, the celebration, the grand finale and farewell of one of the most remarkable careers in sports.

Tonight at Camden Yards, the Orioles played their last game of the season. First there was a 45-minute tribute to their longtime star and beloved local hero—he was born in Havre de Grace, Maryland. The groundskeepers even contributed their bit of homage, mowing a huge 8 in the center-field grass, signifying Ripken's uniform number.

All this for a man who transformed, to a large degree, the concept of shortstop, proving that a big man could be nimble enough to play a demanding position that was usually the province of shorter, springier water bugs.

123

He broke numerous fielding and hitting records. And he broke a mark for endurance that combined skill, strict adherence to conditioning, intelligence, and the will to play through injuries.

In the process, the national attention lavished on him for his pursuit and then his bettering of Lou Gehrig's record for consecutive games is credited with helping to bring baseball out of the malaise it had suffered after the players' strike of 1994.

When Ripken broke Gehrig's mark of 2,130 consecutive games on September 6, 1995—Ripken's streak began on May 30, 1982, and ended at 2,632 games, on September 20, 1998, nearly 17 seasons without missing a game—it made him a national sports figure like few other athletes before or since.

On June 19, Ripken, 41 years old and playing in his 21st year in the major leagues, all with the same team, announced that he would retire from baseball at season's end.

From that point forward, a cheering farewell tour took place in the major-league towns the Orioles visited, a tour capped, perhaps, with the 2001 All-Star Game, his 19th. Ripken was named an American League All-Star as an honor for career achievement, his statistics this season hardly meriting his inclusion on the team. No matter. He homered—Ripken has a history of responding in dramatic situations—and was named the game's most valuable player, becoming the oldest player to claim the award and the only player to win it twice for the American League.

Ripken's final game, filled with sentiment, hardly lived up to his career achievements. He went 0-for-3, lining out to the wall in left in his first at-bat, then popping out to short. In his last at-bat as an Oriole, tipping his cap to a standing ovation before stepping in to bat, he flied out to center field. The Red Sox beat the Orioles, 5–1.

"I've been thinking these last few days about what I'm going to miss, and I think most of all it will be what went on outside the white lines of the playing field, away from the playing field," Ripken said Friday. "Sure, I'll miss the competition, the tension of the games, but I think it'll be the journey, the sitting around in the stadium, on the buses, the horseplay in the locker room, the camaraderie—the people—that I think I'll miss most of all."

Did he believe, as some do, that his longevity record obscured his other significant accomplishments, from two league Most Valuable Player Awards to leading the league in fielding percentage four times, in assists seven times, and double plays eight times? How about his 3,183 lifetime hits, 1,695 runs batted in, and 431 homers?

"I never felt it obscured anything," he said. "The people who know the game know what I've done on the field beyond playing often. I just tried to play the game, and play it well."

David Cone, the starting Red Sox pitcher in Ripken's last game, said: "He's such a class act. Cal should be the model for all professional athletes. He stays in incredible shape—you'd have to be to play all those games—and he's such a consistent performer, which you'd have to be to post up those numbers for 21 years. He's never had a season in which his numbers were glaringly different. And even at the end, he was still the toughest out for me in the lineup."

And this despite Ripken's .239 batting average, a career low. Not everyone was impressed with Ripken's consecutive-game streak. Bobby Bonds, a coach with the Giants, called it "idiotic." He said everybody needed a rest, and that it had to hurt the Orioles at times for Ripken to continue his streak when he was ailing and a more able body was available. Ripken replied: "People are entitled to their opinion. But their opinion doesn't always make it a fact."

To the accusation that Ripken was selfish in pursuit of Gehrig's record, to the exclusion of team considerations, Gene Lamont, a Red Sox coach who managed against Ripken when they were both in the minor leagues in the late 1970s and then when Lamont managed the Chicago White Sox, said: "If he's selfish, everybody's selfish, because every player who got that close would have wanted to break the record that everybody said would never be broken. I know that when I was managing against him, I was hoping he'd take a day off."

Ripken's streak nearly ended a handful of times, when he sprained an ankle or a knee, but he continued playing. On August 2, 1997, in Game 2,423, he considered leaving with lower back pain but stayed in the lineup and singled in his next at-bat and homered the next day.

The streak endured through Ripken's move from third base to shortstop and back. In 1982 Earl Weaver, then managing the Orioles, believed that Ripken the third baseman could be an excellent shortstop and moved him there. It was also in early '82 that Ripken ran into the most difficult period of his career.

"I went into an early slump and thought every day that I'd be sent back to Triple A," Ripken said. "But Earl showed the patience to let me grind it out, which is what I've done my whole career, grind it out."

Davey Johnson convinced Ripken before the 1997 season to move back to third. Ripken bridled at first, but eventually agreed to the change. Some teammates expressed displeasure when, on the road, Ripken would stay at a different hotel, to avoid crowds.

Other teammates, like Ripken's good friend, outfielder Brady Anderson, would note that if those guys did what Ripken did, they could establish some rules for themselves, too.

"I never played carefully to avoid injury, but I never dove for a foul ball two rows deep in the stands, either," he said. "I played for today, not for tomorrow, and whatever came around was part of the game."

He said he would now devote his energies to a baseball complex being built for youth in Aberdeen, Maryland. For many, the memory of Ripken the player will not be forgotten, particularly the passion with which he played. He said he got that from his father, the late Cal Sr., a coach and, for a period in the late 1980s, Cal Jr.'s manager with the Orioles.

"My dad not only taught me the value of hard work, that when you work hard good things happen," Ripken said, "but he taught me to enjoy what I was doing. He exposed me to the joy of the game. In the end, baseball for me was fun."

Last night's career-ending final inning found Ripken in the on-deck circle. There were two outs and a man on second and the crowd was chanting,

"We want Cal." It was up to Brady Anderson to get on base, but on a 3-2 count against reliever Ugueth Urbina, Anderson struck out.

With most of the fans still in the ballpark, still cheering, Ripken made a tour around the park chauffeured in a red convertible. His teammates and the Red Sox players stood in front of their dugouts and watched. Then Ripken came to shortstop, where a microphone had been set up.

For minutes, he couldn't speak, he was so emotionally caught up in the moment. When he gathered himself, he thanked the fans for "sharing your love of the game with me." He said he had lived "a dream" playing for his hometown team and he hoped that "I had made a difference."

He left his particular stage for the last time, to a thunder of fireworks and applause.

Game 7: A Stack of Goose Eggs

October 27, 1991

MINNEAPOLIS, MINNESOTA—Nothing was happening, nothing, nothing, nothing, nothing but increasing tension. The zeros on the scoreboard last night in the Metrodome were dropping inning after inning after inning, as if a row of hens were working overtime. It appeared that the best and concluding moments of this baseball season—maybe the best of any baseball season—might last forever.

This was the seventh game of the World Series, and, after three, four, five, six, seven innings, nobody could score. People tried: The Minnesota Twins got a runner to third in the third inning; the Atlanta Braves did likewise in the fifth. But nothing happened. The pitchers, Jack Morris of the Twins and John Smoltz of the Braves, were matching sets of excellence, bookends of bravado.

It was preposterous. It couldn't get more dramatic. It did.

In the eighth, both teams loaded the bases with one out, but the Twins turned a double play to end the Braves' threat. In the bottom of the inning, the Braves did precisely the same thing to the Twins, behind Mike Stanton, who had replaced Smoltz.

It went into the ninth inning, 0–0. That is, 16 zeros. Nothing had happened, and it just kept on happening. And into the 10th: zero, of course, to zero. The longest Game 7 with no score in the history of the World Series.

And there it ended. Dan Gladden hit a broken-bat double, and there was a sacrifice bunt and two intentional walks, and then with the bases loaded and a pulled-in outfield, Gene Larkin, a seldom-used infielder, stepped up to pinch hit. He was facing Alejandro Pena, now on the mound for the Braves. The noisy home crowd of 55,000 was on its feet and creating a snowstorm by waving its white homer hankies. And Larkin responded. He looped a fly ball over the outstretched glove of left fielder Brian Hunter, for a single to score the lone run of the game.

Suddenly it was over. Suddenly the Twins had won. But the Braves did not lose. They just didn't win the World Series, is all.

Sometimes the gods are just. Sometimes even they, taking time from their flutes and lyres and various dalliances, will determine that we, too, down below, could use a bit more pleasure, especially in these times of gloomy national recession and despairing world affairs and the football season. And so they, along with Kirby Puckett, in the guise of a mere mortal, conspired to give us one more game of baseball.

Not just any game, of course, but a seventh game of the World Series. And not just any World Series, either. But one that has gone from the dramatic to the melodramatic, from suspenseful theater to the old Saturday afternoon serial thriller.

Four of the first six games between the Braves and the Twins had been decided by one run, and three had been determined only in the home half of the final inning, to break up a tie game—one concluding in the ninth inning and one in the 12th, with plays at the plate, and, on Saturday night, in the 11th, with Puckett's game-ending home run.

But we needed this game, Game 7, and that's the simple truth. It was only fitting and proper. It was all so unlikely, all so upside-down, but this seems to restore the cosmic balance: two teams that finished last in their divisions the year before win the pennants. Each team knowing in its heart that it cannot lose, that the fates have ordained that this is their season.

Each team understanding that it has come this far, that it has done it by coming from behind not only during the season, but in game after game, and thus overcoming all the odds fashioned by Las Vegas and Olympus.

Each team has had its improbable heroes: Mark Lemke, brought in for defensive purposes, hits a trio of triples, and is prominent in winning Games

3, 4, and 5; Scott Leius, who was only iffy on making the team in spring training, homers to win Game 2; and Jerry Willard, who had left baseball for a season a few years ago because he was going nowhere, is called in to pinch hit and hits a sacrifice fly to win Game 4. And finally Larkin.

It just had to come down to the wire, to a photo finish.

The Twins went up two games to none, and then the Braves came back to take a 3–2 lead, and then the Twins tied it up, three games each.

The dream season would end on a dream: Game 7 of the World Series. "Every kid has dreamed about this," said Jack Morris on Saturday night. "When I was a kid, my brother and I used to play Wiffle ball and I pretended that I was Bob Gibson and he was Mickey Mantle."

But since this is real life, we know that the gods can be cruel, and, using us for their sport, may turn dreams into nightmares.

Ask Charlie Liebrandt, who got knocked out of Game 1, and then in Game 6 was brought back in relief to start the home half of the 11th inning. He faced one batter, Mr. Puckett, and threw a total of four pitches. Two were balls and two were strikes, including the last, which ended up in the left-center-field bleachers.

After the game, a large group of reporters gathered around Charlie Liebrandt's locker. After a long period in the trainer's room and the shower, with most of his teammates gone, Liebrandt, lean, grim, a cup of beer in his hand, and his eyes looking only straight ahead, parted the crowd around his locker. "Nothing tonight, guys," he said to the newsy assemblage.

There was nothing tonight, guys.

Except, of course, for the memory, and the dream, and the nightmare.

And there was the tingling anticipation that all this set up: Game 7. It had to be. And better than anyone could have imagined.

As the scoreboard, in its way, had been reminding us: oh, oh, oh yes.

Frank Saucier: The Man for Whom Eddie Gaedel Pinch Hit

July 21, 1991

WHEN IT OCCURRED, FEW who happened to be involved ever thought that this, above everything, is what they would first be remembered for. It was Bill Veeck's brainstorm that produced a midget to pinch hit for a member of the St. Louis Browns in the second game of a doubleheader against the Detroit Tigers on Sunday afternoon, August 19, 1951.

For most associated with that game, and that moment, it is their fate that they, like Veeck, would often be recalled for having participated in it. They include Bob Cain, the Detroit pitcher, and Bob Swift, the Detroit catcher, who hunkered on his knees to make a target for Cain for the minute strike zone, and especially Frank Saucier, the Browns outfielder, who was replaced by the midget.

This afternoon, Veeck, who died in 1986, and was one of the great showmen and baseball owners, will be inducted into the Baseball Hall of Fame. And as a part of the celebration, a tiny uniform shirt will go on display in the hall, too. It is a St. Louis Browns jersey, and on the back is the number "1/8." It was the shirt worn by Eddie Gaedel, the 3-foot-7, 65-pound midget.

"In the second game," wrote Veeck in his autobiography, *Veeck as in Wreck*, "we started Frank Saucier in place of our regular center fielder, Jim Delsing. This is the only part of the gag I've ever felt bad about. Saucier was a great kid whom I had personally talked back into the game when I bought the Browns. Everything went wrong for Frank, and all he has to show for his great promise is that he was the only guy a midget ever batted for."

"I shouldn't have been in the game to begin with," said Saucier from his home in Amarillo, Texas. "I was suffering from acute bursitis in my right shoulder and couldn't swing a bat. Nor could I throw."

Saucier knew nothing about the midget project, which was a closely guarded secret by Veeck and a handful of his intimates.

"I had been undergoing treatment for my shoulder," Saucier recalled. "Then that Sunday morning Zack Taylor, our manager, told me I was starting in right field. It was right field, and not center, as Bill wrote in his book. I couldn't understand it because I hadn't played in a couple of weeks, but I thought, 'Well, we'll just see where this goes.'"

Saucier, now 65, and a financial consultant who had also been in the oil business in the Panhandle, recalls all this with a laugh, now. In the bottom of the first, Saucier was scheduled to be the leadoff batter for the Browns. "As I started to the plate, Zack said to me, 'No, wait a minute, we've got a pinch hitter.' I looked around and here comes Eddie, with about three miniature bats on his shoulder.

"I just laughed. I thought this was one of the greatest acts of show business I'd ever seen, and still do. But the umpire didn't. It was Ed Hurley, and he said to Taylor, 'You can't do this.' And Zack said, 'Yes, I can, I have the contract right here in my pocket.'"

"I remember Zack hollering to Eddie, 'Don't swing!' So Eddie bent over and his strike zone was about an inch high. He walked on four pitches, of course. As he trotted to first base, he stopped and tipped his hat to the crowd and waved and then when he got on first, Jim Delsing went out to pinch run for him. Eddie came back to the dugout and sat down beside me. I said, 'Eddie, you were kind of showin' it up a little bit there, weren't you?' 'Man,' he said, 'I felt like Babe Root.'

"I've never felt bad about being pinch hit for by a midget because I probably should never have been with the Browns to begin with."

His only year in the big leagues was 1951, like Gaedel, who never played again. Saucier, injured most of the time, played in only 18 games, most of them as a pinch hitter, and got one hit, a double off Mike Garcia.

"I was making more as the leading hitter in the Texas League with San Antonio than I would have made as a rookie in the major leagues, so I was content," he said. "I had also invested in an oil well. And in February of 1951, lo and behold, the well began flowing 150 barrels natural a day. So I quit baseball. But Bill Veeck called me in July and said he wanted to see me. We talked all through the night, with him trying to convince me to play. Finally, he did.

"He was on crutches, and before he left I asked him, 'What are you doing on those crutches?'

"'Well,' he said, 'I got shot in the leg on Guadalcanal.'

"I said, 'Don't you have a false foot?'

"He said: 'Yes, I do. But I want to tell you something.' And he kind of chuckled. 'When I go to make a deal and my position is not very good, I go on crutches. But when I'm going to make a deal, and I'm in the driver's seat, then I wear my false foot.'"

Saucier, a Navy deck lieutenant in World War II, was recalled to active duty in January 1952 for two years during the Korean War. He was sent to the naval station at Pensacola, Florida "Bill came down there to try to get me released," said Saucier. "'I've got to protect my investment,' he said.

"I said, 'Bill, you can't do this.'

"He said, 'I can try.'

"He went to two admirals there, and got nowhere. Then he went to Washington. 'I've got important people there and I've got I.O.U.s I can pick up from them,' he said. But he couldn't get me out."

Saucier would never play big-league ball again, but his memories of Veeck and the Browns remain vivid. Satchel Paige was on that team, too, and Saucier recalled: "Satchel was amazing. He was around 50 years old and for two or three innings he still had great control and velocity. We used to talk a lot when we traveled on trains. I guess he grew up on a farm in the South, and he hated mules. He told me: 'Stay 'way from mules. You can't pull 'em and you can't push 'em and if you turn your back on 'em they'll bite your ear off.'"

Saucier still gets several letters a week asking for his autograph. "I guess Gaedel helped make me famous in a trivia sort of way," he said. "Eddie died about 30 years ago, and the last time I saw him was when I was stationed in Pensacola. The Ringling Brothers circus came to town and I went to see it. I had heard Eddie was with a circus and I saw him there, tumbling out of a small car with a bunch of other midgets.

"I talked to him later. Oh, he was happy to see me, an old teammate, you know. I asked how he was getting along. 'Well,' he said, 'it ain't baseball, but it's a livin.'"

Executing the Potato Play

September 3, 1987

IN A MINOR-LEAGUE BASEBALL game in Williamsport, Pennsylvania, the other night, the catcher threw a potato wildly in an apparent attempt to pick a runner off third base.

When the base runner reached home plate he was surprised, as was the umpire, that the catcher had the ball and tagged him out.

The runner and the umpire were surprised for good reason. They thought that the thing thrown by the catcher and still being retrieved by the outfielders was the ball in the game. It turned out to be only the potato in the game. A white potato, as it were, which had been shaved cleanly by the catcher, Dave Bresnahan of the Williamsport Bills, a Cleveland Indians team in the Class AA Eastern League.

It was a costly play for Bresnahan, who had sneaked the potato into his glove before the pitch. It cost his team a run, cost him a $50 fine, and also cost him his job. The Indians' director of player development, Jeff Scott, released him right afterward.

"I had checked the rule book a few days ago and found nothing in it that says you can't throw a potato in a game," Bresnahan said yesterday by phone from Williamsport. Which is absolutely true. The rule book also has no ruling against throwing a watermelon in a game. But that's another issue.

Before the pitch, Bresnahan had told the plate umpire that he had a problem with a string on his glove, and went back to the bench to get a new glove. In that glove was the now notorious white potato.

Back behind the plate, potato in glove, Bresnahan gave the pitcher the signal, then just before the ball was thrown, Bresnahan deftly switched potato to bare hand, caught the ball in the glove, and threw the potato intentionally wild to third.

"When I tagged the runner," said Bresnahan, "the umpire looked stunned. He realized that the potato was in the outfield, and now called time out.

"I didn't know why he called time out, but he said the runner was safe.

"I really thought they'd say, 'Do it over,' like a net ball in tennis, and get a laugh out of it. But the umpire didn't have any sense of humor about it at all. Maybe in a week he might. I think he thought I was trying to show him up, but I wasn't.

"I was just trying to put some fun into the game. I mean, it's not like it was the seventh game of the World Series. We're in seventh place, 26 games out of first. It was the 137th game of a 140-game season. The ump said, 'You can't do that!' I said, 'Why not? Where's the rule against it?'

"He said, 'You just can't, that's all.' I guess he was referring to his personal rule book."

Bresnahan makes a distinction between what he did, and the recent outbreak of corked bats and scuffing of balls to get an edge.

"What I did was just to liven up a dull end of a season," he said. "The Phillies, they thought it was funny. My teammates thought it was funny—and had encouraged me to do it. The fans and management thought it was funny. You know they're having a Potato Night at the ballpark. Come to the park with a potato and you get in for a buck. I think tickets are $2.50 or $3 otherwise.

"Everybody thought it was funny except the umpire, and the Cleveland management."

The "prank or practical joke," admitted Scott of the Indians, "was kinda funny, but I think the game, once you get on the field, is sacred. You can't tamper with the integrity of the game. It disrupted the flow of the game, and I can't accept that."

Bresnahan, 25 years old, holds a business degree from Grand Canyon College in Phoenix, his hometown. This is his fourth year in the minor leagues and it appears, with a .149 batting average in 52 games this season for Williamsport, that this might be the end of the line for him.

It is a long way from the career of his great-uncle, Roger Bresnahan, the Hall of Fame catcher for the Giants and the Cubs, among others, in the early years of this century. It was great-uncle Bresnahan who introduced shin guards in 1907, and who, following a severe beaning, is credited with being the first to experiment with a batting helmet.

"I guess ingenuity is in the Bresnahan blood lines," said Scott.

"All I knew about my great-uncle," said Dave Bresnahan, "is that he was called the Duke of Tralee—that's in County Kerry where my grandparents are from—and he used to catch Christy Mathewson."

Dave Bresnahan said he couldn't believe that he would be released for this. As for the fine, he said his teammates wanted to pay it for him. What he did the next day was come to the park with a sack of 50 potatoes and a note pinned to it and put it on the desk of his manager, Orlando Gomez, who had removed Bresnahan from the game immediately after the incident.

The note read that he couldn't pay the fine, but that he hoped the manager would be satisfied with the potatoes. The note concluded, "This spud's for you. Bres."

Well, some thought the idea of throwing a potato in a game was half baked, others expectedly weighed in with its being sweet.

Whatever, the result was that Dave Bresnahan was going back home. Did he have any plans for the future? "Sure," he said. "Run for governor of Idaho."

Vince's Story (With Assists from Mickey Lolich and Al Kaline)

December 25, 1986

WHEN THE HOLIDAY SEASON rolls around and talk of miracles is in the air, Mickey Lolich sometimes remembers a boy named Vince, and wonders what happened to him.

In fact, the thought of Lolich was triggered by the arrival recently of the ballot for the Baseball Hall of Fame. One of the names on it for the third straight year—he has received only a modest number of votes in the past—is Mickey Lolich, who pitched for 16 years in the big leagues, mostly with the Detroit Tigers.

Besides having won 25 games in one season, and having started, completed, and won three games in the 1968 World Series—in the seventh game he defeated Bob Gibson and the Cardinals, 4–1, and was named the Most Valuable Player in the Series—besides all that, Mickey Lolich stood out because, from the neck down, he looked like Santa Claus in a baseball uniform.

Six feet tall, and weighing as much as 225 pounds in his playing days, Lolich sported a pot belly ("Got it from home cooking," he said, "I rarely drank beer") but still threw hard and well and long.

He could hit (he had a home run in the World Series) and he could field. "That belly of his never seemed to get in his way when he was on the mound," said Rod Carew. "But I always marveled at how well this chubby guy bounced off the mound after bunts or taps. I always thought that the fatter he got, the faster he got. He seemed to defy the law of nature."

"The fatter you get," Lolich said recently, with his easy laugh, "the faster you get in perpetual motion. I'd come off the mound to field a bunt and just let my weight propel me. But I pitched a lot—one year I threw 376 innings—so you can't tell me I was out of shape." Lolich now earns a living from, perhaps not surprisingly given his penchant for munching, the Mickey Lolich Donut Shop in Lake Orion, Michigan, some 50 miles from Tiger Stadium, the scene of many of the triumphs.

Lolich was someone many guys in the stands could relate to. "People used to say to me," Lolich recalls, "'Hey, it's nice to see you in the major leagues. You look human, and not like all those golden gods.'"

But Lolich and his teammate Al Kaline were gods to Vince, who in 1977 was 14 years old. Lolich and Kaline ran a one-week baseball camp for boys, in Ypsilanti, and Vince was one of the campers.

"He was a black kid who lived with his mother, was overweight for his age, and retarded," said Lolich. "He didn't know how to put a key in a door. He was confused about things like that. When he put on a T-shirt, he put it on backward.

"We didn't know about Vince, and just accepted applications and let it go at that. We really didn't notice him the first day at check-in, but we discovered on the second day that basically he could do nothing in the way of sports."

Lolich and Kaline became "quite concerned" that Vince might get hurt, and their attorney suggested that Vince be sent home. The attorney called Vince's mother, and she broke down in tears.

She said Vince idolized the Tigers, and that he worshiped Al Kaline and Mickey Lolich. Vince would sit in front of the television set and watch ballgames wearing his Tiger cap and baseball glove.

"He lives and breathes the Tigers, and exists only for baseball," she said. She said she was a cleaning lady and living on that and welfare. Vince had never been to a Tiger game because she couldn't afford it, and she had to take odd jobs to come up with the money to send Vince to the camp.

"It would be the greatest blow to him if he were sent home," she said. "I don't know what effect it would have on him."

"When Al and I heard the story," said Lolich, "we said, 'What choice do we have?'"

So Kaline and Lolich called a meeting of the 90 or so campers—all but Vince, who was taken for a walk by one of the counselors. "Al and I explained the situation to the kids, who had been teasing him and calling him 'Fatty' and 'Stupid,' the way kids can be cruel when there's someone different among them," said Lolich. "We told them it was Vince's life dream to be here, and we'd appreciate it if they could accept him and try to help him.

"They did immediately. They helped him get dressed, and put food on his tray at each meal, and took him to the ballfield. One couple of kids would stand around him to protect him in case of a line drive. It was really something to see. He couldn't play, but he coached first base, and he cheered hard. Vince was a great cheerleader. He was in his glory, he was having the time of his life.

"On the last day, I pitch to all the campers, and Al and I decided to let Vince bat. He had tremendous problems making contact with the ball. Al was on the on-deck circle, and called advice: 'Get your hands up, Vince, get your bat back.' And he'd walk over and show him.

"I had moved in, but I still threw overhand. The first pitch was a strike down the middle, and the umpire naturally called it a ball. Vince swung at the next pitch and missed. And then, lo and behold, on the next pitch the miracle happened. Vince hit the ball! He tapped a slow roller to the shortstop.

"Vince chugged to first, and the shortstop—God bless him, I wish I could remember his name—juggled the ball on purpose, and threw to first just as Vince was one stride from the base. Vince beat the throw and both teams were jumping up and down, yelling and screaming.

"Later that night, there was an awards banquet, and Vince got the award for most improved player.

"Vince was given a standing O, and he put his arms around Al and me and gave us a big hug. He said, 'I'll never forget this as long as I live.' And that's when Al and I both cried."

Can the Cubs Really Be for Real This Time?

May 2016

THE CHICAGO CUBS HAVE gotten off to a swift start in the National League, posting for all of April the best record in the major leagues.

"I'm not getting sucked in again," said my cousin Errol. "It's only April, for God's sake." Errol, like me, is Chicago born and raised. He has remained living in the city, while I have spent the last nearly 50 years living and working in New York. But...

It's odd, of course, maybe even weird. You grow up following a team—in my particular case, the Chicago Cubs—and you can move to Nairobi or the Arctic or even Pittsburgh, and your heart (and, most assuredly, not your head) still follows the boyhood team through thick and thin. In the Cubs' case, through the years, frequently thin and thinner.

I began following the Cubs when I was eight years old, in 1948. For the next 20 years the Cubs finished in what was then known as the second division. That is, for the two eight-team American and National Leagues, when a team finishes in fifth to eighth (or last) place, it's the second division. (As it happened, they finished tied with Cincinnati for last in '48). Meanwhile, you grow up thinking that the team you root for will eventually lose. This is not great on the psyche, to be sure, though I guess it's a great lesson for dealing with life's inescapable adversities, or so I am told by sympathetic souls (like my sweet spouse).

None of the players that were my heroes in those days—Eddie Waitkus, Andy Pafko, Johnny Schmitz, Hal Jeffcoat, Phil Cavarretta, Swish Nicholson (shortly after, Hank Sauer)—not only no longer play for the Cubs, they have all shuffled off this mortal coil. And yet, I follow this team with heightened anticipation, as in years past, regardless of whether it makes sense or not. The Cubs have indeed on occasion started fast, only to succumb to what we in those earlier years, particularly, called, inevitably, the June Swoon.

The Cubs had some exciting, even winning teams, in 1969 and 1984 and 2003 especially. But something terrible would happen to squash our enthusiasm—in '69 the blame was too many days games, though the other teams played in the hot Chicago sun, too; in '84—why did they leave Sutcliffe in so long?!; and in 2003 it was poor Steve Bartman, wearing a headset like a co-pilot, reaching for a foul ball, and, essentially, being ushered into the Witness Protection Program from that point on.

Last season, the Cubs were good, very good, and made it to the League Championship Series, and all they had to do was beat the Mets in order to go on to the World Series. It is a matter of wide knowledge in this nation and Canada that the Cubs had not played in a World Series since the last year of World War II, and had not won a World Series since 1908 (what's that saying around Chicago—"Anyone can have a bad century"?). Well, the Cubs last year were well past any June Swoon. Now, it was Fall Flop. They surrendered to the Mets in four straight.

As a professional journalist, I of course adhered faithfully to the axiom, "No cheering in the press box." Retired now, I am liberated from those requisite bonds. I watch the 2016 Cubs on television and see, again, a true contender. Are my eyes deceiving me? Is my heart? I also look at their uniforms that indicate CUBS, CHICAGO, and the red "C" on the blue cap and recall my tender youth when the uniforms had similar insignias (and wonder: at bottom am I rooting for, well, the cap?). I see a very good double-play combination, from Zobrist (or Baez) to Russell to Rizzo. And I recall the double-play combinations in my youth—Bob Ramazzotti to Roy Smalley to the grandstands, Miksis to Smalley to the grandstands, Terwilliger to Smalley to—well, that was the tenor of those teams. I tell myself, Ghosts Past.

And on the mound now, there's Arrieta, the 2015 Cy Young Award winner, and off to a sensational start, and Lester and Hammel and Lackey also can look dominating. Rondon has been a stopper out of the bullpen. Bryant crushes balls that can break windows across Waveland Avenue from Wrigley Field. Fowler is a demon in center. Rizzo is a master at first base. Jason Heyward was a great outfield acquisition from the Cardinals. The manager, Joe Maddon, is becoming as beloved to Cubs fans as Mayor Daley was to precinct captains. And the brains behind the operation in the front office, Theo Epstein, is no longer deemed the Boy Wonder. He is now the Adult Wonder.

And so, dear reader, it is true. Despite all that I have experienced as a Cub fan for nearly 70 years, after all the disappointments, not to mention the occasional moist eye, it's official: I'm sucked in.

Yes, For Real They Were

November 4, 2016

THE CUBS—THE TEAM I had rooted for since a boy growing up on first the West Side of Chicago and then the North Side—made the playoffs, and did it with the best record in the major leagues. To these supposedly objective septuagenarian eyes (remember, no cheering in the press box, a dictum I subscribed to for nearly 50 years as a sportswriter, so the phrase "supposedly objective"), the Cubs are the best team in baseball, and their winning of 103 games (losing only 58), some eight games better than any other team in the Majors, is reflective of their standing in the baseball world.

The playoffs have a decidedly bittersweet taste since it is recalled how the very good Cubs of 2015 got swept, of all embarrassments, by the Mets in the National League Championship Series. But of course it is a new season, a new team, a new October. In the National League Division Championship series, the Cubs go up against the San Francisco Giants, who have won the World Series for the last three even years, 2010, 2012, and 2014. Oh, oh. Cubs losing 5–2 going into the ninth inning in AT&T Park. Looks like a deciding Game 5 is in the near, tremulous future. But the Cubs erupt for four runs, in the ninth, to win 6–5! Hard to believe!

Next, the Dodgers in the National League Championship Series. The Cubs go down 2–1, and win Game 4, win Game 5, and win Game 6, 5–0, beating Clayton Kershaw, said to be the best pitcher in baseball, and who beat the Cubs in Game 2. Kyle Hendricks shutout pitching, and homers by catcher Willson Contreras and Rizzo, sealed the deal: the Cubs go to the World Series for the first time in 71 years. Hard to believe!

As an honorary (no longer working) member of the Baseball Writers Association of America, I was able to purchase tickets for the World Series games (face value: $285 each, and could have fetched $3,000 or more), and requested only those for Games 3, 4, and a possible Game 5, in Wrigley Field. (The first two games, and, if need be, Games 6 and 7, would be played in Cleveland against the Indians in Progessive Field.) I had box seats far down the left-field line. The fact that the beer vendor in the nearby aisle would obscure my sightline to the batter's box, and the hot dog vendor would do the same regarding my sightline to the pitcher's mound, and the fact that on virtually every pitch had fans leaping up in front of me, didn't quite diminish the thrill of being in this old, and for me, deliciously familiar, ballpark.

Some things, of course, had changed. There was the World Series bunting that, growing up, we'd only see in black and white on television as the Yankees played again and again in the Series. And there were the rooftop bleachers across Waveland and Sheffield avenues that gave their neighborly touch to the august proceedings. It was late fall and the ivy on the walls had started to turn brown. I had been against installing lights in Wrigley Field, believing it would take some charm from the Friendly Confines. But it was done on August 8, 1988, and now I had to admit that the whole electronic setting was spectacular.

Needless, to say, with the excitement of the games, the atmosphere was electric, as well. The great, green, hand-turned center-field scoreboard was still prominent, but so were the two ultra-modern Jumbotron screens above the right-field and left-field bleachers.

I was thankful for the left-field one, because the plays that I missed due to the beer and hot dog vendors and the soaring, roaring fans in front of me, I was able to catch up with on the screen replays. (I was used to sitting and watching games from the press box, where none of my colleagues would be jumping up—except when sandwiches were passed around). And how different from the games I remembered going to as a boy, sneaking into the daytime ballpark, and sneaking down to the box seats, and trying with my friends to nestle in unseen among the, in those days, crowds of generally 6,000 or 7,000. Now for this World Series game there were more than 40,000 jammed into the ballpark, most of the fans standing even with, as I've noted, tickets for seats.

It had looked like curtains after the Cubs had fallen behind three games to one—losing one game in Cleveland and two on cool, windy nights in Wrigley Field—and a line from Shakespeare intruded on my mind (certainly too maudlin in the circumstances of a mere ballgame, but intruded nonetheless): "As flies to wanton boys are we to the gods; they kill us for their sport." But, hold on, Lester in Game 5 was on his game, so was closer Aroldis Chapman, throwing, as the saying goes, bullets, and aided by a Bryant homer, the Cubs made a sweet, narrow comeback to win, 3–2, and force Game 6 in Cleveland. Won that, a 9–3 blowout, behind Arrieta and a grand-slam blast by Russell!

And now the crucial Game 7. Home in Manhattan, I saw the game on television in my living room, with an old friend, Ike Herschkopf. He had asked to watch the game with me—I was reluctant to see it with anyone since, I knew, it was going to be a rather emotional experience. "Okay, Ike," I said, "but there has to be serious concentration." And he, Queens-bred, was true to my word.

We all know what transpired. The Cubs went up 5–1, and Maddon for some reason that I refuse to believe made sense, removed Hendricks midway in the fifth though he was sailing along. Lester enters, and the Indians score a pair. Okay, it was 5–3, and then the aged (well 39 years old is aged in baseball terms) catcher David Ross whacked a solo homer to make it 6–3, Cubs. But then in the eighth, and the Cubs just six outs from winning it all, the Indians scored three runs to tie the game! If this didn't look like Hell has yawned widely for the Cubs—well, nothing but goose eggs on the scoreboard in the ninth for either team.

Going into the 10th, and, my God, the rain came, a rain delay! Rough, rough to take as we sat and wondered: would it rain for the next day, or two days, or whatever? Imagine waiting it out. Who was concocting this suspense, anyway? Who knew when the game would resume, and Ike expressed regrets but had to be heading home—it was getting well past bedtime in New York. I was wide awake.

And then suddenly the rain stopped. The groundskeepers ran out like lemmings and pulled back the tarp on the infield—the rain had lasted only about 15 minutes.

The Cubs came out and scored two in the top of the 10th. No need now to recall how, though young Schwarber, our Paul Bunyan and Babe his blue ox rolled into one, had something significant to do with it. But what mattered was that he and they put us a leg or more up on the Indians. 8–6 Cubs. And now the Indians' bottom of the 10th. Napoli goes down swinging. One out. Ramirez grounds out. Two outs, just one to go…but Guyer walks, takes second. Davis drives him in with a single up the middle. Now 8–7 Cubs. Runner on base. Pinch hitter Michael Martinez comes to the plate. A home run would win the game for the Indians. More important, a home runs loses the game for the Cubs, loses the World Series for the Cubs, devastates the dreams of so many life-long fans. But still, there are two outs…

Martinez swings—and taps a slow roller toward third base. Bryant races in, fields the ball cleanly, rifles a perfect throw to Rizzo. The first baseman snares the ball and leaps up, followed instantly by the rest of his bounding teammates. The Cubs win the World Series—the World Series! I sat there in a kind of disbelief. I don't remember if my eyes were moist—my wife, Dolly, says they were—but I know I felt an uncommon, what, happiness, joy—relief?

Whatever it was, I know one thing: I got sucked in, from April to November, and forever glad I had.

McGwire and Sosa: An Unforgettable Race for a Revered Record

IN A YEAR, 1998, that saw continued fighting in Kosovo, a peace accord in Northern Ireland, and President Clinton accused in a White House sex scandal, in America, as well as in other parts of the world, considerable attention nonetheless was drawn to a rare, but thrilling event. It took place on baseball diamonds in the States, with particular emphasis on the old, ivy-walled Wrigley Field in Chicago and the newer construction, Busch Stadium, in St. Louis.

The red-headed, goateed, muscular, big-as-a-building Mark McGwire, first baseman for the St. Louis Cardinals, and Sammy Sosa, the effervescent Dominican right fielder for the Chicago Cubs, were engaged in a pursuit for the major-league single-season home-run record, perhaps the most hallowed record in American sports.

Ted Williams, one of the greatest hitters in baseball history, once said that "hitting a baseball was the hardest thing to do in sports." Whether he was right or not—that seeking to connect on a 95-mile-an-hour fastball, or a sharply breaking pitch, from 60 feet, six inches from home plate was the most difficult assignment in the realm of sport—it certainly ranks high in that category.

Meanwhile, the McGwire-Sosa race essentially began in the spring, went through the summer, and reached its climax in the early autumn.

Every day, fans opened their newspapers to read whether Sosa had caught up to McGwire, and whether either had hit a home run, or two, or three.

Fans streamed into the ballparks where their teams were playing in record numbers.

Baseball has been called a fabric, or symbol, of America, combining much of American history (its opening opportunities to minorities, for one thing), its ideals (of supposed sportsmanship, as well as cutting corners to get ahead), its strivings (to win, to be first, to be larger than life as a champion), along with outsized heroes like Babe Ruth, and, in this season, Mark McGwire and Sammy Sosa.

For many in 1998, the hope was that the home-run race was so spine-tingling that they wished it would go on forever.

It all began on Opening Day in April with a bases-loaded home run by McGwire. He homered in his next three games. On May 19 he reached 20 homers faster than anyone in any season ever, then became the fastest to reach 30 homers, the fastest to reach 40.

Meanwhile, Sosa kept pace, especially with his spectacular 20 home runs in May. Home runs continued to boom off his bat, but he remained one, two, or three homers behind McGwire. In what seemed a game of home run cat-and-mouse, Mark McGwire is playing Tom to Sammy Sosa's Jerry. This was as good a race as anything at Epsom or Churchill Downs, or even that cycle competition in France.

McGwire and Sosa had put a new face on a rivalry. McGwire, son of a Southern California dentist and Sosa, from an impoverished background in the Dominican Republic, had been as close to brotherly love as possible under the circumstances.

"People have looked at athletes these days as greedy or arrogant and then they see Sammy and I truly respecting one another, and liking one another," said McGwire. "Two guys from two different backgrounds and countries appreciating what the other is doing."

It was in early August and McGwire had told reporters, "There's more important things in the country than worrying about my hitting a home run."

Shortly after, having had a great response to that view, he revisited it. "I had got kind of testy," he said, after having endured a short slump. "I hadn't realized just what all this meant to people. That reaction by me never happened again."

McGwire had been a big (6-foot-5, 245-pound), strapping ballplayer since he broke into the major leagues in 1986 at age 22 with the Oakland A's, and was a home-run slugger from the start. Sosa, on the other hand, had been a skinny, 6-foot, 165-pound 20-year-old when he broke in with the Texas Rangers in 1989. He was traded that year to the Chicago White Sox by the Rangers' managing partner, one George W. Bush.

After Sosa grew more muscular and began hitting home runs in his fourth full season in the major leagues, Bush, who had once desired to become the baseball commissioner, said that one of his biggest mistakes (some thought he said "only" mistake) was to trade Sammy Sosa. The two remained friends, and Sosa excused Bush, saying, "I was young and raw, and I probably would have traded me, too."

"What a great year, what a historical year," said McGwire, in mid-August of 1998. "Wouldn't that be something if both Sammy and me hit—what is it?—62 or 63 homers each? September 27 is the finished product"—that is, the end of the regular season.

Before the game, in sleeveless blue T-shirt, and his prodigious arms folded casually during conversation, McGwire said he is only now beginning to understand what the pursuit of the home-run record by Sosa and him has meant to America—and maybe the world.

"It's amazing," he said, standing in front of his locker in the Cardinals clubhouse. "I've seen the editorials and the front-page stories about what this means to people. Just today I got a letter from the Prime Minister of Japan and from Bob Dole." (Dole was the Republican candidate for president who lost to Bill Clinton in 1996.) He said he found it "incredible" that he has had even bigger headlines than President Clinton.

Sosa, 29 in 1998, liked to say that he was pulling for McGwire, at 34, to break the record, and for the Cubs to reach postseason play. "I'm not thinking about chasing nothing," he said. "Just get in the playoffs." But he admitted to taking great pleasure in all the attention surrounding that home-run business.

"It's like a great gift," he said. He had spoken often about the mean circumstances in which he grew up in the little town of San Pedro de Macoris, where he shined shoes and picked oranges to help his widowed mother put food on the table. "I'm happy to go do my job and everybody go crazy. I love it. Oh, what a country!"

Just before the Cubs and Cardinals met for a two-game series at Wrigley Field, beginning Tuesday night, August 18, Sosa and McGwire surprisingly and outwardly expressed the seeming joy they were sharing publicly. After Sosa took batting practice before the game, he looked to the Cardinal side of the field and saw the team doing stretching exercises. He made a beeline for McGwire, who was twisting on the ground. A phalanx of reporters and cameramen followed Sosa.

"Get away! Get away!" McGwire shouted, laughing. Then he got up, and he and Sosa hugged. And then they parted. It seemed that neither had time to whisper any kind of sweet nothing in the other's ear.

Neither player hit a home run that night. Sosa and McGwire had collectively been 0-for-9, and struck out six times. Sosa said he wondered if they were trying too hard.

But the next afternoon, August 19, the chase to surpass the home-run record in baseball took a dramatic turn. Three dramatic turns, in fact, as the Cubs' Sammy Sosa grabbed the major-league home-run lead from the Cardinals' Mark McGwire only to see McGwire grab it back.

When Sosa lined a home run into the left-field bleachers in the fifth inning, it gave him 48 for the season, one more than McGwire.

Sosa was ahead in the race for the first time all season, and as he ran past McGwire, who was standing impassively by first base, and completed his home-run trot, many in the sell-out crowd of 39,689 who jammed into the ballpark launched into a roaring, "Sammy! Sammy!" chant.

What was McGwire thinking as Sosa cruised by him?

"Not much, really," he said after the game. "Just that Sammy's an awesome player."

As, of course, was McGwire, who over the next five innings answered in home-run fashion not once but twice. He sent one baseball clear out of

Wrigley Field in the eighth inning to tie the game, and another into the center-field bleachers in the 10th to reclaim the home-run lead with 49 and, for good measure, lead his team to an 8–6 victory.

At this point, McGwire was on pace to hit 64 homers—he had 38 games left in the season—and Sosa 62, with 36 games remaining.

The national news media had been dogging their steps for several months.

In the third inning, Sosa lined a shot to left field that looked like a home run to almost everyone in the park, including Sosa. He observed the flight of the ball admiringly on his jog to first base. Alas, the ball hit about three feet from the top of the wall. The Cardinals' John Mabry fielded it, whirled, and threw cleanly to second base, where Sosa, who had realized too late that he had better start running, was out by so large a margin he did not even attempt a slide.

When Sosa did hit one out of the park, in the eighth inning, he was cheered so enthusiastically that he emerged for a curtain call. He waved his cap, then retreated onto the bench where he celebrated on this hot and humid afternoon by pouring a cup of water of his sweaty head.

When McGwire was walked by Mark Clark on a 3-2 pitch in the fifth inning, boos rang from some precincts of Wrigley Field. Fans want to see the march to history, and feel deprived when the slugger—even one wearing the opponent's uniform—is not permitted to swing.

Cardinals pitcher Rich Croushore received the same medicine when he walked Sosa in the seventh inning.

And what did McGwire and Sosa talk about on first base? "We talked about building a golf course together," McGwire said with a smile.

And what was Sosa thinking in right field when McGwire hit his 49th homer?

"I'm thinking, 'He's the man,'" said Sosa.

As the McGwire-Sosa race ever more dominated the news, it was recalled that there were two other historic two-man races for the major-league single-season home run record, both ending in the record being broken.

The first was in 1927, when Yankee teammates Lou Gehrig and Babe Ruth, who held the record at 59, set in 1921, went head to head for much of the season. From April to the middle of August, Gehrig not only matched Ruth homer for homer, but by August 10 he held a 38 to 35 lead. In the end, Ruth fought off the challenge with a charge that began in mid-August and lasted to the end of September and left him with the record 60 homers, to Gehrig's 47 (Ruth hit 17 homers in September to Gehrig's three). Observers recalled that it was a story in America to rival Lindbergh flying solo across the Atlantic Ocean, which occurred in the same year.

In 1961, another pair of Yankee teammates, outfielders Roger Maris and Mickey Mantle, captivated much of the nation with their race for the record. Mantle, the Golden Boy of the Yankees, was clearly favored by a majority of fans, while Maris, who sometimes appeared sullen, was the dogged underdog. And it was Maris who came out on top, hitting 61 homers to Mantle's 54. However, the then baseball commissioner Ford Frick, who had been a friend of and ghostwriter for Babe Ruth, essentially made a concession for Ruth in the record book—sometimes mistakenly called an asterisk, but there was no asterisk. Frick kept Ruth in the record book for home runs because his was a 154-game season (actually 155 games, because there was one tie game), while baseball expanded for the first time to 162 games, in 1961, and this was noted alongside Maris' accomplishment. Again, the race for home runs dominated much of the news, even in John F. Kennedy's first year as president of the United States.

On Tuesday, August 25, 1998, McGwire returned home to Busch Stadium after a nine-game road trip and a giant step toward reaching the home-run record for a season. He departed with 47 homers, and returned with 53, two in front of Sosa and eight short of 61 set by Rogers Maris 37 years earlier.

He remained eight behind Maris, with 32 games left on the Cardinals' schedule.

When McGwire left St. Louis for the road, there was no controversy about muscle-building supplements. When he returned, that morning's *St. Louis Post Dispatch* read, EFFECTS OF ANDRO ARE HOTLY DEBATED.

Some 15,000 fans, who had come two hours before game time, stood along the Cardinals' dugout and filled sections of the lower land upper-left-field decks, lustily cheered McGwire when he stepped into the batting cage for batting practice.

An elderly woman held up a poster: WHEN I GROW UP I WANT TO BE JUST LIKE MARK.

Many of the Marlins stopped their activities, whether it was stretching in front of their dugout or playing catch, and watched, just like the fans. Derrek Lee, a rookie first baseman for the Marlins, edged forward on the dugout steps.

The park grew silent at 5:46 as McGwire waved his bat in anticipation of the throw from the batting practice pitcher. McGwire swung at the first offering and sent it soaring into the lower-left-field deck. The crowd oohed. He hit the second and third pitches into the upper deck. He failed to homer on the next three pitches.

At 5:47, as other teammates had moved quickly in and out of the batting cage taking their turns, he hit one homer in four swings. At 5:48, he went one homer for three. At 5:49 it was one for two, and, in his last trip in the batting cage, at 5:50, getting one swing, he provided the fans with one more treat to remember by lofting a pitch deep into the upper deck, above the neon sign that reads, BIG MAC LAND.

Applause rang around the stadium as he moved to the dugout. McGwire's batting practice homer state: 7-for-16.

Just before Lee took the field, he shook his head. "That was awesome," he said. "He's the best. That's incredible what he just did."

On Friday, August 28, in the top of the fifth inning in Busch Stadium, a small, unobtrusive figure in a small corner of the center-field scoreboard, where a moment before it read McGWIRE 54/SOSA 52, it now read, SOSA 53.

McGwire handicapped himself on August 29 when he argued so belligerently about a called third strike in the very first inning that he virtually forced the home-plate umpire Sam Holbrook to throw him out of the game. The fans booed the umpire lustily, and threw baseballs, golf balls, bottles, and other bric-a-brac onto the field. They wanted to see McGwire swing for the fences. It was like relieving Hamlet of his lines in his own play, or removing the fiddle from Itzhak Perlman when he headlined to play with the New York Philharmonic, or packing the house for Nureyev and then trotting out someone to do a tap dance. But no riot ensued, since many of the 47,627 fans left the ballpark, since the fans generally leave after McGwire's final at-bat. And McGwire himself, of course, was not around to fully respond at the plate to Sosa's 53rd home run, which went up on the electric scoreboard above the center-field bleachers. The next day, however, McGwire made amends with his 55th home run. And Sosa belted his 54th, inevitably dogging McGwire.

At around that time McGwire was discovered to have a bottle of andro-stenedione on a shelf in his locker. It is an over-the-counter supplement and called a precursor to testosterone, the male hormone, because it is converted to testosterone in the body. It was legal in Major League Baseball and in the National Basketball Association—though banned in the National Football League and by the National Collegiate Athletic Association and the International Olympic Committee. Higher testosterone levels are said to speed recovery from workouts and help build muscle mass during workouts. Doctors, meanwhile, are not sure of the side effects.

But an inquiring public asked, was it McGwire or his pharmacist who was responsible for splintering seats in the bleachers and the upper decks?

McGwire has an obvious, and remarkable, natural talent, especially for hitting a baseball long distances, consistently. He broke home-run records in college, at the University of Southern California, and had orbited home runs in his 11 previous seasons in the major leagues, first for Oakland and then with the Cardinals. Most of that time there was no suspicion of body-altering drugs. He, like Sosa, also maintained a rigorous weightlifting program, and it was said he studied films of pitchers with the intensity of a used-car salesman reading the fine print in a contract.

Manager Tony La Russa of the Cardinals said, "You can't teach timing in hitting a baseball, especially when you're talking about hitting a 93-mile-an-hour slider. And if it was just muscle and strength generating those home runs, then you'd have every weightlifter and offensive lineman come off the street and start hitting balls over the fences."

On the afternoon of August 30, Sosa homered in Denver to tie McGwire for the home-run lead, at 54, only to have McGwire, almost exactly seven hours later, blast one out of Busch Stadium, and lead the Cardinals to an 8–7 win over the Florida Marlins.

With that homer, a 500-foot shot, McGwire drew ever closer to catching Roger Maris' record of 61 in a single season, in 1961. McGwire had 26 games left in the season, Sosa had 25.

On September 1 McGwire hit his 56th, tying the National League record. Sosa had moved within a home run or two of McGwire several times in the previous few weeks—after McGwire had held the lead for virtually the entire season—and even went ahead once. But each time, Sosa makes McGwire uncomfortable, McGwire unloads.

On September 7, McGwire propelled home run No. 61, to tie Maris, and the next day, with Maris' family in a box seat in Busch Stadium, he cracked the 62nd. The fans erupted in cheers, and, he recalled, "I was like floating around the bases." In a classy gesture, he went over and hugged the Marises. He had hit his record-breaker in 145 games, so there would be no alleged asterisk alongside his name in the record books.

Neither McGwire nor Sosa stopped there. Oddly enough, Sosa actually took the home-run lead when he hit his 66th, with about a week to go in the season. Just 45 minutes later at Montreal, Big Mac tied Sosa at 66 and quickly took the lead in the following days.

McGwire finished with 70, to Sosa's 66, ending a breathlessly delightful baseball season for the millions of fans in American and beyond. McGwire's team failed to make the playoffs, while Sosa's did, but were quickly eliminated. Sosa, with a higher batting average than McGwire, and more runs batted in, and on a team that had a better season than the Cardinals, was named National League Most Valuable Player.

The record, however, would be short-lived. Just three years later, the Giants' Barry Bonds passed McGwire by hitting 73 homers.

By now, however, the reputations of all three sluggers, McGwire, Sosa, and Bonds, were somewhat tarnished. All three had been accused or suspected of taking bodybuilding drugs. Before a 2005 congressional hearing in Washington on steroid use in the major leagues, McGwire refused to talk about any drug use he might or might not have indulged in. He told a congressman, "I'm not going to go into the past or talk about my past. I'm here to make a positive influence on this." He added, "My lawyers have advised me that I cannot answer these questions without jeopardizing my friends, my family and myself."

To many, this was tantamount to an admission of guilt. Sosa, too, when asked in the same hearing about drugs, categorically denied the use of them. But suspicions remained. Sosa's career diminished. He left the Cubs and played poorly for Baltimore and then in 2006 was out of baseball, though he attempted a comeback in 2007.

McGwire retired from baseball in 2001, due to injuries. In 2007, he was eligible to be elected to the Baseball Hall of Fame. His non-testimony testimony at the hearings soured a great number of the baseball writers who vote for the Hall. Despite a truly Hall of Fame career with the astounding number of 583 homers in his career, he was denied entry, gaining only 23.5 percent of the votes, as star contemporaries Cal Ripken Jr. and Tony Gwynn went in easily.

For his part, Gwynn, the former San Diego outfielder, seemed genuinely sorry that McGwire wasn't voted in. He said he remembered when McGwire "was able to bring a town and country together" when he hit 70 homers.

But McGwire was not alone in that memorable time; there was Sosa, too. And, despite what followed, their great contributions to a glorious time in America, particularly, should not ever be forgotten.

Solace for Mitch Williams

October 31, 1993

HICO, TEXAS—A pale moon, like an eavesdropper, had appeared above the modest red wood ranch house here in central Texas. In the cool early evening, Mitch Williams, in that now familiar scraggly beard and sweatshirt, jeans, and black cowboy boots, sat on the deck and looked out over the broad, flat 600 acres he owns, which, he says, when giving directions to it, is "in the sticks, four miles from paved roads."

It was here that Mitch Williams came immediately after the World Series. It was here he came to get away. To get away from the madness and taunts and death threats and police protection that his performance in the World Series had generated. To get away "from blowin' that last game," as he described it, to get away from "achin' inside."

The tranquility here, the isolation, the peacefulness is what the man known as Wild Thing craved.

When the Philadelphia Phillies returned home from Toronto after losing the sixth and final game at Toronto to the Blue Jays, they returned with only 24 of their 25 players. Mitch Williams wasn't on the flight back. Williams, who had come in in the ninth inning to protect a 6–5 lead, had thrown the last pitch of the World Series, the one that Joe Carter hit for a home run with runners on first and second in the bottom of the ninth inning, giving the Blue Jays an 8–6 victory.

"Can't hear planes, trains, cars—nothin'," said Williams, on his deck Thursday, just five days after the last World Series game. "Can't hear nothin' except when the river is runnin'. Then you can hear the river." As darkness descended, however, one could only hear crickets.

How has he slept since that last game? "Slept better the last four days than I have all year," he said. "The reason?" He smiled. "I'm down here."

He hadn't slept well in the week before, especially after two phone calls to the Phillies office threatened Williams' life after Game 4, which he also "blew," as he said. In the house he had rented for the season in Moorestown, New Jersey, he was up most of the night. "We were scared," said his fiancée, Irene Iacone, who, with her three-year-old son, Damon, is with Williams on the ranch. "Every time he heard a creak—and that housed creaked a lot—Mitch was up and looking around, looking out the window. He had that 9-millimeter pistol at arm's reach all night."

Two local policemen patrolled the house that night, one in the front and one in the back. When the team flew to Toronto the next day, Williams received permission from his manager, Jim Fregosi, to skip the workout so he could get some sleep in the hotel room.

In his hotel room after the last game, when, as Iacone recalls, his eyes were red from pain, from holding back tears—"Oh, he felt so bad, and every time I looked at him I began to cry, and he tried to console me"—he called Iacone's sister and boyfriend, who were staying in their house. He was told the windows had been broken because of rock throwers. "While we were on the phone with them," said Williams, "the police were arresting people outside the house."

And when the Phillies returned to Philadelphia after the last game, Williams and Iacone and Damon were on a flight to Dallas. "If it had just been me, I'd have gone back with the team," Williams said. "But this was Irene's first year with me, and I didn't want to put her through all the things I know we were going to hear, stuff I'd hear at times all year—'You bum.'"

So Williams, the 6-foot-4, 205-pound left-hander, went back to Texas, to the place with the wrought-iron fence at the entrance with the nameplate 3 & 2 RANCH. "Appropriate name, isn't it?" he had said with a smile.

He is aware, meanwhile, that that last pitch, on a 2-2 count to Carter, will likely place him in baseball's all-time hall of infamy. He knows about Ralph Branca's pitch to Bobby Thomson that cost the Dodgers the pennant in 1951. He listened when someone told him that Branca had gone to a priest afterward and asked, "Why me, Father?" And the priest had supposedly said, "Because the Lord felt you were strong enough to carry the burden."

"I've always believed that God will never give somebody something they can't handle," said Williams, drinking a soft drink from a can. "I feel I can handle this. I said in the clubhouse after the game, if there's anybody here who can handle it, it's me. I'd rather this be put on my shoulders than any of my teammates."

It was remembered that immediately after the home run, Phillies first baseman John Kruk, Williams' good friend, hugged him in the clubhouse. What did Kruk say to him? "Nothing," said Williams. "What could he say?"

Fregosi told him, "Mitch, if it hadn't been for you all season, we wouldn't have got this far." And when the other players tried to stand and shield him from the news media at his locker after the game, he would have none of it. "I'm going to face the music," he said. And he sat there answering questions from wave after wave of reporters. It was an impressive, and moving, moment.

"I wasn't going to sit there and make excuses. I lost the game, and I said so. I know that the reporters have a job to do, and that is to cover us in the games. I respect that. And I also know that the last thing a guy wants to do is stick a microphone in my face after I've just blown the World Series. But they have their job, and I have mine."

Williams said it was the hardest thing he has ever had to do as a ballplayer. He talked about the "terrible pitch" that catcher Darren Daulton had called for: a fastball high and away, and he had thrown it low and inside. "I just jerked the ball," he said. "Carter thought it was a slider. That's how bad the pitch was."

Williams said that with two men on—he had given up a walk and a single—he had gone through several scenarios in his mind, but none with the actual result. "I thought about Carter hitting a double-play ball, or him hitting a fly ball and the runners advancing to second and third, but then there would be two outs. I had no doubt in my mind that I was going to save the game. But he hit the hell out of the ball, and I said, 'Wow, I hadn't thought about that.'"

When did Williams know the pitch was gone for a home run? "As soon as he hit—I dropped my head," said Williams. "I didn't even look. I walked to the dugout. I didn't even hear the crowd screaming. Nope, none of it."

He said he wasn't aware that Carter had jubilantly jumped as he ran down the base line. "I remember I jumped about nine feet in the air when I pitched the last out to clinch the pennant," he said, about his saving the sixth game of the playoffs against the Braves. "All the tension and all the excitement was pent up for so long, for 162 games of the season, and then it was all released at that one moment. It was wonderful." The feeling would not last long. "It's amazing how much difference one week can make," he said.

He said he was convinced that he could handle the consequences of that pitch, and that this place, in Texas, was the best place to get all of that out of his mind. "But," said Iacone, "I'm sure some of those thoughts pace through his head."

Why did he feel above all others on his team that he could handle the agony of this defeat? "Because of 600 games in the big leagues," he said. "I'm a closer. My job is to come into the game when it's on the line. I said before the playoffs, 'My job hasn't changed.' And I've said all along, 'You have to have a short memory to be a closer. Nothing you did yesterday has any bearing on what you do today, or tomorrow.' And when that last game was over, I said that the next game is what's important. Even if the next game is next year."

As he spoke, he was anything but Wild Thing—a name derived from a pitcher in the comedy movie *Major League*, who, like Williams, had a blazing fastball but constant control trouble. Williams, this night, appeared a sensitive, reflective young man, one who turns 29 in three weeks.

Williams has been pitching in clutch situations since at least when he graduated from high school in West Linn, Oregon, in 1982 and signed a professional baseball contract at 17 with the San Diego Padres. Four years later he was pitching in the big leagues with the Texas Rangers. He was traded to the Chicago Cubs before the 1989 season—he made the All-Star team that year—and then was traded to the Phillies in 1991.

Some fans have said that there is no way Mitch Williams can return to pitch for Philadelphia, even though he has one year remaining on his contract, in which he earns $3.5 million a season. There was speculation that the Phillies' front office had questioned whether Williams could again pitch effectively for the team. A column by Hal Bodley in Friday's *USA Today* was headlined: TIME FOR WILLIAMS TO LEAVE PHILLIES. But Williams doesn't want to leave Philadelphia.

"Why, because of a handful of fans?" he said. "I love it there, love the situation, the ownership, the players, the pitching coach, the manager. It's where I want to be. I've never been on a team where everyone is so team-oriented. No me, me, me, I, I, I, like most teams. If Kruk, for example, gets punched out four times in a game and we win, he's ecstatic. That's the way it was down the line. There was no quit in that team, no quit in any of us."

"As bad as I felt," Williams said about the end of the World Series, "Darren Daulton came over to me in the clubhouse and said, 'All year I've been tellin' hitters what's comin', and wouldn't you know, in a World Series someone finally believed me!' I appreciated that. We had just lost the World Series and the guys were concerned with picking me up.

"I was achin' inside at that time, and they knew it. I felt I had let my teammates down in a crucial situation of the sixth game of the World Series. But they know I tried with everything I had. It just didn't turn out."

Williams' eyes appeared to moisten a little as he spoke, though it might simply have been the reflection from the porch lights, now turned on because it had grown dark. "There shouldn't be tears," he said. "I mean, a ballgame is a ballgame. Sadness is when someone like Dennis Byrd is possibly paralyzed in a football game. But winning or losing a ballgame, that's just the nature of the game."

He said his perspective comes from his parents, who divorced when he was 12 but with whom he remains close. His father, Jeff, is a machinist in

Oregon, and his mother, Larrie, works in a company's shipping department. "We were a lower-middle-class family, and I know that a lot of people in this world work a lot harder that I do, and without the recognition and earning the kind of money I do," he said. "I've been blessed that I play a game for a living. I mean, I know that I could be out digging ditches."

Meanwhile, there was farm work to do. Along with his brother, Bruce, a former minor-league pitcher who tends the ranch when Williams is away, Williams will feed the five horses, the 15 head of cattle, and the two goats. The brothers will plow the field to plant hay. They might also go fishing for bass and prepare to hunt deer when the season opens this week. And Williams is getting ready to marry Iacone in New Jersey on December 26.

He said he had received phone calls from a number of people, including Bill Giles, the president of the Phillies, and Lee Thomas, the team's general manager. "They asked me how I was doing," said Williams. "I said, 'Fine, I'm doin' fine.'" He grew quiet now and took a sip of his soft drink. He looked out into the darkness. "I love it out here, it's so quiet," he said. "And look at that moon—a full moon—beautiful, isn't it?"

IV.

*THEY DID MAKE
A NAME FOR
THEMSELVES*

The Extraordinary Life and
Times of Ping Bodie

THE QUESTION WAS POSED *to Joe Torre, the esteemed manager of the New York Yankees: "Do you know who is believed to be the first Italian American to play in the major leagues?"*

"Before Ernie Lombardi?" he asked.

"Yes."

"Before Tony Lazzeri?"

"Yes."

He gave it more thought. Finally he said, "I don't know."

"Ping Bodie," came the reply.

"Who?" said Torre.

If Ping Bodie hadn't existed, someone would have had to invent him. In fact, someone did. Two people, as it were: Franceto Sanguenitta Pezzolo and Ring Lardner.

A 1961 obituary in the *Sporting News* told some of the story, under the headline PING BODIE, COLORFUL PICKET AND OLD-ERA SLUGGER, DEAD: "Frank S. 'Ping' Bodie, one of the most colorful characters the game ever produced, died of cancer at Notre Dame Hospital in San Francisco, December 17, at the age of 74."

It went on to say that Bodie, whose real name was Franceto Sanguenitta Pezzolo (sometimes Americanized, so to speak, to Francesco Stefano Pezzolo, or Pizzola) spent nine seasons as an outfielder with the White Sox, Athletics, and Yankees during a playing career that began in 1908 and ended in 1928.

"He compiled a .275 batting average in the majors, but no player ever had more confidence in himself than Bodie, who became a favorite of writers with tales of his power with the bat," continued the obituary notice. "In describing his home runs, Ping used such phrases as 'I whaled the onion,' 'I crashed the old apple,' 'I rammycackled the old persimmon,' and 'I really hemstitched the spheroid.' He was the inspiration of some of the stories in Ring Lardner's *You Know Me Al* series, and it was an unsuccessful steal of a base by Bodie which prompted Bugs Baer to write his famous line, 'Ping had larceny in his heart, but his feet were honest.'"

When Bodie was with the Philadelphia Athletics, he held out for a larger salary than the owner-manager, the legendary baseball genius and tightwad Connie Mack, was willing to surrender. Bodie had led the Athletics in runs batted in the year before, and was thinking quite elevated thoughts about himself.

"I ain't bragging about myself or anything like that, but I got to admit I'm the only real ballplayer Connie's got," he told a reporter. "I and the Liberty Bell are the only attractions left in Philadelphia."

Shortly after, it was only the Liberty Bell, as Bob Creamer wrote in his biography, *Babe*, "for Mack sold the unsigned Ping to the Yankees."

It is often thought that the first Murderers Row in baseball was the Yankees of the late twenties led by Ruth, Lou Gehrig, and Bob Meusel. In fact, the Yankees of a few years earlier were first called Murderers Row, with Wally Pipp and Frank "Home Run" Baker and Ping Bodie.

Since the major leagues in the early part of the century were dominated by English, Irish, and German players, other ethnic groups found that the best way to assimilate, beyond pure talent, was to change one's name. One pertinent example was the Jewish players, such as Reuben Ewing of the Cardinals, Phil Cooney of the Yankees, Harry Kane of the Phillies, and Sam Bohne of the Reds, to name but four. Each of them was born Cohn or Cohen. Another, the Polish Hall of Fame Slugger, was born Aloysius Szymanski, and changed his name to Al Simmons.

Short but powerful and built like a beer keg at 5'8", 195 pounds, Bodie burst upon the scene in 1910 when he hit the then phenomenal number of 30 home runs for the San Francisco Seals of the Pacific Coast League. In the major leagues that season, no one belted more than 10 homers. Of course, the Pacific Coast League wasn't the major leagues, but it was Triple A, just a level below.

Bodie was front-page news. And his output was impressive enough to influence Jimmy Callahan, manager of the White Sox, to have the Chicago ballclub draft Bodie.

Bodie was now a member of the White Sox, but he started his rookie season, 1911, on the bench. After reading a complaint by Charles Comiskey, owner of the club, that his team couldn't hit, Bodie stalked into the boss' office.

"Put me in the lineup," Bodie said, "and I'll show you some hitting of the old apple." Comiskey ordered Callahan to play Bodie, and Bodie lived up to his boast.

He batted .289—only two other teammates hit for higher averages. He didn't get close to the 30 home runs of the season before, and hit but four. But he was productive in another way: his 97 runs batted in were significantly better than any other White Sox player and were good for fourth in the league, behind three future Hall of Famers, Ty Cobb, "Wahoo" Sam Crawford, and Home Run Baker.

While Chicago had a substantial Italian population, Bodie's popularity transcended that ethnic connection. He was a drawing card because of his ebullient personality, as well as his considerable skills as a ballplayer. In his second season with the White Sox, Bodie batted .294 and hit five homers. His RBI production fell to a less impressive but still creditable 72.

"Numerous funny stories were written with Bodie as the 'goat,'" the *Sporting News* reported, "some of which were true, but the majority were new to Bodie until he saw them in print."

This one, however, was true: Bodie made an agreement with White Sox management not to drink liquor during the season. While Bodie seldom touched the hard stuff, he did like beer, and that put on weight, something the chunky Bodie could ill afford.

One day after a doubleheader in St. Louis against the Browns on a hot afternoon in which both games went into extra innings, Bodie found himself in a dilemma.

"When it was over," Bodie said, "I noticed a lot of dust had gathered in my throat. I went to Tony Faust's, a famous St. Louis restaurant, and asked a bartender to prescribe something for my condition. He prescribed a large stein of beer and I was prepared to lift the giant foaming mug to my lips when who should walk in but Manager Callahan.

"Callahan pointed to the stein and hollered: 'That will cost you exactly $500.' I told him: 'You're wrong. It's going to cost me $500.10. I've already paid a dime for this beer.'

"But it turned out that the beer didn't cost me anything. About two weeks before the close of the season, Comiskey called me to his office and gave me a check for $500.10. He not only refunded the fine but paid for the beer."

The story grew and grew, and changed in the telling, like some Homeric saga. Callahan apparently said that he rescinded the fine the next day—after Bodie had gotten three hits.

This was also the time when Ring Lardner was covering the White Sox for the *Chicago Tribune*, and with his exquisite eye and ear and sense of humor took in the language and behavioral patterns of this new sociological phenomenon known as the "modern" ballplayer, which included, to be sure, Ping Bodie, with whom Lardner was in almost daily contact for seven months of the year.

The first of Lardner's famous "Busher" stories was sold to the *Saturday Evening Post* in 1914, Bodie's fourth season with the White Sox. He published five more, which became the contents of the bestseller and acclaimed classic *You Know Me Al*, which continues to be the best selling of Lardner's numerous books. They are stories of a faintly literate pitcher for the White Sox named Jack Keefe who writes letters to a friend named Al Blanchard. The outpouring of his trials and tribulations as a ballplayer, salary negotiator, and lover are depicted with slang, dialect, or baseball argot.

"Readers and baseball fans liked to speculate about who was the original Jack Keefe," wrote Donald Elder, in his biography *Ring Lardner*. "Ring's colleagues saw in him something of the braggadocio of Ping Bodie, the White Sox outfielder, and Frank Smith, the pitcher; his alibis reminded them of Ed Walsh." In addition, Hugh Fullerton, another star Chicago sports columnist of the day, saw in Keefe the traits of Solly Hofman, Jimmy Sheckard, Frank Schulte, and Lew Richie of the Cubs. "All of which indicates that there was no single original of Jack Keefe."

Lardner himself, in a preface to the first edition of *You Know Me Al*, wrote: "The writer has been asked frequently, or perhaps not very often at all…who is the original of Jack Keefe?" And added: "I have heretofore declined to reply to it, as a reply would have stopped the boys and girls from guessing… and I may as well give the correct answer. The original of Jack Keefe is not a ballplayer at all, but Jane Addams of Hull-House, a former Follies girl."

Whether Bodie luxuriated or recoiled from the possibility that he was a model, or one of the models, for Jack Keefe, the plain fact is that after his splendid start with the White Sox in the first two years, he trailed off.

He hit .264 in 1913 and a dismal .229 in 1914. It seems his outgoing personality and lack of production drove Callahan to sell Bodie back to the San Francisco Seals after the 1914 season.

Bodie vowed that he would do such good work that he would someday come back to the majors and "show up Callahan."

He returned to the San Francisco Seals of the Pacific Coast League, where he again hit with his former power and consistency. In his two seasons back in the Bay Area he hit 19 homers and batted .325 in 1915, and walloped 20 homers and batted .303 in 1916.

Writing in the *New York Tribune*, Wood Ballard said, "Ping was such a demon with the ash that Connie Mack recalled him from the bushes and put him to work in the outfield for the Athletics."

Bodie was such a favorite with the fans because he "played to the gallery, which in baseball parlance means the bleachers," wrote Ballard. "And the gallery gods liked it and kidded Ping and Ping kidded them."

Ballard had a leaning toward description, and here is Ping Bodie illustrated:

> There is an apparent anthropoid stoop to Ping's broad shoulders, which seems to lengthen his long arms which dangle the more as he trots to and from his place in the outfield...These characteristics may have been affected in his early baseball days to attract the attention of the gallery, for Ping is something of an actor. However they are a part of him now...
>
> Bodie seldom strikes out. His batting average may fall, but it is because he stings the ball where some fielder can handle it. And Ping is usually good in the pinch. He grips his bat well down on the handle, puts all the strength of his powerful arms and shoulders into the blow and wades into the ball.
>
> Because of his apparent awkwardness he is faster than he really seems, and what he lacks as an outfielder of the first rank he makes up to a big extent with his bat.

In a time when ballplayers felt that a laugh was more important than a sectioned briefcase, when any goofy shenanigan was more intriguing than an addition to his stock portfolio, Ping Bodie was game for any amusement. One of those came during spring training with the Yankees in Jacksonville in 1919.

"The contest for the heavyweight eating championship of the world between Percy the Ostrich and Ping Bodie of the Yankees drew a packed house to the South Side Pavilion last night," wrote W.O. McGeehan, in his column in the *New York Tribune.* "Percy the Ostrich quit on the eleventh platter, and Sheriff Donahue, the referee, declared Bodie the undisputed eating Champion of the world."

The match was promoted by the Jacksonville Chamber of Commerce, which had been advertising Percy as the world's greatest eater. Colonel T.L. Huston (who, wrote McGeehan, "foots the fodder bill for Bodie"—he was co-owner of the Yankees) "laughed at these pretensions, and the challenge followed."

Since Bodie was the challenger, he could choose the *cuisine de guerre*. He selected spaghetti. McGeehan described it as a boxing match, round for round. This was the conclusion:

> Round 11: The ostrich barely waddled from his corner. Percy's eyes were bloodshot and his sides were heaving as he toed the platter. He was a badly beaten ostrich. Bodie was almost finished with his platter when Percy dropped to his knees. The timekeeper began to count. Bodie ferociously downed the first morsel and stepped back to survey his fallen antagonist. As the timekeeper muttered the final ten, the ostrich sank back to rise no more.

How Francito Sanguenitta Pezzolo, born October 8, 1887, in San Francisco, the son of Rose De Martini and Joseph Pezzolo, both born in Italy, became Frank S. "Ping" Bodie was explained by Bodie:

"My folks bought a house when I was a youngster from a man named Dwyer," Bodie told a reporter in 1918. "The Dwyers had a boy, Jack, about my age, whose nickname was Ping. When we moved into the house and Jack moved out he left the Ping behind him and the neighbors hung it on me. As for the Bodie, I don't know. Some bloke must have wished it on me when I began playing ball. Anyway, by this time, it's mine. I couldn't get rid of it if I wanted to."

That's not how Ping's older brother, Dave, remembered the change of the last name. After the *Sporting Life* periodical had written a piece about Bodie, Dave wrote a letter to the editor saying that Ping's correct last name is Pizzola.

> He took the name of Bodie from our uncle—my mother's brother—when he started to play ball because he thought all the fans would josh him. Both Frank and I were born here in San Francisco at the old house on North Beach. Corner Vallejo and Pacific streets—what they call Telegraph Hill. Frank is here now, and we both wish you would correct what you said in next week's "Sporting Life."
> Yours truly, Dave Bodie (Pizzola).

The remark about the concern that fans might "josh" him for his name suggests that a purely ethnic Italian name was not what ball fans of that era were accustomed to.

Bodie also gave the impression that "Ping" came from the sound of his 52-ounce bat striking the baseball in the Dead Ball Era. "You should have heard me crash the old apple," he said.

The mystery of the name thickens, however. Did the Pezzolos, or Pizzolas, like Dave Bodie, change their names to Bodie because Ping did, or was there yet another explanation?

And Bodie gave yet another version:

> All of the boys in our family of 16 kids took the name of Bodie because it was the name of a California town where my father was a gold miner. A friend of the family named Jack Dwyer was nicknamed Ping and he didn't like it. Once, when I was two years old, he said, "That kid can't defend himself, so I hereby give him the name of 'Ping.'"
>
> So "Ping Bodie" became my legal name. My father didn't like the boys' adopting the name of Bodie, but he was more angry with me than the others, because I became a national figure, and the first player of Italian descent to reach the majors. He said I should have carried the name Pezzolo to fame.

Ping was, as one writer of the time termed it, "a swashbuckling youngster" growing up in his native San Francisco. McGeehan, who couldn't resist comical allusions to Bodie, said of him: "He's one of the rock-rollers of Telegraph Hill. They keep their territory free of invaders by pulling rocks out of the summit and rolling them down the streets."

Bodie, who was a product of the San Francisco sandlots and the Telegraph Hill section, San Francisco's "Little Italy," dropped out of high school after his first year and began his career as a professional infielder in 1906 in the California outlaw league. After one year he was transferred to the outfield and from 1908 through 1910 played for the San Francisco Seals of the Pacific Coast League.

In his four seasons with the White Sox (1911–14), he hit a total of 20 home runs. In his next to last season in Chicago his batting average sank to .264, though he slugged eight homers, and he hit .299 with three homers in 1914, playing in just 107 games (compared to 145 in his first season). He was sent back to the minor leagues, back to San Francisco.

Bodie complained that the decline in his hitting was all Callahan's fault. Bodie liked taking a whack at the first pitch, and Callahan had instructed him to be patient. Patience led to falling behind in the count. "I was always a first-ball hitter," explained Bodie, "and I always thought I had the advantage, because the pitcher would send up the first one mighty careful in attempting to make sure of the range and the groove. Callahan made me stop hitting the first one, and that gave the pitchers the percentage on me."

Baseball magazine sided with Bodie: "If a man has developed a batting style of his own, and has made his attack effective by cracking the first one, why try to make him change?…If a man is known to possess a keen lamp and a sharp swing, and is also famous as a first-ball hitter, the burden, the weight of trouble, all shift upon the pitcher."

The *New York Tribune* suggested another side to Bodie's plummet with the White Sox, referring to Bodie as "the 'comedian' who had fallen into evil ways around the gay life of Chicago's stockyard."

Bodie was described as possessing "an even temper that wins. He is congenial, a great mixer and likes to talk, and he can be entertaining in a baseball way." Perhaps at times he was too great a mixer.

Back with the Seals, for two seasons, he was hitting the ball with his onetime vigor. He batted .325 and hit 19 homers in 1915, and hit .303 with 20 homers the following year.

He returned to the major leagues with the Athletics in 1917, when he batted .291 in 148 games, and was traded to the Yankees the following March for first baseman George Burns.

"The presence of Bodie in a Yankee uniform should furnish many a merry quip for the metropolitan journalists who recount baseball anecdotes," wrote W. J. Macbeth in the *New York Tribune*. "Ping is a temperamental cuss, like most geniuses…

"He proved one of the most dangerous hitters of the Mack clan," driving in 74 runs, to lead the last-place A's in that department, and hit .291, second best among A's regulars. His seven homers tied for third in the American League. "He was serious, at least, in his endeavors," continued Macbeth, "and campaigned through the year pounds lighter than he had been as a member of the White Sox."

He hit .256, .278, and .295 in three full seasons with the Yankees, and was with them in 1921 when they won the first of their pennants. However, he didn't finish the season with them, and missed his chance to play in a World Series. He was traded to the Red Sox in August of that year. He didn't play a game with the Red Sox.

When Yankees officials turned down his demand for a one-half World Series share, he refused to report to the Red Sox and returned home and spent the next seven seasons with Vernon and San Francisco (Pacific Coast League), Des Moines (Western League), and Wichita Falls–San Antonio (Texas League).

When Babe Ruth joined the Yankees in 1920, he was assigned to room with Ping Bodie and did so until Bodie was traded to the Red Sox late in the 1921 season. Years later, Bodie recalled that period:

> Ruth, as I remember him, had a great personality. He was a perennial big kid. I guess he never really grew up. But that's one of the reasons we all loved him. He had an overpowering amount of energy, both on and off the field, and was always on the go. During one period, the Babe was hustling around so much after dark that when a reporter in Wichita Falls, Texas, asked me how I liked rooming with the Babe, I replied, "I'm rooming with a suitcase." I thought that was the best way I could describe the Babe's continual battle with manager Miller Huggins' curfew.

In 1925, Bodie, now a minor league player, was in the news again. This time for an odd twist on a divorce case. He filed suit for a divorce from Anna Bodie, to whom he was married in 1908. The Bodies had a son and a daughter but had not lived together since 1923. Bodie charged that in

August 1922 his wife started a story among their acquaintances that he was a bootlegger and a "common drunk," and that she made the further false statement that he was crazy. However, his principal complaint was that five years earlier his wife had begun to send derogatory telegrams about him to Judge Kenesaw Mountain Landis, the commissioner of baseball; Miller Huggins, manager of the Yankees; E. Lee Keyser, manager of the Des Moines club of the Western League; and Eddie Maier, manager of the Vernon club of the Pacific Coast League. These messages, he said, attacked his character and conduct. Bodie was granted the divorce.

Bodie wound up his career in 1928 with the San Francisco Seals, hitting .347, at the age of 40. But he said he'd had enough. He bought a gas station, and then a diner, yet kept his hand in baseball by playing in semi-pro leagues.

One day he ran into Pat Monahan, a scout for the Boston Red Sox. Monahan was bemoaning the scarcity of good ballplayers and the terrible time a scout has in finding major-league starters in minor league settings. He got no sympathy from Bodie.

"Why, you've got the softest job on earth," said Bodie.

"Soft huh, scouting seven years for a tail-end ball team?" Monahan replied with indignation.

"Soft is right," said the irrepressible Bodie. "You couldn't go wrong if you tried to. Any ballplayer you pick up is bound to go better than those the Red Sox are losing with."

When Bodie's filling station fell on hard times during the Depression, he tried a brief comeback in 1931 with Oakland. But his skills had eroded with age. He was now 43 years old. He was recommended for a job in Hollywood as an electrician on movie sets. He held the job for the next 31 years. He was said to be a favorite of such screen stars as Charles Boyer and Carole Lombard.

"I ran across Bodie in a jungle on a Universal Pictures set recently, while the Giants were playing exhibitions around Hollywood," wrote Ken Smith, a sports reporter for the New York *Daily Mirror*, in 1948. "Lon Chaney Jr., stalking through the foliage, suddenly went into a trance that transformed him into a gorilla or something. The director yelled 'Cut' and a round man wearing a Yankees baseball cap stepped briskly and incongruously into the jungle, pulling a sound track wire from beneath a banana tree.

It was Ping Bodie—and it is a pleasure to report that he can still go to his right or left when it comes to setting up movie stages, or grabbing baseballs."

Smith described Bodie as "one of the great colony of Italian ballplayers from the San Francisco hills—the DiMaggios, Tony Lazzeri, and Frank Crosetti." But added the ethnic description that Bodie "was one of New York's most famous spaghetti destroyers in his day." In a less politically correct atmosphere, such illustrations went virtually unnoticed—unless, of course, one was Italian and resented it.

When, in 1919, Bodie left the Yankees in spring training because he said he had personal and urgent business to attend to in New York, manager Miller Huggins did not give him permission to leave and a contretemps ensued, with Higgins saying he wanted to trade Bodie. The situation was described this way in the *New York Tribune*: "The temperamental Italian, in a word, is on the market." Another reference to Bodie stated: "Ping Bodie is his stage name. Ping needs a stage name. Pezzolo wouldn't look well in a box score."

In *Ethnicity and Sport in North American History and Culture,* Carmen Bazzano wrote that "the Depression years…proved to be a bonanza for Italian-American baseball players." He wrote that some have argued that the decline of Nativism—the practice or policy of favoring native-born citizens over immigrants—accompanied the economic hardship of the Depression, and proved instrumental in the acceptance of the new immigrants in baseball. "While it is difficult to substantiate (this) argument, the fact remains that during the 1930s many Italian players began finding their way to the major leagues. By the close of the fourth decade, so many of them were active in the majors that the National Italian American Civic League issued an 'All-Italian Team' for 1939."

On the set of Universal Pictures, Smith of the *Mirror* sat down with Bodie and reminisced. "Bodie is still stout, quick-actioned, happy and philosophical," wrote Smith. He proceeded to draw the old ballplayer out.

"I don't go to many games but I follow the scores," Bodie said. "I'd much prefer watching sandlot kids play. They have that will-to-win. The professionals go through their games as though it was a day's work. I don't mean all of them nor that they aren't giving their best. But there is that tendency to say: 'You do or you don't, a fellow can't do anything more.' Buy in my time there was more all-out determination to win."

Even at his retirement at age 73, Bodie had not lost his confidence as a hitter.

Did he think he could still hit? a friend asked. "Give me a mace," Bodie shot back, "and I'll drove the pumpkin down Whitey Ford's throat."

Stan Wasiak: A Minor-League Lifer

STAN WASIAK REMEMBERS THE morning clearly. It was in March 1950, at the spring training camp in Vero Beach, Florida, and he was beginning his seventh season as a second baseman in the high minors of the Brooklyn Dodger organization. He was 30 years old, and not advancing.

Branch Rickey, the Dodgers' president and general manager, was sitting, as usual, on an elevated chair behind the screen in back of home plate, and he asked to see Wasiak.

"I had no idea what he wanted," Wasiak recalled recently from his home in Mobile, Alabama. "He was wearing an old fedora, thick glasses, a bow tie, and he had a pair of socks sticking out of his suit jacket—why socks, I don't know. He had those bushy eyebrows and that deep voice, like a preacher.

"He said to me, 'Wasiak, I like the way you hustle, and the way you think out there. I believe you'd make a f-i-i-ne manager in the Dodger organization.' I was completely surprised. I hadn't even considered managing. I said, 'Thank you, Mr. Rickey, can I think about it?' He gave me a day.

"The offer was really flattering, coming from a man like Mr. Rickey, and, though I thought I still had a chance to make the majors—the dream was still there—I accepted. I figured it was a good opportunity to stake out a future in the game and maybe make the big leagues as a coach or manager."

Thirty-two seasons later, until the end of last year, he was still a manager in the minor leagues. He had handled clubs in 17 cities, from Class D, formerly the lowest classification, to Class AAA, currently the highest.

He had traveled with his young charges by bus, starting with a tiny school bus with broken springs, and gone thousands and thousands of miles over the back roads of America. No one has ever managed in the bushes for so many straight years. Few, surely, would have wanted to.

His teams have won 2,286 games. Only two minor-leaguers ever won more, and they managed longer, though not consecutively. The years tell on Wasiak. He is 5-feet-8 and 160 pounds, with a face as rugged as parchment. He is chunky and has bowlegs. "I used to have a pretty good shape," he said, "but I guess all those bus rides rearranged it."

He is known, of course, as the King of the Minors. But for the first season in the last 33, His Minor Highness is not sitting on his splintered throne in the dugout. He is not managing the Class A Vero Beach Dodgers, his current team, because he is home recuperating from hepatitis, which developed after he had open-heart surgery last summer.

Wasiak, who is 62 years old, is healthy now. "And so anxious to get back he's like a caged animal," said his wife, Barbara. But the Dodgers, following doctor's orders, have given him the year off, with full pay.

He says he misses putting on the baseball suit, misses the anticipation of a game, misses working with the kids. He has managed young players in ballparks with lights dimmer than street lamps, with clubhouses so small only half the team could dress there at a time, and with stands so empty that people couldn't talk too loud because everybody in the park would hear them.

Despite all that, a number of Wasiak's players went on to the major leagues. From Roger Craig, who pitched on the first team Wasiak managed, Valdosta, Georgia, Class D, in 1950, to Steve Sax, with Vero two years ago and now the rookie starting second baseman for the big club in Los Angeles.

Rudy Law, now with the White Sox, played for Wasiak at Lodi, California, in 1977 and credits him with making a major difference in his career. This was Law's second season in pro ball, and he was discouraged. "Stan relaxed me, gave me confidence," said Law.

"The first week at Lodi," Wasiak recalls, "Rudy would make an out and be so low he'd stay down the right-field line and sulk. I spoke to him. 'Rudy, that's not professional. It looks like you're just thinking of yourself. It doesn't help you or the team. You're a good hitter, an outstanding hitter. Get back to the bench and get 'em next time.'"

Wherever Wasiak goes, the question invariably arises: "How come, Stan, you never made the big time?" "After a while, it gets under your skin, but I say something like 'I could've, but I just don't like the towns.' I've been getting laughs with that line for years."

He managed Class AAA ball in Albuquerque, New Mexico, for three years—the majors a step away—but was returned to the lower minors. "I think I got the reputation of being too easy," he says. "Reputations travel fast in baseball."

Al Campanis, general manager of the Dodgers, says: "I don't think Stan wants or likes to be a disciplinarian. He wants to treat his players like men, and when he can't, I think, he feels frustrated. But he's got a great rapport with young players. It's an art, a technique. Stan's a valuable man for us down there. You know, there are a lot of people who work for a company for 30 years and never become president."

In the winter of 1977, the Atlanta Braves were looking for a manager. A wire-service article mentioned that one of the candidates was Stan Wasiak.

"Just the fact that someone thought enough of me to consider my name was a thrill," said Wasiak. He didn't get the job; Bobby Cox did. Cox had played for Wasiak at Salem, Oregon, in Class C ball.

"Sure, I'd be lyin' if I said being in the minors all these years didn't get me low sometimes," he said. "I'm not braggin', but I'm just as good a strategist as any of 'em up there. And I'm a winner—I've proved I can win."

In 1978, in honor of his 2,000th managerial victory, the Dodgers honored Wasiak at Dodger Stadium. He threw out the first ball of a game.

"It was first class all the way," he recalled. Peter O'Malley, the Dodger president, drove him back to the hotel in a limousine. "And I flew out the next morning. It had been great, but, no question about it, I felt like Cinderella after the ball." He laughed softly. "And then I went back to the salt mines."

Jack Lazorko: Up and Down, and Once Again

MAYBE YOU'VE NEVER HEARD of Jack Lazorko, the 37-year-old right-handed pitcher who is as compact as a tugboat and is called "Il Bulldog" in Italy, "El Bulldog" in Latin America, and "Zork" in the States.

Maybe you've never seen him play, his dark brows over intense hazel eyes, armed with an assortment of pitches from forkballs to knuckle curves to sliders to fastballs that dip and fastballs that rise—none of which will blow anyone away, as he describes it, but all of which are invariably around the plate and always carry a purpose.

While he is hardly a household name, fans in hundreds of the most unlikely towns around the world plus a legion of people in baseball—from players to executives—knows him, or of him. After all, he played for or with or against many of those in baseball. Maybe most of them.

"Sometimes," he said, "it feels like all of them."

Few baseball careers have been anything like Jack Lazorko's, who was born in Hoboken, New Jersey, and grew up in River Edge to the north, and who has called so many places home since then that, he says, he has single-handedly kept map makers in business.

Maybe you haven't followed his career for the past 16 years, as he played for nine major-league organizations and 17 of their teams, and maybe a dozen more teams in the Caribbean and Mexico and South America and Europe. This year alone, he has worn the uniform of the Yankees (in spring training) and of the Norfolk Tides, the Mets' Class AAA team. When a call was made recently to the Tides' executive office, it was asked whether Jack Lazorko was there.

"Not anymore," came the reply. Gone after seven games.

It is, in a nutshell, the story of Jack Thomas Lazorko's baseball life.

"I've been released by more teams in more leagues in more countries and in more languages than anyone in the history of baseball," Lazorko said one day last week. "And I'm the only man to have been released by both the Mets and the Yankees in the same year—within four months!" He shakes his head and smiles wryly. "Unbelievable."

Unbelievable because, as he said recently at his home here, "I always seem to be the 11th man on a 10-man pitching staff."

He is currently unemployed. Again. But that could change tomorrow. Or the next day. He is ready. He says he has learned to pack in 10 minutes, and that's for a six-month trip, if necessary. He asks two questions of his new team: "What color spikes do you wear?" And "what color sleeves?" He has in his closet piles of various colored baseball shoes and piles of sweatshirts. In his attic above the garage are several dozen suitcases, hanging bags, and equipment bags. One day last May his wife and children drove into the garage, and the seven-year-old, Mitch, noticing that the foldable stairs to the attic had been pulled down, said, "Oh, Daddy's got a job."

"But this year might be the turning point, when I start to think of something else, a normal job, maybe like coaching," said Lazorko. "It's come to that."

Lazorko has played at all levels of amateur and professional baseball, from rookie league to the major leagues. He has played in the United States and Canada and Mexico and Latin America and Europe, for teams ranging from the El Paso Diablos to the Tulsa Drillers to the Phoenix Fire Birds to the Wichita Aeros to the Asheville Tourists to the Sun City Rays (in the Senior League) and on to, among others, the Calgary Cannons, Edmonton Trappers, Los Mochis (Mexico) Caneros, Santurce (P.R.) Crabbers, Valencia (Venezuela) Magallenes, and Parma (Italy) Angels. Just recently he joined a team called the Hollywood Legends, which played and won a weeklong European tournament in Belgium.

Maybe you weren't aware of Jack Lazorko's brief pitching stints in the major leagues in parts of five years in the 1980s with Milwaukee, Seattle, Detroit, and California (twice) as a spot starter, middle reliever, and infrequent closer—and that it took him three years to notch his first victory in the big leagues (he has five victories against eight losses, two saves, and a 4.22 earned-run average in 69 games.) The last time he appeared in the major leagues was in 1988, with the Angels.

Maybe you didn't see him pitching with his customary aggressiveness in the dead heat of Managua, Nicaragua, where he and his teammates were protected from antsy local fans by soldiers bearing machine guns, or hurling in the midnight sun in Skelleftea, Sweden, just a three-hour bus ride from the North Pole.

And maybe you haven't seen him throwing in recent days at a screen with a roped-off strike zone in his small backyard here, in this bedroom community just northeast of Dallas, hoping for one more chance at the big leagues, or Japan, or somewhere.

"Every year we say, 'This year, this year won't be crazy like the last one,'" said Brenda, his wife of 15 years. "And every year turns out to be crazy, like the last one, only more so."

"Every year we start out with a plan," Lazorko said. "We have Plan A, Plan B...This year we're on Plan Double Z, and the summer has only just started."

"A lot of people think ballplayers have it made," said Brenda. "They don't realize that only a relative handful do. And they don't realize the stress involved. Jack has played for 16 one-year contracts. Every time he pitches, his livelihood is on the line. It's got to a point when I'm at a game where I hate to hear the organ play. I know Jack's coming into the game and my stomach starts to churn."

Brenda is a petite blonde with an even disposition, which she has needed, and with the inner strength of a tiger, something that has also been required.

"Oh, the times we've had," she said. "Like twice we've bought Christmas trees in places, once in Puerto Rico, once in the Dominican, and we've been sent somewhere else, and we had to sell the trees. Then there was the time we were on a road trip in Hawaii with the Edmonton team and Jack got the call to the big leagues for the first time, to go immediately to play for the Brewers in Baltimore. Well, we had one suitcase, and Jack took it. I had to buy another suitcase to get home with the kids."

Brenda Nanney and Jack Lazorko met when they were in college together at Mississippi State in 1978. He graduated that year with a degree in business administration. The next year Brenda, who got a degree in fashion merchandising, went to visit Jack in Sarasota, Florida, where he was playing in his second professional season.

"As soon as I got there, he was sold to Asheville," she said, speaking of his move from the Houston Astros organization to that of the Texas Rangers. "Right then I should have known."

In the first five or six years of their marriage, they moved 50 or 60 times. "Then we just started to lose count," she said. "It seems that every time I unpacked everything, we were traded or sold. It was like a bad omen. Even when we were in one place for a while—like we were in Tulsa for a full year—I still kept all my cosmetics in the bag."

This spring training Lazorko snared a tryout with the Yankees, after many appeals, including some to his former teammate at Mississippi State, Yankee manager Buck Showalter. "Jack," said Showalter, "is a survivor."

Reggie Jackson came by the clubhouse and noticed the name taped to the locker. "This can't be the same Lazorko who pitched for Seattle years ago," he said. "Yeah, Reggie, that's me," said Lazorko, from behind Jackson. Lazorko was released by the Yankees in March.

In April, he sent letters and visited teams and called managers and general managers and player personnel directors nationwide and in foreign lands looking for a job. His phone bill for the month was $249. At the end of May he caught on with the Mets and was sent to pitch for the Norfolk Tides. After two games, he was released.

"I got belted a little in the first game, where I gave up two runs in two-thirds of an inning," he said, "but I was a little rusty, not having pitched in a game in two months. But Clint Hurdle, the manager, threw me in the next day and I gave up just one hit. The next thing I know, it's hit the road, Jack."

He is always so close, he feels. So close to reaching his dream of having a fulfilling career as a major-league pitcher. This, he says, is more important even than the big bucks he would receive. He sees players he played with in the minor leagues, pitchers like Tom Henke and Ron Darling and Tom Candiotti, among others, making millions of dollars.

The most he ever made was $125,000, when he pitched for Edmonton on a major-league contract. In contrast, in his early years in the minors, his first contract was for $500 a month in A ball, around $1,500 in AA ball, but as much as $15,000 a month in Class AAA. But in his lean years, "to make ends meet," he said, he had to pitch winter ball and, on the side, sell radio advertising, storm windows, and meat from the back of a truck.

In recent years, though, he has earned a regular, if generally modest, living (especially when you factor the expenses for his peripatetic existence) for Brenda and their three children, 11-year-old Jake, seven-year-old Mitch and three-year-old Nicky—all of whom travel with him.

The Lazorkos lived in Italy last season, renting a fourth-floor walk-up in Parma, where he made $90,000 and was named the most valuable player in the Italian League as well as in the championships, which Parma won. He pitched and won the last two games on the same day.

"Traveling the way we have, the kids have got an education you wouldn't believe," said Brenda.

Back in Texas, where Brenda was raised and where, Lazorko said, one can conveniently catch nonstop flights to almost anywhere in the world, the Lazorkos live in a nicely appointed two-story brick house on a street appropriately named Meandering Way.

Lazorko has been careful with the money he has earned, and has been able to buy the house as well as keep up a college fund for his children. "And we've managed to save some—not a lot," said Lazorko. "But I'm going to have to find a job soon. These kids drink a lot of milk."

So Lazorko was on the telephone trying to sell himself and his pitching arm to a rather reluctant clientele.

"Oh, he's not in?" said Lazorko, in the kitchen, the American League Red Book and the National League Green Book, loaded with team phone numbers, on the table before him. "Well, could you tell him Jack Lazorko called? Would he mind calling me back? He'll know what it's about it. Thank you."

Lazorko shrugs, checks another number.

"We want to go with younger guys," he hears from some people he calls. Or: "We're full right now." Or: "We don't have any spots open." Or: "I'll take your number and I'll call if somebody goes down."

That's exactly why the Mets called in May. "To be brutally honest, we just needed an arm," said Gerry Hunsicker, the Mets' director of player personnel. "Some guys went down with injury, we had a few other things happen, and Jack had been calling me, so I told him, 'Okay, but it might not be for very long.'

"Jack's a good guy to have on a ballclub. He gives you everything he's got. I knew him when he was in college. I coached against him, when I was at Florida International University. That was 20 years ago. I remember him as a kid with a strong arm. A pretty good-looking pitcher with above average fastball and definitely major-league potential.

"But the realities now are that we got kids we're developing. Kids with a future ahead."

Said Buck Showalter: "At this stage for Jack, he needs pinpoint location where he can throw the breaking ball for strikes at will, and he just has to be a cut above the others. I like Jack, and I've always loved his attitude. But I felt his stuff came up just a little short."

Lazorko said: "If I get lit up whenever I go out there, that's one thing. Then I know it would be time to hang 'em up. But that doesn't happen. I keep guys in the ballpark, I keep runners on base, and I'm one of the best fielding pitchers in the game."

Brenda does not discourage her husband in his pursuit. And the kids, apparently, have not suffered. Jack tutored them in Italy, and Jake spent his ninth birthday climbing the Matterhorn with his folks and his 10th birthday climbing one of the pyramids in Egypt, until a security guard told him it wasn't allowed.

"Everyone has his level of frustration," said Lazorko. "Some guys who play 15 years in the big leagues are frustrated that they haven't made the Hall of Fame. Some guys who played 10 years never got in a World Series. We had a great college team and eight guys were drafted by big-league teams, but only one of us ever made the Show. How do you think those other guys felt? And me? I still love the challenge of setting up the batters, and getting them out."

But something else gnaws at him. "I just want a little more, just to prove that I was a real, contributing big-league player, and not a fringe guy."

It is nighttime, and warm. The black Texas sky is sugared with stars. Crickets are in harmony. Jack Lazorko has switched on the garage lights and they throw a gentle glow on his backyard.

Diagonally, the yard, from the corner of where the red-brick garage meets the house, to the now-shadowed gray picket fence and the roses that line it, is just a little more than 60 feet, six inches, the distance from the pitcher's mound to home plate.

At the far end is the screen, a backstop, and just below the roped strike zone is a large netted bag that catches most of the balls that he throws. "What's great about this is that I can keep my arm in shape, and don't need a catcher," said Lazorko.

He is wearing a dark-blue Yankee T-shirt and gray Yankee shorts and rubber-soled cleats. He is standing on the concrete walk in the corner, where he has placed a pitching slab. Behind him is his living room, and through a picture window his wife can be seen sitting in a leather chair watching television. A leather bag of some 125 baseballs lies on the patio table near him.

He begins to throw, slowly at first, stretching his stocky body. Then he begins to throw harder, testing his assortment of pitches, almost but not quite skinning his knuckles on the bricks of the garage wall.

This is his routine when he is, as he says, "between jobs." He pitches to batters in his imagination, batters he is familiar with, like most of the lineup of, say, the Oakland A's, whom he had been watching earlier on television. And he throws in what he calls "situations." "Otherwise," he said, "you're just throwing and not thinking."

He's pitching now to Rickey Henderson with a man on, and going inside with a fastball and low and away with his slider. Next, Mark McGwire is up. Lazorko throws a curve. "Uh, oh," he said, "I hung that one. Home run." And he grunts. He is sweating now, plucking up one ball, deciding what to pitch, and letting go. This is work. This is pleasure. This is Jack Lazorko's life.

"If I were called up, I could pitch tomorrow," he said, breathing deeply after throwing a high hard one. "Tomorrow."

He took another ball from his bag, and looked down to get the sign, with, maybe, Ruben Sierra at bat in his mind's eye.

"I just need the opportunity, is all," he said. He wound up and threw. The ball thumped against the shadowed screen—for a strike.

The San Diego Chicken,
Feathers and All

THE CHICKEN, AS USUAL, was packing them in. This was his first appearance in Omaha, and long lines formed to enter Rosenblatt Stadium, home of the Royals, a Triple A baseball team in the American Association. Cars kept driving into the parking lot, stirring up dust. Soon the ballpark would be filled with 13,659 spectators, the third-largest crowd ever here. The previous game had drawn 1,803.

When the Chicken finally appeared in the second inning, the crowd greeted him with a standing ovation. Dancing, hopping, scurrying—or however it is a chicken ambulates—this phenomenon in an eight-foot-tall orange and furry and long-beaked costume glowing in the park lights repaired to first base and dismissed the Omaha Royals' coach there with a flick of his feather.

The crowd, pardon the expression, egged him on. Now he went through a series of pantomime routines that brought howls: he gave a flurry of signs to the batter, he fell back flat as a board when the umpire called the strike, and he did the heebeejeebees to discombobulate the pitcher.

Eventually, he ran around the bases, diving head first into third, a la Pete Rose, then backed up and did it in slow-motion replay. He flapped at the umpire in the manner of Billy Martin, and later came out with a white smock, Groucho Marx eyebrows and mustache and an eye chart, and tested the umpire's sight.

Then the Chicken—that is, Ted Giannoulas, the man within the pullet—went up and worked the stands, followed by an adoring and ever-growing claque of kids.

This is, obviously, not your run of the mill fowl. This chicken is incorporated, has five persons on his payroll, including an office staff in San Diego that books him throughout the country, a valet who travels with him and combs and fluffs his wattles and tail. And if you ever have to reach him immediately, just check the San Diego telephone listings; he's there under "Chicken, The."

From May through October of this year he has only 10 open dates. He expects to make a half-million dollars this year, and perhaps double that figure by 1982. Since 1974, when he began doing San Diego Padres games at $2 an hour while employed by radio station KGB, he has grown in popularity to a remarkable degree. And since 1979 when he took his act on the road—in the tradition of ballpark slapstick artists like Max Patkin and Al Schacht—he has enjoyed enormous success. For example:

- Last season, the Yankees played an exhibition game at Columbus, Ohio, against their top minor-league team. They drew 15,000. The Chicken came in two weeks later and drew 20,123, a record. This year, he returned and drew that figure plus 38.
- He was invited to conduct the Denver Symphony Orchestra before a game in June, and the crowd of 16,349 was the most to attend a game in Mile High Stadium this year. He has also filled the house in major-league parks, including Wrigley Field and the Seattle Kingdome.
- He was a special guest speaker for a recent Reader's Digest seminar on motivation and success, because, he said, "I have made chicken salad out of a chicken suit." He told the Digest group, "Zeal is the key. You have to believe in what you do. I eat, sleep and think chicken."

In 1979, when Giannoulas wanted to expand, and travel around the country, KGB said sure, if you split the profits. But Giannoulas said that KGB was reneging on a promise made when he began that if he ever did expand he could keep all his earnings. Giannoulas was sued by the radio station, and he won his case—but with the stipulation that he redesign his costume.

He had been barred from appearing at San Diego Stadium for two months, during the court proceedings, but when he reappeared, it was highly publicized. He was brought into the stadium atop an armored truck and inside a giant papier-mâché egg. The ballplayers took him down, and then he hatched from the egg to tremendous applause from the 47,000 fans. Television programming was interrupted in San Diego to bring this event live to local viewers.

"It was tremendous," Giannoulas said at breakfast last week. "And all this for a chicken." He laughed, but he didn't mean to disparage himself. He takes himself seriously as a comedian, and perhaps he should. He has drawn accolades from such as Rodney Dangerfield and Bill Cosby (who called him "Chaplinesque") and, if imitation is truly the sincerest form of flattery, he should be all puffed up: imitators range from the Phillie Phanatic to the federal government's Woodsy the Owl, who says, "Give a Hoot—Don't Pollute."

"Well," says Giannoulas, with a smile appearing from under his black mustache, "even Elvis had his imitators."

Giannoulas has his detractors as well. A sports columnist in Chicago called his act "boring." One of the few major-league ballparks he has yet to crack is Fenway Park. "Management there is pretty conservative," he said, "I can't get a date."

And once Lou Piniella, the Yankee outfielder, got so angry at his antics— after striking out—that he complained to the umpire and threw his glove at the Chicken.

"He missed," Giannoulas said, "but that's the kind of day Lou was having. I asked the umpire if I should cool it, and he said, 'No, if Lou had gotten a hit he'd be laughing like everyone else.'"

Players and managers and umpires are surprisingly cooperative. "It's entertainment and that's what, in the end, they're all in the park for," Giannoulas said. "I know the game and I never detract from the dignity of it. And I end my act with the seventh inning, so as not to interfere with the conclusion of the game."

Players even make suggestions. Roger Craig, when serving as pitching coach for the Padres, gave him the idea for the eye chart, and Pete Rose jokingly threatens to sue for royalties for the head-first slide.

Giannoulas, 26, was born in Canada but moved to San Diego as a youth. He describes the act as being "a kind of fuzzy Harpo Marx." "I'm not a mascot, I try to be a visual comedian," he says.

But his verbal shtick has been good enough to get him on talk shows such as Johnny Carson. When asked if it gets hot inside that 12-pound chicken costume, Giannoulas says, "Sure, but if you can't stand the heat, stay out of the chicken."

And to a question about how his mother feels about his being a chicken, he says, "She thinks I'm a doctor in Wisconsin." At breakfast, he ordered a strawberry waffle. "What's wrong with eggs?" he was asked. "I don't like them," he said, "but I definitely encourage the eating of eggs and chicken. It helps eliminate the competition."

Hercules Payne: The Spring Training Phenom

February 21, 1990

HERCULES PAYNE, A 22-YEAR-OLD rookie pitcher, couldn't wait to get to spring training. He hurriedly packed up his belongings, jumped into his car—a red Javelin, though, as his reputation expanded, camp gossip would turn it into a long white Cadillac—and drove straight from Pine Bluff, Arkansas, to Fort Myers, Florida, where the Kansas City Royals trained.

Hercules wheeled into town at 4:00 on that February morning in 1971, the first player to arrive. Only when he began to unpack did he realize his glove and baseball shoes were still at home.

"I have wanted to get to the big leagues for soooo long," he explained, "and wanted to get here so quick that I just plain forgot to pack 'em."

The next day, Hercules walked onto the field in his new Royals uniform, a pair of white high-top sneakers and a catcher's mitt that he had borrowed. He looked like a man not from Arkansas, but from Mars.

His true name was Mack Payne, but he was called Hercules because of, as he called it, "my physique." He was a bodybuilder, at 5-foot-10, 195 pounds, with a small waist and a roosterlike chest. He also had a wide smile, bowed legs, and a most unorthodox windup, twisting into a knot, his left arm covering his eyes, and then letting fly.

He recalled hearing that Nolan Ryan's fastball was clocked at 101 miles an hour; he believed he could throw harder. He wanted to pitch nine innings immediately, but the Royals manager, Bob Lemon, thought it might be a little too soon in spring training.

So Hercules Payne settled for throwing batting practice. He wound up and his first pitch sailed over the screen. "I was just experimenting with my knuckleball," he explained.

Since there are no real baseball spring training stories these days, this reporter turned his lonely eyes to Hercules Payne. In the midst of a lockout and closed-door negotiations between owners and the players' union, the suspension of spring training, regardless of the length, is the suspension of dreams. And no one ever symbolized the dreams of a young player, and the embodiment of hope that spring training represents, more than Hercules Payne.

He had been signed off the campus of Arkansas AM & N, a predominately black school later renamed the University of Arkansas at Pine Bluff, where he had been an outstanding right-handed pitcher for two seasons. He had gone there from Leland, Mississippi, his birthplace. "I grew up in the field choppin' cotton in the sun," he said recently. "And to be able to sleep all day and then play ball all night and get paid for it—oh man, oh my goodness—it was unbelievable! A lot of players today just don't appreciate it."

In March 1971, Hercules said: "I signed for a measly $5,000. But I'm not interested in the money. I've got my chance now for the big leagues. I am the happiest person in the world."

He had pitched part of the previous season for the Class A Waterloo team, with a 2–3 record and a respectable 3.93 earned-run average, and impressed the parent club enough to merit a tryout.

On the Royals team bus and in the clubhouse, Hercules sang and whistled church songs and rock-n-roll, and retains happy memories of teammates such as Lou Piniella, who, he said, "was always crackin' jokes but he'd do anything for you."

Hercules, young, fast, and wild, got his chance to pitch. Lemon sent him against the Yankees, and had him warm up in front of their dugout. "To intimidate 'em, I guess," Hercules recalled. He held them hitless for three innings, however, and walked only two of the edgy Yankees.

He pitched three innings each against the Baltimore Orioles and the Washington Senators. No one got a hit off him, though he walked many. He remembers loading the bases on walks against the Senators and then, with two outs, striking out huge Frank Howard.

But Hercules' pitching shoulder ached. He was afraid to tell anyone because he hoped to make the team. But he was farmed out. "I was disappointed," said Hercules, "but Mr. Lemon said I needed a little more control and I'd be back in no time. That brightened my eyes."

Hercules never returned. His shoulder grew worse. He soon dropped out of baseball, went back to school for a degree in education, and today is married, has a son, and teaches adults in Pine Bluff who seek a general equivalency diploma for high school.

"I was brokenhearted about baseball, and for quite a few years I couldn't watch it on television," he said. "But I can now, and still root for the Royals."

What stands out for him about the spring of 1971? "I remember Mrs. Kauffman, the wife of one of the owners, saying players weren't allowed to go without socks outside the clubhouse, even with shower shoes," he said. "I thought that was great. It was big-league. And to this day, even when I throw out the garbage, I always wear socks."

Emil Verban:
The Antelope Returns

July 7, 1985

WASHINGTON, D.C.—To his left was one great home-run hitter, to his right was another great home-run hitter, and together the three of them had hit a career total of 1,034 major-league home runs. Their lockers, simply by coincidence, had been placed in a row in the National League clubhouse for the recent Cracker Jack Old-Timers' Baseball Classic at R.F.K. Stadium in Washington.

Above the cubicle on his left was the name Willie McCovey, who had hit 521 home runs, and above the cubicle on his right was the name Eddie Mathews, who had hit 512 home runs.

Inscribed above his locker was his name, Emil Verban, who in 1949 hit the only home run of his seven-year major-league career as a second baseman for the Cardinals, Phillies, Cubs, and Braves.

With his gold-rimmed glasses glittering, and carrying a discernible paunch under his light-blue summer suit, Verban, gray haired at age 69, hurried into the clubhouse, fairly tore away at his clothes, and quickly climbed into his baseball suit. He had a pair of baseballs with him and turned to Mathews. Would Eddie autograph the balls? Verban then asked others like McCovey and Aaron and Wilhelm and Banks and Koufax to sign his baseballs.

"Know who that is?" he said to someone nearby, as an elderly, bow-legged man in an American League uniform came in. "That's Luke Appling."

Then: "Hi, Luke," said Verban. Appling returned the cordiality, though it wasn't certain whether he knew his greeter's name.

After a while Verban took a seat in an empty cubicle and looked around, seeming almost forlornly out of place among the host of great names.

What was an obscure player like Verban doing here?

Verban, it turns out, is a popular figure in Washington, though he lives in Lincoln, Illinois. There is a Washington-based Chicago Cubs fan club and it is named in his honor, the Emil Verban Memorial Society. One of its members is President Reagan, who broadcast Cub games on the radio in the 1930s.

The society was founded 10 years ago, when the Cubs were spending, as they often did, a considerable amount of time in the lowest depths of the National League standings.

The name Verban was chosen by club founders as a symbol of the Cubs. To some it was a joke. But to at least one man, it wasn't so funny.

"I didn't think I was a mediocre ballplayer," said Verban. "And when I first heard about this fan club, I didn't care for the idea.

"You know, I've never seen a guy who put on a uniform who I felt I'd have to take my hat off to. I thought that at my position I could play with the best, except maybe someone like Frisch or Hornsby, who had other things, like more power. But I could make the double play as good as anyone, and I don't think anyone ever covered more ground."

Verban hadn't played in the major leagues since 1950, but his records are as clear to him as if it all happened the other day. He played in two All-Star Games and one World Series, making up one half of the Cardinals' double-play combination with Marty Marion in the 1944 Series against the St. Louis Browns. "I hit .412 and in one game went 3-for-3," he said. In 1947, he struck out only eight times in 540 times at bat. "Someone told me that's an all-time record for second basemen in a season," he said.

He recalled that he had led the league in putouts and assists and double plays. He also led two years running in errors—one of those years, 1949, was his only full one with the Cubs—but perhaps the error mark was an oversight by Verban, or he considered it not significant in light of the ground he could cover.

"And I had a lifetime batting average of .272," he said. "With an average like that today, I'd be making a ton." His highest salary was $22,000.

There are about 10 Hall of Famers, excluding pitchers, who have lower career batting averages than Verban, and two were seated beside him: McCovey batted .270 and Mathews .271.

"Nowadays, with this Astroturf and these gloves that are as big as a bushel basket, I would never have made an error," he said, laughing, and pounding his fielder's mitt.

"Look at this." He extended his glove. It looked ancient. It was black with stubby fingers and cracking leather and no strings between the fingers and a skimpy webbing. "This is the glove I used in '44, when I was a rookie, and played in the Series," he said. "I used other gloves later, but I've always kept this."

He smiled. "That was in the days when they called me 'the Antelope,'" he said. "That was my nickname. I got it because I could move pretty quick. But in those days I was 148 pounds straight up and down. Now I'm 195 pounds. I've attained my full growth. I guess now they'd call me the Elephant."

Verban, a real-estate broker in commerical property back home, said: "You know, I came to like the Emil Verban Memorial Society. It gave me more exposure than I ever got as a player. I get about 10 letters a week from people wanting my autograph.

"And last year they had a banquet here and I was the featured guest. They had congressmen and a bunch of important people. And I was invited to the White House with my wife, Annetta, and my son, Dr. Emil Verban Jr., and my daughter, Barbara Kivittle. The president was very nice. He said he was glad to meet my acquaintance. He said that they had picked the right man for the name of the society, that it was someone who got the most out of his abilities. It was a thrill."

Verban became a member of the society last year. "They gave me number 7," he said, "my number with the Cubs."

Then the venerable Verban went out to warm up for the game. He played catch with a bat boy. In the five-inning game, he was inserted as a pinch hitter in the last inning. Batting against Mickey Lolich, Verban hit a ground ball to the third baseman, Eddie Yost.

Verban's old wheels churned, but the throw beat him to the bag. He had given it a good try, as he always had, and pulled a muscle in his leg as well.

Ralph Branca Looks
Back, Back, Back...

IT HAPPENS LESS FREQUENTLY these days, but, more than 55 years later, 55 years after the fact of that shattering moment that will not die, it is mentioned to Ralph Branca, or he is prepared for it to be mentioned.

Branca, his hair gray but looking fit and younger than his 82 years, sat in the canopied outdoor restaurant of the Westchester Country Club, in Rye, New York, where he lives with Ann, the woman he married just 17 days, by chance, after it happened, 55-plus years ago. They occupy a five-room apartment with a terrace that has "a view," said Branca with an easy smile on his broad face, "of the skyline of Manhattan and the bridges." Over lunch, iced tea, and a chicken Caesar salad ("no croutons, please"), he recalled his days as a major-league pitcher, the drama and the joys, and the uncommon life he led after that long-ago moment.

"Ralph is a very intelligent man who has an understanding of the world and his place in it," Bobby Valentine, the onetime manager of the Texas Rangers and New York Mets, and the son-in-law of Branca, said in a recent e-mail. Valentine, who married Branca's daughter Mary, is now a manager with the Chiba Lotte Marines of Japan's Pacific League. He said his father-in-law "has always been understanding of my situation, whatever it was, and when things were bad, Ralph has always been there."

It is hardly surprising that he would be understanding. At first, in the moments and hours and days—maybe even years—after it happened in the haze of a late afternoon, at 4:11 PM, on October 3, 1951, in the Polo Grounds in upper Manhattan, he was burdened with it. How do you deal

202

with personal disaster, even if it comes in the form of a game that little boys can play?

As time went on, however, he slowly came out of, as he called it, "shock." At some point he began to talk openly about it, and even joke about it. He would be invited to speak to various groups, whether it was about baseball or at investment conferences (he is the long-time head of Strategies for Wealth, dealing in financial advice) or as a guest in college classrooms, he had a running gag:

"After two questions from the audience, I'd say, 'Isn't somebody going to ask me how I felt?' It was always the third question."

Looking back, it all seems so mundane, if not silly, that people should invest so much of their hearts and emotion in a game, even that particular game:

Essentially, a pitcher, Ralph Branca of the Brooklyn Dodgers, comes in to pitch in relief in the bottom of the ninth inning in that quirky, horse-shoe shaped ballpark on Coogan's Bluff. His team was ahead 4–2, there were two men on base, and two were out.

He delivers a pitch, a pitch "at the chin" that would have been called a ball had the batter, Bobby Thomson of the New York Giants, let it sail by, but Thomson took an uppercut swing and lofted a fly ball that, as Branca recalls, he pleaded silently, "Sink, sink!"

But let's backtrack to give a sweep of the situation: Branca's Dodgers were leading 4–2, two men were on base and two were out. This was the third and final playoff game, the tie-breaker, for the National League pennant. (The Giants had won the first game, the Dodgers the second.) If Branca gets Thomson, the Dodgers head for Yankee Stadium to play in the World Series the following day.

Branca entered the game to pitch to Thomson after his manager, Charlie Dressen, phoned from the dugout to the bullpen to have him relieve the starting pitcher, Don Newcombe. Branca had been throwing well in the warmups and felt strong.

"I felt confident, maybe overconfident," Branca recalled, "but even with the pennant on the line, I didn't feel scared."

A 6-foot-3, 220-pound, hard-throwing right-hander, Branca, then 25—with "golden muscles in his pitching arm," as the former Dodger president Branch Rickey had once described him—whizzed his first pitch down the middle to Thomson. He let it go for strike one. "It was about a 93-94 mile-an-hour fastball," recalled Branca.

The Dodger fans in the crowd of 34,320 howled with anticipation at the called strike. It silenced the Giants fans, who had been on their feet as their team rallied to score one run in this ninth inning and now, after two outs, had managed to put those runners on first and third.

It may be difficult for current fans to truly contemplate the intense rivalry between these two teams, from adjoining boroughs of New York City. After all, both the Giants and Dodgers departed by the end of the decade for California. Their ballparks, the Polo Grounds and Ebbets Field, were reduced to rubble by the wrecking ball, and apartment building constructed in their place. But if, in that era of flannel uniforms and players quaintly leaving their gloves on the field when they came in to bat, it wasn't a matter of life and death for fans of the winners and losers, it was surely the sporting equivalent.

Years later, Newcombe himself recalled the rivalry: "Just the names of the players in those days could get you juiced up—we had Jackie and Campy and Furillo and Erskine and Duke and Reese, they had Dark and Willie and Maglie and Jansen and Monte Irvin." And to add unnecessary spice to the mix, the Giants manager was the combative former Dodger manager, Leo Durocher.

And, in the current climate of the glut of sports and teams, it may be difficult to contemplate how important baseball was in the American culture. "There were only 16 teams in Major League Baseball at the time, where there are 30 now," recalled Branca. "And the only postseason was the World Series. A playoff occurred only when two teams were tied for first place at the end of the season, and our playoff was only the second in National League history. Now there are playoffs after playoffs. The NBA, the NFL, the big tennis and golf tournaments, auto racing, none of it had the hold on fans as baseball did. From a standpoint of general interest, the other sports were in their infancy. Television was in its infancy. Baseball was king. Baseball in New York took on a kind of cult obsession. And in Brooklyn especially, the fans had a passionate love affair with our team."

Add this to the fact that the Giants had made a fantastic comeback at season's end. They had trailed the seemingly uncatchable Dodgers by 13½ games by August 11. But the Giants won a blistering 37 of their remaining 44 games while the Dodgers stumbled and squandered their lead, putting their fans in a panic. To even create a playoff situation and tie the Giants for first place on the last day of the season, the Dodgers had to beat the Phillies—in 14 innings yet—on a home run by Jackie Robinson.

Branca, in 1951, was still one of the most formidable pitchers in baseball. In his first full season in the big leagues, in 1946, he was, at age 20, the starting pitcher in the first playoff game in National League history, but lost to the Cardinals. The next season he won 21 games, tied for second in the league. He made the All-Star team that year, and the following two seasons, as well. He suffered a shoulder ailment in 1950—had a 7–9 record—but had recovered by the following fateful season to post a 13–12 record and a respectable 3.26 earned-run average. He was fourth in the league in allowing fewest hits per inning, and fourth in the league in strikeouts per game, with just over five. He started the first game of the '51 playoffs and pitched a solid eight innings, giving up three runs on just five hits, but one of those hits was a home run to, who else? Bobby Thomson, with a man on. The Dodgers lost 3–1.

Now, Branca hoped to end matters decisively by striking out Thomson. From the mound, he looked down to Roy Campanella, a broad, squatting target behind the plate, for the sign for his second pitch. One finger: Fastball. Yes, he'd throw it high and inside for a ball, setting up Thomson for a curveball strike on the outside corner.

Alas, it wasn't to be.

Branca gripped the ball with a hand so large he could nearly touch thumb and middle finger around the sphere. He wound up and threw, his body so low while unleashing his pitch that his right knee, as usual, scraped the ground. Lean Bobby Thomson swung and the batted ball flew skyward and began to dip and dip, but fell just beyond the hopeless reach of the left fielder, Andy Pafko, who slumped against the wall in frustration. The ball landed five rows deep in the stands, as fans scrambled for it.

"The Giants win the pennant! The Giants win the pennant!" screamed Russ Hodges, the Giants' radio announcer, into his microphone in the broadcast booth, as three Giant runners jubilantly circled the bases.

An 18-year-old Dodger fan living on East 17th Street in the Flatbush section of Brooklyn named Maury Allen, who later became a distinguished New York sportswriter, had cut class and gone to a high school friend's home down the street from where he lived with his parents to watch the game.

"My friend was one of the few who had a TV set in those days," recalled Allen. "As soon as Thomson hit the home run I bolted out of his house, slamming the door, and ran to my apartment, slammed the front door, slammed my bedroom door, and fell sobbing onto my bed. I wouldn't come out of my room. My mother called me for dinner but I refused to move from my pillow. I didn't come out of my room until the next morning. A lot of us Dodger fans felt it was the end of the world."

As Branca turned from the mound and started toward the center-field clubhouse, the number on his uniform, as the great sports columnist Red Smith wrote, "looked huge. Thirteen."

Some few minutes later, after this most wrenching 5–4 loss, a photographer took a now famous shot of Branca slumped on the clubhouse steps, capless, his head buried in his hands in complete despair.

Later, after he had showered, Branca went to the stadium parking lot, where he was met by his wife's cousin, the priest Pat Rowley. "I remember saying to him, 'Father, why me?'" said Branca. "And he said, 'Because God knew your faith would be strong enough to bear the cross.'"

Has it? Branca was asked. He nodded. "I think so, yes," he replied.

It has been some cross to bear.

The moment has been called "The Miracle at Coogan's Bluff." The home run has gone into legend as "The Shot Heard 'Round the World." In 1998, the United States Postal Service issued a stamp of the home run which, along with 14 other subjects, was to represent the 1950s in its Celebrate the Century program (along with, to name two, "Drive-In Movies" and "*I Love Lucy*"). The term "walk-off home run" had not yet been invented. But that's what it was, the game ended, the pennant decided, on that one pitch, that one swing. Nothing quite like it has ever again taken place in baseball.

Forty years after the home run, in the May 27, 1991, issue of *The New Yorker*, Roger Angell, the superb baseball writer for that magazine, noted that Thomson's home run "stands as the most vivid single moment, the grand exclamation point, in the history of the pastime." Nothing, it seems, has happened to change that observation.

After his long-planned wedding in mid-October of 1951, Branca, like most players, had to work during the off-season to supplement his baseball income—he sold insurance. The highest salary he earned in baseball was $17,500, in the 1949 season, about $5,000 above the average for players that year. (Branca, in off-seasons, also completed two years at New York University.)

Fred Wilpon remembers Branca well. "He was a kind of idol of mine," said Wilpon, chairman of the board and CEO of the New York Mets. Wilpon had been a rising pitching star and Brooklyn Lafayette high school teammate of Sandy Koufax in the early 1950s. He said Branca "was used as an example by my parents. Ralph had gone to New York University, and my parents said, 'See, there's a fine, intelligent young man who went to college before he entered baseball.' I had wanted to follow in that path." (Wilpon suffered an arm injury, ending his baseball career, but did graduate from the University of Michigan.)

In 1952, Branca injured his arm in spring training and struggled on the mound. "Some people wrote that I had trouble pitching because it was psychological, that I was suffering from the after effects of the home run," he said. "But it wasn't. It was soreness in my arm. Maybe, though, I was trying too hard to come back, pressing too hard to make good."

He pitched in only 16 games in 1952—he had appeared in 42 the season before—and finished with a 4–2 record. He was traded to Detroit the next season—the arm never fully recovering—to the Yankees the following year, was in the minor leagues in 1955, came back to Brooklyn in 1956, pitching in one game, with two shutout innings, and then was released, his baseball career over. He was 30 years old. He had spent part or all of 12 seasons in the big leagues (he first appeared briefly for the Dodgers in 1944, when he was 18), finishing with a fine 88–68 won-lost record.

But it was with the Tigers, in 1954, when Branca was told something that stunned him, and years later would stun followers of baseball.

"Thomson knew what I was going to throw him," said Branca, the smile on his face disappearing. "Ted Gray, a pitcher on the Tigers and a friend of mine, said to me one day, 'Ralph, I don't know if I should tell you, but…'

"He told me that a guy on the Giants, a reserve outfielder named Lucky Lohrke, had told him that the Giants had a system for stealing signs in that series. They placed a man with a telescope in Leo's center-field office. When he saw Campy give a sign, he relayed it to the Giants' dugout by a buzzer system.

"Stealing signs was not all that unusual in baseball—but at this moment in the season, well…" He paused. "They made heroes out of those guys. I thought—I think—telling hitters what was coming was the most despicable act in sports history."

In his book, *The Echoing Green: The Untold Story of Bobby Thomson, Ralph Branca, and The Shot Heard 'Round the World*, published in 2006, author Joshua Prager detailed the revelation. He quotes Giant catcher Sal Yvars telling him that he relayed the sign of the pitch to Thomson.

Thomson, however, said he had no foreknowledge of the pitch he belted for the historic home run.

"Thomson denied it to me," said Branca. "I like Bobby, but I was disappointed that he wouldn't admit that he knew what was coming."

For his part, Thomson said, "I wasn't nervous when I came to bat, I was numb."

Thomson later told Branca: "I was just thinking as I walked to the plate, 'Give yourself a chance—watch and wait, watch and wait. Don't be too anxious.'"

Years later Thomson told this reporter: "I try to downplay the home run. I'm grateful people remember, but life goes on." Could Thomson possibly empathize with Branca? "I guess you can get a little tired of hearing about that homer. And I know it's been kind of a burden to Ralph. He once said, 'Why me?' But I remember the next day, when we were playing the Yankees in the World Series, he took a picture with me and he was joking and choking me. I thought it took a lot for him to do that, and said a lot about Ralph Branca the person."

Branca added that he and Thomson have done some card-signing shows together: "We're friendly, but we're not really close."

Branca said, "People talk about the homer less and less. Young people aren't so tied to it. To them it's ancient history, like the Civil War."

Some of the responses he's heard over the years about the home run have made him laugh. "One guy said, 'I was in Ebbets Field and saw Thomson hit the homer.' I said, 'You must have had very strong binoculars to see through the buildings all the way to the Polo Grounds.' Another guy said, 'I was in a motel room in Kansas with a woman and the game was on the radio and you knocked me right out of bed!'"

When Branca left baseball he went into the life insurance business full-time. "And I made a success of it," he said. "They used to have something called the $1 million round table—when a million dollars was a lot of money—and it brought together guys from across the nation who had sold a million dollars or more in insurance for the year. I made the round table for a number of years. You work on commission in this business, and you have your ups and downs, but overall I was fairly consistent.

"Strange thing is that my quote notoriety, or being so-called infamous, for throwing that pitch, didn't hurt my business. I was never shy about being in the public. I've been out of baseball for more than 50 years and people still recognize me on the street. I know who I am. And if a client is curious about it, I'd talk with him about it. Most people are well-meaning. But there are some who like to zing people. You'd hear stage whispers ('Bobby Thomson'). Okay, but how many guys play big-league baseball? How many guys have dreamed of it? I did it."

He and Ann, a graduate of Marymount College, also brought up two daughters: Mary became a dental hygienist and Patti became a special education teacher in the Westchester school district.

Ralph became a superb golfer (handicap went as low as 4 but is much higher today) and still enjoys playing in charity events. He has always had an exceptional singing voice. A baritone, he has sung the national anthem at ballparks and Hall of Fame induction ceremonies. "I still put on the radio when I'm driving and sing along with the songs," he said. "I did it as a player," driving the 40 minutes from his home in Mt. Vernon, New York, to Ebbets Field. "I've always found singing uplifting."

For 16 years, until 2003, Branca was president and CEO of BAT, the baseball assistance team, which has provided funds for more than 1,500 needy or indigent ex-major-league players and their families (Branca was also one of its co-founders, among a few that included Joe Garagiola and Warren Spahn). "For example, we got a prosthetic for my old teammate, Sandy Amoros, when he lost a leg," said Branca. "He had been living above a garage in Miami, and we got him an apartment. For him and many other players and families that were having hard times, we paid rent and put food on the table, and got clothes for them. We get requests, we look into them, and then see if it's something we can do to help."

Branca also cited a former World Series Dodger pitcher, Nick Willhite, who was found homeless, a drug and alcoholic addict, and on the verge of suicide. He called an old teammate, Stan Williams, to say good-bye. Williams wisely suggested contacting BAT. Willhite did, and was rescued. He recovered in a rehab center to the extent that he was re-united with his family and took a job with the Utah Alcoholism Foundation Center in Salt Lake City.

Who are the players who need help? Some didn't make a lot of money in baseball, or squandered it in bad investments. Some, like Amoros, didn't have any other particular skills other than playing baseball, and some, like Willhite, had some business setbacks, got depressed, went to the bottle and the coke, and suffered a downhill spiral after that.

Branca and the other executives had an annual BAT dinner in January in Manhattan which, along with old-timers' games, raised millions of dollars for the organization.

Branca was asked how he would like to be remembered in baseball. "I guess first, my work with BAT," he said. "And then that I was a pretty good young pitcher. I started two playoff games, in 1946 and 1951. I made three All-Star teams, and was the starting pitcher in one of them, in 1948. From 1947 through 1949, I won 48 games and lost 26. People forget how good I was."

He sat back in his chair on the veranda, still thinking about how he'd like to be remembered. "And," he said at last, "as the guy who threw the home-run pitch." He smiled at his ironic joke.

From across the table, Ralph Branca appeared to be a man who, for over half a century, had indeed been strong enough to bear his singular cross.

Bobby Thomson and the Shot Heard 'Round the World Stamp

April 8, 1998

THEY ARE GOING TO make a stamp commemorating a home run—not any home run, to be sure, but the one called "The Shot Heard 'Round the World."

And just when one may be legitimately wondering how the United States Postal Service can possibly consider a long blow in a baseball game on October 3, 1951, between two New York teams, the Giants and the Dodgers, still of any interest—an internecine piece of competition, after all, with adversaries long gone from the scene—there is a tall, white-haired, soft-spoken gentleman from Watchung, New Jersey, to remind us.

"One day some 20 years after it happened, I get a call from a man in Boston," said Bobby Thomson, now 74 years old, and as lean as when he was an outfielder for the Giants. He sat in an office in midtown and wore a gray suit and blue tie and a pair of spectacles. "The man says, 'I've wanted to call you for a long time and tell you where I was when you hit that home run and what happened when you did. Do you mind?'

"I said, 'No, go ahead.' I wasn't doing much and I've heard so many stories about where people were, and I know they like to talk about it. Sometimes I tune out. But not this time. He had taken the effort to call, and it was long distance."

The man said that he had been in the Marines, on the front lines in the conflict in Korea. "We were all spread out, and I'm in a bunker and my best buddy is the craziest Giant fan ever and he is listening to the ballgame," the man told Thomson. "This is a no-no. I mean, if the enemy hears us, one shot could take us all out. But he keeps the radio real low. And then the big moment approached."

The "big moment" arrived after the Giants had been behind the first-place Dodgers by 13½ games in August, but made a tremendous comeback, moving into a tie for first place in the National League pennant race on the final weekend of the season, causing a two-of-three-game playoff. The "big moment" arrived after the series had been tied, 1–1, and the Dodgers were leading, 4–1, going into bottom of the ninth in the Polo Grounds. The Giants had scored one run and had two runners on with one out when Ralph Branca came in to relieve Don Newcombe.

The "big moment" arrived when Thomson came to the plate.

"And then," said the former Marine on the phone from Boston, "when you hit the home run to win the game—well, my buddy got so excited he shot off his rifle! And then the whole place erupted! People started shooting on the right of us, and the left of us, and the enemy started firing back. I remember one of the commanders hollering, 'What's going on here!' My buddy got killed in action about a year later. But I promised myself, for his sake, that one day I'd tell you the story."

"And I told him that I'm glad he did," Thomson said.

Thomson, a semiretired paper salesman for the Stone Container Company, has no elevated sense of self. When asked how the old Marine got his phone number, he said: "I'm in the phone book. I'm nobody special."

Of the 264 homers he hit in his 15-year major-league career, not another approaches the renown of that 1951 shot. Of all the home runs ever hit, it is generally considered the most dramatic because the one swing—the last swing of the game—not only reversed an imminent defeat, not only won the game, but also won the pennant.

"And it was in what people called 'The Golden Age of Baseball,'" Thomson said, "when in that entire decade every year had the Giants, Dodgers, or Yankees, or two of them, in the World Series. And we had this rivalry with the Dodgers in which we hated each other.

"I remember before the series, Leo"—Leo Durocher, the Giants manager—"told us, 'If they throw under our chin, we go two for one.'"

After allowing the home run, Branca wept openly, lamenting, "Why me? Why me?" And Branca had a tough time dealing with it over the years. Did Thomson ever feel sorry for Branca? The mild-mannered Scot said without hesitation: "No." And while he and Branca have often been reunited in recent years and are a twosome at sports card shows, and are friendly, a residue of the old rivalry obviously remains.

And what happened to that home-run ball?

"The next day we opened the World Series in Yankee Stadium, and as I was about to enter the Stadium a man said to me, 'I've got the ball you hit yesterday and I'll give it to you if you give me two tickets to the game,'" Thomson recalled. "I said, 'Stay right there.' I ran into our locker room and grabbed our clubhouse man, Eddie Logan.

"'Eddie,' I said, 'get me two tickets for today's game quick. A man outside has the home-run ball I hit yesterday and he'll trade it for two tickets.' Eddie laughed. 'Eddie, what are you laughing about?' He said, 'Look over there.' On the shelf of my locker were about 10 baseballs, with notes. Eddie said, 'Each one is the home run you hit yesterday.'"

Thomson shook his head. "After that, I gave up," he said. "Who knows, the ball just may be down a sewer somewhere."

Pete Gray: One-Armed Brownie

August 1971

WHAT IS PETE GRAY doing today?

"Don't do nothin' but play a lot of golf," he said by telephone from a tavern in Nanticoke, Pennsylvania. "I shoot in the 80s, usually. Once shot 79."

Pete Gray plays golf left-handed. That is, with the left hand only. Just as he played outfield, hitting .218, with the St. Louis Browns in 1945. He lost his right arm when he was six years old. He is 54.

"Just got out of the hospital," he said, speaking rather loud as if unaccustomed to phones. "Ulcers. Used to drink pretty heavy. Lost weekends, that kind of thing. But I don't drink any more.

"Say, could ya hold on for a minute? I got a cigarette here, I wanna take a couple puffs of it."

The phone banged and dangled against the wall. Gray does not have a phone in the 12-room house where he lives with his mother and brother. You can reach him by calling the tavern down the block. If he's not playing golf, he'll answer the phone, sometimes.

He says he doesn't have a home phone because people would be callin' all the time. Like the Hall of Fame in Cooperstown. According to a local man, the Hall of Fame has been trying to get Gray's glove for its collection. "But Pete says the glove is somewhere in his cellar and he'd just as soon let it rot there," the man said.

"Hello," says Gray, "back on."

He says he weighs about 145 pounds now ("pretty thin") after the ulcer operation, about the same as he weighed during his one big-league year.

"People always ask me, how did I throw?" he said. "Well it's impossible to describe. The way I done it was all in one motion. I'd catch the ball and stick the glove under the stub of my right arm."

And hitting? "When I was a kid I'd go up to the railroad tracks in town and take a stick and throw up a rock and hit it for hours and hours. My father was always mad because I was late for supper. Developed a pretty good wrist, though."

The year before he came up to the Browns, he played for Memphis, stole 65 bases, and was named the Most Valuable Player in the American Association. These were the war years and the caliber of professional base-ball was at low ebb. But in 1945—or any year, for that matter—for a one-armed man to play 77 major-league games and bat .218 and hit six doubles, two triples, drive in 13 runs, and strike out only 11 times in 234 at-bats is quite a feat.

"I packed 'em in all over," recalls Gray. "There were 65,000 in Cleveland the first time I played, and I hit a triple my first time up. When we played the Yankees the first time in New York, our team was introduced before the game. Luke Sewell was our manager. He said, 'Pete, you stay here, be the last one to come out on the field.' I got a standing ovation—just to make an appearance! But I done a pretty good job, too."

Gray lost his arm when he fell off the running board of a huckster's wagon and his arm caught in the spokes of a wheel. Soon, however, he was playing baseball in the streets of Nanticoke, a coal mining town of 20,000 persons, six miles from Wilkes-Barre.

"By the time I was 16 I was better than the other kids," he said. He came to New York in 1939 for the World's Fair, and took his glove along because he had read that there were big-league tryouts in Brooklyn. He eventually caught on in the Canadian-American League, and in his first game dived for a fly ball and broke his collarbone. He wound up hitting .381. The next season he moved up to Toronto where he got a late start; he had come down with the grippe.

After 1945, he bounced around the minors—Toledo, Elmira, Dallas—haggling over contracts and having drinking problems. In 1950 he played for the House of David club, and two years later got a call to play in an outlaw league in Canada.

"And that was it," said Gray.

He says that except for baseball he has never worked a day in his life, though an old *Sporting News* clipping said that he had left the Dallas team to return to the billiard parlor he owned in Nanticoke.

A local woman says that Gray doesn't seem to have much money, but doesn't seem to care about it either. He plays golf almost every day, she said, and she thinks his buddies pick up the tab.

"And Pete refuses to go on public assistance," said a man who works in the Nanticoke post office.

Gray was asked what he lives on.

"Nothin', never done no work," he said. But what do you use for money?

"Well, I saved some from baseball," he said, reluctantly. "I did a lotta gamblin'. My mother, she rents six rooms in the house and she gets a check because my father died of black lung from the mines, you know."

Gray says he's a celebrity in town. "Wouldn't you think so?" he said. Though he seems proud of his baseball career, he hardly seems to revel in it.

"It's done," he said. "They don't run the railroad here anymore. It's all weeds where I used to hit the rocks. And the ballfields I played on, they're all woods. Time changes."

Could there ever be another one-armed big-leaguer?

"I don't know," he said. "I see that some high school kid's been playing with one arm. But you gotta put a lot of time in, like I done."

Jim Abbott:
He Did It with One Hand

December 25, 1992

NEWPORT BEACH, CALIFORNIA—One looks for turning points. How is it that he has come this far, this way? Maybe it was the time when Jim Abbott was five years old and came home from school, angry and tearful, and held up the steel hook a doctor had recommended he use for a right hand. "I don't want to wear this anymore," he told his parents.

Other children were afraid to play with him and, in the way that small children can be cruel, called him names like "Mr. Hook." Even then he struggled not to appear different. He never wore the hook again.

Or maybe it was the time when he saw that his parents had learned to tie a shoe with one hand so they could teach it to him. He, unlike them, was born with just one hand, his left.

Or maybe it was when his father in a park in Flint, Michigan, taught him to throw a baseball and then remove the glove ever so smoothly and swiftly from his right wrist and place it on his left throwing hand in order to catch his dad's quick throw back, and then switch the glove back again in order to throw.

He developed the technique so skillfully that when he was pitching in high school, the story goes, the first nine batters on an opposing team tried to bunt for hits. He threw the runners out each time.

"That story has grown out of proportion," Abbott said. "It was only five or six batters."

Or maybe for Abbott, the 25-year-old pitcher recently obtained by the Yankees in a trade with the California Angels, there was no single turning point. Maybe it was simply the concept that his parents, Mike and Kathy Abbott, had come to live by, that Jim, except for the strange fate of having been born with one hand—there is a stub with one small finger-like protrusion where the right hand would be—was as normal as any other kid, and should think of himself that way.

Four years ago, Abbott became the first and only one-handed pitcher in baseball history, and one of the elite who can throw the ball at speeds of up to 94 miles an hour. Abbott also accomplished something else that, while not singular, is rare. He went from the campus of the University of Michigan to the Angels, their first-round pick in the amateur draft. He has never spent a day in the minor leagues.

Abbott's parents were married at 18 and had Jim when they were still 18. There was a time early on when they felt sorry for themselves, but they soon overcame the shock and influenced Jim not to feel sorry for himself, either.

Kathy Abbott recalled that occasionally Jim drew stares from people. "Oh, yes, because of Jim's hand," she said. "I'd forgot about it."

"I never heard Jim ask, 'Why me?'" said his father recently. "And as he grew up, I watched the way he handled himself around people. He's always had a lot of friends, always laughed. Even when some people have said insensitive or cruel things. Like a reporter asking, 'Is anyone else in your family deformed?' But Jim is always a gentleman. I don't understand how he does it. His dad is now taking lessons from him."

"My parents kept me in the mainstream; they never shielded me," Abbott said, sitting recently with his wife, Dana, on a stuffed white couch in their ground-floor apartment here. Outside, near the window, stood a palm tree. Inside, there was a small, decorated Christmas tree. Abbott said he felt blessed. "When we moved into a new neighborhood, my father said, 'Jim, go out and meet the kids. Say, I'm Jim Abbott. Ask to play in their game.'"

One can somehow still picture Abbott, now 6-foot-3 and 215 pounds and looking husky in a short-sleeve blue shirt, blue jeans, and worn running shoes, as that blond-haired, open-faced, seeking boy. He recalled that his parents always supported him but never pushed him, that they emphasized he should do whatever came naturally, and that he could just about realize whatever dreams he had, including, eventually, pitching in the major leagues.

"I will always be thankful to my parents for how they dealt with it," he said. "They were young. They were alone. There were no support groups. Really, I look back with admiration."

Pitching for a mediocre Angels team that, as it happened, often didn't play well behind him or hit well for him, he managed to post commendable statistics. Last season, for a team that tied for fifth place in the American League West, Abbott compiled a 2.77 earned-run average, fifth best in the league, although his record was 7–15. The year before, he was 18–11, with a 2.89 ERA. In his two previous seasons, his records were 12–12 and 10–14 (and in those 14 losses his team scored a total of 15 runs).

"He pitches his heart out every time," said Rod Carew, the Hall of Famer and the Angels' batting coach. "But he pitched with incredibly bad luck. He could win 20 games for the Yankees, easy. I'd put him in the category with Catfish Hunter and Nolan Ryan, some of the greatest pitchers I faced. And he's a terrific guy to be around. I hated to see him go."

On the bench, Angels players laughed among themselves how Abbott, with his cutting fastball and hard slider, broke five or six opponents' bats a game. And they would take pleasure in observing other players watch Abbott field a shot through the box, handling his glove so fast that it was nearly sleight-of-hand. "Did you see that!" players in the other dugout exclaimed. "Did you see that!"

Why, then, did the Angels trade Abbott? A contract dispute seems at the crux. Abbott was at the end of a one-year contract with an option. The Angels offered a four-year contract at $16 million. Abbott's agent, Scott Boras, had asked for a four-year deal for $19 million but made it clear that this was negotiable. At this point, it seems, Jackie Autry, who runs the team for her husband, the old troubadour-cowboy Gene Autry, and the general manager, Whitey Herzog, decided they would show Abbott and Boras who was boss and traded the pitcher for three Yankee minor-league prospects.

"I was surprised," said Abbott. "I just thought I'd spend my whole career with the Angels. It's kind of easy to get it into your head that you're indispensable. And then suddenly I was traded and felt a real sense of rejection. And there were the concerns about coming to New York—just a big, looming city. As great a city as it is—and I've always loved to visit there—I wasn't sure. You hear a lot of horror stories. And I was concerned about Dana making the transition because she was born and raised in Southern California. But she seemed excited about it."

Dana Douty lettered in basketball and earned a degree in economics from the University of California at Irvine last year, shortly before she and Abbott were married.

"Jim's such a fierce competitor that going to the Yankees will just be another challenge for him," she said. "He even hates it when I beat him in gin rummy."

"But I'm getting better," Abbott insisted.

"You are," she assured with a smile, "you are."

Despite his boyish looks, Abbott hardly seems one to be intimidated, even by New York City.

"I like the team the Yankees are putting together," he said. "I like the players they've recently picked up, like Jimmy Key and Wade Boggs and Spike Owen and Paul O'Neill, and plus, of course, it's a privilege to play with guys like Mattingly—or should I call him Don?" He smiled. "Or Mr. Mattingly?" He was half serious.

"And I have no problem with anything I've heard about George Steinbrenner. I mean, it sounds to me like he wants to have a winner in the worst way. I love that."

Abbott spoke about a phone call from Yankees manager Buck Showalter. "You'll like the fans," Showalter told Abbott. "They stay for the whole game and hang on every pitch, and they know baseball. They'll cheer you when you do well and boo when you don't. But there's an excitement at Yankee Stadium that's different from Anaheim."

"The call pumped me up," said Abbott. And while he didn't want to say anything bad about the Angels, a team that "gave me a chance," he was nonetheless upset when he read something an Angels executive had said: "Oh, people are unhappy to lose Abbott only because he's a one-armed pitcher."

"I have an arm," said Abbott. "I don't have a hand."

Abbott is not the only one-handed player in major-league history. There was Pete Gray, the one-armed outfielder for the St. Louis Browns in 1945. "I didn't grow up wanting to be another Pete Gray," said Abbott. "I grew up wanting to be another Nolan Ryan."

Abbott was always a good athlete, and sports has helped give him a sense of stature that he might not have had otherwise. He became a high school pitching sensation and then got a scholarship to Michigan, where he majored in communications and was so brilliant a pitcher (and a capable batter, too) that in 1987 he was named amateur baseball player of the year. In 1988, he won the Sullivan Award as the best amateur athlete in the country.

With all that, he is not pleased when, for example, people have come to him to autograph a baseball that Pete Gray had signed. While Abbott admires Gray, he doesn't want to be thought of as an oddity.

Gray, for all his remarkable achievements and ability, was still kind of a sideshow in the major leagues, a wartime player used primarily to draw crowds, a player who would be introduced last to the fans in pregame introductions. Gray batted .218 in his one year in the big leagues. Abbott is one of the finer pitchers in baseball, and, after four seasons, an established one.

"I just don't think all of this about me playing with one hand is as big an issue as everyone wants to make it," said Abbott. "I don't try to run from the attention about it, I just accept it."

Abbott received so much mail with the Angels—as many as 300 letters a week—that the public relations department regularly piled it into shopping carts when he was on the road. Many of the letters were from children who were physically handicapped or disabled, or from parents of such children.

"Some of the stories are unbelievable, so tragic," said Abbott. One letter came from an eight-year-old girl who had been attacked by a mountain lion and lost an arm. Another boy had lost an arm when fireworks exploded.

"I try to write them all back. But sometimes there's really not much I can say. I don't really believe in this stuff about ballplayers as role models. But if I can be of help to anyone, if anyone can take something from the fact that I'm a baseball pitcher, then fine.

"But when I'm out on the mound pitching, I'm pitching because I love it, because I like the challenge of trying to get people out. I'm not pitching because I want to prove anything to anyone."

In every city he travels to, parents bring their children to meet him. "There was this one boy, about seven years old, who came into the clubhouse with his parents," Abbott recalled. "He had only parts of two fingers on one hand. He asked me if kids were mean when I was growing up. He said they called him 'Crab' at camp. I said, 'Yeah, they used to say that my hand looks like a foot.' I said to him, 'Do you think that teasing is a problem?' He said, 'No.' I said, 'Is there anything you can't do?' And he said, 'No.' And I said, 'Well, I don't think so either.'

"Then I looked around the room and said to him, 'Look, I'm playing with guys like Dave Winfield and Wally Joyner and Dave Parker. I'm playing with them and I'm just like you.' I'd never said that before, that I was thrilled to be here and it didn't matter if I had two good hands. But I put myself into his shoes and remembered what I was like at his age. And I'm sure that kids need someone to relate to. But so do their parents. Most of the time I think it's my parents these people should be talking to, not me."

While there were surely grim moments in his background, much of it, he says, he has blocked out. Like, perhaps, his feelings of self-consciousness as he tried to hide the stub of his hand from view. Even now, perhaps subconsciously, his father said, he still sometimes does.

But Abbott, meanwhile, tries to look forward, not backward, which is why he has turned down numerous movie and book offers.

"I'd hate to be held to what I said or thought when I was 21 years old," he said. "But anyway, a book on me would be boring. Like, 'Oh yeah, he pitched a great game.' Or, 'When he was losing with the Angels he got booed.' Not great literature."

It was near the end of day, the sun was setting behind the palm tree and the Christmas tree, and the Abbotts rose to get in some late Christmas shopping.

They entered the apartment garage, where a set of his golf clubs in a red golf bag leaned against the wall. Abbott climbed behind the wheel of his cream-colored minivan. He was asked: is there anything he can't do that he wished he could?

"Yes," he said, after a moment. "I'd love to play the piano."

Lou Brissie: Left for Dead, Then a Major-League All-Star

December 8, 1994

YESTERDAY, DECEMBER 7, THE 50th anniversary of the day that changed his life and contributed in a harrowing way to making him one of the most remarkable figures in American sports history, Lou Brissie did nothing different to mark it. No reason to. He woke beside his wife in their home in North Augusta, South Carolina, felt the ache in his left leg that has never left him for a single day over this half-century, and prepared for work as a state supervisor of job trainees.

"Sometimes, when people know that I had pitched in the major leagues, and see I have some trouble gettin' around, they ask if I injured my knee playin' ball," he said yesterday by telephone. "I tell 'em, 'Well, no, it was a little something I got in the service, and that's it.'"

Brissie, now 70 years old, his hair thinning, still big at 6-foot-4½ and still looking fit, can walk unaided, though with a slight limp, for short distances. Otherwise, he must rely on a cane or crutches.

And he remembers: It was on December 7, 1944, in the Apennines in central Italy as American soldiers moved up against German positions, that an advance echelon, with the 20-year-old Corporal Brissie, got into trouble.

"They unloaded everything on us," he recalled. "The shell that hit me killed 11 men. I was the closest when it exploded, but I got mine mostly in the legs. The others were hit mostly in the throat and the head."

Brissie crawled to a creek, where he hoped to get some protection, and passed out. He was left for dead until one medic carried him off. In the Army hospital in Naples, a doctor said he must amputate his left leg.

"Doc, you can't!" said Brissie. "I'm a ballplayer. You have to try to find another way."

Before entering the military, Brissie had been a promising left-handed high school and then freshman college pitcher at Presbyterian in South Carolina. Connie Mack, manager of the Philadelphia A's, wrote him while he was in service and promised him a tryout on his return.

The Army surgeon, Dr. William Brubaker, who would become a lifelong friend of Brissie's, found a way to save the leg. Brissie was the first person in the Mediterranean theater to be given the new drug penicillin, and Brissie underwent surgery—the first of 23 operations on his leg—in which 30 bone fragments and 5½ inches of skin bone were removed.

Now began an amazing story, beginning with his return on a stretcher to America to his wife and infant daughter, seeking to regain his health and use of his leg in veterans hospitals and never forgetting his dream of pitching in the big leagues, though often being told by doctors: "You must understand your limitations, young man. Think about other things you can do."

Brissie began throwing a baseball on crutches. He was soon free of them. He hooked up with a sandlot team in 1946, wore a bulky aluminum brace that was made to protect his leg but drew stares, went through tearful disappointments, then adjusted his pitching stride and learned how to field bunts. He joined the Savannah Class AA ballclub and began winning games. In 1947, he was called up to the A's. "It took my breath away," he recalled.

On opening day of 1948, he started against the Red Sox. In the sixth inning, Ted Williams hit a line drive off his leg brace. It made a clanging noise heard throughout the ballpark. Brissie collapsed. Williams ran from first base to the mound. "Are you all right?" he asked. Brissie looked up from the ground. "Why don't you pull the damn ball?" he said. They both laughed.

Brissie, despite battling infections and pain, became a standout pitcher, making the American League All-Star team in 1949. He was traded to

Cleveland in 1951 and retired from baseball two years later, refusing to be sent back to the minor leagues.

"I knew I was a symbol to many veterans trying to overcome problems," he said. "I wasn't going to let them down."

Today, Brissie says he identifies in a manner with Jim Abbott, the Yankees' one-handed pitcher. "He was innovative, and it seemed, like me, he never thought of failing." Brissie is also distressed about the baseball strike. "There's not going to be a winner. That's the tragedy."

Last summer, for the first time in nearly 50 years, Lou Brissie returned to Italy, visiting military cemeteries at Anzio and other sites.

"I found a lot of old friends there, and thought about those times," he said. He paused for a moment. "I didn't handle it as well as I thought I would."

V.

GEORGE STEINBRENNER

I'm Like Archie Bunker

THERE IS NOT A MORE controversial figure in sports than George Michael Steinbrenner III. Possibly the most famous thing about George Steinbrenner is his trap door through which his managers seem to disappear.

Second-most famous is his vault, or that which is contained therein. It is from this green arsenal that he has, it is often said, built the New York Yankees into "The Best Team Money Can Buy."

Steinbrenner became principal owner of the Yankees in 1973, a period in which the once-great Yankees were foundering. Under his leadership, they rose, in three seasons, from fourth place in the American League East standings, to league champions in 1976. In 1977 and 1978 they repeated as league champs and went on to win the World Series each time. They made the playoffs in 1980—but lost to Kansas City—and are now assured of a mini-playoff spot this year, having won the first part of the split season in this strike-ravaged year.

When Steinbrenner took over, the Yankees had drawn less than 1 million fans at home for the first time in 28 years. Since then, attendance has risen each year and they drew more than 2 million fans for five straight seasons.

Steinbrenner has been great at capturing headlines, and making melodrama out of his dealings with and coarse criticisms and abrupt dismissals of players and managers, including and especially the slugging right fielder Reggie Jackson and the two-time former manager Billy Martin. (Steinbrenner has gone through five managers in the last three years—more than any other team in baseball.) He was also the most flamboyant owner in acquiring free agents.

For all this, friends of Steinbrenner—some people may be surprised that there is such a group—say that beneath his gruff, fleshy exterior there beats a gruff and fleshy heart, but a heart nonetheless. Besides the Yankees, Steinbrenner has many business holdings, including the Bay Harbor Inn on the Gulf of Mexico here.

He was educated at Culver Military Academy and Williams College. He has made his fortune developing and expanding the American Shipbuilding Company of Cleveland—his hometown—and Tampa, a company he inherited from his father, Henry.

George Steinbrenner is pictured often in the press, but there was one candid view of him on national television that remains in many minds:

In last season's third and final playoff game against Kansas City, a Yankee base runner, Willie Randolph, was thrown out at home plate in an important play. Steinbrenner jumped up in his private box and stormed out of the ballpark, the camera catching him uttering an obscenity. Later he would condemn his third-base coach, Mike Ferraro, for sending the runner home—even though it took a perfect relay and perfect throw to get Randolph. Steinbrenner's action seemed the essence of an arrogant, petulant, boorish poor sport.

"Okay, I can understand how you'd think that," he said, sitting at a table in the hotel restaurant which has the motif of a Yankee clipper sailing vessel. "But you have to understand how I feel. I'm like Archie Bunker, I get mad as hell when my team blows one. But there are 5 million Yankee fans just like me sitting in front of their TV sets with beer and hollering the same thing when Ferraro sends Randolph home and he's out. I want this team to win, I'm obsessed with winning, with discipline, with achieving. That's what this country's all about, that's what New York is all about. Fighting for everything—a cab in the rain, a table in a restaurant at lunchtime—and that's what the Yankees are all about, and always have been."

In print tie and green sport jacket, Steinbrenner, at the age of 51, is as thick-chested as an old football coach, which he once was; he is jowly with hair cut short and gray, and blue eyes that have counted many a house. When he makes a point with his puffy, but surprisingly small hands, his 1977 championship ring—his first—with the diamond-studded NY emblem, flashes.

"So I flew off the handle. My mother was watching the game on television, and when I spoke to her—I always call my parents to tell them why I did what I've done—she said, 'Dear, did you say what I thought you said?' You have to know my mother, she's a Christian Scientist, a very gentle person. And I said: 'I didn't know the camera was on me, Mother, but I said it. Because that's the way I felt.'

"People get on me for blasting players in public," he said. "But some of them are making hundreds of thousands of dollars for playing a kid's game. I mean, the game should be fun but it's also serious work. Look at Rick Cerone. The other night in Milwaukee he makes an error that costs us the game. You've got to produce for these people—these folks, these construction guys and cab workers—they deserve the best. This is their recreation after a grueling day. Cerone makes $440,000 a year, this is after I rescued him from the scrap heap at Toronto, where he was making $100,000. And as soon as he comes to New York he takes me to arbitration and wins with some garment-district arbitrator who knows nothing about baseball. And if Cerone doesn't do well is he gonna return the money to me? Hell no. It's a new age, and these players are making more than some big corporate executives. So I've got a platform where the little guy doesn't, and I use it."

Does that platform entitle you to interfere with your managers, like calling the dugout and ordering them to do certain things? "Stop. I never called the dugout. What you're referring to is the Gene Michael thing." Michael was dismissed as Yankee manager September 6 after less than one season on the job. "Bill Bergesch, my vice president in charge of baseball operations, called the dugout, I didn't. Bergesch told Stick"—Michael's nickname— "that he thought we should have a practice on the following day—an off day—because we were screwing up pathetically on fundamentals. But Stick said we didn't need a practice, we needed a rest."

Did Bergesch or you think the team needed a practice? "I did." But even if you didn't directly call the dugout, isn't that interfering with your manager? "No, I suggested or recommended that he have a practice period and he said, 'If I do, I'm telling the players that it's your idea, not mine.' Isn't that childish? I said, 'Well, put the blame on me, I don't care.' He didn't like that, either."

It was suggested to Steinbrenner that Michael obviously felt it would be a loss of dignity to tell the players to do something he truly did not believe was right.

"I'm the boss, I'm the leader, and he should have shown more loyalty. No one anywhere keeps a job acting that way. And then he went public with this, and with him saying that I kept threatening to take his job. That wasn't right either."

But you had gone public earlier in criticizing Michael. When the Orioles had swept the Yankees in a series in Baltimore the press asked you if Michael's job was in jeopardy.

"And I said I didn't know. I'm not a phony. I wasn't going to give a vote of confidence if I didn't feel it. I told it straight." You said that in the Michael case, you felt like a "father scorned." "I was disappointed," he said, "Stick knew I expected better from him. It reminded me of my father toward me. He was a great track man in the '20s. He was the low hurdles champion in 1927. I ran track, too. Well, my dad would see me win three races and come in second in the last and he'd show disapproval that I hadn't won all four. But I don't want to get into my personal life."

Steinbrenner said that, when he decided to dismiss Michael, it was only after he consulted with his strategy board: Bergesch; Lou Saban, the club president; Cedric Tallis, the administrative vice president; Bill Livesey, the director of player development; and Bobby Hofman, the director of scouting.

Does the strategy board ever overrule you? "Many times. Let me tell you, this is one of the most democratically run operations there is. All of us have a say."

You ever overrule them? "Once. It concerned Bobby Brown. I think the kid has a hell of a future as an outfielder. But they thought he was trouble.

The vote was 5–1. I was the one, but I made my vote count for six, and Bobby stayed."

Do they ever overrule you? "Yes. Certainly. Many times." Can you think of one? He paused. "Not offhand, but there were a lot. But Gene should have known what I was like. He worked with me in the front office for a couple of years. I've got a quick temper, but I calm down. Like in my office in Tampa. I've got a secretary there that I fired 100 times. But she never leaves. No kidding. She understands me. I come in the next morning and she's there, and we both go about our business."

Do you say hello? "I grump at her. That's my hello." What if Michael had decided to show up in the dugout the day after you dismissed him? "It would have been a little crowded." "But Gene's thing was different," Steinbrenner said. "I thought he showed disloyalty. And if there's one thing I want, it's loyalty. That's first and foremost.

"You know, there's something else that gets me. Sportswriters write that I don't care about people and that I fire 'em and just throw them into the street. That's a damned lie. I do care about them, and I make sure they land okay. Like Dick Howser. I made a mistake in taking him away from his job as baseball coach at Florida State. Well, when we had a parting I paid for the mortgage on his house, and I kept him on as a scout. And I paid the full salary of his contract. And remember, Dick, for all our disagreements, never said that he wouldn't come back as a manager for me.

"I thought Dick missed details. I'm a great detail and organization man. Like the other day, I called up to make sure our heaters were set for the play-offs—which are a full three weeks away. A physicist I know said that warm wood will hit a ball better in cold weather. I want to be ready.

"And I'm an innovator. Take minor-league teams. They used to have just one coach—he drove the team bus and shagged balls and every other damned thing. When did he have a chance to coach or manage? Now I have three coaches on each minor-league team—including a pitching coach—and a good one—for each team. That's the first that this kind of thing has ever been done. And six of our seven minor-league teams have won their league championship for two years in a row.

"We also spend more than any other team on scouting and player development—$4 million a year. That's why I get mad when people say it's just money that has turned this club around. It's a lot of thought and a lot of hard work."

Is it because of this concern for detail that you once lost your temper in your hotel restaurant when you found ice chunks in the ice cream?

"Let me tell you about that. I was with some businessmen and we got served this ice cream with big chunks of ice in it, in my own restaurant. I called over the waitress. 'Miss, look at this ice in this ice cream. This is no way to serve ice cream. Get the manager.' And I demanded to know who was in charge of the food quality."

It was said that you were loud about it and other diners turned around. "I want things done right. And there was no excuse for those ice chunks in the ice cream." He has dismissed employees for committing transgressions on this level—he says he makes his standards clear—but in this case none lost his job.

Understandably, Steinbrenner strikes fear in the hearts of some of his employees. But not all. "I know that a guy like Lou Piniella writes on the blackboard in the locker room when I'm in New York, 'Col. Clink's in town.' Or, 'Attila the Hun has arrived.' And I get a chuckle that Graig Nettles wears a T-shirt that says FIDO on it because he says he's always in my dog house.

"I can take that. But what I didn't like about Nettles is when he turned down an invitation for the Yankees to go to a luncheon that I thought was important. He said, 'Why should I go to an affair when I'm in the circus?' The Yankees are no circus—they are tradition, they are the greatest and most famous sports team in the world—and I resented his remark. His agent later apologized to me for Graig.

"I'll tell you what I hate, I hate being called an ogre in the press. I'm no angel, don't get me wrong, but the man with no dents in his armor, let him step forward. I try to do the best I can. And sometimes—as much as I don't want to—I have to inflict pain, but I also inflict some joy.

"I'm not a tentative leader. I make a decision and then I've got to go hell bent for leather. People in this country don't want tentative leaders. That's why they voted Carter out of office—overwhelmingly. There are too many underachievers in this country. I want my guys to perform up to their abilities, and beyond. And God knows they're getting paid enough money to do it. I can't be a nice guy about it. Church choirs are filled with nice guys. This country was built on people with guts who wanted more than they had—like the people in those little covered wagons who went West and fought the weather and the Indians.

"But I think I can get the most out of somebody by doing it the way I do. I don't do it passive. I don't know how. Maybe if I were smarter I could. Sometimes I wish I could change. But I haven't."

And sometimes, he said, he is grossly misunderstood in his relations with players. "Like Reggie Jackson. He was lousy at the plate for much of this year. In the outfield, well, he's never been Baryshnikov to begin with. I love calling him that. He laughs when I say it, too. Anyway, now, it was serious. We didn't know if it was physical or mental. Friends of his said he was down about this being the last year in his contract and that I wasn't showing him enough attention. Well, I can't walk around with a badge, I Love Reggie, no matter how much he has delivered for me in the past, and he's been absolutely great until this last season. I've got 24 other guys who want the same kind of attention. So Reggie was hitting .199—after batting his all-time highest average, .300, last year—and my people are telling me they never saw him look so bad. Obviously something is very wrong. It had to be either physical or mental. I thought we ought to give him a complete physical examination to begin with, to make sure he's okay there. He refused. He told the newspapers I was trying to embarrass him, humiliate him. Completely false. He was afraid to go, to maybe find out that something was seriously wrong. But I ordered him to go, and he got a clean bill of health. Even his eyesight was 20-15 and he discovered that he really didn't even need glasses at bat. So I said to him, 'Reggie, now don't you feel better that it's not physical?' He said that he did feel better. So I told him, now we know the problem is upstairs."

Upstairs meaning? "The head. And right after that he started pounding the hell out of the ball. Some of these guys—they're something. I remember when I called Thurman Munson into my trailer in training camp in Fort Lauderdale. I wanted to make him captain of the Yankees. We hadn't had a captain since Lou Gehrig, and I thought Thurman was as important to the Yankees as Gehrig was back in his day.

"Munson said, 'I don't want to be no damn captain.' I said, 'You're going to be the damn captain.' So he walks out with his head down the way he used to walk. Sometime later, he comes to me and says he wants to resign as captain. He says: 'Some guys resent me being captain. They salute me when I come in the room.' I said: 'You can't quit on the team now. We're in fourth place. We need you to lead this team.' And by God, he did. We went from 14 games down to winning the pennant.

"And after we beat the Dodgers in the last game of the Series, we're in the locker room and champagne is flowing and everyone's hollering and I hear Munson call me. 'Come over here,' he says. And I do and he hugs me. And he says, 'I'm building a new house and I wonder if you could get me a replica of the championship trophy to put in it.' I said I thought I could. I started to walk away, and he calls, 'Hey, wait a minute,' like he was trying to impress a few of the ballplayers around him by giving the boss orders. He said, 'Could they write on the trophy—Captain of the Yankees?' I said, 'You got it.'

"And the next year Thurman was gone. It was the saddest day of my life when I heard the news that his plane crashed. We fought like cats and dogs, but we got along great." Steinbrenner paid for all the expenses for Munson's funeral—including flying the entire Yankee team to Canton, Ohio, for it.

Another of Steinbrenner's favorite players was Catfish Hunter. Steinbrenner recalls with fondness the sixth and final game of the 1978 World Series against the Dodgers. "I'll never forget it. It was in New York. I saw the manager, Bob Lemon, and asked him who was pitching. He said Catfish. I said that's great. You see, Catfish was the cornerstone of the Yankees. He came to us and taught us how to win. He was a wonderful guy, and one of the all-time best competitors. He knew how to pitch. Everybody loved Catfish. Now he was coming down to the end of his career—he retired after the next season. So now I went to the training room where he was getting his arm rubbed down. I was thinking about this movie I once saw, called *Angels in the Outfield*, with Paul Douglas. A great old film about an old pitcher who gets a last chance and wins the big game. Great film. So I walk into the training room, and Catfish is there and so is the trainer, Gene Monahan. I said, 'Cat, I want to tell you—you're gonna do it tonight. I know it. There's this film,' and I started telling him about it, and he's got his arm back and Monahan has stopped rubbing and they're both staring at me like I'm crazy. I didn't care. I said, 'You're gonna do it.' And damn it, he beat the Dodgers, 12–2, and we won the championship."

Steinbrenner is a prominent donor to numerous charities, and, as the saying goes, doesn't hide his light under a bushel. "I've put 79 kids through college. Disadvantaged kids. Kids who thought no one cared about them. But someone does. I think businessmen have a responsibility, not just to buy 10 tables at some affair, but to go one-on-one. One day I read in the papers that a seven-year-old girl had a piece of a board pierced through her head, and she had one operation, which she owed $6,000 on, and she needs another operation to save her life, and her family doesn't have the $6,000 the second operation costs. She's going to die otherwise. I called up her home. They couldn't believe it was me. I said, 'Come to my office, I'll send a check to pay for the two operations.' Her parents later sent me a letter thanking me for saving their little girl's life."

He also likes to make projects out of some of his players. He talks this season of "salvaging" Reggie Jackson. And he tried to do the same with Billy Martin. He dismissed Martin once and then "anguished" that he had done the wrong thing.

"I hired him back because I thought it was the right thing to do. But when he got in that trouble in Minnesota, I called his friend and said, 'Whatever you do, tell Billy to tell the truth.' If he had said, 'The guy was pestering me, Boss, and I couldn't take any more and I belted him,' I'd have said, 'Fine, I could understand that, I'd have done the same thing.' But he comes out the next day: 'I'm innocent. The guy slipped and fell.' Well, later he admitted the truth. I just couldn't accept him doing that, I couldn't close my eyes to it. So Billy had to be let go. And it hurt. I like Billy, and he's a genius as a baseball manager."

Being so demanding and quick-tempered, did Steinbrenner feel he could ever work for a man like Steinbrenner? He thought for a moment. "We'd fight a lot, we'd fight a hell of a lot. But, damn it, like I always say, nothing worthwhile is easy."

Analyzed by Freud

May 2, 1985

SIGM. FREUD, AS THE good doctor signed some of his correspondence, departed from this vale of tears nearly half a century ago. Yet his wisdom in many matters lives on. Recently, Dr. Peter Berczeller, who, like Dr. Freud, was born in Austria, and who now practices medicine on, and follows the Yankees from, Second Avenue, wondered aloud what Sigm. might have cogitated about the latest undertaking of the principal owner of the Yankees, the fantastical Herr S.

A clue, perhaps, may be found in the newly published *The Complete Letters of Sigmund Freud to Wilhelm Fliess, 1887–1904*. An interview follows that uses this text. The answers were chosen with careful selectivity by this typist, but the words, whether they would have been approved in the context or not, are Sigm.'s.

Q. Dr. Freud, how are you feeling now after Herr S.'s firing of Yogi Berra and his hiring for the fourth time of Billy Martin?
I have not yet really overcome my depression…On my side of the tunnel it is quite dark.

Q. Sorry to hear you're so ill over the recent events.
My state of health does not deserve to be a subject of inquiry…There was a recrudescence of the suppuration of the left side, migraines rather frequently, the necessary abstinence is hardly doing me much good. I have rapidly turned gray.

Q. Could you guess at how Met fans are feeling about this?
The sun and the stars are shining…

Q. Have you given much study to the case of the principal owner?
I shudder when I think of all the psychology I shall have to read up
on the next few years. At the moment I can neither read nor think. I
am completely exhausted by observation.

Q. Did you have any idea that Herr S. would make this move?
So my premonition of something ominous turned out to be right.

Q. You mean that Yogi was fired only 16 games into the season?
I find it sad that the interval is so short.

**Q. Yankee fans appear to be deeply depressed. Any words of advice
for them?**
I seem to remember having heard somewhere that only dire need
brings out the best in man. I have therefore pulled myself together…
A basket of orchids gives me the illusion of splendor and glowing
sunshine; a fragment of a Pompeiian wall with a centaur and faun
transports me…

**Q. On the subject of Herr S., it seems to most laymen that he has
a compulsion or fixation or obsessional idea or some other oddball
thing that they can't quite put a finger on in regard to firing people,
particularly managers. He hadn't fired a manager in over a year
until last Sunday. Can you relate to such an itch as Herr S.'s in any
way? What about your quitting smoking?**
After seven weeks…I began again…From the first cigars on, I was
able to work and was the master of my mood; prior to that, life was
unbearable.

**Q. Does that mean that firing people, like smoking for you, makes
him feel better?**
It is a question of psychic mechanism that is very commonly employed
in normal life: transposition, or projection. Whenever an internal

change occurs, we have the choice of assuming either an internal or external cause. If something deters us from the internal derivation, we naturally seize upon the external one.

Q. Does that mean, Doc, that he has to blame people other than himself?
In every instance the delusional idea is maintained with the same energy with which another, intolerably distressing, idea is warded off from the ego. Thus they love their delusions as they love themselves. That is the secret.

Q. Are you saying that this is the answer?
That is the material we have. No one really has a clear picture…

Q. But?
The whole business is uncanny.

Q. Many Yankee fans and some local journalists have advanced the notion that Herr S. should sell the Yankees and stick with his shipbuilding business. Your thoughts?
I vaguely sensed something I can express only today: the faint notion that this man has not yet discovered his calling.

Q. But if he continues as principal owner, what might this mean for Yankee fans?
Gloomy times, unbelievably gloomy.

Q. What do you foresee for the Yankee fans in the near future?
Fathomless and bottomless laziness, intellectual stagnation, summer dreariness, vegetative well-being…

Q. Even for you?
In times like these, my reluctance to write is downright pathological.

Q. Granted that you are not a prognosticator as such, but how do you think the Yankees will do this year?
Fluctuat nec mergitur.

Q. Pardon?
It floats but it does not sink.

Q. I think I follow, Doctor: floating is not sinking, but it's not sailing, either. In other words, no pennant in the offing?
Pour faire une omelette il faut casser des oeufs.

Q. Oh?
"To prepare an omelet, one must break eggs."

Q. Yes, yes, eggs plural. There has to be more done than just a changing of managers. And the bottom line, then, is that you're still down at the mouth about all this?
Life is miserable. Life is otherwise incredibly devoid of content.

Q. Well, how do you plan to spend the rest of the baseball season? I notice you are packing. Are you going someplace?
Italy…the journey will take in San Gimignano-Siena-Perugia-Assisi-Ancona—in short, Tuscany and Umbria. In Italy, I am seeking a punch made from Lethe—the dead drank from Lethe, the river of forgetfulness, upon their arrival in the underworld…Here and there I get a draft.

Q. Thank you, Doctor. Many of us would love to drink a draft of forgetfulness with you.

VI.

EXECUTIVE BRANCH

Marge Schott: Oh, the Troubles She and Her St. Bernard Caused

CINCINNATI, OHIO—She was in a hurry as she strode to the elevator behind the press box, trailed by her small party and the smoke from the cigarette clenched between her teeth. This was in Riverfront Stadium, home of the Cincinnati Reds. The woman, with her salt-and-pepper hair cut short, was sturdily built and wore a white-and-red sweater and fire-engine red slacks— the colors of her team—and brown loafers.

At the elevator, she turned her back to the steel door and kicked it with repeated thuds. Very shortly, the elevator door slid open.

"Hello, Mrs. Schott," said the elevator operator, looking concerned.

"What took you so long?" she said to him in a kind of raspy voice.

There were times when Marge Schott, owner of the Reds, kicked so hard for the elevator—it was her signal—that the heel of her shoe fell off. Sometimes her kicks destroyed the electronic sensory device of the elevator.

Such scenes took place regularly over several summers, and now Schott, sitting several weeks ago behind the cluttered desk in her stadium office, recalled them. "I'm very impatient. Sometimes women are that way." She smiled and nodded in agreement with herself.

The remarkable behavior of Margaret Unnewher Schott, 63 years old, doesn't stop at the elevator door. The recent disclosure of a deposition taken in a suit filed against her by a former employee revealed that she has made racially and ethnically demeaning comments, including use of the word "nigger."

247

The controversy over her remarks has plagued her now for several weeks and, for many, has transformed her image from that of a quirky eccentric known best for parading her St. Bernard around Riverfront Stadium into a mean-spirited, insensitive woman.

It has also drawn scrutiny from her fellow owners and others in and out of baseball. Hank Aaron has publicly called for her suspension, as has Abraham H. Foxman, national director of the Anti-Defamation League of B'nai B'rith, who said Schott had "tainted and sullied baseball."

There are strong indications that baseball's executive council will seriously review the situation at its next meeting, on December 7, and could fine or suspend her. Peter O'Malley, the Los Angeles Dodgers president, was quoted in the *Los Angeles Times* as saying: "If the statements attributed to Marge Schott are accurate, I believe Mrs. Schott should resign as chief executive officer."

In an interview last Wednesday, Schott rejected much of this newly publicized portrayal, and yet acknowledged, wittingly or otherwise, some of the substance that has prompted it.

"I'm not a racist; I've never meant any harm," she said. "I'm so sick of all this. It's discouraging. I wish they'd stop all this falseness."

In her deposition she either acknowledged, or did not deny, using words like "nigger" and "Jap" and terms like "money-grubbing Jews."

"But if and when I've used them," she said last week, "it was only kiddingly." They were "joke terms," she said. She denies calling Eric Davis and Dave Parker, two former black players, "million-dollar niggers."

"Of course, nigger is a demeaning word," Schott continued. "But I know that blacks call it to each other, too. I've been in the business world for 24 years and never had any problem with discrimination. I've got a Jewish manager in my car dealership who is like a son to me. And it hurt when it was reported that I called Eric and Dave nigger this or nigger that. I love Eric. It hurt me when they booed him here. I love his parents, really good people. I called Eric the other day and explained to him that it wasn't true. I tried to call Dave, too, but haven't reached him yet."

While only one of her 45 front-office employees is black, Schott said that that wasn't the whole story. "Look on the field; you see black players for the Reds," she said. "They're part of the organization, too."

Regardless of the backlash she has encountered, she has continued to use some of the terms that have gotten her into trouble. Recently, she pointed out gifts to a visitor in her office that she said she had received from "the Japs" while in Japan touring with a group of Reds players. She made the comment without a seeming concern or understanding of its pejorative implications.

When speaking about a visit last week from Bill White, the president of the National League, she recalled that she used the word "Jap" in talking with him. "Bill said to me, 'Marge, will you quit that!'" She laughed. "I said, 'Bill, I didn't know it was so bad. But I'll stop.' I didn't mean to insult the Japanese; I love them. I have great respect for the way they've come back in the world."

In her deposition, she also acknowledged keeping a Nazi swastika armband in her home. When asked about that last week, she explained: "It was a gift I got several years ago from a worker in one of my car agencies. He took it off a dead German. It's what they call, what, 'memorabilia'? It's no big deal. I keep it in a drawer with Christmas decorations."

Earlier this month, recalling that she had family members in Germany who had suffered during World War II, she said: "Hitler was good in the beginning, but he went too far."

The controversy around Schott was stirred by the former team controller Tim Sabo, who sued Schott last year for $2.5 million. In the suit, Sabo, who is white, contended that one of the reasons he was dismissed was that he did not approve of her use of racial and religious slurs. Sabo's case was dismissed on the ground that Ohio's "at-will" doctrine of employment allows an employer to fire or hire as he or she sees fit. But some of her statements in the deposition sounded either racist, bigoted, arrogant, stupid, or callous, or all of the above.

Those who have worked closely with Schott in baseball say that while she is capable of being "very, very charming when she wants to," she can also be vicious, vindictive, and surpassingly ignorant, especially when it suits her purpose.

A widow of 24 years, Schott runs a major-league baseball team with a 123-year history that today may be as famous for its mascot, her St. Bernard named Schottzie, as it is for any of its players.

She recently fired her third general manager in eight years, Bob Quinn, and a manager she liked, Lou Piniella, recently quit in disgust.

She fired Quinn just two seasons after he helped engineer a World Series championship. Actually, her lawyer gave Quinn the bad news. "I can't fire people face to face," she said. "I'm a wimp about it."

Quinn, who spent three seasons with the Reds, had won praise for his 1990 feat. And he had been hailed by peers and press alike for the trades he made in the months leading up to the 1992 season.

The Reds began the 1992 season as a strong contender in the National League West but a series of injuries to key players made it hard for them to compete with Atlanta. Still, Cincinnati finished with a very respectable 90 victories. Some baseball people, like John Schuerholz, the general manager of the Atlanta Braves, were stunned at Quinn's dismissal. "Bob Quinn did the best job of any G.M. in baseball," he said.

Two days before Quinn's firing, Piniella, the field leader of the 1990 championship team and for the following two seasons as well, did what many had expected. He resigned. "I just didn't want any more," he said. "I left there on good terms. I honored my contract. I just didn't want to be renewed."

What Piniella didn't want any more of was an organization that too often reflected its owner, either by being idiosyncratic, or eccentric, or worse.

Before the disclosure of her deposition, Schott was viewed by some as a grande dame, the queen bee of the Queen City. The populace appreciated a certain rough-hewn charm in her, and even considered her a civic hero because she purchased her hometown team in 1984 when there was a threat of it being sold to outsiders, and possibly being moved.

Scott had been a limited partner in the Reds since 1981 and became the president and chief executive officer after the purchase. "I bought the team with my head and not my heart," she said. "It was Christmas time, and you know how women are at Christmas. You buy things and charge it."

Yet despite this expenditure, she is often portrayed as cheap, even though her player payroll has risen from $15 million in 1990 to $37 million last season. She has been accused of selling employees day-old doughnuts ("that's ridiculous," she said). But she admits having charged Piniella for donating three bats from the Reds for a charity (she is, to be sure, active in several charities of her own choosing), and she once made Quinn pay his way to the All-Star Game.

Schott's dog was part of the reason for Piniella's leave-taking. Actually, Piniella had to deal with two dogs, since the original Schottzie died in 1991 at age eight, and Schott bought the second dog, sometimes called Schottzie 02, last spring.

It was dismaying for Piniella to see a dog have the run of the field during practice, and he was insulted to have to pose for pictures wearing a baseball cap with the stuffed likeness of Schottzie's large face on the brim.

Schottzie 02, while adored by the owner, is often reviled by many others in baseball, including a number of players from the Reds, who have complained about dog excrement littering the field during warmups. One Cincinnati pitcher, Tim Belcher, grumbled last season about Schottzie 02 bothering him while he was warming up. It is an embarrassment, say many of the players. A travesty, a joke. "Look," said one, "it's just not professional to have a dog running around the field when you're out there working. It's wacky."

"I get their chewing gum on my shoes," Schott said of the players. "They should be happy I don't have a horse, right?"

"Our club," said one former Reds executive, "was a laughingstock in the league."

White, the National League president, once called a team executive of the Reds, and asked, "What do you think I should do about the dog?"

"At the very least put her on a leash," the executive replied.

So far, Schottzie 02 has remained unleashed.

Despite the all the criticisms of her quirkiness, she has presided over a team that was losing money when she bought it and that now operates in the black. Profits last year were estimated conservatively at $15 million.

She weathered the stormy Pete Rose years, in which she was virtually a bystander as Rose battled gambling problems that concluded with his banishment from baseball. "I like Pete a lot," she said, "and my greatest thrill in baseball was the night he broke the hit record."

After Rose surpassed Ty Cobb's hit record in 1985, Schott presented Rose with a Corvette. "And I learned later that he sold it," she said. "That hurt me. Women do get hurt a lot."

Schott generally keeps a distance between herself and the decisions of her baseball people. She does not pretend to know baseball, and would be hard-pressed to define a sacrifice fly, or a squeeze play. She says her favorite play is the Wave, in which she participates from her box seat in Riverfront Stadium.

A few years ago, in salary negotiations with a player's agent, the agent mentioned Barry Bonds. "Who's he?" she asked.

And on the day Don Baylor was hired by the Colorado Rockies as manager, she was asked if the development took the pressure off her to seek a minority manager. "Why?" she asked. "Is Baylor black?"

Her lack of knowledge about baseball, and her mistakes about things not directly connected to the sport, make some shake their heads. A few years ago there was a meeting of owners in a Chicago hotel and Schott arrived so early that she was seated for some time at the conference table before any of the other owners showed up. Later, she was overheard speaking on a public telephone to her office. "Hey!" she said. "Why didn't you tell me there was an hour difference between Cincinnati and Chicago?"

But she has more to do, she believes, than just run a baseball team or study geography or time zones. She says she was just a spoiled housewife when her husband, Charles Schott, died and left her with a car dealership and a huge inheritance. Coming in without any real knowledge of the business, she learned it.

She also keeps a close watch on all the various odds and ends associated with the Reds. "I'm a saver," she said. Some have extended that description, calling her a hoarder. Those people refer to a large room in Riverfront Stadium that is filled with goods left over from various giveaway days: caps and batting helmets and bats and balls and, according to one source, candy bars that date back eight years and calendars of the original Schottzie that were printed in 1986 and 1987. And some of those items she still tries to sell.

Her office, meanwhile, is a kind of cathedral to stuffed animals—many of them St. Bernards of various sizes and shapes, and many of them wearing Reds caps.

She regularly refers to being a woman in a man's world, and that she had to overcome slights and abuse. She talks about "the buddy system" and the "little boys club" that is the fraternity (with a sole sister) that makes up the group of major-league owners. She was the only one of them, for instance, to abstain on the vote that ended the reign of Fay Vincent as commissioner of baseball. "I didn't like what some of them were doing," she said, "how seven teams for example were getting in bed with the Cubs on their superstation, and I didn't find out about this until late. So I thought, if they want to play their games with each other, let 'em. I don't want any part of it."

When she took over the team, some of the baseball men who were suddenly working for a woman hardly spoke to her. "And it took me a couple of months to get my own parking space at the ballpark," she said. "The only one who talked to me was the elevator operator."

She tells people that she knows some employees try to take advantage of her. That may be why she charged Piniella for the bats (she didn't press the issue, and he didn't pay) or why she is niggling about sending her executives to some baseball meetings. ("All these men do there is play golf," she said.)

She still lives in the huge house on 70 acres in a leafy Cincinnati suburb left her by her husband. It is gray stone with turrets and slate roofs and, she was told by painters, "360 openings, which includes windows and doors." It looks like a castle.

"It's a man's house, isn't it?" she said as she walked around the large, rather dark, rooms. She still keeps the clothes from her husband in a closet.

"People have asked why I don't move. I tell them I've gotten used to the place."

"When you're left alone, after your husband dies, there is insecurity," she said. "For any woman. But especially for me. You see, my father was Achtung-German. He used to ring a bell when he wanted my mother. When I was 21 and went to vote, he told me who to vote for. I said, 'Yes, Daddy.' And I was that way with Charlie and Charlie's father. So men have influenced me a lot. And when I didn't have one to tell me what to do, it was hard to get my footing. I have. But there's still insecurity. I mean, it's still a man's world."

She walked into another room of the house and opened a secret door that was built during Prohibition in order to hide liquor. "Kids love to come here because of all the nooks and crannies in the house, like this one," she said. "I have a big Christmas party for kids every year. Charlie and I never had kids. Oh, we tried, but we couldn't manage it. We once had 22 St. Bernards here, though. Drove my husband nuts. I said, 'They're just pups. We'll get rid of them when they grow up.' He said, 'Grow up? They're up to my waist already!'" She laughed and lit up another cigarette.

"Then another time I began collecting bees. Had 'em all over the place. Had bottles and bottles of honey. Everything was sticky. That drove Charlie nuts, too.

"But I always felt guilty about not having children. It was a tragedy to us, my biggest heartache. I have four sisters and they had 10 kids in 11 years. They're like rabbits. But since I never had kids—I don't know—maybe I want my ballteam to be like family.

"If I could have a team of only sweet guys, I'd love it, but they probably wouldn't be able to play ball too well. And I want families to come to Reds games. We're still the lowest price ticket in the major leagues. And we have hot dogs that cost only a dollar. People say, 'You sell hot dogs for a dollar? I can't believe it!' But how else could families afford a day at the ballpark?"

As soon as she swung open the kitchen door, Schottzie 02 bounded up to greet her. "Hey little baby, hey little baby," she said, hugging the dog.

Marge Schott handed Schottzie a biscuit and the dog ate it lustily. Schott watched and smiled. Then she returned to another room, one with heavy drapes and knickknacks on the shelves. "I don't hire maids because I have so much junk I'd never know what's missing," she said.

She sat down in a tall dark wooden chair in the large room and lit up another cigarette. She was alone. In the other room, Schottzie 02 was barking.

P.K. Wrigley:
Reclusive Owner Speaks

July 22, 1973

CHICAGO, ILLINOIS—"I'm loose," said Phillip K. Wrigley, actually standing there in person in his white shirt sleeves, a little smaller in physical build than one might expect from a genuine mystery man, and a little hunched from his 79 years of cowering from the public glare.

He does exist! He was talking to his prospective interviewer and asking him into his office. He was standing there pouchy-eyed and a bit floppy-eared but not dour-looking at all as some of the stiff old photographs show him. There was a sort of comfortable old Home Sweet Home sampler look about him.

Chicago Cubs owner Phillip K. Wrigley may not be exactly the Howard Hughes of baseball but he's the closest thing to a multimillionaire hermit the sport has.

Wrigley has owned the Cubs for 40 years. The team has not won a pennant since 1945. From 1947 it spent 20 straight record-smashing seasons in the second division despite some of the weirdest contrivances by its owner. In recent years the Cubs have gained fame for late-season flops. But now they just might stay on top.

So people are wondering again, who is this mystery man?

Who, in fact, is this unswerving individualist who has done everything from withstand the pressures of putting lights in his ballpark (the Cubs are the only major-league club to play only day home games) to pay for the

256

families of his players to accompany the team on a road trip to try a system of rotating managers.

Wrigley hasn't been to Wrigley Field, home of the Cubs, in over 10 years. He got tired of being fawned over by the ushers when he came to his special box. Then he tried sitting incognito in various parts of the park. He was always being discovered by gaping fans and being photographed by the press ("and always with my mouth open").

So this gigantically rich fellow (estimated daily income of $10,000) does not go to Wrigley Field at all (in fact, he hardly ever went—even when the team won a pennant in 1945, he stayed in his office and wrote personal letters to fans explaining why everyone couldn't get tickets) but slips into the white wedding-cake-like 32-story Wrigley Building on the north bank of the Chicago River, where he conducts the business of the largest chewing gum company in the world.

It is here that to the man in the street Wrigley may become a disembodied voice. Everybody who works in the executive offices of the gum company answers his own phone.

His father taught him that they were in the five-cent business. "But even if it's a 10-cent business now," says Wrigley, "we should still remember our level."

"Hello, hello, I wanna talk to Mishter Wrigley," says the caller with the sudsy voice.

"This is Mr. Wrigley."

"Oh."

"What can I do for you?"

"Well, I'm watchin' the game here and your jerk manager oughta yank the pitcher. Use your influence, huh?"

Click.

Wrigley had been watching the game on television, as usual, in his wood-paneled office. Just as the caller hung up, the manager went out to the mound and changed pitchers.

Wrigley, now, says, "The guy probably turned to his pal on the stool and said, 'Boy, do I get action!'"

(It is one of Wrigley's favorite anecdotes.)

Being uppity is anathema at the gum place, thus the answering of one's own phone. But phones are still a modern necessary evil to Wrigley, who says, "My ambition is to live in a cave without any telephones and a big rock over the door."

He says that "my cave" is the Wrigley House on Lake Geneva. He never answers any of the 21 telephones in the place, whether one rings in the master's bed dressing room or the hall-coat closet or the stable shop or his enormous workshop or anywhere near any of the house's 11 bathrooms.

When asked, "Is it true that you earn over $3 million a year?" he says, "I don't know. Money has never really interested me," and the listener believe this man with the clear blue eyes and avuncular visage.

He has never appeared on television or radio. He has made only two speeches that anybody knows about. Both were after receiving awards. He said, "Thank you," the first time. The second time he burst wide open. He said, "Thank you very much."

So it was shocking when he took out a full-page ad in the Chicago papers on October 3, 1971, to condemn a "Dump Durocher clique" as he called it. It was headlined: "This is for Cub fans and anyone else who is interested" (the latter surely included some disgruntled players). He ended with: "(Leo) is running the team, and if some of the players do not like it and lie down on the job, during the off-season we will see what we can do to find them happier homes." Signed: "Phil Wrigley."

Two things are noteworthy here. One is that Durocher was fired two-thirds of the way through the next season (Wrigley knows when he can go no further with a problem) and second, he spelled his name correctly (part of the Wrigley legend is that sometimes he even spells his name incorrectly).

Misspelling your own name sounds nearly as eccentric as something Howard Hughes might do. Wrigley does not see himself in that mold at all.

"Howard Hughes goes into a hotel in Las Vegas and when he can't get a room, he buys the place and fires the manager," said Wrigley. He smiled to himself at the probable scene. Then a story occurred to him.

"A fella had a flat tire in front of an insane asylum," said Wrigley. "Several of the inmates came to the bars and watched him take off the back tire and start to put on the spare. But he accidentally kicked all of the nuts (Wrigley probably meant "lugs") down an open manhole. He didn't know what to do.

"One of the inmates called out, 'Why don't you take one nut from each of the other wheels and put them on the fourth and then fix it up as soon as you get to the nearest service station?'

"The driver looked with such amazement that such an intelligent idea should come from the inmate.

"'I may be crazy,' said the guy behind the bars, 'but I'm not dumb.'"

Bill Veeck: "And the Circus Came to Town"

October 20, 2005

THE SENTIMENT WAS HARDLY unusual.

"I loved the guy," Billy Pierce, the former White Sox pitcher said the other day about Bill Veeck, the former owner of the team. "But you'd be out with him at dinner and he'd be smoking a cigarette and dropping the ashes into his peg leg. I mean, it was a bit disconcerting."

Mary Frances Veeck, who was often at her husband's side at such dinners, confirmed Pierce's recollection. "But," she explained, "Bill only used the false leg when there wasn't an ashtray handy."

The flamboyant, the irrepressible, the innovative Veeck, who died at age 71 on January 2, 1986, is being honored in absentia this week with the return of the White Sox to the World Series for the first time since 1959, his first year as the majority owner. (The Sox, making their first Series appearance in 40 years, lost to the Los Angeles Dodgers in six games.)

This year, the Series will open Saturday at U.S. Cellular Field against the Houston Astros. These White Sox seek to wipe out any memory of the 1919 team, which had eight players, including Shoeless Joe Jackson, indicted on charges of throwing the Series to the underdog Cincinnati Reds.

Veeck, with a bright, boyish look in his eye even when his face aged and wrinkled, was often referred to as the Barnum & Bailey of Baseball for his stunts, and the Pied Piper in the way he drew fans to the ballparks. He owned three major-league teams—the Cleveland Indians, the St. Louis

260

Browns, and the White Sox—and a few minor-league teams, and almost all of them set attendance records.

Indeed, he sent Eddie Gaedel, a midget, to the plate for the Browns in a 1951 game. (He walked.)

At season's end, Veeck used signs to poll the fans about the Browns' strategy for manager Zack Taylor, who sat in a rocking chair and wore slippers. (The other team said this was "unbaseball," but the Browns won.) He also brought pennants to two teams, the Indians (in 1948) and the White Sox, who had gone a combined 68 years without one.

Before the White Sox ended their drought in 1959, Veeck entertained fans at a game that May with midgets dressed in spacesuits who landed on the field by helicopter.

"Of all the unusual things my father did in baseball," said Mike Veeck, 54, the owner of five minor-league teams, "my favorite hands down was the exploding scoreboard."

The 130-foot scoreboard at old Comiskey Park loomed beyond center field; when a White Sox player homered, it set off fireworks, screeching sounds, and 10 electronic pinwheels.

"Do you know where he got the idea?" Mike Veeck said from Mount Pleasant, South Carolina. "From a William Saroyan play, *The Time of Your Life*, that he saw with my mother. Near the end of the play there is a pinball machine that goes off like crazy. Dad couldn't stop thinking about it."

Mary Frances Veeck said she had thought that the scoreboard "wasn't very genteel."

"I mean, if you do something well, shouldn't you just be modest about it?" she said Tuesday. "But the fans loved it, and I came to love it, too. And Casey Stengel, when he managed the Yankees, had an answer for the quiet scoreboard when one of his players hit a homer. He had four or five of his men light sparklers in the dugout."

Stengel managed Veeck's minor-league Milwaukee Brewers in the early 1940s. Veeck liked Stengel as a character, but also respected his baseball acumen when many thought he was a clown.

"Bill had empathy for people that others didn't consider normal," Mary Frances Veeck said.

She laughed, for there were some who wondered about Veeck's state of mind. But Pierce, among others, saw the other side of him.

"He knew how to put the pieces together for a team," Pierce, 78, said by phone from his home here. "And about midway in the 1959 season, he made a deal for Ted Kluszewski, and it brought us the power we were lacking, and that made a huge difference on our way to the pennant."

Veeck had bought the majority rights to the White Sox from the original owners, the Comiskey family. "We never had a box," Mary Frances Veeck said. "Bill liked to sit out with the people."

Mike Veeck recalled: "I'd walk into the park with him. He'd be holding my hand and he had this funny gait, and everyone would say hello to him: the vendors, the security guy, the receptionist. It was all so joyous. And then the team winning the pennant. For an eight-year-old kid, it was like I had died and gone to heaven."

Veeck was in ill health and sold the team in 1961, but he returned as head of the White Sox in 1975 to keep them in Chicago. He still had flair. In 1976, the White Sox wore hot-weather uniforms: Bermuda-length navy shorts with white pullover tops. The experiment lasted three games. In 1979, a Disco Demolition Night devolved into the fans burning records on the field and caused the White Sox to forfeit a game.

With failing health and finances, Veeck sold the team after the 1980 season.

The exploding scoreboard and a shower in the bleachers to cool off fans on steamy days are Veeck's legacies to U.S. Cellular Field, the White Sox home since 1991.

Hank Greenberg, the Hall of Fame slugger who was a partner of Veeck's with the Indians and the White Sox, said before his death in 1986 that Veeck was the only owner he ever knew who really cared about his players. As a kind of affirmation, Minnie Minoso, who had played for Veeck, wore a White Sox uniform to his funeral.

In 1986, Greenberg told *The New York Times*: "Bill brought baseball into the 20th century. Before Bill, baseball was just win or lose. But he made it fun to be at the ballpark."

Branch Rickey brought Jackie Robinson to the Brooklyn Dodgers in April 1947, breaking the major-league color barrier, and three months later, Veeck broke the color barrier in the American League by acquiring a 23-year-old outfielder named Larry Doby for Cleveland. In 1948, Veeck signed Satchel Paige, a Negro League pitcher who was in his forties. Many in baseball thought this was another stunt. Paige went 6–1 and contributed to the Indians' pennant drive.

Doby and Paige are in the Hall of Fame, as is Veeck, whose election in 1991 came as a surprise to some in the baseball fraternity. After all, he was considered a maverick, often an irritating one, by most of the other owners. He surely made himself even less beloved when he and Greenberg were the only executives to testify for Curt Flood in his 1970 suit over baseball's reserve clause.

Veeck was a Marine on Guadalcanal during World War II when an antiaircraft gun recoiled into his leg. The leg became infected, and in 1946 part of it was amputated. Never one to wallow in self-pity, he threw a party for himself and danced the night away on the new wood limb.

Mary Frances, who had six children with Veeck, remembered that sometimes when she changed the sock on his leg, she would forget about the ashes.

"We had a cream-colored rug in our bedroom," she said, "and I'd have to clean up the spots. But Bill and I, we were together for 35 2/3 years exactly. The other day, I was with a friend whose husband had recently died, after 55 years of marriage. I envy that. Sure I do. But Bill and I—we had great years. It was a romance from beginning to end."

Bart Giamatti: "The Green Fields of the Mind"

September 2, 1989

"IT BREAKS YOUR HEART," Bart Giamatti wrote about baseball, in an essay titled "The Green Fields of the Mind." "It is designed to break your heart. The game begins in the spring, when everything else begins again, and it blossoms in the summer, filling the afternoons and evenings, and then as soon as the chill rains come, it stops and leaves you to face the fall alone. You count on it, rely on it to buffer the passage of time, to keep the memory of sunshine and high skies alive, and then just when the days are all twilight, when you need it most, it stops...And summer [is] gone."

The baseball season wasn't over yet, but it was nearing its end, and Bart Giamatti, who loved baseball, who loved it with all his heart, had the end of the division races to look forward to, and the championship series, and the World Series. These would be his first as the commissioner of baseball.

And then after that, after the twilight of the season, was the end of summer, the end of baseball. The time that breaks your heart. Yesterday, on Martha's Vineyard, Bart Giamatti died. Near season's end. And we are all the poorer for it.

There was more to Giamatti than baseball, of course. He was a Renaissance scholar and teacher, a former president of Yale, and a lover of language. He could use the most beautiful sentences and phrases and metaphors, even over linguine in an Italian restaurant, speaking perhaps about Matteo Boiardi, the 15th century poet, whom he admired, or Bobby

Doerr, the 20th century second baseman, whom he once tried to emulate in the sandlots of South Hadley, Massachusetts, where he grew up.

And the language was elevated but it wasn't haughty. After his beloved Red Sox failed to win yet another championship, he wrote, "Mutability had turned the seasons and translated hope to memory once again."

He became the president of the National League and then, about two years later, on April 1 of this year, he succeeded Peter Ueberroth as commissioner. Why would a university man become involved in baseball? Because it was interesting, he said, and because he loved baseball.

And suddenly he was embroiled in the Pete Rose affair. Now, this erudite man, this most cultured and civilized and warm and generous and witty man, was called upon to make some unexpected and agonizing decisions.

He knew what Rose meant to the game, and liked Rose personally, but he had to be fair, to himself, to Rose, and to baseball.

"Let it also be clear," he would say, "that no man is above the game." He believed that he was the keeper of a nearly sacred flame, that baseball was an "enduring national institution." And when he was battling in the courts to maintain the integrity of the office of the commissioner, as he saw it, he said he would not compromise, he said he would fight to the end.

He had been criticized as an ivory tower guy who was in over his head in a street fight of this nature. And when he made what appeared a disastrous error, signing a letter to a judge in Cincinnati who was sentencing Ron Peters, one of Rose's chief accusers, and said Peters had been "truthful" to Giamatti's investigator, the judge thought Giamatti jeopardized impartiality.

But Giamatti maintained that he would be impartial to Rose in a hearing, and never wavered. Eventually, Rose did. And the ivory tower guy proved to be a street fighter, and banished Rose for life for conduct that he determined was harmful to baseball. Giamatti went by the rules. He was tough, but left open a door for mercy for Rose, providing that Rose would in some way have to "reconfigure" his life.

He might have become the best baseball commissioner we've ever had. He had brains, sinew, and the best wishes of the game. And he was honest.

It may be written in days to come that the stress from the Rose entanglements hurried his death. I say not necessarily. Yes, there was tension from this case, which absorbed the entire five months of his abbreviated regime, but he was also at peace because he knew he had done the right thing.

The Rose case had been concluded the way he felt was best for baseball. He had done what was necessary to keep intact that beautiful and transporting national game that he loved so much.

"Boiardi's deepest desire," Giamatti wrote, "is to conserve something of purpose in a world of confusion. He knew that chivalry is an outmoded system, but he wants to keep something of its value, its respect for grace and noble behavior."

So did Bart Giamatti, dead much, much too soon at age 51.

Marvin Miller: Master Bargainer

February 15, 1999

ONE DAY IN THE late 1970s, Bowie Kuhn, then the commissioner of baseball, invited Marvin Miller, then the executive director of the Major League Players Association, to lunch for the first and only time. At one point Kuhn said to Miller, his adversary of more than 10 years: "Look, Marvin, you've beaten the owners at every turn. And now the owners need a victory."

Miller, as he recently recalled, couldn't believe his ears. "Bowie," asked Miller, "are you suggesting I throw the game?"

Miller did not, and the owners continued their losing streak. The owners lost at every turn, as Kuhn said, because one man had on his side the insight, the foresight, the experience, the courage, and the style—unruffled, unflappable, undeterred—as well as the United States Constitution and labor law. Miller led the players, often at dramatic junctures, out of virtual subservience and into the democratic system of America.

A man of medium height, with a mustache and a quiet, patient demeanor, Miller took over in 1966 as executive director of a loosely organized group of ballplayers, with assets of a file cabinet and about $5,400. He shaped them into what many believe is the most successful union not just in sports, but in the history of American labor.

Not only did he work to raise the level of earnings—the average salary of a major-leaguer when he began was $19,000 a year; it is now $1.4 million—but he helped improve playing conditions, from padded outfield walls and better-defined warning tracks to safer locker rooms. He even helped

267

improve play, according to Henry Aaron, allowing players more financial freedom to remain in better shape during the off-season instead of having to work at jobs like insurance salesman (Aaron) or sporting goods salesman (Andy Pafko). He was also instrumental in improving scheduling, such as negating night games on get-away days. And he gave players the freedom that other American workers had—his cataclysmic battle for free agency ended the reserve clause, which had prevented players from bargaining for their services on the open market. As a result, a greater number of teams won pennants than ever before, attendance figures broke records season after season, and the value of teams increased (the Yankees were purchased for $10 million in 1973 and today are worth $600 million or more).

Along the way, he also took one of the poorest benefit plans and built it into one of the best.

Jim Bunning, now a United States senator and a Baseball Hall of Famer who, along with Robin Roberts and Harvey Kuenn, led a players' committee to hire someone to lead their meager union, once said, "The two proudest things I take out of baseball were the perfect game I pitched and being part of the selection group that chose Marvin Miller as executive director."

Aaron, the home-run champion and now senior vice president of the Atlanta Braves, once said, "Marvin Miller is as important to the history of baseball as Jackie Robinson."

And Roberts, the Hall of Fame pitcher, said: "I don't know of anyone who changed the game more than Marvin Miller. His legacy is that, through his work, ballplayers for the first time attained dignity from owners. He changed a monopoly into a more realistic setup. He deserves to be in the Hall of Fame."

Two weeks from today, on March 2, the Veterans Committee of the Baseball Hall of Fame in Cooperstown, New York, will gather and vote on the inclusion of new members in their shrine. One of the leading candidates is Orlando Cepeda, the fine first baseman whose best slugging years were with the Giants and Cardinals. His recently published autobiography, *Baby Bull*, written with Herb Fagen, ably presents the case for Cepeda, who was once imprisoned for 10 months in Puerto Rico for possession of marijuana.

Cepeda's baseball accomplishments should merit him selection to the Hall of Fame, just as Miller's do.

But in his way, Miller, who was born in the Bronx in 1917 and who retired in 1985 and lives in Manhattan, is as controversial a choice as Cepeda. Miller is still resented by owners, but shouldn't be. Owners, who feared a thinning of their substantial pocketbooks, had presented him as an ogre from the moment he took his position. He was painted by them as one among "union goons" for his work as chief economist and negotiator for the United Steelworkers.

Kuhn declared on the witness stand in a courtroom that free agency would "ruin" baseball.

When Miller once went to a spring training camp to talk with players in an outfield meeting—they were refused use of the locker room—the Astros' manager, Leo Durocher, fungoed baseballs in an attempt to hit Miller.

But virtually by himself, one decent man, with knowledge and the mission to do the best job possible, beat the owners with their teams of lawyers and press agents, time after time after time.

And despite the overwhelming resistance, he helped improve both the game and the lives of players—and, as it turned out, the lives of the owners, as well. And not just in baseball, but, eventually, in all team sports in this country.

The Veterans Committee would distinguish itself and do what is right and unequivocally just by voting Marvin Miller into the Baseball Hall of Fame.

VII.

BALLPLAYERS' WIVES

Johnny (Lois) Vander Meer:
"He's Gone Fishin'"

June 13, 1988

THE PHONE CALL LAST week to Johnny Vander Meer's home in Tampa, Florida, didn't fall on deaf ears, it just didn't fall on Johnny's ears.

"No, Johnny's not home," said Lois Vander Meer, his wife of 48 years. "He's gone fishin'." "Is there any way to reach him?" "Not that I know of. He's somewhere in the Okeechobee." "When will he be back?" "I don't know," she said. "It depends on the fish."

"I'm sure there have been other calls for him, after all, this is the 50th anniversary of—"

"Mister, this phone has been ringin' off the wall all week. That's why he went fishin'." "Oh?" "He just got tired of answering the same questions over and over again. He said he'd just had it. After 50 years, what else can he say about it?"

Regardless, Vander Meer will be back from fishing at least by Wednesday night, for he has agreed to throw out the first ball for the Astros-Reds game in Cincinnati. Wednesday, June 15, marks the 50th anniversary of Vander Meer's second no-hitter in a row. Five pitchers have pitched two no-hitters in the same season. But only one man has pitched two straight no-hitters, and within a space of five days, and that was a 23-year-old left-hander for the Reds in 1938 named Vander Meer.

Lois Vander Meer was asked, "What do they ask him?" "They ask how he did it." "What does he say?"

"He says: 'All you have to do is read last year's paper. I gave the same interview.'" "Did you know Johnny then?" "Yes." "How did you hear about that second no-hitter?" "I didn't hear about it." "What do you mean?" "I was there. With his parents, who had come up from Midland Park, New Jersey." "What was it like that night?" "It was very exciting." "Anything else?" "What else is there? It was very exciting and you didn't know if he was going to do it or not."

No reason, then, to go into detail about the drama that built during that second no-hitter, and the near carnival atmosphere that surrounded it.

Vander Meer had pitched a 3–0 no-hitter against the Boston Bees in Cincinnati on Saturday, June 11, and then came to Brooklyn to pitch what would be the first night game in the history of Ebbets Field.

The capacity crowd of 38,748 filled the park quickly—not to see Vander Meer, but to see this curiosity, the first night game in Brooklyn, which would be played under 615 floodlights.

The game was delayed about a half hour, with Vander Meer unhappily having to warm up three times. In celebration of the lights, Jesse Owens gave a running exhibition and a bomb exploded behind second base to signal the playing of the national anthem by a uniformed band.

Few surely gave any thought to the possibility of a second straight no-hitter.

"It had never been done and no one even considered it," said Lois Vander Meer. "What about Johnny?" "He didn't, either."

But there he was pitching hitless ball into the sixth inning, the seventh, the eighth, and now the ninth.

With one out in the ninth, and the Reds ahead, 6–0, Vander Meer walked Babe Phelps, Cookie Lavagetto, and Dolf Camilli to load the bases. He later said that he wasn't tired, but that he was just bearing down too hard.

The next batter, Ernie Koy, hit a grounder to third and the third baseman, Lew Riggs, threw home for the force out.

Now Leo Durocher came to the plate. And Vander Meer, he later said, told himself, "Go to Powder River." Powder River was the name of excellent Western equipment, and Vander Meer was telling himself to go with his best pitch, the fastball. Durocher lined the first pitch foul into the right-field stands. Then, on a 2-2 pitch, Durocher hit a lazy fly to center field, which Harry Craft caught for the final out.

Four days later, he pitched two hitless innings before giving up a hit in the third to Debs Garms of the Braves.

The closest anyone has come to duplicating Vander Meer's feat of back-to-back no-hitters was Ewell Blackwell in 1947, who after pitching one no-hitter had one out in the ninth inning against the Dodgers for his second straight no-hitter, when it was broken up with a single to center by Eddie Stanky.

Vander Meer was still a member of the Reds, then, and said he was on the steps of the dugout, ready to run out and congratulate Blackwell.

But he had also said that every time somebody pitches a no-hitter, he kind of holds his breath to see if they'll pitch another in their second start.

He had also said that it was one of those records that could be tied, but probably could never be broken.

Vander Meer never quite equaled those two days in 1938—no one else has either—though he did pitch in the majors for a total of 13 seasons. He finished with a 119–121 record. He won 18 games in his best season. He led the league in strikeouts three times, and threw 30 shutouts.

Vander Meer is now 73, and retired from his job as a field manager for a beer company.

Lois Vander Meer was asked, "Does he do anything else these days besides fish?"

"Sometimes he'll get a call from friends in the Little League down here, and he'll help out."

She met Johnny when he was a pitcher for her hometown team, the Scranton Miners. "What did you like about him?" she was asked.

"Everything. He was quiet and unassuming and had good morals—still has—and he had blond, curly hair and the nicest dimples." "He still has those dimples?" "Certainly, but," and there was a little laugh, "he may not have all of that curly hair." "Otherwise he's the same?" "The same. Why, should he be any different?"

Nellie (Joanne) Fox: The Phone Rings

March 6, 1997

IN HER HOME IN Chambersburg, Pennsylvania, Joanne Fox anxiously awaited the phone call that would say whether her late husband, Nelson Fox, would finally make the Baseball Hall of Fame.

The call would come after the vote of the Veterans Committee, which was meeting yesterday in Tampa, Florida. Fox, the former Chicago White Sox second baseman, had come so close in 1985, his last eligible year on the baseball writers' ballot, getting 74.68 percent of the vote. He needed 75 percent.

Last year, he came in second to Jim Bunning on the 15-member Veterans Committee ballot.

Joanne Fox waited in the home she shared with her husband until his death from skin cancer in 1975, at age 47. She waited in a room that contained one of the bottle-handled bats he used, as well as, on a wall, the Most Valuable Player plaque he won for leading the White Sox to the 1959 American League pennant.

One of Fox's teammates, pitcher Billy Pierce, had called every year after Fox failed to make the Hall, to share her disappointment—along with the Nellie Fox Society, an organization of fans in Chicago, which campaigned for his election.

And for those of us in Chicago in those exciting baseball years starting with the "Go Go Sox" of 1951, when such players as Chico Carrasquel and Minnie Minoso and Jim Busby and Fox scratched out runs and challenged the mighty Yankees, the image of Fox remains vivid—the intense, crouching left-handed batter choking up on the thick bat, and the comical, stout wad of tobacco in his cheek.

"Nellie was very annoying," recalled Jerry Casale, a former Boston Red Sox pitcher and the owner of Pino's Restaurant in Manhattan. "He'd never strike out and he might foul off 20,000 pitches. He could hit to all fields, and he was a great bunter. He could do a million different nice little things."

Fox was exceedingly competitive, and tricky. "Fox played a good game in the field at second base," Casey Stengel once said, "and he'd stand up at the plate and barber and keep the boys irritated. And he'd even walk by and step on the resin bag for our bats, and make the resin run out."

And Ted Williams, in his autobiography, *My Turn at Bat*, wrote: "You couldn't underrate that Fox. He was always blunking or blooping one to win the game in the ninth inning."

The way it all began was with that old pickup truck rattling into the dusty driveway of the ramshackle ballpark in Frederick, Maryland, in March 1944. The Philadelphia A's were preparing for the season there because major-league teams couldn't go south to train during the war. The truck came to a stop and three people emerged from the cab, a moon-faced lad of 16 with a big cigar in his mouth and his parents. They had made the 50-mile trip from their home in St. Thomas, Pennsylvania, in order to meet Connie Mack, the A's manager, and present them with their son, Nelson Fox, a first baseman.

The youth was relatively short for a first baseman, at 5-foot-9, and rather slight, at 150 pounds. He was a first baseman, he would tell Mr. Mack, "because, well, I have the mitt." Mack gave the kid a look, and liked what he saw, and signed him. He sent him to the minor leagues and switched him to second base. Mack brought him up to the A's in 1947—the Foxes were married shortly after that—primarily kept him on the bench, and then traded him in 1950 to the White Sox.

It was there, under manager Paul Richards, that Fox developed into one of the best second basemen of his time, a 12-time A.L. All-Star, four times leading the league in hits, and finishing a 19-year big-league career with a .288 batting average.

Fox's manager in his later years with the White Sox, Al Lopez, said yesterday, "He was a good man for me." But Lopez had found some fault with Fox. Lopez thought he could be a selfish player, and when Lopez was a member of the Veterans Committee, it was known that he did not cast his vote for Fox.

Then yesterday came the news: Tom Lasorda, the extroverted former manager of the Los Angeles Dodgers, was voted into the Hall of Fame on the first try. And an old Negro Leaguer, shortstop Willie Wells Sr., also made it.

And then the phone rang in the home of Joanne Fox. After a moment, she picked up the receiver.

"Nelson Jacob Fox," she was informed, "has been voted into the Baseball Hall of Fame."

"Thank you," she said. "Thank you."

Steve (Cindy) Howe: The Story as Lived by Cindy Howe

May 17, 1991

SHE HAD PRETENDED SHE was sleeping. Her husband stirred in bed beside her, then he rose and went down the stairs to the living room. Quietly, she followed him. She saw him pull from behind a cabinet a small packet of cocaine. As he was about to pinch some of the contents, he looked up.

"There was," she recalled, "the look of the caged animal when he saw me. He was filled with guilt, and terrified."

This scene took place in January 1989, in their home in Whitefish, Montana, and Steve Howe, who had been a star relief pitcher for the Dodgers, who had been out of baseball a couple of years, and been in eight rehabilitation centers over five years to treat his alcohol and drug problems, and who had been clean for about a year, dropped the bag, and slumped on the couch.

Cindy Howe had vowed that if he slipped one more time, she would throw him out for good, and separate him from their two children, Chelsea, then six years old, and Brian, one.

"I knew he loved us, I knew he didn't want to live without us, and I loved him, very much, and I knew he had tried, but this was it," she said the other day in Yankee Stadium.

Howe begged her to stay. She called their local pastor and Steve, she said, cried and cried. "But he went through a great inner healing," she said. She stayed. Howe has been clean ever since.

280

She met Howe when he was pitching in a summer league in her home town of Fairbanks, Alaska—he was from Michigan. They were married in 1979, he was 21 and she was 19, and it was all wonderful. He was Rookie of the Year in 1980, and pitched in the World Series against the Yankees in 1981. But he had begun to "party," as she says, and he had virtually no tolerance for alcohol or drugs. He was soon hooked. She once had one of his drug dealer friends arrested.

"No one really understood cocaine in those days," she said. The Dodgers sent him to rehabilitate for 28 days, and, she said, "they thought he was cured. They wanted him back."

Home life for the Howes was terrible. Steve would go to the store for a carton of milk and not return for three days. Cindy would not cover for him when the Dodgers called asking where he was. They fought over that.

Every time he came home after a bout he was "very sorrowful," she said. Once she thought he was dying. He came in and fell to the floor and had lost all muscle control. He threw up and lay in a fetal position twitching. "He was like a ghost in there," she said.

She felt sorry for him, but she was sick of it, and filed for a legal separation. They came back together. The Dodgers released him. The Twins picked him up, and he fell again, and they released him. The Rangers picked him up, and he abused again, and he was released again.

He bounced around, in the minor leagues, in the Mexican League. His family traveled with him. "Our kids adore him," she said. "Everybody likes Steve. Even my parents, who suffered along with me. Steve's a wonderful, caring, loving person. He's just goofy and flaky and likable and lovable. He's just been very sick."

They had gone through all of his earnings—at his best, he made $325,000 a year from the Dodgers—and last year in Salinas, California, in Class A ball, he was earning $1,600 a month and because of their expenses with two homes, two cars, two kids, and travel, needed about $4,000 a month. "We'd get checks in the mail from ballplayers, and from friends," she said.

Then Steve had an operation on his arm—his second—and a blood clot in the lung nearly killed him. They returned home to Whitefish and lived "day to day," said Cindy Howe.

Howe's agent, Dick Moss, called all the big-league teams last winter asking for a tryout. He had not pitched in the major leagues in four years. "Steve knew he could still pitch, though," said Cindy Howe, "still throw the ball over 90 miles an hour." Most teams said no to him. The Yankees said maybe. Howe got on the phone to Gene Michael, the Yankees general manager. "C'mon, Stick," said Howe, "give me a chance."

Howe threw, the Yankees liked what they saw, and signed him. "I was almost in tears when we got the word," she said. He was soon sent to Columbus, the Yankees' top farm team, and pitched well. Cindy and the family continued to travel with him, and to hook up with religious support systems and "establish relationships of sobriety" in the towns he plays in.

Last Friday Howe was called up to the Yankees, pitched against Oakland and retired the side. Howe, who now is tested for drugs almost daily, hopes he and his family have found a home. "It's still day-to-day, always will be," Cindy Howe said, "but it's like a miracle. We're back together as a family, and Steve's back to being a person and not an addict, and for good, I really believe, and after eight rehabilitation centers and two arm surgeries, he's back in the big leagues, and grateful."

·   ·   ·

Howe retired after from the Yankees and major-league baseball in 1996. Ten years later, on April 28, 2006, Howe's pick-up truck rolled over in Coachella, California, and he was killed. The toxicology following the autopsy indicated that he had methamphetamine in his system. He was 48 years old.

VIII.

THE OTHER SIDE
OF GLORY

The Shooting of Eddie Waitkus

2002

I HAD NO IDEA she was there, lurking, as it were, in the crowd, perhaps even rubbing shoulders with me.

This was after Chicago Cubs games in Wrigley Field in 1948 and, particularly, Cubs–Philadelphia Phillies games in the spring of 1949. I was a boy of nine in 1949, she a girl of 19. We were both, it turned out, starry-eyed over the ballplayers—she over a particular player—as they came out of their clubhouses under the shaded stands, hair all showered and slicked back, looking like tanned gods and stuffed with thick shoulders into their light-colored sport jackets.

Most of them scribbled autographs for the swarming fans as they walked and then hurried on and disappeared inside their cars in the players' parking lot—or the team bus for the visiting players—leaving behind a trail of awe and aftershave lotion.

My friends and I went regularly from our neighborhood on the West Side of Chicago to the ballgames at Wrigley Field and across town at Comiskey Park, home of the White Sox. All the players and coaches—anyone with a major-league uniform—interested us, though of course we had our favorites. One of mine was Eddie Waitkus, a smooth-fielding first baseman who had been traded from the Cubs to the Phillies in the winter after the 1948 season—another one of those inexplicable Cubs trades that sent one of their best and most popular players away and doomed the team to perennial bottom-of-the-standings finishes. Waitkus was also her favorite but in a completely different way—in an obsessive, homicidal way, as it turned out.

Her name was Ruth Ann Steinhagen, and she lived with her parents and sister on the North Side, a short distance from Wrigley Field. While I was often in the crowd of fans that sought the autograph of Waitkus and others, Steinhagen often stood apart, with bizarre thoughts running through her head.

I had a special attachment to Waitkus because I played first base, too, in our sandlot games. In my Lawndale neighborhood, it seemed that first base was less than a glamorous position. I was one of the younger kids in the games but tall for my age, and the older boys sought out pitcher, or shortstop, or center field. I'm not sure how I found my way to first base, but I did—I either gravitated to it or was shunted to it—and beseeched my parents to buy me a first baseman's glove, a three-fingered "claw" model. The glove was impractical in that you could only play one position with it. But I liked first base—you were, after all, in on most plays.

And I admired Waitkus, who had what I perceived even at that age as a cool and buttery style around the bag. He was left-handed, and I was a righty, but I still tried to emulate his unique, if somewhat comical, little midair jitterbug of stretching for a throw, catching a ball, and toeing the base all in one wondrous motion.

He was six feet tall, lean, with sharp Slavic features, and as I recall, from those long-ago days after games, warm, rather slanted eyes. And after games among the fans, he demonstrated a patience and bonhomie, though a slightly shy one, that many of the other players lacked.

Steinhagen was smitten with Waitkus, even built a shrine in her bedroom to him with photos of him. She learned Lithuanian because he was of Lithuanian descent. She wanted to marry him—though he had no idea she even existed—and knew that would never be. Her parents grew deeply concerned at the depth of the infatuation but thought it might just be a teenager's phase and would pass.

"As time went on, I just became nuttier and nuttier about the guy. I knew I would never get to know him in a normal way," she said in a report prepared by the chief of the Cook County behavioral clinic in response to an order from the felony court, which found her deranged. "And if I can't have him, nobody else can. And I decided I would kill him."

She purchased a secondhand rifle, checked into the pink, castlelike Edgewater Beach Hotel where the Phillies stayed while in Chicago, and sent a message to the front desk for Waitkus, signing it with a pseudonym. Waitkus, a bachelor, read the note, which asked him to come to her room, room 1297-A, and which said only that it was important. He found the note mysterious and decided to follow up. It was close to midnight, June 14, 1949.

Stories in the following day's newspapers that I and everyone else, I imagine, read with stunned disbelief described what had happened next. A banner headline in the *Chicago Tribune* read: EDDIE WAITKUS SHOT: QUIZ GIRL.

The bullet that tore through the chest of Eddie Waitkus shortly after he walked into Ruth Ann Steinhagen's room ripped a hole through my idea—a nine-year-old boy's fantasy notion—that sports was not a part of the real world and that sports heroes were greater than mere mortals.

The rifle shot that exploded in that hotel room that night in Chicago, some 10 miles from where I lived, remains with me, 50-plus years later, and with the nation, as well. The incident is now not only a part of our national history—baseball with its long ties to our hearts and minds also indeed remains in many ways our national pastime—but it also provided a scene in our literature and in our print and celluloid mythology.

In one of the most dramatic moments in *The Natural*—a novel by Bernard Malamud, published in 1952, which years later was made into a Hollywood motion picture starring Robert Redford—an unsuspecting big-league player named Roy Hobbs is shot in a hotel room by a woman, a stranger, wearing a black veil.

Fortunately, Waitkus survived. Not only that, but incredibly the following season, he was the star first baseman as the Phillies, known as "The Whiz Kids," went on to win the National League pennant. He batted a healthy .284 and played in every one of the team's 154 regular season games as well as in the four close World Series games that the Phillies lost to the Yankees.

How the shooting affected his life; how he was washed up as a baseball player after the 1955 season, at age 35 after an 11-year career; how life began eventually to unravel for Waitkus personally, professionally, and physically; I knew little of this. But one day after having written a column on the passing of Waitkus and recalling the shooting, I received a letter from out of the blue from Edward Waitkus Jr., a lawyer living in Boulder, Colorado.

"In every dismal event," he wrote, "there is something positive which comes out of it. While recovering from the shooting my dad met my mother." This was in Clearwater Beach, Florida, where Waitkus was sent for rehabilitation and Carol Webel was vacationing with her parents, from Albany, New York. "Had it not been for this horrible event in his life, my sister and I would probably not be here. Life is very ironic. I think sometimes that all horror that comes to us has a reason…

"It was a miraculous recovery from the shooting that Dad made, winning Comeback Player of the Year the following season and getting into the World Series. He said the Series was the high point of his career…

"He had always told me he understood the four years of his career lost to serving in World War II. 'Everyone went,' he would say. He, however, never quite accepted being shot, that is, the time lost because of the shooting."

In a subsequent conversation, Ted Waitkus, as he is generally called, remembered as a boy feeling the deep indentation in his father's back that was made from the several surgical incisions required to save his life. His father told him that it was hard to believe that "a little bullet could make you feel as though six men had slammed you against the wall."

"My dad was an easy-going, trusting guy at the time and kind of flippant with women," said Ted Waitkus. "He walked into her hotel room and said something like, 'Well, babe, what's happening?'…I guess she was a fanatic in the way the guy who shot John Lennon was. Then she went into the closet, took out the .22, and shot him. The first thing he said was, 'Why'd you do that?'"

The shooting, said Ted Waitkus, changed his father a great deal, "as you might imagine." He went from being "outgoing" to "almost paranoid about meeting new people."

On the morning of September 16, 1972—a little more than 23 years after the shooting—I opened *The New York Times* and happened to run across a modest-sized obituary notice on Edward Stephen Waitkus, former major-league first baseman. He had died of cancer at age 53.

I remember reading the Waitkus obituary and thinking how the shooting was the beginning of a heightened awareness for me of senseless violence and mindless, heart-breaking tragedy. Many more times I would experience the terrible gut feeling of helplessness, befuddlement, and rage over such events. It was there after the murders of John and Robert Kennedy and Martin Luther King, after the insane cult murders of Charles Manson and the preventable slaughters in Vietnam. It is there to this day with the genocides in eastern Europe and Africa, the mad suicide bombings in Israel, the seeming eternal conflicts in places like Norther Ireland, and the unspeakable attacks on the World Trade Center and the Pentagon.

But when I read the Waitkus obituary, it was only weeks after I had returned from the 1972 Olympics in Munich, where the 11 Israeli Olympians had been murdered by Arab terrorists.

I learned the phone number of Waitkus' younger sister, Stella Kasperwicz, and spoke with her. She told me Eddie had retained an interest in sports and had watched the Olympics. She said he had talked about the shooting of the Israelis.

"Eddie thought it was awful," Mrs. Kasperwicz recalled. "He said that none of us will ever be the same because of it."

I understood, I told her. I said I also felt that way about a similar incident that had occurred many years before, when I was a boy growing up in Chicago.

Ferguson Jenkins: A Terrible Turn in the Road

January 3, 1993

GUTHRIE, OKLAHOMA—In the morning, Ferguson Jenkins had noticed that the hose to the large red vacuum cleaner was missing, but he paid little attention to it, never once imagining what terrible use it might be put to.

Then in the late afternoon, around 5:00, the phone rang in the kitchen of his ranch house here. The date on the calendar on the wall was Tuesday, December 15, 1992, two days after Jenkins' 49th birthday. Jenkins was outside, smoothing the red clay in the driveway with a shovel, when his ranch foreman, Tommy Christian, answered the phone.

"Sheriff Powell!" he called to Jenkins from the doorway.

Sheriff Powell? Jenkins recalled thinking. *What can he want?* The last time he had spoken to Doug Powell was two years earlier, after a robbery at the Jenkins ranch.

From the driveway, Jenkins could see that the sun, weak all day, was disappearing behind the hills and two man-made lakes on his 160 acres. It was getting cool as a wind picked up in this isolated area of the plains, about eight and a half miles north of Guthrie, the nearest town, and about 40 miles north of Oklahoma City.

Jenkins was wearing a green windbreaker, green baseball cap, jeans, and work boots. This is a working farm, with eight horses, 52 head of beef cattle, and 60 acres of wheat, and Jenkins dresses for it. So did his fiancée, Cindy Takieddine, who lived with him, his adopted 12-year-old son, Raymond, and his three-year-old daughter, Samantha, the child he had with his wife, Maryanne, who was seriously injured in a car crash in December 1990. Her death in January 1991 came just four days after the announcement that Fergie, as everyone calls him, had been named to baseball's Hall of Fame.

The election had been the culmination of a 19-year career in the major leagues, mostly with the Chicago Cubs and Texas Rangers, in which Jenkins won 284 games, was a 20-game winner seven times, won the National League Cy Young Award in 1971 and the American League Comeback Player of the Year Award in 1974, and then finally retired in 1983.

Jenkins is a big man. At 6-foot-5 and 225 pounds, he is about 20 pounds heavier than in his playing days, but he carries his weight well, with a graceful, slope-shouldered walk. Having learned that the sheriff was on the phone, he entered the two-story redwood house, walked past the Christmas tree that Cindy had decorated for three days, took the receiver, and was told that the sheriff wanted to see him in Guthrie. Within 15 minutes, Jenkins arrived in town in his pickup.

"I have some horrible news, Mr. Jenkins," said Sheriff Powell. "And there's no easy way to tell it. "Cindy Takieddine and Samantha Jenkins were found dead of carbon monoxide poisoning. They were found in a Bronco pickup on a rural road near Perry."

"No, you're wrong, Sheriff," said Jenkins. "You're wrong. I'm picking up Samantha at 5:30 at her day-care nursery." He looked at his watch. "In about 10 minutes."

"It was a positive I.D., sir. And a note was left."

"Call the day-care center," said Jenkins. "You'll see; Samantha's there."

Powell called the center for Jenkins, and put the call on a speakerphone. Samantha Jenkins was not at the nursery.

"Mr. Jenkins was devastated," recalled Powell. "This was one of the hardest things I've ever had to do as sheriff, or deputy, in Logan County. Mr. Jenkins is highly admired here. He's been a model citizen, and always willing to speak at civic or school or church groups. As famous as he is, that's how down to earth he is. He rode up to Perry with my undersheriff to identify the bodies, about 30 miles. All the way there and all the way back he never said a word."

It was back in Powell's office that he learned that Cindy, a tall, 44-year-old blonde, had stopped at the day-care center and picked up Samantha, whom she had dressed at home that morning in a green party dress with white sash and white stockings and black shiny shoes, saying it was for a Christmas party at the nursery school. But no party was scheduled.

Before Cindy and Samantha left home that day, Jenkins went to town to buy groceries. It was the last he saw them alive. "There were no arguments," recalled Jenkins. "We were civil to each other."

"She didn't look or act no different," said Christian, the foreman.

After picking up Samantha at the day-care center, Cindy would drive to the deserted road. She affixed the vacuum cleaner hose to the exhaust pipe of the Bronco, ran it up through the back window, sealed the window with the duct tape she had taken from home along with the hose, and, with the ignition still running, climbed into the back seat and held Samantha in her arms. The coroner's report estimates that this happened around noon.

A few hours later, a pumper on a nearby oil rigging spotted the car, with two bodies slumped in the back seat, and he phoned the police.

On the day after Christmas, 12 days after the tragedy, Ferguson Jenkins loaded his pickup truck with unwrapped Christmas presents, and returned them in Guthrie to Wal-Mart, Sam's Wholesale Outlet, and Anthony's Clothing Store. They included a jogging outfit and sweaters for Cindy. For Samantha, there were Cabbage Patch dolls, a Minnie Mouse towel set, a Beauty and the Beast towel set ("She loved Beauty and the Beast," said Jenkins), coloring sets, a large box of crayons, a sweater that had Santa Claus and reindeer and the word CHRISTMAS across it, and matching socks.

When Jenkins returned home from the stores, his three daughters from his first marriage, to Kathy Jenkins, were in the house. The girls, Kelly, 22, Delores 21, and Kimberly, 15—all in college or high school—had come down from their home in Chatham, Ontario, where Jenkins was born and raised, to celebrate Christmas with their father, as they did every year. But this year, they had also come to go to the funeral of their three-year-old half-sister.

Jenkins' 86-year-old father, who is in a nursing home in Chatham, had not made the trip for the funeral. "Said he couldn't take it," said Jenkins. It was his father, Ferguson Jenkins Sr., to whom Jenkins dedicated his induction into the Hall of Fame and who sat proudly in attendance in a wheelchair.

Jenkins had told the gathering at Cooperstown: "My father was a semi-pro ballplayer and he played in the Negro Leagues, but he didn't make the major leagues because he was limited by history"—the color barrier in big-league baseball that existed until 1947.

"But he has outlived that history," Jenkins continued. "I always told him that anything I do in baseball, I do for the two of us, and so now I feel I'm being inducted into the Hall of Fame with my father."

Jenkins' mother, Delores, has been dead for several years. She had become blind after complications while giving birth to her only child. "I remember she always walked with a white cane and always made sure that my baseball uniform was sparkling clean and my baseball shoes were polished," Jenkins has recalled. "I'm not sure how she knew, but she never let me out of the house to play ball unless I was all in order."

Jenkins grew up playing baseball and hockey and basketball, and was often the lone black in those leagues in Chatham. "I heard 'nigger' a lot," he recalled, "but I was always determined to make people respect my abilities. I always wanted them to say, 'Hey, watch that black guy, he's good.' And I did get into some fights, mostly in hockey, and lost a few teeth. But I came out of it."

He left home after signing a contract with the Philadelphia Phillies when he was 18, having just graduated high school, "a tall, skinny kid of 155 pounds," he said. "My father was a cook on shipping lines in the Great Lakes, and my mother was home alone a lot. I've always felt kind of guilty leaving her, but I knew I had to pursue my career."

Three years later, at the end of the 1965 season, he was called up to the Phillies, as a relief pitcher. In his first game, he replaced the veteran Jim Bunning, whom, he recalled, he had badgered for pitching help.

"How do you grip the ball? How do you throw your slider?" Jenkins would ask Bunning. The next season Jenkins was traded to the Cubs, and Leo Durocher made him a starter. Jenkins would learn his craft well while pitching in Wrigley Field, the smallest ballpark in the major leagues.

With the often lackluster Cubs teams, he pitched in bad luck. He still shares a record for the most 1–0 losses in a season, five, in 1968, in games against pitchers that included Bob Gibson and Don Drysdale. Still, he won the Cy Young Award in 1971, with a 24–13 record, leading the league in complete games, with 30, innings pitched, 325, and strikeouts, 304. He won 20 games six straight seasons for the Cubs, and then fell to 14–16 in 1973. The Cubs responded by trading him to Texas in a move that stunned him, and much of baseball.

The next year, 1974, Jenkins won 25 games and the American League's Comeback Player of the Year award. Like his former teammate Ernie Banks, he was never on a pennant winner. He came close, however, during the 1969 season when the Cubs, leading for much of the season, faded in the stretch as the Mets won the National League's East Division, and then the pennant and World Series.

Jenkins was traded to Boston in 1976, traded back to Texas in 1978, released after the 1981 season, and then signed as a free agent by the Cubs. He pitched two more seasons and then retired, two months short of his 40th birthday. He caught on as a pitching coach in the Rangers organization, where he spent several years with their Oklahoma City Class AAA team before being given his release three years ago.

Jenkins was always one of the most gentlemanly of ballplayers, and was thrown out of a game only once, when he threw a few bats onto the field in a pique. "Fergie, I'm sorry," said the umpire. "I'm going to have to ask you to leave." Jenkins had one other incident of greater notoriety. In August 1980 he was arrested in Toronto on a charge of carrying in his luggage small amounts of hashish, marijuana, and cocaine.

He was suspended by baseball commissioner Bowie Kuhn, but soon was reinstated by an arbitrator who said that Kuhn could not rule on Jenkins before the courts did.

But while Jenkins was found guilty of possession of drugs in December 1980, no police record exists. At sentencing in the Ontario Provinicial Court, Judge Jerry Young told Jenkins: "You seem to be a person who has conducted himself in exemplary fashion in the community and in the country, building up an account. This is the time to draw on that account." Judge Young then wiped the slate clean for Jenkins.

It was while he was with the Oklahoma City team that he found that ranch house. He and Maryanne, whom he had met and married while with the Cubs, had loved the house at first sight, he said. Both liked the solitude it afforded, and the beauty of the landscape there. Her son, Raymond, by a previous marriage, was then eight, and his father had died and Jenkins had adopted him. "I call him Fergie usually," said Raymond, a bright, good-natured youth, "unless I want something. Then I call him Dad."

Ray, who had known only cities, had to make adjustments to farm life, and did, getting to learn how to care for and ride horses, and, at paternal urging, to paint posts, too, not always with pleasure.

Adjustments for him, and for Jenkins, would grow increasingly harder when Maryanne was injured in a car accident near their home, and, after a month in intensive care, died of pneumonia. Samantha was then six months old.

When Cindy Takieddine, divorced and working as a secretary in a law office in Los Angeles, read about Jenkins' election to the Hall of Fame, she called the Cubs to try to locate him, to congratulate him. She managed to get his home phone number. She had met him when he was a young player with the Cubs and she was 19.

They had struck up a friendship, although Jenkins says it was never a romance, and he hadn't seen her in about 15 years. When she learned from Jenkins on the phone that his wife had died, she offered to come with a girlfriend to Guthrie on her vacation, and help him any way she could. He accepted.

"They cooked, they took care of the house, and they watched over the kids," Jenkins recalled. The girlfriend soon went back home, but Cindy stayed and they fell in love.

Six months ago they became engaged. He said she started feeling pressure from friends about marriage. "It'll happen, just not right away," Jenkins told her. Meanwhile, she was a great mother and, essentially, a great wife, Jenkins said. She traded her white slacks for farm overalls. She was a talented decorator around the house, putting, as the foreman, Christian, called it, "the woman's touch on it, with all them frills and friggles." He added, "And she was always a lady."

Cindy kept the checkbook in order and looked over the endorsements and the personal-appearance schedule for Jenkins, who flew periodically to card shows, fantasy camps, and speaking engagements. She grew to be a loving and concerned mother to Raymond and developed a close bond with Samantha. Cindy also seemed to take to farm life, and was active in classes in town, particularly ceramics. She made angels and deer heads and a Santa Claus for Christmas that was placed on the mantel above the fireplace in the living room.

"There were some spats between Fergie and Cindy, sure; what couple doesn't have spats on occasion?" said Lemoyne Hardin, a family friend. "But it was pretty clear that they got along just fine."

A lot of mail came to Jenkins, much of it asking for autographs, and sometimes Cindy would open it up, see that it was from a woman, and throw it away. When Jenkins found out, he said that was not right, that it was his personal property. If she wanted to open his mail, he would be happy to do it with her.

Tension seemed to increase when a sports reporter from Cincinnati called the Jenkins home in early December and Cindy answered. He asked whether it was true that Jenkins had accepted a job as a pitching coach in the Cincinnati Reds organization. Cindy had known nothing about it, and it angered her.

"Cindy knew I was talking with front-office people," said Jenkins. "But I hadn't told her about the Reds, hadn't shared it with her. But I hadn't signed the contract. I still have the contract, unsigned." At his kitchen table recently, he took out a briefcase, and two pink contracts, and showed them still unsigned.

"I told her that baseball had been my life, and that I still had a dream of one day being a pitching coach in the major leagues," he said. "But I said nothing is certain yet, I hadn't made any definite decision about baseball. But she was concerned. She said she was nervous about having to spend eight months alone at the ranch, and she wasn't sure how she could manage the place.

"I told her that she could come visit me wherever I was. It appeared I'd be with the Reds' minor-league club in Chattanooga and that things would work out. Not to worry. I think that's what troubled her. I think so. I don't know for sure. I never will."

Jenkins sighed. "I sit here and I seem calm," he said. "But my mind is racing 90 miles an hour. The other night I woke up about 3:00 in the morning and came down here and just looked around. I said, 'Why? Why? Why did she have to do it? Why if she's unhappy, chop off her life like that? And take the baby with her?' Okay, be angry at me, but don't punish the baby."

After Jenkins had returned the Christmas presents, he remembers "getting short" with his daughters. The suicide and homicide, the Christmas season, all of it was bearing down on him, "smothering me," he said.

"I apologized to my kids," he said. "I told them, 'Your dad's just not having a good day.' They understood, I think. I said to myself, 'Fergie, get a grip.'

"But I knew I needed help, needed to talk to someone. I thought of calling 911. But then I thought about a chaplain I'd met in the hospital where Maryanne had been. I needed answers and I thought a clergyman might know. I called and told him it was urgent. He said to come right over. We talked for about three hours.

"He told me that God will not put more pressure on an individual than he can handle. Well, I don't want any more pressure. I don't want any more grief, any more sorrow. I really don't know how much more I can take. But talking to him was a big help. And I had talked to a priest, too. He told me he thought that Cindy had had a chemical imbalance. But I'm going to be going to some support groups now. I think it's important."

Jenkins is a Baptist, and says that despite his agonies he has maintained a belief in God. "People tell me that God has his reasons," he said. "I'm hoping somewhere down the road he lets me know. I certainly can't figure it out."

The suicide note that Cindy left on the front seat of the Bronco provided no answers for him, either, he said. He took out the letter that was written in pen on the back of a lumber-company receipt. It read:

"My last statement. My name is Cindy Backherms Takieddine. My address is in my purse. Contact Ferguson Jenkins. He can claim the bodies.

"Fergie said opening his mail is a gross invasion of his privacy—truly immoral. But ruining someone's life and telling them to get out the best way they can—that's immoral. I am to leave with what I came with. I was betrayed.

"I cannot leave and go away without Samantha. I love her more than life itself and cannot envision my life without her. She has been my child for almost two years.

"To all those who love me and Boog please forgive me—I had no way out." Boog was Cindy's nickname for Samantha.

"We had been talking," said Jenkins. "We talked a lot. We worked things out a lot. I never wanted her to leave. I never said that. I don't understand what she meant by betrayal. I just don't know. I just don't know. I've got so many questions. And no answers."

Jenkins was now on the white porch overlooking his property, as the sun, on an unseasonably warm day, reflected on the lakes and the cattle that were grazing, and on the horses. "My uncle Coleman said I should blast the house, that it's unlucky," he said. "I even thought of it. But this is my home, where I'm going to stay. And I'm going to have a priest bless it."

Jenkins ran a hand against his graying temple and looked out at the farm that he loves so much. "It's much quieter now with just me and Raymond," he said. "But we're trying to make it, trying to get things done. And I'm trying to be his dad as much as I can."

Jenkins said he still isn't sure about the Reds job, and who will stay with Raymond if he does go. "I still have things to figure out," he said.

Later that evening, in the dark, he drove for dinner into town to a pizza parlor with Raymond. The lights from the pickup truck reflected on the red clay farm road.

Raymond seemed to be doing all right. His father talked now about the computer game Raymond had been promised for Christmas if he did well in school, in the seventh grade. He had produced a 96 average, and received the game. Raymond talked about the computer game and what he wanted to do when he grew up. "Probably mess with computers," he said. Jenkins smiled.

"Oh, Raymond," said Jenkins after a moment, "it's supposed to start getting cold and rainy tomorrow. I think you'll have to take the horses into the barn."

"Okay, Fergie," he said, quietly and respectfully. "I'll remember."

Father and son sat, lost in thought. Jenkins, in his green baseball cap, was silent behind the wheel. The only sound in the night was the rattling of the truck on the road.

Bruce Gardner: So Close, Yet So Far Away

(written with Murray Olderman)

Los Angeles Police Department Death Report: File #71-045 104
Date/Time deceased discovered: June 7, 1971. 0900 hours

Interviewing officers: Det. Richard Ortiz, Det. George Kellenberger

Officers notified of possible suicide at Bovard Athletic Field (baseball field), University of Southern California campus.

Officers observed deceased lying on his stomach on the grass. Deceased was in an open area of the baseball field approx. 18 ft. n/w of the pitcher's mound. Both hands were partially under the face and neck, with the left hand clutching a Smith & Wesson .38 spcl. Rev., 3" barrel.

The deceased had a gunshot wound to the left temple with an exit wound in the right temple. The body was rigid. The bullet that passed thru the head could not be located.

Next to the body, officers found a laminated plaque with the deceased's name on it, naming him as All-American Baseball Player of the Year for 1960. Under the right portion of the body clutched in the right hand was a laminated plaque of a B.S. degree from Univ. of So. Calif. issued to Bruce Clark Gardner.

Approx 3 ft. from body toward pitcher's mound was full-page type-written statement taped to smooth wood board and resembling the laminated plaques. The note indicated possible suicide. It was unaddressed and unsigned.

300

AT 6:00 THAT MORNING, Bruce Cameron, a USC caretaker, had seen a body lying prone on the baseball infield, but he didn't approach it. He thought it was a student sleeping off a drunk. A couple of hours later, he and Mitharu Yamasaki, another campus caretaker, came closer. At Heritage Hall, where the USC athletic offices are housed, Virgil Lubberden, who often got to work early, saw them through a window. Jess Hill, then director of athletics, told his assistant to see what was going on.

"He was sprawled out, face down," Lubberden recalled. "I didn't realize at first it was Bruce. It was just unbelievable when I found out who it was."

At the Glasband-Willen Mortuary on Santa Monica Boulevard in Los Angeles, the crowd of mourners was so huge—about 500—that nearly half of them had to stand outside during the funeral service for Gardner.

Marty Biegel, the basketball coach at Fairfax High School, which Gardner had attended, delivered the eulogy with tears in his eyes. "Why? Dear God, explain to us why a 32-year-old man like Bruce, so young, who had so much to give to so many, takes his life."

Bruce Clark Gardner won more games—40—than any pitcher in USC history, including Tom Seaver, Bill Lee, Jim Barr, and Steve Busby. Before he ever pitched a varsity game, he was offered a $66,500 bonus by the Chicago White Sox. He was handsome, intelligent, sensitive, and articulate. In junior high and high school, he was president of the student body. He was a talented pianist and entertainer. Nearly everyone who knew him came away feeling better for it.

Ron Mix, an All-American football player at USC and an All-Pro with the San Diego Chargers, knew Gardner well in college. "Bruce was a guy who seemingly had everything that God could bestow on one person," remembered Mix, now an attorney. "He was very bright—one of the top students in our class. He was a first-rate, decent person. If you could design your own life, what you'd like to be, you'd come up with a Bruce Gardner."

And yet, one June night nine years ago, Bruce Gardner, with most of his life left to live, walked out to the pitcher's mound at Bovard Field and put a bullet through his head.

In retrospect, it really ended for Gardner seven years earlier when he was released by Salem (Oregon) of the Northwest League. In 1960, fresh out of USC, he had signed a modest bonus contract of $12,000 with the Los Angeles Dodgers. The next year in the minors he won 20 games. Then he hurt his arm. By 1964, his professional baseball career was over. At 25, Bruce Gardner, who had been brilliantly successful all his young life, considered himself a failure.

He returned home to Los Angeles, his life-long dream of making the major leagues shattered—a dream he once had every reason to believe would become reality. Now lost, confused, his future unclear, Gardner began to feel frustration and bitterness.

Until now, Gardner's lengthy suicide note was never made public. Nor were the contents of his four thick, meticulously kept scrapbooks—15 x 13 art-form black naugahyde-covered books with 20-ring acetate pages—which he started to keep at 17.

At first, the scrapbooks tell a love story between Gardner and life. There are numerous photos of his parents, of young Betty Fegen, a pretty, 25-year-old blonde when she met Joe Gardner, and dark-haired, round-faced Joe ("robust, singing, smiling, friendly," wrote Gardner).

Betty and Joe married in 1937. Joe worked in an automotive parts store, and later started his own gas station. Gardner was born October 30, 1938. Baby pictures and photos of Gardner with his parents—he resembled his father—dominate the early pages. Happy childhood, happy family.

And then, suddenly, a funeral notice: "In memory of Joseph J. Gardner." Under it, Gardner wrote: "March 3, 1941, my father, Joe Gardner, died of strep throat, probably complicated by his own rheumatic fever as a boy"—and, ironically—"his death just preceded the use of penicillin."

Gardner included in his scrapbooks a poem—"The love and heart of my father"—composed when Gardner was nine:

When he had a heart
When he had a soul
God had to take my

Father to his goal
I dreamed of him too
and when I was
two years old he
had to go to his
goal. And after 7 years
I saw his grave.
My father was
very kind and he
loved everybody that
was good and he said,
Never do anything that
you will be sorry for,
and his last words were
God bless you, and I
hope he did.
This is the end
of my story.
So, so long.

Despite his father's death, his boyhood seemed full and joyous—Cub Scouts, Halloween costumes, singing in a synagogue choir. And, at 10, he began to write about what would be the love and consuming passion of his life: baseball.

October, 1948: "Today was Halloween," he wrote. "I went trick or treating. I also thought about baseball. I made believe that I was the second Babe Ruth. When *The Babe Ruth Story* came to a local theater, I went in at 2:00 and came out after midnight. I sat through the main feature twice just to watch the Babe three times."

And later: "I had seen someone in school with a Marty Marion glove and I thought it was the greatest. I remember pulling my mother by the arm to the sporting goods store. No one was ever more willing to drop everything to play baseball than I was."

And at 12, in 1950: "Ever since I have been playing baseball, it has been my ambition to one day be in the big leagues."

He was becoming a standout sandlot pitcher, as well as a model student. He wrote original poems, won "posture" contests, represented his school in citywide oratorical contests, and was elected president of the student body of Bancroft Junior High in 1953.

"The election would be decided by the candidates' speeches," Gardner wrote. "I was last. This helped make the difference, because their weaknesses built up the dramatic strength of my speech. The scuffling during their speeches turned to silence during mine. I could feel the riveted attention to the last sentence. I won."

He also played the piano—at least partially out of a sense of commitment as the only child of a widowed mother. "After my dad's death, her life became a sacrifice," Gardner captioned one photo of his mother, who was working as a secretary at Temple Israel. "She went without things for herself so that I could have a baseball glove, piano lessons, braces on my teeth, and a million other things. May I die on the spot if I try to forget it."

And he added: "I can't imagine how much different it would have been for Mother if Dad had lived."

When Gardner was about 10, Samuel Fegen, Betty's father, came to live with them in their two-floor, three-bedroom apartment in the primarily Jewish Fairfax district of Los Angeles. An orthodox Jew born in Russia who achieved prosperity through real estate investments in the U.S., Fegen was a strict man who would get up every morning at 4:00, tuck his fringed prayer shawl into his black pants, and walk to the synagogue to pray.

Under his grandfather's influence, Gardner was bar-mitzvahed, an occasion he describes glowingly. But this is the last mention of religion in the scrapbooks.

Meanwhile, there was growing tension in the house. "The grandpa was always accusing Bruce of stealing, of doing something wrong," recalled Barry Martin Biales, who would become one of Gardner's best friends, the executor of his estate, and, ultimately, the owner of his scrapbooks. "Bruce would get upset, being accused of things he never did. And his mother, she was very frugal. There was a lock on the telephone. It was like a twilight zone in that house."

Not surprisingly, Gardner sought support outside the home—usually in the form of father figures. He found several, invariably baseball coaches—Bob Malcolm, his junior high school coach; Frank Shaffer, his coach at Fairfax High; and Tony Longo, father of his friend, Mike Longo, and coach of Gardner's American Legion team. "I practically raised Bruce," Tony Longo would say later. In the summers, Gardner's friends had a routine: meet at school, go to the beach, play baseball at a local park. But Gardner would skip the beach to wait for Longo to take him to play baseball.

Gardner's devotion to baseball was paying dividends. He gained a reputation as a left-handed pitching star in sandlot, American Legion, and high school ball. Large crowds watched and cheered him.

Although he did not have a blazing fastball, he did have pinpoint control. And his concentration was intense. Art Harris, a boyhood friend and teammate, recalled: "There was always the sense of Bruce being a loner. When he was pitching, he seemed like a stranger in a crowd."

Something Gardner especially liked, he wrote, "was to pitch quickly, to force the action by pouring strikes past the hitter." He put himself on a strenuous running program, and he felt this gave him unmatched endurance and the capacity to work quickly. Friends remembered him running up the steps of the Fairfax bleachers in 90-degree heat in a sweat suit. "I honestly believe I ran more than any athlete in the history of Fairfax," he wrote.

In high school, Gardner was an honor student (he would finish 76th in a class of 403 in a school with a high academic reputation), student body president, honorary mayor of Los Angeles for a day, and a piano player and singer who entertained at school assemblies.

Larry Wein, a neighbor and later a high school coach, remembered one incident. "Every kid grows up looking for a hero. In my case, it was Bruce Gardner. In fact, he was a hero for a lot of kids. I lived across the street from Fairfax, and I remember one time I was out on the track, running with my father. Bruce came over and asked if he could work out with us. That blew my mind. I mean, my hero was asking if he could work with us."

Gardner's high school was a stream of successes. He made the varsity at 16, was 11–2 as a junior, and 18–1 in his senior year, leading his team into the city finals.

Major-league scouts came to his games. One was Harold (Lefty) Phillips of the Dodgers, considered a highly astute judge of baseball talent (he later managed the California Angels). Sometime after Gardner's senior year in high school, Phillips filed the following confidential scouting report: "Has good stuff for 18-year-old but might be as good now as he ever will be. Real intelligent boy—might be too smart, know-it-all type. With a little more pitching and knowledge and experience should go into AA or at best AAA."

The Dodgers were anxious to sign him, even sending Larry Sherry—a former Fairfax High School pitching star and then a minor-leaguer in the Dodger farm system—to persuade Gardner. But Gardner had already turned down an offer from the Pittsburgh Pirates of $4,000, and the Dodgers' offer had not been enough to keep him from college. On the advice of high school coach Shaffer and his mother, he had opted for an athletic grant-in-aid to USC.

A primary reason for attending USC, only 10 miles from his home, was Rod Dedeaux, the finest college baseball coach in the country. Dedeaux's sales pitch—that he'd work to get Gardner a bonus later and that a college education was worth $100,000—made sense to Betty Gardner. She was part of a tradition that found solace and power in learning. Sports, at best, were harmless diversions; at worst, a waste of time.

Gardner, in his desire to attach himself to an older man, sensed Dedeaux would fill the void. A graying, paunchy ex-ballplayer, he had become a wealthy trucking magnate in L.A. But, like Gardner, Dedeaux loved baseball first. That accounted for his USC salary—$1 a year. He pursued his job with fervor: "I have one set of rules—do everything absolutely right." With his devotion to discipline and a methodical approach to all things, Gardner seemed a perfect match for Dedeaux.

The freshman team at USC was coached by Joe Curi, which was fine for Gardner. "Curi, loved me because I didn't complain and I was always ready," he wrote. "I was 10–0 for the season and held the USC varsity to a 0–0 tie.

I was USC's freshmen athlete of the year over my teammate Ron Fairly and shot-putter Dave Davis. I was quickly becoming the best unsigned prospect in the United States."

This, it seemed, was likely to change quickly. Bob Pease, Gardner's manager on a sandlot team and bird dog for the White Sox, recommended him to Hollis Thurston, Chicago's top scout on the West Coast. Gardner, accompanied by Tony Longo, was flown to Chicago for a tryout.

Gardner threw to a catcher in the bullpen at Comiskey Park. The big leagues. For 20 minutes, Thurston, Longo, manager Al Lopez, general manager John Rigney, and farm director Glen Miller watched the 6-foot-1, 185-pound southpaw.

Then Thurston turned to Longo and said, "We'll take him." He mentioned a big bonus figure. Longo said, "You'll have to talk to his mother." Gardner was only 18, and needed his mother's consent to sign.

The big number was $66,500, enormous in 1957. Gardner rushed home to tell his mother the news, Betty Gardner was not moved.

"Bruce came over to my house to talk with my father, who he was very close to," said Biales. "He looked sad. He told us about the offer, and said his mother wouldn't let him sign. My father said, 'Are you kidding? That kind of money doesn't come along every day.' Bruce said he had pleaded with his mother. I remember him saying, 'I was in tears. I asked her to, please, just sign it. I can go to school in the off-season. I'm ready now.'"

Longo couldn't believe it. But he understood. "Bruce was a good boy, the kind of kid you want for your own. He had fights with his mother, but who hasn't? When it was done, he listened to her. It's not like today. When a parent told you to do something, you did it."

Apparently, Mrs. Gardner was influenced greatly by Dedeaux, who emphasized the value of a college education—and that Gardner would get an even better deal after he graduated as a star. "I didn't approve of his signing, because I felt he needed security for the future. I wanted to help him become a success and make a lot of money. The trouble, I suppose, was that he felt I was interfering with his goal." (Betty Gardner remembers her son fondly—"he was magic, a wonderful, adorable person"—but finds it too painful to say much more about him now.)

Several of Gardner's USC teammates would leave school after signing major-league contracts, including Ron Fairly and Len Gabrielson. But Gardner, the dutiful son, stayed and, on the surface, seemed happy. "I don't know of anyone who enjoyed college more than Bruce," said Dedeaux.

Star athlete, excellent student, popular with the coeds, handsome. Gardner tried out for a bit part in the campus play, *Damn Yankees*. He won the lead—playing Joe Hardy, the man who loved baseball more than anything else in life—and was a hit. He had never sung or danced on stage before.

On the field, Gardner made All-League in each of his three varsity years. In his last two (27–4), he made All-NCAA District 8, and, in his final year, he was All-American. In 1960, he was named player of the year, after leading the Trojans to the final game of the College World Series (USC lost).

And he liked and respected Dedeaux. Don Buford, a USC teammate and later a major-leaguer: "Most of the guys who played for Rod felt the same way about him. Playing for Rod was, in some ways, like playing for a major-league manager, he was that good. But most of us looked on him as more than a coach. We relied on his judgment, even in personal matters. Bruce and I were only children. Both our fathers died when we were young, and we were both raised by our mothers. We didn't talk about it much, but, in some ways, it created a bond between us."

Dedeaux remembered Gardner as a friend: "One of the finest boys we ever had. There was never a more cooperative guy in any way."

In 1958, the season after not being allowed to accept the White Sox bonus, Gardner wasn't satisfied with his performance. He wrote: "I had my first poor year. I won almost all my games—13–1, with a 2.62 ERA—because we scored so many runs. But I lost a good deal off my fastball, probably because of losing so much weight." (Gardner had dropped 15 pounds to 170.)

There is a photo of Gardner, customary smile on his face, with three other USC pitchers. Next to the photo, he wrote in his scrapbook: "I look happy on the outside, but I'm thinking, 'What am I doing here? I should be in professional ball now, establishing my credentials.'"

He also wrote about leaving the practice field terribly upset. "I was running away. But who to? My grandfather? My mother? Rod Dedeaux?"

On May 21, 1958, Phillips amended his scouting file on Gardner: "Poor rotation on curve and hangs lots of breaking balls. Poor deception on change-up. His stuff is inconsistent. Poor pitching rhythm. Question his mental setup, don't believe he will stay with the game if the going gets tough. He has gone backward."

During Gardner's senior year, his grandfather died, which caused some family problems. His grandfather's will had been changed shortly before his death, leaving everything to Betty Gardner and nothing to his other daughter and three sons. (Two cousins estimated the inheritance at more than $100,000, although Mrs. Gardner wouldn't confirm the figure.)

"Bruce went to see his aunt and uncle," recalled Biales, "and they did not want him in the house. 'Go tell your mother to give us the thousands she took,' they told him.

"'Why blame me?'" he said.

"'We don't want you showing up anymore,' they said."

This disturbed Gardner, who had a great sense of family. Growing up without a father, he had clung to his relatives. But as he was hurt, so he would turn around and exhibit kindness to others. "He'd be at a party," Biales said, "and he'd see a wallflower, a plain girl sitting by herself. 'That's unfair,' he'd say. 'She's not having a good time.' And he'd ask her to dance."

After Gardner's senior year, Phillips upgraded the scouting report: "Tall, rawboned, long arms, good agility. Best fastball tails away high and outside. Sharp-breaking curve. Should be signed for somewhere in the amount of the first-year draft price." Translation: a bonus of $12,000, to be paid out in three $4,000 installments. Gardner agreed. Phillips signed him.

Gardner was smiling in newspaper photos of the signing, but he later wrote: "I cried that night. I had thrown away three baseball seasons. I had thrown away a very important amount of money. And though I had a college degree, I couldn't see its importance. I was older, and there was something wrong with my arm. It took me a long time to warm up the last few games at USC."

The severity of his arm problem was never spelled out, but the arm was strong enough for him to enter professional baseball at the highest level of the minor leagues, the Dodgers' AAA team in Montreal in the International League.

Oddly enough, however, by major-league standards he was less of a prospect than after his freshman year. At 18, he didn't have the outstanding fastball. But he might have developed one. At 21, he didn't have that fastball, and he never would.

Dedeaux thought it was a good deal anyway. "If he had signed after his freshman year," said the USC coach, "he would never have been sent to a AAA team. He'd have started much lower in the minors."

Perhaps. But the White Sox might have taken special care of him, bringing him along properly to protect their investment.

Montreal was a rude awakening. "He goes to Montreal," said Biales, "which is like 42 games behind, and they had all these greasy old ballplayers. Bruce is knocking on hotel doors, 'Hello, this is Bruce Gardner reporting.'

"'Get the hell out of here, you punk kid. I got a broad in here.' He had to sleep in the lobby. You know, they broke him in at Montreal. He had been a virgin. The guys said, 'Hey, we got to take care of this kid.' So they took him out and got him laid.

"Some people wonder if he was a homosexual, and couldn't face that fact in his macho sports world. If he was, I never knew it. He loved women, loved their bodies. He had a lot of affairs as he got older."

To the hardened veterans of pro ball, Gardner must have seemed vulnerable. Clean-cut, seemingly naive, a musician, college kid. There were few collegians in pro baseball then, and only a few had degrees, as Gardner did. Many players had not finished high school. Some veteran managers had not even attended high school.

Gardner wrote to Dedeaux: "Boy, what a difference. Pro ball isn't the glamorous life everybody thinks it is."

Johnny Werhas, a USC teammate who later played for the Angels and the Dodgers, felt that a lot of baseball people simply didn't understand Gardner. "They thought he was an oddball. But I tell you, he was way ahead of his time. He was eating health foods way before the fad. He went to chiropractors before anyone else. Once he removed all the hair on his left arm, as an experiment, to cut down wind resistance. People laughed, but years later swimmers like Mark Spitz and other athletes were doing the same thing." He also stood on his head doing yoga in the dugout. He said it brought more blood to his pitching arm.

After some undistinguished appearances at Montreal, where his record was 0–1, he reported for his first spring training at Dodgertown in Vero Beach, Florida, in 1961. The facilities were first-rate, but the caliber of baseball minds did not impress Gardner. "I can't believe these people," Gardner told Biales. "The only smart guy I met there was Walter O'Malley." O'Malley owned the Dodgers and once gave Gardner $100 for playing his favorite song on the lounge piano.

That first spring, Gardner still had not gotten over a case of mononucleosis. "Mononucle-what?" said one of the coaches. "Get out there and run. When I was your age, Gardner, I never had this mono-stuff you're talking about." Gardner's response? "Go tell Roy Campanella when you were his age, you never got in an auto accident." Campanella, the great Dodger catcher, was paralyzed for life after an auto mishap.

Gardner, who was supposed to be assigned to Greenville in AA classification, was sent instead to Reno of the California League, Class C. "What a waste," Gardner told a friend. "I'll probably win 40 games. I should be pitching AAA ball."

Gardner was 20–4 at Reno. In his Dodger scouting report, Reno manager Roy Smalley described Gardner: "Excellent attitude, exceptional aptitude. Improving steadily, has endurance, good fielder, hits well, mentally tough. Has a chance to make majors." Smalley did not mention Gardner's occasioned habit of standing on his head in the dugout, sometimes while the national anthem was being played.

The official 1962 program of the Dodgers lists a handful of players with exceptional promise on their minor-league clubs. One was Gardner: "Former Trojan Bruce Gardner topped the California League in four departments. His 20–4 record gave him top victory total, and best percentage (.833). He also pitched most complete games, 18, and was the ERA leader with 2.82."

After the season ended, Gardner went to Fort Ord, California, to fulfill a military obligation. He was to serve six months and be out in time for spring training. But the Cold War escalated into the Berlin Crisis, active duty rosters were frozen, and Gardner injured his arm in maneuvers—possibly one time when he fell off a truck. Finally released in July, he was assigned to Spokane, a AAA team in the Pacific Coast League.

At the time, his mother was staying with one of Gardner's paternal aunts in Oakland. She begged him to take her along to Spokane. He didn't want to, but he couldn't stand to see her cry. So he piled everything he had in the world—including his mother—into his car and took off. He met the team on the road in Seattle and sent his mother on in the loaded car to Spokane to find an apartment.

Gardner had made $600 a month in Reno. He expected a minimum raise to $800 and thought he would probably get $1,000. He received a new contract for $700. And that wasn't the worst of it. "I came into Spokane at 7:00 in the morning—and there my mother was in the car packed to overflowing and no place to go," he wrote. Apparently, only two places met Betty Gardner's standards of frugality. "One was a dingy basement apartment. The other was a fucked-up, dilapidated Chinese hotel. I put my hand over my forehead and eyes and just sat still. I gave up. We took the Chinese hotel. I went to sleep on an empty, unmade cot and later got up and went to the ballpark like a POW. This was early August, 1962, and around this time Marilyn Monroe committed suicide. And this idea for the first time entered and cemented itself in my mind." It was also the first time Gardner had used any profanity in his writings.

He finished 1–5 in Spokane. There were hysterical shouting matches with his mother in which Gardner dredged up old hurts about not signing the big bonus contract. He was suffering, his arm hurt, and he was failing as a pitcher. "I didn't sleep nights," he wrote. "Instead, I took piano lessons in Spokane. After each game I would go to the studio and beat the piano until morning. I even smoked cigarettes for the first time. Then I could go back to the Chinese hotel and sleep all day on that shitty cot."

Spokane manager Preston Gomez's succinct report in Gardner: "Says arm hurts. So have to wait for him to get better before make determination."

There is still vagueness about the origins of his arm problem. But it was clear the snap in his pitches was diminishing. So was his confidence as he prepared for another season. He wrote: "In spring training, Tommy Lasorda didn't even say hello. [The year before, Lasorda had held Gardner up as an example of how to throw the difficult "drop" curve.] It's a game of survival of the fittest. A 20-game winner fits. A one-game winner doesn't. My pitching was forced. I had trouble getting anything on the ball."

During his years in the minors, there is no mention of his father in the scrapbooks. Two photographs put in about this time are noteworthy, though. One shows Gardner's father in a dark suit, buttoned up, smiling, with his arm around a friend. In the photo directly below, taken more recently, Gardner is posed and dressed identically—with his arm around the son of his father's friend.

In 1963, he was assigned to Salem (Oregon) in Class A, pitched poorly, and was sent to Great Falls (Montana) in the Pioneer League. His last night in Salem was spent with a girl named Jo. "It was the most beautiful time I'd ever had. In the morning she brought her baby over (from a previous marriage), made breakfast. I dreamed of life as it should be, packed everything I owned again into the car and traveled to Great Falls."

There, getting by on guile, he was 10–4 with a 4.07 ERA. And the dream of a major-league career persisted. That December he sent Christmas cards with a picture of himself in a Dodger uniform.

Betty Gardner still worried about her son. Early in 1964, she wrote to Fresco Thompson, vice-president of personnel for the Dodgers:

> May I introduce myself? I am Bruce Gardner's mother. Confidentially, I am concerned about my son. Could you give me any infor-

mation about his future with the Dodgers? How fast is his ability as a pitcher? How is progressing, etc.?

I am very proud of my son and eager to help him make good. He is very ambitious and loves baseball very much. I wonder if there is anything I can do to help him achieve his aspirations.

P.S. Of course, I would not want Bruce to know that I am writing to you as he may think I am being too forward.

Thompson responded:

You are, undoubtedly, aware that Bruce began his professional career by winning 20 and losing 4 in 1961. For some reason, he has been unable to recapture the form which he showed in 1961.

At spring training in 1962, he indulged in self-diagnosis and self-treatment of real and imaginary ills. On two occasions, I personally went to his room to see why he had not reported for practice. Each time I found him in bed with what he had diagnosed as a respiratory condition. He was treating himself despite the fact that we had a full time Doctor and Registered Nurse on the premises at all times.

He then began visiting chiropractors in Vero Beach and elsewhere for soreness in his arm. Mrs. Gardner, in all my baseball experience, I have never heard of one of these bone-poppers curing a baseball player of anything.

Baseball is a difficult and demanding taskmaster. One must, during the baseball season, apply himself solely and diligently to becoming a ballplayer. This I do not think Bruce does at times. With most youngsters in the Dodger Organization, baseball is the end. With Bruce, this is not so; baseball is a means to an end. What that end is no amount of probing and delving has uncovered.

Gardner discovered these letters in 1968 and put them in his scrapbook. He wrote: "Boy, oh boy. Some of things she says in that letter sure hurt. 'Proud of my son and eager to help him make good.' How come we never discussed this? She didn't seem proud in 1957. It's a little late now.

"But Fresco's answers are as ridiculous as my mother's questions. 'How fast is his pitching ability?' Her main question was 'etc.' That's Jewish for 'I don't know what I'm interested in asking so you tell me.'

"So he tells her that I was sick in 1962. Since I was actually sick during 1961, that's also the year that I had my successful season. He forgets I was in the Army in 1962. Then I suppose he convinced my mother I wasn't really dedicated. Fresco had a real talent for: thinking, over-eating, over-drinking, and using the word 'taskmaster.'"

Gardner's last training camp was in 1964 at Vero Beach. "Bruce was the hardest working guy I ever saw," said Jimmy Campanis, his catcher that final season. "He would run and run and run." But he broke an ankle practicing slides and wasn't ready to pitch again until early summer, when he reported to Salem. A rule of thumb among major-league teams is three years to rise in the minors. Salem was Gardner's last chance.

"Good kid," recalled his last manager, Stan Wasiak. "Hard worker, high-class boy. But sometimes I got the feeling he thought he was above me, in intellectual status."

At the ballpark, Gardner struggled to a 2–2 record in 19 appearance, finished none of his three starts, and had an ERA of 5.40. An old USC teammate, Marcel Lachemann, played in the same league that year and thought Gardner pitched "almost like an amateur. It was sad watching it." He was nearly 26-years old, a faded prospect.

"I was up in the press box late one night after a game," remembered Bob Schwartz, sports news editor of Salem's morning newspaper, the *Oregon Statesman*. "I saw Bruce on the field, fully dressed. He was standing on the mound. I'm sure he didn't know I was there. He smoothed the rubber with his foot, then walked around the mound. I went back to work. When I finished, he was gone."

In a confidential Dodger report, a scout wrote: "Has no future." Gardner concurred. "My arm could only take an inning," he wrote. "Damaged by now." But he felt bitterness toward the Dodger organization: "Too many kinds of people that can't be decent unless you're leading the bandwagon."

From the scrapbooks: "Notice of Official Release. September 30, 1964. You are officially notified of the non-disposition of your contract. You are released unconditionally. Fresco Thompson."

Gardner now faced the classic dilemma of the former pro athlete, the onetime star: What do you do when the cheers stop, when the lifelong dream collapses? Whom could he blame? Whom could he strike back at? He was not a violent person. He never even threw at a hitter. He remembered when Marilyn Monroe committed suicide, how he felt. One day, about a month after he was released, Gardner went to Vernon, a small town near Los Angeles, and bought a .38 Smith & Wesson blue steel pistol in a pawn shop.

He told Biales: "I went home to plan to kill myself, but the phone rang and got my mind off it."

Biales was stunned. "Are you serious?"

"Yeah," said Gardner. "Everything's so low. The baseball's over and there's nothing left for me."

On June 4, 1965, Betty Gardner, now having frequent shouting matches with her son, again wrote to Fresco Thompson:

> My son seems so unhappy at the end result of his baseball career.
>
> I hate to see him so unhappy. It is partially due to a scout making a high offer one day and reneging the next day, that has caused Bruce to be this way.
>
> I think perhaps if he could in any work with baseball (which has been his dream since he was 10 years old) that he would not now be so depressed. Do you think there is any phase of the game he could fit into?

Thompson responded two weeks later:

> I am indeed sorry that Bruce appears to be so unhappy due to the fact that he is now out of baseball.
>
> I must say that Bruce has absolutely no one to blame but himself for his present predicament. We gave Bruce every opportunity to

take full advantage of his God-given baseball talents. He appeared, however, to have many other things on his mind.

I regret that I cannot advise you of some other phase of the game in which he might fit. Professional baseball is an exacting taskmaster and in order to succeed, a full-time effort is required.

Gardner wrote: "Now my career is over. Eight years late and now my mother is concerned. My mother's philosophy is to get concerned when it's too late. But create the predicament by not using reason beforehand. She says a scout reneged. I guess because I didn't sign. He didn't renege. She shouted 'No' at me. I'm afraid the shadow of Rod Dedeaux in the wings made her unable to move in any direction.

"Quit bothering the wrong man [Fresco Thompson], Mother! Looking back, I don't see what I could have done differently except to quit baseball earlier. My life taken away."

Outwardly, Gardner seemed to adjust. He was a real estate salesman, then sold mutual funds. He dressed nattily and flashed jewelry. In 1968, he won a trip to Bermuda and the next year was awarded another trip—to Puerto Vallerta, Mexico—for his sales success.

There he fell in love with a "beautiful, intelligent, and charming girl" from Vancouver named Donna. He wrote a song about her the first day he met her, "with the sound of xylophone and mariachi in my mind."

> ...there wasn't anything such
> as tomorrow
>   They would wine and dine and
>   laugh,
>   And the day just seemed like
>   half;
>   She was the essence of his life—
>   such a Madonna.
>   But when it came time to leave,
>   How his soul would ache and
>   grieve;
>   It tore his heart to have to say,

Manana Donna, manana Donna,
It's so hard to be apart,
For you have entered in my
heart,
Life is too short to want to say,
manana Donna…

He visited her in Canada but soon concluded, "Her enthusiasm didn't equal mine."

There were other girls—exotic Latins he met in some of the strip joints in which he played the piano—and for a time there was a serious liaison with a slim blonde named Pat. But they all faded, too. He complained that he could never get the girl he wanted.

In 1970, his mutual funds career collapsed because of a slump in the market. Friends and relatives who had invested with him lost money—and he felt guilty about it. He trained to become a bank manager for a savings company, but he was let go after four months. He was told he didn't have the background for the position.

"In the last two weeks of 1970, I became very despondent and thought of ending my life, which hasn't been a rare thought for me for over a decade now," he wrote.

His cousin, Paul Fegen, remembered Gardner's disillusionment with life "because he couldn't make of himself what everyone else thought he should have. He was disappointed that he couldn't make money, because in school he was always the hero. He was like an aging actor who no longer could get parts. With Bruce, it happened suddenly."

Gardner still maintained an interest in baseball, and often went to games at Dodger Stadium with Biales. He would sit high behind home plate, watch the pitcher intently and say, "That should be me out there." Periodically, he visited the Dodger clubhouse to look up old teammates who had made it—Campanis, Lefebvre, Werhas, Fairly. "I didn't sense any bitterness or envy in him," said Werhas. "He seemed happy for me."

So to the world at large, Gardner maintained a smile. And he still went out of his way to extend a kindness. In December of 1970, he organized a surprise party for the managers of his apartment building, Arthur and Virginia Searles. He wrote a letter to the apartment building owner, Mr. Meltzer, describing the good job they did. The Searles framed the letter.

"But you know what else Bruce did?" Virginia Searles would later ask rhetorically. "He deliberately sent the invitation to Mr. Meltzer a day late, so he wouldn't be there. Mr. Meltzer wasn't the friendly type, and Bruce felt he didn't appreciate us as much as he should. When Mr. Meltzer called me, he said, 'I would have come to the party but I got the letter a day late.' All of us in the building thought it was a wonderful joke."

To earn a steady living, Gardner took a job as a physical education and health teacher at Dorsey High School in southwest Los Angeles. It's a predominantly black school, with a small percentage of Asian students. Gardner also coached the junior varsity baseball team to a 13–2 record, winning a championship for the first time in the school's history.

The star of the jayvee squad was Vassie Gardner, no relation. Vassie Gardner is black. He was a pitcher; he is now an outfielder with Chattanooga of the Southern League.

"Mr. Gardner reminded me of the coach on the TV program, *White Shadow*—only he was years ahead of it, and he was for real," said Vassie Gardner. "We were mainly a black team, and it was hard for me to believe a white guy would really care for me. He thought I had the potential to make the major leagues. But I was running loose on the streets. He'd call my house to make sure I was all right. Once he asked me to move in with him. He'd kind of adopt me.

"Guys used to joke around, say Mr. Gardner's funny. Because of the way he walked. Real straight. But he wasn't effeminate. He scared the hell out of me when he got mad.

"One day, I was late for practice. He told me to take a lap around the field. I told him I wasn't going to do it. Oh, did he get angry. So I said, 'Well, I better run a lap.' About halfway, I ducked behind a backstop on the other side of the field. As soon as I stopped, I felt someone grab be from behind. It was Mr. Gardner; he'd been running behind me. He wrestled me to the ground. He was strong. And he began hitting me in the stomach. Playfully, not really hurting me. 'I'm tired of your bullshit,' he told me. 'You're going to start doing things right, and you're going to get your ass out here and become a ballplayer.'

"He talked about his career. Something messed it up, a bad arm. He was my man. I wish he was still living. It happened too fast; I was just getting to know him."

Ironically, at the same time he was having this kind of impact on his players, Gardner was telling friends and relatives how he hadn't found anything worth doing, how useless he felt. And aimless.

Jim Lefebvre, his teammate at Salem and then with the Dodgers, saw him sitting alone in the box seats in Dodger Stadium one day in 1971. "I went over to him and asked him how he was doing. He said, 'Oh, okay.' I asked him what he was up to, and he told me he was coaching junior high school. I asked how he liked it. He said, 'It's not what I want to be doing.' His eyes had a vacant quality. He seemed alone, inside himself."

On the first Thursday in June of 1971, his boyhood buddy, Art Harris, saw Gardner at Dodger Stadium at the city high school baseball championship game. *Good*, Art thought to himself, *he's with some other people.* Harris was sensitive to Gardner's loneliness. Then Harris spotted Dedeaux and Casey Stengel, a close friend of Dedeaux, walking down the aisle together. "Bruce turned around and saw Dedeaux," Harris said. "Rod gave him the usual, 'Hi, Tiger.' Bruce's face turned as white as a gym towel. Looking back, I know now he was already planning to kill himself."

Bruce Gardner, sensitive and dedicated, wasn't trained to handle failure. When Al Campanis, the Dodgers' vice-president for personnel (and father of Gardner's teammate, Jimmy), was asked what he remembered most about Gardner, he said: "He didn't win."

On Friday afternoon, June 4, 1971, Vassie Gardner was playing basketball in the Dorsey gym and turned to see his coach staring at him. "He was just standing and watching me," he said. "I never saw that stare before. I guess he knew he was going to go away."

Gardner stayed in all of Saturday and Saturday night. He fastidiously arranged his book shelves. In his bedroom, there was a neat pile of *Playboy* magazines, which would later shock one of his aunts. His clothes in the closet were hung meticulously in sections—pants, suits, coats. Stacks of record albums neatly flanked his stereo. The blond wood furniture was dusted. The seascape oil painting on the wall behind the stereo was perfectly straight. The lid of the piano was pulled down over the keys.

On Sunday, Virginia Searles, the manager of his apartment building, saw Gardner neatly folding his wash in the laundry room. She said, "Good morning, Bruce." He said, "Good morning." That was it. She knew Gardner was a private person, though friendly. If he didn't want to say anything more, that was fine.

That was the last time anyone saw Bruce Gardner alive.

At 11:30, Arthur Searles made his nightly security check around the building. He noticed that Gardner's Buick LeSabre was parked in an odd place. The driveway had 18 individual carports on each side, with Gardner's spot designated No. 1, his apartment number. He always parked it there. Perfectly. This night, the car was parked on the incline at the end of the driveway. Since Searles saw no light in Gardner's apartment, he decided not to knock. Gardner—"such a thoughtful neighbor"—would take care of the problem the next day.

At that moment, Gardner was probably lying in bed in the dark. Apparently, he had made the decision at least as far back as Friday. Ken Bailey, the tennis coach, had seen Gardner grading books for his four gym classes. Bailey thought it was odd. School didn't close for two weeks.

Sometime after midnight, it is presumed Gardner rose from his bed and began his final preparations.

The chronology is uncertain, but he probably sat down at his Remington manual typewriter to type his suicide note. He poured himself a shot of Scotch. He kept the liquor for guests, because he never drank. But in times of distress, he would often do something out of character—like the time in Spokane when an argument with his mother drove him to his first cigarette. As he typed up two copies of the suicide note—and a will, which he left in the roller—he drank some more. (He would eventually consume the equivalent of four highballs, according to the coroner's report.) The will gave most of his $3,000 estate to Biales. He left $1 to his mother.

Gardner then placed one copy of the suicide note into the last page of his scrapbook and carefully taped the other note onto a wooden board.

He washed his glass and returned the bottle of Scotch to the cabinet.

He shaved, brushed his dark brown curly hair—cut short because he didn't like the way it kinked.

He put on a tan sport shirt with thin collar, a black sweater, blue-striped slacks, and black loafers. Then he slipped into a brown corduroy jacket with leather buttons.

He gathered the three plaques he would carry with him: the baseball All-American certificate, his USC diploma, the suicide note.

From the back of his top drawer in the bedroom, he removed the pistol and put it in his jacket pocket.

Before leaving, he made his bed. A detective would say later that the apartment was so tidy it looked as if Gardner had been expecting guests.

He picked up the plaques, closed the lights, walked outside, and double-locked the door. It was cool in Los Angeles for a June morning, 57 degrees. He buttoned his jacket. It was about 3:00 AM.

He put the three plaques in the car, and backed out onto Cattaraugus Avenue.

The route he usually took was through a quiet neighborhood of small, single-story homes to the Santa Monica Freeway. The divided concrete strip is invariably quiet at that hour. On the left are the lights of Beverly Hills and the Hollywood hills. Two of his closest cousins, Paul Fegen and Arlene Rosenthal, were asleep in large homes in the high section—the kind of luxurious homes Gardner never had. He drove past the Fairfax Avenue turnoff, exit to the neighborhood in which he was the big star. He drove past La Brea, the exit he would normally take to Dorsey High School. The exits rolled by—Crenshaw, Arlington, Normandy, and finally Vermont and the turnoff to USC. He almost certainly clicked the right-turn signal. He was a careful driver, never got a ticket, followed all the rules of the road.

At Jefferson Boulevard, he would turn left, then right on McClintock to the USC campus. The security guardhouse, built on a small island at the entrance, was empty. He turned into 34th Street and parked halfway down the block. Bovard Field was only 300 yards away. It was quiet.

Gardner got out the car with his three plagues, the gun in his pocket. He walked past Founders Hall, then through the slightly dewy hedge to the baseball field. The gate was locked. He climbed over the wooden fence, probably at its lowest point—along left field—where it was seven feet high.

The moon was three nights short of full, and it cast a bright light, creating shadows on the field. Gardner walked across the moist grass to the pitcher's mound, surrounded by empty stands which were once filled with fans cheering for him. He placed the suicide note on the grass at the edge of the circle. He walked a few feet more and lay down, halfway to second base. He lay straight. When they found him, he wouldn't be crumpled and awkward. His right elbow cradled the All-American plaque and his degree. With his pitching hand, he removed the pistol from his jacket pocket, then raised it to his temple.

Only the typewritten note nearby would be left to explain.

> Let my blood be the pathetic proof to those who have heard Rod Dedeaux say that a college education is worth $100,000 more in a man's lifetime. Because it is so deceitfully true. The man who starts at $800 a month versus the one who starts at $600 a month will wind up, after 40 years, with $100,000 more.
>
> And isn't that enough reason to shatter the hopes and dreams of an 18-year-old boy who has the opportunity to sign professional baseball with offers high in five figures?
>
> They keep him in college, don't let him believe that he could do anything with that kind of money but squander it. Don't ask what it is the boy wants to accomplish, because he might tell you that he would like to go into professional baseball, especially in light of the fact that many know baseball have regarded him very highly. And that it's his love.
>
> Then don't look too carefully at the facts. Don't think that a good student—president of Bancroft Junior High and Fairfax High—with

the determination of a winning miler, captain, and three-year cross-country runner, and the excellence of an All-City pitcher, could possibly have the wherewithal to make decisions concerning his own life.

Since he is too young to sign for himself, scare his mother. It's even easier, because his father passed away when the son was three. Let the mother feel that her boy will be wandering skid row if he leaves college. So that when he begs her to let him sign, she has nothing but shouts of "no." Do all these things carefully, Rod Dedeaux, and you will have an All-American. And his mother will get her vicarious college degree. Don't let any of his advantages get in the way of your National Championship.

He'll have graduated before your half-truths become the realities of his place in the world. And then he'll wonder where is the magic in the education you don't seek, and why so much energy is compulsively wasted in containing his bitterness and moving one foot in front of the other to get to each day's meaningless job. Where his $800 a month won't buy the home he's never had, meet the friends he's never entertained, nor call the mother he never wants to see. To what direction have the fragments of his broken heart discarded his ability to give and receive love?

But given another 32 years—in retirement he'll be able to look back with that overpowering joyful knowledge that some people in their work-a-day world jobs didn't earn the $100,000 more that he did in his. And that's when he'll hug his diploma and die of unhappiness. But somehow I don't need to wait anymore for that day. I reached it years and years ago.

I saw no value in my college education. I saw life going downhill every day and it shaped my attitude toward everything and everybody. Everything and every feeling that I visualized with my earned and rightful start in baseball was the focal point of continuous failure. No pride of accomplishment, no money, no home, no sense of fulfillment, no leverage, no attraction. A bitter past, blocking any accomplishment of a future except age.

I brought it to a halt tonight at 32.

6-6-71

IX.

VIEWPOINTS

Shoeless Joe: His Confession

June 24, 1989

IN THE CURRENT MOVIE *Field of Dreams*, Shoeless Joe Jackson and seven teammates of the Chicago White Sox—the historically besmirched Black Sox—who were banned from baseball for allegedly throwing the 1919 World Series to the Cincinnati Reds, are sentimentalized and glorified.

"Is this heaven?" one of them asks, when a ballfield is erected and they emerge from what might be assumed is a place down below to play ball forever in the friendly confines of an Iowa cornfield.

"Shoeless Joe batted .375 in the Series, hit the only home run, and didn't make an error," someone says in the film. "How could he have thrown the Series?"

Of course, it's possible. It's possible to not hit in the clutch, or to miss a sign, or a cutoff man, or to short-leg a fly ball in left field, with none of this embossed in the box score.

Beyond this, in this year of the 50th anniversary of the Baseball Hall of Fame in Cooperstown, the senate in South Carolina, Jackson's home state, on Monday passed a unanimous resolution asking organized baseball to exonerate him, with hopes of his one day being elected to the Hall of Fame, since his career batting average of .356 is third-highest in baseball history.

Jackson through the years maintained his innocence, until his death in 1951. But at 3:00 PM on September 28, 1920, Jackson was called as a witness to the grand jury of Cook County investigating the scandal. The transcript was recorded in a signed confession, and then swiftly disappeared because, it is believed, of a cynical deal cut between the White Sox owner, Charles A. Comiskey, and the gambler Arnold Rothstein. The lack of hard evidence helped Jackson and his teammates to be found not guilty in court.

Three years later, when Jackson sued Comiskey and baseball to be reinstated—Commissioner Landis had banned him despite the court's decision—the confession mysteriously resurfaced, and Jackson lost the suit.

Recently, the confession reappeared in an exhibition about the scandal at the Chicago Historical Society. Jackson's testimony is conflicting and compelling. Following are excerpts:

Q. (by assistant state's attorney Hartley L. Replogle): Did anybody pay you any money to help throw that Series in favor of Cincinnati?
A. They did.

Q. How much did they pay you?
A. They promised me $20,000 and paid me $5,000.

Q. (Did Mrs. Jackson) know that you got $5,000 for helping throw these games?
A. She did…yes.

Q. What did she say about it?
A. She said she thought it was an awful thing to do.

Q. That was after the fourth game?
A. I believe it was, yes.
(Jackson said that Lefty Williams, the Chicago pitcher, was the intermediary between him and the gamblers.)

Q. When did he promise the $20,000?
A. It was to be paid after each game.
(But Jackson got only $5,000, thrown onto his hotel bed by Williams after the fourth game. Jackson was asked what he said to Williams.)
A. I asked him what the hell had come off here.

Q. What did he say?

A. He said (Chick) Gandil (the Chicago first baseman, and player ringleader) said we all got a screw...that we got double-crossed. I don't think Gandil was crossed as much as he crossed us.

Q. At the end of the first game you didn't get any money, did you?

A. No, I did not, no, sir.

Q. What did you do then?

A. I asked Gandil what is the trouble? He says, "Everything is all right." He had it.

Q. Then you went ahead and threw the second game, thinking you would get it then, is that right?

A. We went ahead and threw the second game.

After the third game I says, "Somebody is getting a nice little jazz, everybody is crossed." He said, "Well, Abe Attel and Bill Burns had crossed him." (Attel and Burns were gamblers in the conspiracy.) (Then Jackson was asked about the fourth game of the Series.)

Q. Did you see any fake plays?

A. Only the wildness of (Eddie) Cicotte (Chicago pitcher).

Q. Did you make any intentional errors yourself that day?

A. No sir, not during the whole series.

Q. Did you bat to win?

A. Yes.

Q. And run the bases to win?

A. Yes, sir.

Q. And field the balls at the outfield to win?

A. I did...I tried to win all the games.

Q. Weren't you very much peeved that you only got $5,000 and you expected to get $20,000?
A. No, I was ashamed of myself.

Q. Where did you put the $5,000 (that Williams gave him)?
A. I put it in my pocket.

Q. What did Mrs. Jackson say about it?
A. She felt awful bad about it, cried about it a while.

Q. Had you ever played crooked baseball before this?
A. No, sir, I never had.

Q. You think now Williams may have crossed you, too?
A. Well, dealing with crooks, you know, you get crooked every way. This is my first experience and last.

The Meaning of Baseball by Some Who Might Know

May 31, 1981

WARS COULDN'T STOP MAJOR-LEAGUE baseball, the Depression couldn't stop major-league baseball; it seems the only thing that could is major-league baseball itself. By the very threat of the players' strike, the idea that the great stadia would be empty this summer—and the crack of bat against ball merely an echo in the mind—gives pause to reflect on baseball and its meaning in the warp and woof of life.

"Whoever wants to know the heart and mind of America had better learn baseball," Jacques Barzun, the social commentator, wrote more than a quarter of a century ago.

"Fundamentally," Barzun said in an interview last week, "things haven't changed. Baseball still reflects our society, it's just that our society has changed."

Baseball, Barzun says, once expressed the unification of America, the teamwork involved. "When we look at the triumphs of American technology on a large scale," he says, "we see the fine workings of a national machinery—everybody in every department cooperating effectively with no gaps in time.

"It was like the making of a double play perhaps. Or a relay in which nine men speedily clicked together to achieve a desired result. It's a beautiful thing to observe.

"But now, the contentions in baseball parallel the enormous unrest in our society—there's more litigation, for example, than ever before. And the star system has gotten out of hand. The teamwork that once marked the beauty of baseball is now scorned, and along with the diminishing appreciation for the rich qualities of baseball, there has developed diminished appreciation for the rich qualities of American life."

But a summer without baseball would not be quite the same for Barzun—who is still a casual fan—or for Jake Rabinowitz, proprietor of A&J Grocery on Second Avenue, who said, "I wouldn't have all the aggravation watching the Mets and Yankees, especially this season, but sometimes they give me pleasure—once in a while they win."

For Roger Angell, a writer for *The New Yorker* magazine, baseball would be missed. "It's part of my summer habits—and maybe my winter habits, too," he said. "I suppose I'd get along all right without it, but I'd rather not. There is a continuity with baseball—and there'd be a feeling of loss with it, like, there goes something else in our lives."

One of the qualities that Angell likes best about baseball has been its relative stability. He wrote: "Within the ballpark, time moves differently, marked by no clock except the events of the game. This is the unique, unchangeable feature of baseball and perhaps explains why this sport, for all the enormous changes it has undergone in the past decade or two, remains somehow rustic, unviolent, and introspective. Baseball's time is seamless and invisible, a bubble within which players move at exactly the same pace and rhythms as all their predecessors."

The late Bruce Catton, the historian, said that "baseball is a...pageant and a ritualized drama, as completely formalized as a Spanish bullfight, and although it is wholly urbanized it still speaks of the small town in the simple rural era that lived before the automobile came in to blight the landscape. One reason for this is that in a land of unending change, baseball changes very little."

But it seems to have often reflected the mood of the nation, and its ambitions.

Mark Twain wrote at the turn of the century that baseball was "the very symbol of the outward and visible expression of the drive and push and rush and struggle of the raging, tearing, booming 19th century."

For many it remained that way into the 20th century. "America was the land of opportunity where even a poor boy could grow up to be Babe Ruth," wrote Douglass Walop, in *Baseball: An Informal History.*

Once those sentiments were expressed about the presidency. But, Walop went on, "Cal Coolidge moved through life with careful sidesteps, smiling sour smiles. Babe Ruth laughed a mighty laugh, strode with the stride of a giant, slamming the door of his Stutz Bearcat and wading through the crowds, long camel hair coat flapping near his ankles, big brown eyes shining, a long cigar stuck between the fat lips, and grinning as they all say, 'Yiya, Babe,' and yelling back, 'Hiya, Kid...Sure, Kid...Atta Boy, Kid, keep swinging from the heels.'"

Surely there were those who resented Ruth making more than the president of the United States, but his larger-than-life qualities overshadowed the money aspect. Today, though, the big bucks intrude on our summer devotions, says Angell: "A lot of people find it insupportable, and against the work ethic, that young men can make so much money. You're supposed to work hard for not much money at something you don't like when you're young, and improve on that as you get older.

"And this idea of players making large amounts of money also says something uncomfortable about our society, where a ballplayer can make so much more than, say, a teacher. But it's not the fault of the players. The money is obviously there. It seems like the owners have a death wish about the game."

Above the noise of the machines in the United Features Syndicate pressroom Raymond Ruiz, in a blue smock, says he has sometimes resented the big money the players are making. "But if I was a player," he said, "and the owners were giving it to me, I'd take it, too. I sure would."

Baseball is part of the tradition of many American families. "It may be on the periphery of our lives, but it is ingrained in our psyches," said Dr. Peter Berczeller, a Manhattan physician. "We grow up with it being an integral part of our childhood, and we never really divest ourselves of it. I still root for the Giants—even though they've moved from New York to San Francisco. And now I see my son following the teams and players, as I did."

At least twice a year, Paul Weiss, professor of philosophy at Catholic University in Washington, and author of *Sport: A Philosophic Inquiry*, says he meets his son, Jonathan, a New York attorney, in Baltimore to take in an Orioles game. "Baseball is something we've shared for a long time," said Dr. Weiss. "It is a beautiful, graceful game and it is social in a way that football and hockey aren't. Those two sports are adventitious. It seems that beating up opponents are of as much interest to fans in those sports as the game itself; and basketball is a sport limited to the technically knowledgeable."

If there is a baseball strike, Dr. Albert Ellis says he is sure to hear about it from some of his clients. "It will disturb a few of them greatly," says Dr. Ellis, a psychologist and executive director of the Institute for Rational-Emotive Therapy. "They're devoted to it, and some of these people have a very low frustration tolerance. They'll whine and scream that there's no baseball."

There are other citizens who have a different view of baseball. "I don't have the slightest interest in the thing," says Lillian Hellman, the playwright. "Mr. Dashiell Hammett spoiled me of all sports. He was such a sports fan—a sports fiend, I should say—that he drove me crazy. He'd be listening to a baseball game and shouting about this player and that, and I'd have to leave the room. He'd holler, 'You're the only person in America who doesn't give a damn about baseball.'"

Not so. "I went to my last baseball game in 1934 in Washington," said John Kenneth Galbraith, the economist, with a chuckle. "It was between the Senators and an otherwise unspecified team. Unless I'm in Washington and unless the Senators come back to town, I don't plan on seeing another." About the possible baseball strike? "I am totally unaffected by these grievous undevelopments," he added.

Baseball doesn't always travel well and it has had its detractors overseas. In the fall of 1924 George Bernard Shaw wrote about an exhibition game in London between the Chicago White Sox and the New York Giants.

"It was as a sociologist, not as a sportsman—I cannot endure the boredom of sport—that I seized the opportunity of the London visit of the famous Chicago Sioux and the New York Apaches (I am not quite sure of the names) to witness for the first time a game of baseball," wrote Shaw. "I found that it has the greater advantage over cricket of being sooner ended."

Perhaps baseball held the kind of impenetrable mysteries for Shaw that it did for Albert Einstein. When Professor Einstein met Moe Berg, the esteemed linguist and major-league catcher, he suggested, "Mr. Berg, you teach me baseball, and I'll teach you mathematics." He paused, and added, "But I'm sure you'd learn mathematics faster than I'd learn baseball."

Such is not the case for Seymour Siwoff, president of Elias Sports Bureau, the sports statistics company. "I'd miss everything about baseball that we grew up with—from the pennant races to the batting averages," said Siwoff. "A real part of our history would be lost. Take for example the box score, it is a treasure.

"Baseball in the summer is like a journey, it's played every day," continued Siwoff. "We follow it. There'd be a great void without it. I'm sure we'd find something to take its place. The question is, what?"

Cooperstown: Village of Facts and Myths

July 2, 1989

LITTLE OF COOPERSTOWN, THAT 19th century village in upstate New York, seems real anymore, not even some of the deeds recorded in its most famous building, a handsome three-story red-brick structure on tree-lined Main Street: the Baseball Hall of Fame.

After all, who could pitch 511 winning games in a career—better than 20 victories a season for 25 seasons? Or win 41 games in a season? Or bat .367 for 24 seasons? Or drive in 190 runs in one year? Or catch a ball with that little piece of leather that resembles a stiffened lump of mud? Or hit a ball with that odd-shaped stick?

Who indeed? But it happened. And that and more will be recalled on the weekend of July 22–23 when as many of the 46 living Hall of Famers (204 are enshrined) as are physically able will make it to Cooperstown to celebrate the 50th anniversary of the diamond pantheon.

There are hard facts supplied there. But numerous tales also suffuse the town like clanking ghosts, and disputes that lend themselves to enduring debates seem to echo in the hallowed halls of the red-brick shrine.

What, for example, is Jake (Old Eagle Eye) Beckley doing deified in the Hall of Fame? Or Ray Schalk (with a career batting average of only .253, the lowest of the nonpitchers embronzed in the Hall), or Tom Yawkey, or Tinker and Evers and, well, yes, even Chance (a trio remembered more for a verse about them than their hitting records—now there's fodder for a wrangle!)?

And where are Nellie Fox and Richie Ashburn and Roger Maris? And Bill Veeck and Marvin Miller? And if Pee Wee Reese wears the spikes of immortality in there, why shouldn't Phil Rizzuto be similarly shod?

And though Shoeless Joe Jackson's scruffy baseball shoes are on exhibit in the hall (wouldn't a pair of his grass-stained socks have been more fitting?), a bust of Joe himself, because of a little matter of allegedly throwing World Series games, is not. And Pete Rose, that all-time hitting hero, is up for election in 1992. If he is found to have wagered on baseball games, and on the Reds, should there be a spot for him anyway on the wall of the hall?

All this seems the most exalted form of what constitutes possibly the most captivating part of what baseball people like to call the National Pastime: controversy. Who's better, the Thumper or DiMag? Or Mays, Mantle, or the Dook? Could Cy Young have won all those games today? Or Cobb have averaged .367? Would he have hit as well as Carew or Boggs? Was Koufax faster than Johnson or Feller, or Smoky Joe Wood when his fires were really stoked? Was Ryan even more rapid than all of the above?

Cooperstown, meanwhile, is a pastoral village (population 2,300) that seems perfect for a Hall of Fame for baseball. It is a living reminder of what used to be, an America that existed before the sprawl of large, industrial cities, and where baseball, if not invented in such a place, as legend has it, then should have been.

The most famous myth about it is the one that Abner Doubleday invented the game of baseball in 1839. The likelihood that Doubleday, the Civil War general who was born in Cooperstown, never played baseball didn't bother the mythmakers.

When in 1905 a blue-ribbon commission was appointed to look into the origins of baseball, a man named Abner Graves sent a letter to the group, and it was weighed heavily by the committee. Graves contended he was playing marbles in front of a tailor shop on Main Street on a day in 1839 when Doubleday explained the game he had invented to a bunch of boys. Much evidence says that this was hogwash. What is fact, though, is that Graves soon after was committed to an asylum.

In 1935, when Graves died in Fly Creek, New York, near Cooperstown, an old, mangled baseball was found in his truck in a farmhouse, and locals, who had already conceived of a museum for baseball in Cooperstown, jumped on the notion that that was a baseball used at the dawn of the invention—that is, in Elihu Phinney's cow pasture off of Main Street.

Among numerous unhappy facts that dispel that lovely story is the one that Doubleday in 1839 was a first-year cadet at West Point, restricted to the post.

Even the most famous member of the family that gave the town its name, the novelist James Fenimore Cooper, sometimes had major problems in dealing with facts. Mark Twain once wrote an essay, "Fenimore Cooper's Literary Offenses," in which he detailed how aspects of some of Cooper's novels, like *The Pathfinder* and *The Deerslayer*, were beyond the belief even of fictional renderings, such as the marksman "who could hunt flies with a rifle."

"Cooper's art has some defects," wrote Twain. "In one place in *Deerslayer*, and in the restricted space of two-thirds of a page, Cooper has scored 114 offenses against literary art out of a possible 115. It breaks the record."

And records, as we take the leap from deerslayers to ballplayers, is what Cooperstown is now most about.

The records of the batsmen and twirlers often make the difference in regard to elevation to this baseball heaven. It is a designation that is supposed to be the ultimate measure of skill and craftsmanship at the plate, on the mound, and around the horn.

Controversy over voting in flanneled personages has been a part of the hall ever since 1936 when the first five players were chosen—Ty Cobb, Walter Johnson, Christy Mathewson, Honus Wagner, and Babe Ruth. In the beginning, only 10-year members of the Baseball Writers of America voted for players to enter the hall. And in 1936, of 226 writers, 11 of them left Ruth off their ballots. What those loose-cannon 11 were thinking of, or whether their pens just ran out of ink, no one knows. But the Babe managed to get in anyway.

In later years, a Veterans Committee was established in order to make up for what are seen as past oversights. This year, for example, Red Schoendienst, who didn't make it via the writers' route, got apotheosized by the Veterans Committee. Carl Yastrzemski and Johnny Bench made it by way of the writers. Al Barlick, the former umpire, is the fourth inductee this year, and selected by the veterans.

Another way to make it to the Hall of Fame is by virtue of the committee on Negro Baseball Leagues. None got in this year, but two years ago Ray Dandridge, a third baseman, was honored.

"It's a credit to baseball," he said, in his acceptance speech, "that they haven't forgotten those of us who people said were born too late."

Nor should it be forgotten that one of the reasons Dandridge would enjoy this proud, teary-eyed day in the sun on the flag-draped steps of the Hall of Fame library, was because of something unexpected Ted Williams said in his induction speech in 1966:

"Baseball gives every American boy a chance to excel, not just to be as good as someone else, but better. This is the nature of the man and the name of the game, and I've been a very lucky guy to have worn a baseball uniform, to have struck out or to hit a tape-measure home run. And I hope that someday the names of Satchel Paige and Josh Gibson in some way can be added as a symbol of the great Negro players who are not here only because they were not given a chance."

A few years later, Williams, whose expressed sentiments were as admirable as his lofty batting records, saw his hopes fulfilled, and Negro League players like Paige and Gibson and Dandridge entered the hall.

For one reporter, the memory of a Hall of Fame visit during induction week was highlighted by one incident.

On the third floor, there is a life-sized cardboard cutout of Willie Mays making that famous over-the-shoulder catch in the 1954 World Series.

On the second floor, he noticed a middle-aged black man in a business suit and with a companion looking at some exhibit. The man was Willie Mays.

"Willie," said the reporter, "what are you doing here? I just saw you upstairs making a great catch."

Mays laughed. "I'm upstairs, too?" he said, in his familiar, squeaky voice. "Yeah," said the reporter. Mays continued looking at the exhibits, but a few minutes later the reporter overheard Mays say softly to his companion, "Why don't we take a look upstairs?"

Of the many legends about baseball, there's the one about a great catch, an impossible catch, a classic catch—it may have been Mays' catch—when someone in the rival dugout exclaimed, "That's the most fantastic catch I've ever seen!"

The manager beside him grunted. "Yeah," he said, "but I'd like to see him do that again."

Such a thing may or may not have ever taken place. But something like it surely did. And in the beauty of a catch of that nature, its human and yet extraordinary qualities, where it ranks in history, is at the core of the fan's interest and delight in the game. It's good for an argument. Such is baseball. Such, it follows, is the Hall of Fame.

Tom Gorman's Final Call

August 17, 1986

WHEN BRIAN GORMAN, SON of Tom Gorman, the former major-league umpire, was in grade school in Closter, New Jersey, a classmate asked Brian one day what it felt like when his father missed a call.

"I don't know," said Brian, "he's never missed one."

And that is how the offspring of baseball arbiters often go through life. Like their fathers, they know that he's always right, at least in his heart, if not specifically on the diamond.

When Tom Gorman died last Monday night, Brian still knew that his dad had never missed one.

It is an uncommon and difficult life being an umpire. In the autobiography that his father wrote with Jerome Holtzman, *Three and Two!*, published in 1979, Gorman recalled how the Hall of Fame pitcher Ed Walsh responded to umpiring. He worked at it for two months after having retired from the Chicago White Sox.

"It's a strange business," he told Billy Evans, the umpire. "All jeers and no cheers. You can have it!" And Walsh quit. But there are rewards. Brian understood from his father what satisfactions can accrue to a man who calls balls and strikes, and safes and outs, and can tell a man earning $2 million a year to go take a shower, and right now.

Brian is now an umpire in the Southern Association, with dreams of making the major leagues, and he learned to love the life of an umpire when, as a boy on summer vacation, his dad would take him for two weeks on a trip through the National League towns. His dad also took his two brothers, Tom Jr. and Kevin, and their sister, Patty Ellen. "He took us each separately, so he could give us each undivided attention," recalled Brian.

He did it before their mother died, suddenly in 1968 at age 46, and the children were then ranging in age from nine to 14. And Tom Gorman kept the household together—with help from neighbors and relatives—even as he continued clocking 100,000 miles or so in his travels as an umpire.

With the kids grown, and Gorman retired as an umpire after 27 big-league seasons—he was most recently a supervisor of umpires for the National League—he married again six weeks ago. He was 67 years old, and life seemed to hold out continued joys.

A few weeks ago, in fact, he traveled to Memphis to watch Brian work some games there, and then sat up at night with his colleagues. "He loved to talk umpiring," said Brian. "And he never gave me secret advice. If he had something to say about the techniques of umpiring, he told us all, and did it in a way that was kind of indirect. But you got the picture."

Brian recalled that three years ago, umpiring his first game, in the Class A New York–Penn League, in Oneonta, New York, he absently looked around the stands between the third and fourth innings, and there, right behind home plate, was a familiar, strong-jawed, white-haired gentleman. "He gave me a nod," said Brian, "and I gave him a nod back. I didn't know Dad was coming. He surprised me. And it didn't make me nervous at all. It felt great to see him."

When Tom Gorman would tell his kids stories of days as an umpire, he told them with delight, and with none of the pain of the jeers, the travel, the lowly days of when he was a young umpire, and the pay: in 1950 in the National League, it was $5,000 a year and he had a nail on the wall for a locker.

He told of the five no-hitters he worked behind the plate, the five World Series, and five All-Star Games, and the great games he was involved in. His favorite was the 1968 World Series opener in which Bob Gibson of the Cardinals struck out 17 Tiger batters.

"He'd correct people on that," said Brian. "He'd laugh and say, 'Gibson only struck out 10—I struck out seven.' There were seven called third strikes."

Tom Gorman recalled a time when Henry Aaron had two strikes on him and the pitcher threw a pitch right above the knees, on the outside corner. "Nobody," he wrote, "could hit a pitch like that. Nobody. And so I yelled, 'Strike three!' The next thing I knew, the ball was sailing into the seats.

"Aaron trotted around the bases and the catcher turned to me. 'Tom,' he said, 'what the hell are you doing?' 'I'm practicing, I said.'"

Brian Gorman recalls that the most important thing for an umpire is to keep control of the game. An umpire must "keep an even keel," and try to calm the irate manager or ballplayer who is arguing a call.

Sometimes, Gorman accomplished this in the oddest way. He told the story of when Leo Durocher, a nemesis of his, raced out of the Cubs' dugout to argue that he had missed a call on Don Kessinger, who was trying to beat out a hit at first base.

"How the hell can Kessinger be out?" Durocher hollered, his veins coming up his neck, his eyeballs popping.

"Leo," said Gorman, "he tagged the base with the wrong foot."

Gorman recalled that Durocher "stopped and looked at me, like I was a nut. He didn't know what to say. I had him stumped... He turned and walked away." Gorman could see Durocher, when he got back to the dugout, talking to some of his players. Gorman could tell they didn't know what he was talking about.

"The game ended an hour later. Our dressing room was behind the Cub dugout and Leo was in the runway waiting for me. As I came in, he said, 'Hey, Tom, I want to talk to you.' 'What is it, Leo?' 'How long have you been in this league?' 'Twenty years.' 'I want to tell you something, Tom,' Durocher said. 'And I'm only going to tell you once. They can tag first base with any foot.'"

Yesterday, in a cemetery in Paramus, New Jersey, Thomas David Gorman, born in Hell's Kitchen in Manhattan, was laid to rest. "When I go," he had told his children, "I want to be buried in my umpiring suit, and holding my indicator."

His wish was granted. His suit was buttoned, and his blue cap with the white letters, "NL," was at his side. In his right hand was an indicator. The numbers read "three" and "two."

No False Modesty for Henderson

May 6, 1991

RICKEY HENDERSON BECAME THE Tarzan in all of us, standing triumphantly at third base and beating his gums instead of his chest.

He had just broken the career base-stealing record, and he was not lost for words. He crowed about it right on the spot, right in front of the crowd of 36,139 fans at Oakland–Alameda County Stadium, and before television cameras that would take his sentiments to millions more later on the evening news.

Most of us attempt a little more dignity when the spotlight focuses on us for achievement. We bow, we shuffle our feet, emit an "Aw shucks," and then depart the stage. The moment we're behind the curtain, we leap nine feet in the air. "I did it, suckers!" we shout. "I damn well did it!"

In a game at Oakland last Wednesday, Henderson of the A's had just stolen the 939th base of his major-league career, a record, and the game was stopped and he was congratulated, and in his brief acceptance speech, he pronounced that "Lou Brock is the symbol of great base stealing, but today I'm the greatest of all time."

It was less than gracious, but it was a fact. He was now, in his 13th major-league season, at the pinnacle of baseball base thievery. Of course, fact does not always excuse the expression of such. You don't generally walk up to an ugly person on the street and say, "My, you're an ugly person." And it seemed inappropriate to boast in front of Lou Brock, whose record Rickey broke and who was intentionally on hand to participate in the celebration.

345

Yet there was some strange charm in Henderson's statement, some poignancy, too, and absolutely some history.

Boasting and gloating have a long and tortuous background. And did Henderson say any more than "Veni, vidi, vici"? Rickey came, Rickey saw, Rickey conquered. And Rickey, like Caesar, said so.

Boasting exists in our fairy tales: "I'll huff and I'll puff and I'll blow your house down." And it was part of everyday speech on the American frontier: "Get out of town by sundown or I'll blow your brains out."

And though a more modest-appearing ethic has often enveloped the sports hero in our culture (didn't pride goeth before the fall?), we've had exceptions, and the swagger in our sweaty stars is becoming increasingly more common.

Once Jack Johnson grinned as he knocked out opponents. Once Dizzy Dean, after his brother and teammate, Daffy, pitched a no-hitter in the second game of a doubleheader, while he had given up a few hits in winning the first game, said, "If I had known Paul was going to pitch a no-hitter, why, I'd have thrown one, too."

And before Super Bowl III, Joe Namath stated, "I guarantee we'll win," when his New York Jets of the stripling American Football League were 19-point underdogs to the Baltimore Colts of the big-daddy National Football League. Namath, though, wasn't so much boasting for himself as he was trying to boost the stock, and the morale, of his team. Many thought it was just the case of a man whistling as he walked through a dark cemetery. But when it was over, and his pledge fulfilled, Namath, in eyes raccooned with lampblack, ran off the field with his right index finger raised: We're A-No. 1, like I told ya.

And there was Muhammad Ali, who told the world that he floated like a butterfly and stung like a bee, and stated his invincibility with "They all must fall/In the round I call," and, as a harbinger to Henderson, allowed that "I am the greatest."

In retrospect, much of Ali's theatrics are considered charming, but many in his time saw Ali as little more than a big-mouthed vulgarian. Essentially, though, Ali did his dance with a humor that Henderson has not yet mastered, or even attempted.

And much of what Ali did was designed to fill up the house on fight night. He learned, as he has admitted, from the perfumed grappler Gorgeous George, a master of staging and ticket hustling.

There was another point to Ali's act, a much deeper motive, conscious or otherwise. It carried a sociological wallop. Ali came along in the 1960s and became a kind of symbol for the black revolution in America.

"Black is beautiful" was a byword in their communities. In churches and meeting halls, black children were taught to say, and to sing, "I am somebody." And to believe it.

No more shufflin'. No more grovelin'. I stand up and I proclaim: "I am somebody. I am beautiful. I hold my head high."

And that's exactly what Ali did. Today he is one of the most beloved figures in the country. When he was introduced in the ring before the recent Foreman-Holyfield heavyweight title fight in Atlantic City, he drew the longest and warmest applause.

And when the ring announcer said, "And the three-time heavyweight champ-een of the world…" Smiling but subdued, now suffering from Parkinson's syndrome, and with one hand holding the top ring rope, Ali extended four fingers with his other hand at his waist, subtly correcting the announcer, showing that he had won the title four times. And even if that fourth title was only the North American Boxing Federation title, the gesture of Ali's was, well, beautiful. Still.

Rickey Henderson standing at third base gave no hint that he had anything of more worldly, historical, or sociological significance on his mind than pure, unadulterated Rickey Henderson. But he had come a long way, farther even than his 16 miles' worth of stolen bases. He was Basic Man, Candid Man, Triumphant Man. Oh, man.

All-Star Game: Whose Game Is It, Anyway?

July 10, 1990

SOME FOLKS STARTING IN the All-Star Game tonight in Wrigley Field, by dint of the fans' ballot, are not having years nearly as fancy as others who will be riding the cushions in the dugout.

Cal Ripken Jr., for one, was hitting nearly 100 points below another American League shortstop, Ozzie Guillen, for much of the season; and Ozzie Smith, for another, will be at shortstop for the National League when either Barry Larkin or Shawon Dunston would seem a better contemporary choice.

What's Boggs starting at third for, when Gruber's having a superior season? And McGwire over Fielder at first base? No way, Jose. Or is there a way, Jose?

"We're not allowed on the field, so I think the fans should vote for the team," said Dave Taylor, a parking-lot attendant across from Wrigley Field. "It gives them a chance to express themselves. You always hear the managers and players and sportscasters talking. This gives a fan a voice, too."

"It's ridiculous for the fans to vote," said Josh Noel, a high school student. "The managers and players are the ones who know what's going on, who see the players every day, and they're the experts. They should vote."

"Who cares?" said Frank Robinson, the Orioles manager. "They're not voting for me."

Right now the fans, as long as they stay on their best behavior, are permitted to select the starting field lineups, and controversies abound.

They were bad boys and girls in 1957, at least those in Cincinnati, and seven Reds were chosen in an unbridled display of ballot-box stuffing. Seven Reds and Stan Musial. And so in 1958, the vote, as in a banana republic, was stripped from the fans because of the embarrassment they caused their baseball superiors.

In 1970, however, that benevolent despot and new commissioner of baseball, Bowie Kuhn, gave the franchise back to the paying customers, where it has resided ever since.

Fans participated in the selection of players for the first two All-Star Games, in 1933 and 1934.

But from 1935 to 1946, managers took over and picked all the players.

Then from 1947 to 1957, the voting for starters was given to the fans.

Some people subscribe to a notion, perpetuated by people who profit from baseball, that the All-Star Game is the fans' game. That is, it's a game designed strictly for the fans' pleasure. And so that's the starting team.

One wonders, meanwhile, well, aren't World Series games, or playoff games, or even the regular-season games for the fans' pleasure as well? And shouldn't fans have a say in who starts in those contests, too?

And no one gives the fans a vote on whether there should be a lockout or a strike, or whether the price for a hot dog at the ballpark should be raised a buck, or a bleacher seat should be upped by a deuce.

As for the games, they are designed, to be sure, to make money. They are a business venture in the form of a public entertainment.

And the money accrued goes to those who make baseball their livelihood.

No one in baseball says it's the fans' game, so the proceeds should go to the fans.

When the fans were re-enfranchised in 1970, it was because the feeling among baseball people was that the game was slipping in popularity; perhaps this little voting bait will help lure them back. It hasn't hurt. Barry Larkin of the Reds also believes the fans should vote. He said this even though his statistics are better than his colleague, Ozzie Smith.

"I feel that Ozzie's the man," he said. "He's been doing it for 10 years. Hey, I filled out a ballot and punched in Ozzie's name, too. So I'm as guilty as anyone."

"Over all," said Will Clark of the Giants, "I think the fans do a good job."

Tony La Russa, the manager of the American League team, said he thought the theories of Sparky Anderson and John McNamara, who would give fans a partial voice in the selection, bear consideration.

Ripken, meanwhile, said he wasn't embarrassed by his selection.

"If you look back on performance in previous years," he said, "you can make a case for me."

Who did he think should vote for the All-Star players?

"I voted when I was a kid, and I don't have any problem with the fans doing it," said Ripken, with only a slightly sheepish and self-interested smile.

Finally, one group is generally left out of discussions on who merits picking the All-Star team.

That group is the owners. And their omission is odd.

After all, it's the owners' game, isn't it?

Batgate: George Brett's Tarriest Moment

July 26, 1983

THE SMOKING GUN IN Batgate—Exhibit A—was wrapped in yellow paraffin and delivered to the American League office on the third floor of 280 Park Avenue yesterday morning.

The smoking gun is 34½ inches long and weighs 32 ounces. But it is not a gun nor does it smoke. It is a baseball bat, made of white ash. It is the now-notorious bat used by one George Howard Brett Sunday night when he hit the home run into the right-field seats at Yankee Stadium that counted for the last out of the game.

"The bat arrived in the office about 10:00, maybe a little before, I really can't pinpoint the time," said Tess Basta, a secretary in the office.

It had been due an hour earlier. When it finally came it was brought in by a man wearing jeans and a shirt, "or whatever," said Tess Basta. "Neatly dressed. I don't know his name, but he works for the Yankees."

Bob Fishel, assistant to Lee MacPhail, the league president, had been told by one of the umpires in the crew Sunday night that it would arrive at 9:00. He was also called at home by Dick Howser, manager of the Royals, and told that the Royals would appeal the game.

The league office would await the physical evidence—the bat—plus the reports from the umpires. Then MacPhail would check precedents and history and decide on whether to uphold or overturn the umpires' ruling.

As the world now knows, Brett came up in the top of the ninth with one man on and the Royals losing to the Yankees, 4–3, and hit a home run. However, Alfred Manuel Martin, the field brains behind the Yankees, rushed out and said Brett had been using an illegal bat. He claimed that the pine tar on the bat exceeded the legal limit of 18 inches from the knob.

The umpires measured it, and the plate umpire, Tim McClelland, gave the signal that upheld Martin's protest. The two-run homer was nullified, and it became the third out, and in an instant turned a lead into a loss. It also turned Brett into a rather unhappy person, and about 25 men were needed to keep him from the umpire's throat.

Fishel, in his office yesterday morning, waited about 15 minutes more for the bat and then went out for breakfast. When he came back, still no bat. Shortly after, Tess Basta informed him that it was here. Fishel came out, took the bat. and then went into his office and closed the door. He would later testify to a reporter that he took the bat out of the wrapping and checked it over.

Reporter: Were there any fingerprints on it?

Fishel: I didn't see any.

Reporter: Are there any now, after you held it?

Fishel: Not mine, I can tell you that. I held it by the ends.

Reporter: As if you were eating corn on the cob?

Fishel: Sort of, but without the margarine.

Reporter: Margarine?

Fishel: Butter's high in cholesterol.

Reporter: Yes, well, where's the bat now, Mr. Fishel?

Fishel: Got it stashed.

Reporter: In the office?

Fishel: Not saying. I don't want to sound mysterious about this, but Lee MacPhail is out of town and won't be back until tonight. I don't want anyone to see it until he does, so he can determine for himself about the appeal.

Fishel said MacPhail would probably not rule on it for "at least another 24 hours." The appeal, as he understands it, will contend that the rule was interpreted too strictly, and that the pine tar on the barrel of the bat in no way aided the distance or the direction of the ball.

"We're going to check every facet of it that we can," said Fishel. "There may have been a reason why the pine tar was up so far on the bat."

At 10:50, Murray Cook, the general manager of the Yankees, arrived in Fishel's office with a video tape of Sunday's events. Simply amicus curiae, of course. Cook, this impartial friend of the court, thought it was nonsense that the Royals had anything to appeal.

Reporter: Why?

Cook: You can't have foreign substances going all the way up the bat. Say you want to bunt, the ball would stick and aid the batter.

Reporter: But his ball didn't stick, it flew.

Cook: (Shrug, smile) Strange, isn't it?

Following up on Exhibit A, a call was placed to Hillerich & Bradsby in Louisville, makers of the Louisville Slugger. Brett's bat, said Rex Bradley, a vice president for the company, is a T-85 Marv Throneberry model.

Reporter: Marvelous Marv Throneberry? The Mets' legend, the guy who did things like hit a triple and miss both first and second base?

Bradley: One and the same.

Reporter: Why is a hitter like Brett using a Marvelous Marv bludgeon?

Bradley: I once asked George the same question. Apparently he picked it up in spring training one year, liked the feel of it, and had us make some for him. It's been about five years, I'd guess. He's used 'em ever since.

Reporter: Any distinguishing characteristics about the bat?

Bradley: There's no finish or lacquer on it. We turn it, brand it, sand it, and send it. George doesn't wear a batting glove, you know. He likes raw skin against raw wood.

The pine tar, Bradley added, is put on the bat so that Brett can touch it to get a good grip. A hitter like Brett, who doesn't get jammed regularly and often gets good wood on the ball, breaks relatively few bats. A bat may last him as long as a week. And as he touches the pine tar, the substance creeps higher on the bat.

Brett said that the bat was a particular favorite. "It's a seven-grainer," he had said.

Most bats, according to Bradley, have five grains. "Each grain or ring indicates a year's growth of a tree," he said. "We don't like to think that there's any difference in a seven- or five-grain bat. As long as the weight is evenly distributed and the rings have grown evenly, it's a good bat."

Five grains or seven grains, it has become for the league office one big migraine. Meanwhile, Bill Guilfoile of the Baseball Hall of Fame called Fishel to ask for the bat. Fishel said not until MacPhail sees it. And probably not after that, either. Someone else requested it first. He lives in Kansas City. "I want my bat back," the person said. "I like it."

Hank Aaron:
An Unusual Tribute

January 15, 1982

ON THE AFTERNOON OF April 4, 1974, a sports talk show was being taped in a television studio in Manhattan. Suddenly it was interrupted. A note had been passed to the host by a producer, and the guest, a sports reporter, waited.

"There's a bulletin," the host said, looking up from the note. "Henry Aaron has just hit a home run for the Atlanta Braves to tie Babe Ruth's career record."

A feeling of relief passed over the guest. In the last decade or so, when a program was interrupted by a news bulletin, it invariably meant that something tragic had happened.

Now it celebrated an individual triumph, one that could be achieved only by the highest dedication to sustained excellence—at that point, it was Aaron's 21st season in the big leagues.

The scope of the accomplishment went beyond the ballpark and beyond that television studio. It touched the nation, which had been following Aaron's pursuit of the record—the home-run mark was generally considered the most unreachable in team sports and was held by Ruth, the most revered American athlete in history.

It touched some negatively, to be sure. Some simply did not want to see Ruth's legendary record broken—a small but malicious number of others

355

did not want to see a black man do it. Soon, some of Aaron's mail—he was getting nearly 700 letters a day -was being screened by the F.B.I. Four days after he hit the homer that tied the record, Aaron belted the 715th of his career and broke the record that had stood for 47 years.

Last Wednesday, Henry Louis Aaron was voted into the Baseball Hall of Fame, and not solely because of that lifetime home-run record—755 by the time he retired in 1976.

"Henry," said Monte Irvin, of the baseball commissioner's office, "owns the National League record book." Not quite, but the record he holds are numerous, including, among others, most runs batted in, most total bases, and most extra-base hits.

But it is home runs No. 714 and 715 for which he will be most remembered. Ruth's record was broken by an unassuming man whose power was recognized early but whose professionalism and dignity over a period of 23 years came to be widely appreciated only gradually. "The thing about Hank," said Eddie Mathews, Aaron's onetime teammate with Milwaukee and Atlanta, and later his manager, "is that he does everything so effortlessly, so expressionlessly.

"He runs as hard as he has to, for example. His hat doesn't fly off the way Mays' does. Clemente ran, and he looked like he was falling apart at the seams. Pete Rose runs hard everywhere and dives head first. Aaron runs with the shaft let out, but you'd never know it. Yet when the smoke clears, he's standing there in the same place as the others."

His teammates, when he came up to the Milwaukee Braves in 1954, called him "Snowshoes" because of the slow way he seemed to drag his body.

But he swiftly demonstrated that he was anything but lethargic. His bat, as they say in baseball circles, was quick. "Trying to sneak a fastball past Hank Aaron," the pitcher Curt Simmons once said, "is like trying to sneak a sunrise past a rooster."

From the start, Aaron seemed to defy convention. When he entered pro baseball with the Indianapolis Clowns—a black team—as an 18-year-old out of Mobile, Alabama, his form seemed wrong: he swung with his weight on his front foot instead of the back one; he held his bat in the palms of his hands instead of in the fingers; and, oddest of all, he batted cross-handed, like someone's aunt at the family picnic.

Only the last would be changed. The rest remained—but who can account for genius. "I may have looked like I was leaning at the plate," he said, "but my bat was ready."

When the bat no longer was, when he couldn't "pick up the rotation on the curve anymore," and his eyes "began playing tricks," he retired at the age of 42.

In his last several seasons, Aaron, who had been a quiet man not prone to controversial or colorful remarks, was given a forum by the press who seemed to have discovered him at last. And Aaron did not shy away. He began to speak his heart. And what he said surprised many.

He criticized the baseball establishment, for example, for not hiring blacks in management, and he also said blacks were not getting a fair shake as players, either: "You know, we're considered super giants on the field, but when we come off the field we go to the back of the bus, again."

Aaron had great respect for Jackie Robinson. "Before Jackie died," Aaron said, "we had long talks. I will never forget that he told me to keep talking about what makes me unhappy, to keep the pressure on. Otherwise, people will think you're satisfied with the situation."

The Braves, upon his retirement, offered Aaron the job of vice president in charge of player development: "I thought I could make a contribution to the organization, and I said I'd take it, but I don't want to sit in an office and stare at the four walls. I want to make decisions." He has, and he still holds that position with the Braves.

But wherever he goes, he is still reminded of the home runs that broke Babe Ruth's seemingly unbreakable record. "The funny thing is that I never saw them," said Aaron. "Whenever I hit a home run, I'm too busy concentrating on touching first base to watch the ball." He said he developed the habit in Class C ball in Eau Claire, Wisconsin, in 1952, where he played after the Braves signed him from the Negro League.

"I was on the road to realizing my dream of making the major leagues," he said. "And when I hit my first home run there, I was so excited, I missed first base and was tagged out. From that day on, I decided if I hit the ball into the stands, I'll know about it, and then I can go into my trot."

"What Would Koufax Have Said?"

SANDY KOUFAX, AT AGE 73 in 2009, hair salt and pepper, more salt than pepper, yet looking as fit as though he still might be able to hurl a few shutout innings in a tight ballgame, wearing a Navy-blue blazer, white button-down shirt, and wine-red tie, natty in that understated but warmly appealing manner that his millions of fans surely would recognize quickly, sat for a film interview. It was for the documentary, *Jews and Baseball: An American Love Story*, for which I was the scriptwriter. The interview was conducted by Peter Miller, the director of the film, and in his apartment on the west side of Manhattan. Miller and Koufax were seated facing each other, a video camera above the shoulder of Miller and focusing on Koufax. The conversation turned to Koufax's striking out 15 New York Yankees in the first game of the 1963 World Series, a World Series record.

Yankee Stadium, that sunny October afternoon, looked immense to Koufax. "You're playing the Yankees in Yankee Stadium, which is an amazing feeling," he recalled. "The Stadium is so tall and then so close to the field, as opposed to other ballparks, it almost feels like you're at the bottom of the Grand Canyon." Whitey Ford, the Yankees' starting pitcher, "came out and struck out the side in the first inning," continued Koufax. "So I came out and struck out the side. It kind of made it feel like, Okay, the game is on…"

And so it was. Koufax began to dominate. Yogi Berra, who was coaching at first base for the Yankees, remembered feeling "lonely there." "No one was coming to see me," he recalled, because most of the Yankee batters were returning to the dugout, their bats useless against Koufax's sizzling fastball

359

and tumbling-off-a-table curveball. To say nothing of his knee-buckling change-up and control that would make pub dart-thrower envious.

I was sitting on a couch nearby, a few feet away from Koufax, and beside his wife, Jane. During a break in filming I took the opportunity to speak with Koufax.

"Sandy," I said, "are you aware of James Thurber's line that the majority of American males go to bed at night dreaming of striking out the Yankee batting order?"

"No," he said. "I hadn't heard that."

"But you did it."

He shrugged, as if to say, that's nice.

"Did you ever dream of doing anything like that?" I continued.

"No, I never have."

That response hung in the air for a moment.

"Well, Sandy" I said, "what *do* you dream about?" A throw-away line, to be sure.

He smiled. "Her," he said, pointing to Jane.

Everyone in the room laughed. Jane beamed. Koufax, not known for his prowess at the plate, had hit this one out of the park.

I tell this story because it is so revealing of Koufax, and the Jewish condition and tradition in America.

Here was a "clutch moment," of sorts—Koufax was certainly used to dealing with crises, with games on the line—and perhaps this was also a moment of indecision, and the Jewish baseball icon chose the right thing to say, and came at it from an unusual or unexpected angle, underscored with a, well, Yiddish sense of humor, as he deflected the question away from himself. One may be taken back over 6,000 years, when Jews, by brains, by innovation, by wit, by self-possession, even by, yes, muscle, sought to overcome or resolve or side-step situations, sometimes with their lives hanging in the balance—which, to say the least, wasn't quite the case with Koufax's response to my question.

At one end of the spectrum, it was nothing more than a cute, though surely sagacious, response. On the other, however, it might well be fodder for, as almost everything else, a Talmudic discussion, with an exploration of the conceivable, historical ramifications. It's a very Jewish consideration, and at this point I will leave it to Hebraic scholars to continue the discourse, if, in fact, one is to be had.

From earliest times in America Jews faced a preponderance of obstacles amid strivings, from when Jews made their first attempt to settle these shores in the 17th century (initially barred from entry by Peter Stuyvesant, the antisemitic governor of New Amsterdam, later called New York, who referred to Jews as "a repugnant race") to their various travails in Columbus' Land, as immigrants were wont to refer to America, to their entrance into, and discovery, as it were, of the world of baseball. The National Pastime would take a passionate hold among newly arrived Jewish citizens and, surely, their off-spring, a hold that continues to the present day. It was to this notion that the esteemed scholar and author Jacque Barzun, French-born but an Americanized citizen, wrote in 1954, "Whoever wants to know the heart and mind of America had better learn baseball."

Mark Twain had a similar take when, in 1890, he commented that baseball had become "the very symbol, the outward and visible expression of the drive and push and rush and struggle of the raging, tearing, booming 19th century." Bart Giamatti, the late commissioner of baseball, echoed both earlier writers in 1998, when he stated that in the early part of the 20th century, "baseball became business as Business and wealth and population boomed across the country, as millions of immigrants poured in, as the tempo of life quickened and the country flexed its muscles. Baseball, increasingly played with increased skill, caught the mood of America and rode it…for the immigrant, the game was a club to belong to, another fraternal organization, a common language in a strange land. For so much of expanding and expansive America, the game was a free institution with something for everyone."

Jews, as well as other new arrivals from all over Europe, blacks, and Hispanics and Asians, found that there was significant truth to baseball opening doors to feeling American. For example, in the 1920s Jews flocked to the Polo Grounds to see the rookie second baseman Andy Cohen play for the New York Giants while Italians cheered Yankee second baseman Tony

Lazzeri, one of the first Italian star major-leaguers, calling from the stands, "Poosh 'em up, Tony" in the hope that their Italian hero would advance the runners whenever he came to bat. Growing up in Chicago, I remember going to Wrigley Field with my father in 1948 to see the Cubs play the Brooklyn Dodgers. I remember the great block of Negroes (as blacks were generally referred to in those days) all sitting together in the right-field grandstands (and nowhere else in the stadium), attired in their Sunday-best suits and dresses and hats, and heartily, if politely, cheering for Jackie Robinson.

The prejudice and ignorance that Robinson had to confront when he broke the 70-year-long color barrier in the majors leagues has been well documented. Some 15 years after Robinson had established himself as one of baseball's greatest players, I interviewed Dixie Walker, then spring training batting coach for the Dodgers. Walker, a Southerner from Alabama, had been a teammate of Robinson's and outspoken in the beginning about his aversion to playing with a black man. "Not only did some of us feel that a Negro was inferior to a white, but we thought they couldn't take the pressure, that they didn't have ice water in their veins," said Walker. "It didn't take long for Jackie, and a lot of the others—Mays, Aaron, Newcombe—to prove us totally wrong."

As a sportswriter, I remember the intense interest and pride that Latinos took in the success, for example, of the future Hall of Fame Pittsburgh Pirate outfielder Roberto Clemente, who became one of Puerto Rico's most revered native citizens. Cubans have exulted in fellow countrymen who succeeded in the major leagues like Tony Oliva, Minnie Minoso, and Aroldis Chapman. And Dominicans have had hundreds of players to cheer for, among them Juan Marichal, and the brothers Jesus, Matty, and Moises Alou. Venezuelans go back to White Sox shortstops Chico Carrasquel and Hall of Famer Luis Aparicio, Mexico to Fernando Valenzuela and Sergio Romo, and Panama to Rod Carew and Mariano Rivera.

I remember the remarkable flock of Japanese reporters crowding into the press box to send back transmissions to fans in Japan hungry for information about their countrymen who has joined the major leagues, from pitcher Hideo Nomo to catcher Kenji Johjima to infielder Kazuo Matsui to outfielders Hideki Matsui and Ichiro Suzuki. Pretty much the same held for the South Korean major-leaguers, like outfielder Shin-Soo Choo and pitcher Chan Ho Park, and the Taiwanese, including pitcher Chien-Ming Wang and infielder Chin-Lung Hu.

On Opening Day 2013, 241 players, or 28.2 percent, of those on major-league rosters were born outside the 50 United States, representing 15 countries or territories, including two from the most distant country, Australia, Arizona Diamondback pitchers Grant Balfour and Travis Blackley. Rugby and cricket are the major sports in Australia, but both Balfour and Blackley discovered the game as young boys, and took to its "complexity," as Balfour described it. Baseball has been in Australia since 1850, when American gold miners first brought the game over, but it never truly gained widespread popularity. But some two dozen Aussies have indeed found their way to the big leagues, including Sydney-born Trent Oetjien, who had played outfield for the California Angels. He said that growing up he was intrigued by the "faster pace of baseball." "Cricket's a little slow, and it can take a couple of days to complete a match," he said. "I wasn't too into that."

Baseball, to be sure, had an even longer history than that played by those American minors in Australia. Fact is, no one knows exactly when or where baseball began—most likely in the 18th century with a version of it in England, called One O'Cat, or Rounders, though it would hardly be recognized in the American ballparks today. But by the middle of the 19th century baseball was emerging as the most popular sport in America, played in sandlots in the country and empty lots in the city. America was made up of people from every other place on earth. And as each new group arrived, they too found baseball.

By the end of the Civil War, the Jewish population in America was a quarter of a million, one-half of 1 percent of the nation. One of the first players to receive money for playing baseball—$20 from the Philadelphia Athletics in 1866—was a Jew of Dutch origin, the outfielder Lipman Emanuel Pike. When the first professional baseball league was organized in 1871, the National Association of Professional Baseball Players, Lipman

Pike was its star. He led the league in home runs the first three years of its existence, hitting as many as six home runs in a season.

When Barry Bonds became the all-time leader in career home runs in 2007, I was charmed to come across a timetable of big-league career home-run leaders. Bonds broke Henry Aaron's record of 755, Aaron broke Babe Ruth's record (714), and down it went to the very bottom, to the first career home-run leader, Lipman Emanuel Pike, known as "Iron Batter" for his stunning ability at the plate. Pike hit a total of 20 home runs in his 16-year career, a seemingly low number, but baseball was different in those days, the ball softer, the outfield stands more distant, a variety of pitches he saw like the spitball that are disallowed today, yet he still sent more baseballs soaring over the fences than any of his contemporaries.

It has not been recorded, to my knowledge, whether Pike endured anti-semitic treatment. He was respected enough to be named a player-manager, for the Troy (New York) Haymakers, the first Jew to become a professional baseball manager. Still, it is instructive to know that big-league players in the early part of the 20th century (some with very short careers, if only a handful of games, and others that played for a number of years) such as the 5-foot-4, 145-pound St. Louis Cardinals shortstop Reuben Ewing (born in Odessa, Ukraine), Philadelphia Phillies pitcher Harry "Klondike" Kane, Chicago White Sox pitcher Ed Corey, Cincinnati Reds star infielder Sam Bohne, and Yankees third baseman Phil Cooney all decided to change their names when they entered professional baseball. Each one of them, it happens, was born "Cohen" or "Cohn." At the time that Harry Kane made his debut in the major leagues, on August 8, 1902, a story in the *Sporting News* noted, "His name is Cohen and he assumed that of Kane, when he became a semi-professional, because he fancied that there was a popular and professional prejudice against Hebrews as ballplayers."

One who did not change his name was second baseman Andy Cohen, who came up to the New York Giants in 1926. He once told me of a minor-league game in which he was being berated by a fan who loudly called him "Christ killer." Finally, Cohen had his fill of it. He went to the edge of the stands and, bat in hand, shouted, "Come down here and I'll kill you, too!"

Another time, he made a very good catch in the field. A fan in the stands shouted, "Just like all you Jews—you'll take anything you can get your hands on." Cohen said, "I didn't mind that so much. It was actually a back-handed compliment."

Despite the increased assimilation of Jews in America, primarily after the Second World War—glass ceilings were removed in corporations, quotas permitting only a certain number of Jews in colleges, including several in the Ivy League, were exposed and eliminated, housing and country club restrictions were eased somewhat—some Jew-baiting and discrimination in and around baseball still existed.

A young Navy ensign, fresh from battle in the South Pacific, returned to the States following the war and embarked on a baseball career, and two years later, in 1947, at age 23, made it to the major leagues as a third baseman with the Cleveland Indians (though he did not stick with the big club until two years later, eventually becoming a four-time American League All-Star, unanimous league Most Valuable Player in 1953, and one of the best sluggers in baseball during his 10 seasons). This was Albert (Al) Leonard Rosen, who grew up in Miami, but in a mixed area and from the time he was a small boy felt, and/or was made to feel, intensely about his Jewishness. So much so that, he said, "there were times I considered changing my name to sound even more Jewish—a name maybe like Rosenthal or Rosenstein."

"Being a Jew in the limelight is a heavy burden," Rosen said, "to be someone that your community, your friends, your associates look up to unwaveringly. When I was a baseball player, I always felt like I wanted to be the Jew that all other Jews could be proud of. I knew the newspapers wrote about what I did and didn't do not only on the field, but off the field as well. And I just felt that it was very important to the Jews that were following my career—even the Jews who didn't know anything about baseball but were proud of their heritage—to have someone they could be proud of."

Hank Greenberg, who would become the first Jewish baseball superstar, first came up to the major leagues nearly two decades before Rosen, with the Detroit Tigers. It was 1930, the nation was in the throes of the Great

Depression, and antisemitism was rife in America and, with the rise of Adolph Hitler, would grow to unimaginably tragic proportions in Europe.

Greenberg was named the American League's Most Valuable Player in 1935. He was continually being sought for appearances, dinners, and other events by the Detroit Jewish community. The child of Orthodox parents, he had grown up in the Bronx, where he sought to be "a good baseball player, not a good Jewish baseball player." He tried to shrug off that burden—an added burden, as he saw and felt it. "While I was very aware not to do anything that would embarrass the Jewish people," he once told me, "it was still hard enough trying to hit a major-league fastball without thinking that the Jewish community was looking over my shoulder."

That changed by 1938, when he pursued Babe Ruth's hallowed record of 60 home runs in a single season. As he was belting home runs 52, 53. 54, 55, he said he was acutely aware of the plight of Jews in Europe. "As time went by, I came to feel that if I, as a Jew, hit a home run, I was hitting one against Hitler," he said. With five games to go in the season, Greenberg had 58 home runs. He did not hit another, though he got several hits and some long outs and foul balls. He was walked a handful of times, but no more than any other slugger of his caliber. It is widely thought by conspiracy theorists that the opposing pitchers did not want a Jew to break Babe Ruth's record, so they pitched around him—"didn't give him anything to hit."

Greenberg, who died in 1986 at age 75, disputed that supposition. "I had enough chances," he said, "I just didn't do it." The facts, as I understand them, bear that out. One example Greenberg liked to tell was his 57th home run, against the St. Louis Browns. He had hit a ball over the center fielder's head, and it bounced against the wall and rolled back toward the infield. Greenberg, not a speedy runner, thought he could get an inside-the-park home run. The third-base coach tried to hold him up, but Greenberg ignored him, thinking he could beat the relay. The throw came in to the catcher and, recalled Greenberg, "I was out by a mile." However, the home-plate umpire, an Irishman named Bill McGowan ("my good friend," said Greenberg), called him safe. The Browns' catcher leaped up and protested. To no avail. Home run No. 57 was entered into the record book.

"Hank Greenberg was the perfect standard bearer for Jews," Shirley Povich, a Jew and the great sports columnist for the *Washington Post*, said. "He was smart, he was proud—and he was *big.*"

Yet both Greenberg and Rosen battled antisemitism in their time—even engaging in fist fights with other players over insulting remarks (Rosen, in fact, was quite handy with his fists, having been a Golden Gloves middleweight champion while still in high school)—while Koufax, who came along several years after Greenberg and overlapped with Rosen only briefly, said he experienced no antisemitism that he was aware of.

However, Ike Davis, the New York Mets first baseman, had a stunning though different awakening into his Jewish identity. Putting together a family tree while in high school in Scottsdale, Arizona, Davis discovered that many of the relatives on his mother's side had perished in the Holocaust (his mother—the former Millie Gollinger—is Jewish while his father, Ron, a former major-league pitcher, is Baptist). Davis consulted his great aunt, who survived the Holocaust, and she told him of the horrors members of his family endured during Hitler's regime. "That's when I realized how brutal it was and how many people were killed," Davis said. His grandfather on his father's side landed in France on D-Day in 1944 and later helped liberate one of the concentration camps. Davis said that his grandfather's experience in Europe made it easier for him to accept the Jewish girl that his son brought home, and would become his wife, and eventually Ike's mother.

Davis has not asked to be a representative for Jewish causes but understands that, particularly in New York City and its expansive Jewish population, he is held up as one who carries the torch of the heritage.

"But I'm not trying to be a role model for any religious reasons," he told Dave Waldstein of *The New York Times*, "I'm trying to be a role model, period, for everyone, by just being a good person, a responsible person who leads the best life he can. That's for everyone, I think."

Rarely has a Jewish baseball player been involved in a controversy that puts him in a negative light, but that happened during the 2013 season, when Ryan Braun, the star outfielder for the Milwaukee Brewers, admitted to taking performance-enhancing drugs during the 2011 season, when he was named the National League's Most Valuable Player.

"I was shocked and deeply disappointed by those revelations," said the 89-year-old Al Rosen, by telephone from his home in Rancho Mirage, California. "Ryan Braun was this clean-cut, impressive young man, and had a reputation comparable to, say, Derek Jeter. Braun is a special kind of athlete, and if you're a Jew in that category, you have two kinds of people following you—those who admire you and want you to succeed, and those who want you to fall on your face because of who you are. As a Jew, I especially follow the progress of Jewish ballplayers. And I revel in their success, as I reveled in Ryan Braun's. He's a tremendous player, but he broke the rules of the game. Being a Jewish athlete is a kind of calling. Imagine, you've reached a level that only a very few reach, and so many wish they could. So I think you have an added responsibility."

Jews take satisfaction not only in the legitimate achievements of Jewish baseball players on the field, but also, in certain cases, their erudition. These are, after all, the People of the Book. Perhaps the most learned of the 21st century Jewish major-leaguers is Craig Breslow, a Yale graduate with a bachelor's degree in molecular biophysics and biochemistry. Breslow, a left-handed pitcher for the Boston Red Sox (in 2013) had been admitted to the New York University School of Medicine several years ago, but deferred acceptance because of his "love of the game." In 2010 the *Sporting News* named Breslow the "smartest athlete in sports," topping a list of 20. He was brought up in Trumbull, Connecticut, with a sense of Jewishness by his parents, Abe and Anne Breslow, both teachers. "Being Jewish is more difficult in baseball...but I try to do what I can in terms of paying attention to holidays," he said. While Breslow has pitched on Yom Kippur, he said, however, that "I was also fasting." Breslow has traveled extensively in the big leagues since his 2005 debut—San Diego 2005, Red Sox 2006, Cleveland Indians 2008, Minnesota Twins 2008–09, Oakland Athletics 2009–2011, Arizona Diamondbacks 2012, and back to Boston. Breslow's journeys illustrates that regardless of impressive brain matter and a 92-mile-an-hour fastball, making it in the major leagues is still a tough go.

In this regard, there has been no one like the inscrutable Morris (Moe) Berg, spy, scholar, catcher. In the baseball press boxes at Shea Stadium and Yankee Stadium in the late 1960s and early 1970s, a man wearing a black suit, a black tie, black shoes—the ensemble never varied—with black hair and a touch of gray at the temples, black eyebrows rather closely knit, and a warm smile, an elegant demeanor, a high intelligence, and an air of mystery was often perceived, and even fostered by him. I would often sit with him, and listen to his insights to the goings-on on the ballfield in front of us, and his stories of long ago.

This was Moe Berg. He was a baseball player whose 17 years in the major leagues with the Dodgers, Indians, Senators, White Sox, and Red Sox produced a lifetime batting average of .243 with 11 stolen bases and six home runs. He was, wrote Terry Hauser in a letter to me, "unmatched for marginality."

Berg, who died at age 70 in 1972, had extended his big-league playing career because managers liked having him around for his wisdom. He knew the pitchers and could help the hitters. On occasion he could knock a pitch off the left-field wall. Berg, the son of immigrant Jewish parents from the Ukraine, graduated from Princeton University, where he had been a star shortstop and magna cum laude with a major in languages. He was a graduate of the Sorbonne, and he passed the law bar at Columbia University while a starting catcher for the White Sox in 1929. Two anecdotes about Berg have met the test of time: "Moe could speak 12 languages but couldn't hit in any of them" and, kidded by other players, including Hank Greenberg, "Moe, you have seven college degrees but you always call the wrong pitch."

Moe told me of the time he returned to Princeton and requested to meet with Albert Einstein, then an esteemed faculty member of the Institute for Advanced Study at the university. They met at Einstein's residence on campus, had tea in a glass, and the professor played the violin for Berg. At one point, Einstein said to his guest, "You teach me baseball and I'll teach you the theory of relativity." But, Moe added, "Dr. Einstein said, "We'd better forget it. You will learn mathematics faster than I would learn baseball."

And he was a spy. While on tour with an All-Star team to Japan in 1934 (Moe was brought along with Babe Ruth and others as an interpreter) he disguised himself in a kimono (black, of course) and from rooftops snapped photos of industrial plants in Tokyo that were supposedly helpful to American bombing missions during World War II. It was also said that Berg, working with the OSS (Office of Strategic Services), a precursor to the CIA, was sent to Zurich in December 1944 to attend a conference at which it was thought that Germany's leading scientist, Werner Heisenberg, might indicate that the Nazis had a devastating weapon, perhaps the atomic bomb. If so, Berg, who was fluent in German, had instructions to assassinate Heisenberg on the spot. The scientist revealed no such new weapon, and Berg, as the story goes, spared his life.

"Moe," I asked him, "is the story true?" In his customary fashion, he put his finger to his lips, "Shhh," he said, even some 25 years after the alleged fact.

I once asked Moe if he had ever written for publication. "Only once," he said. "A treatise on Sanskrit."

One day shortly after I was browsing in a second-hand bookstore and ran across an old collection of *Atlantic Monthly* articles, and one, written in1940, was entitled "Pitchers and Catchers." The author was Moe Berg.

The piece was all Moe, smart, insightful, and fun. Such as: "At first, the super-speed of Grove obviated the necessity of pitching brains. But, when hissed began to fade, Lefty turned to his head. With almost perfect control and the addition of his fork ball, Lefty fools the hitter with his cunning. With Montaigne, we conceive of Socrates in place of Alexander, of brain for brawn, wit for whip…"

When I next saw Berg at the ballpark, I said, somewhat perplexed, "Moe, you told me you never wrote for publication." And I produced the book.

He looked at it, looked at me, and smiled.

"You caught me," he said.

This piece began with an anecdote about Sandy Koufax, and it seems fitting to end it with one that may say something about how being Jewish shaped his identity. The fact that Koufax did not pitch on Yom Kippur, which happened to fall on the first day of the 1965 World Series, was a matter of pride for the Jews across the country. "I had always taken Yom Kippur off, and felt I should do the same, even if it was the World Series," Koufax said. Koufax pitched Game 2 against the Minnesota Twins, lost, then won Game 5 and returned with just two days' rest to pitch a three-hit shutout, 2–0, to give the Dodgers the World Series victory.

I had heard an anecdote about that Series and wondered about its veracity. Don Drysdale, the other ace on the Dodger pitching staff along with Koufax, started Game 1 and was removed by manager Walt Alston in the second inning in the midst of a six-run scoring outburst by the Twins. One day in the 1980s, when Drysdale was a broadcaster, I ran into him and asked if the story was true. "Yes," he said. "When Alston came to the mound to take me out of the game, I handed him the ball and said, 'I know what you're thinking, Skip. You're wishing I was a Jew too.'"

I think we should go with the way Drysdale told it to me.

This is not the only example, to be sure, of how Jews have often succeeded in America and in the National Pastime, but few, from where I sit, are funnier.

Wrigley Field: The Boy, the Man, and the Ballpark

ONE BRIGHT BLUE AND gold summer morning in 1971 I stood behind the batting cage in Wrigley Field in Chicago in my official capacity as a 31-year-old sportswriter while the Cubs in their home white uniforms took batting practice. I was wearing a sport jacket, sunglasses, and wielding a notebook and pen. It was all a disguise: I was faking it, for I was again 11 years old and I knew that at any moment one of those dreaded blue-uniformed ushers with epaulettes and a cop's hat and scuffed black shoes would escort me out of there by the scruff of the collar.

The latter had been a scene played out numerous times in my childhood growing up on the West and North Sides of the city, when my friends and I would sneak into the ballpark (when workers' eyes were elsewhere we'd slip through the vendor's gate, or slide down an ice-laden chute that stuck out like a long tongue from a beer truck through a ground-floor window, or scale a turnstile, or blend angelically into a church group getting off a bus) and, once in, sneak down to the box seats at game time. We might be in those seats for an inning or so when—oh, oh, here he comes! "You kids got tickets for them there seats?!"

That summer morning in 1971 was among my early experiences of being in Wrigley Field as a professional journalist, and one in which, gratefully, an usher didn't suddenly appear to check my non-existent ticket stub. I had carefully tucked in my pocket my baseball writer's pass—I was then writing for Newspaper Enterprise Association, a feature syndicate based in New York, where I now lived—and I was official. I stood there taking in the beautiful old ballpark—from the sweep of the double-decker stands, to the team pennants of the major-league teams flying, like the lists at Camelot, on the rooftop circling the stands and on the great, green-and-white, hand-operated scoreboard above the bleachers in center field, to the lush ivy-covered outfield walls to the striking red-brick low wall that separated the box seats from the emerald ballfield that, now, nearly sparkled in the sunlight.

Growing up, I was hardly aware of how special the park was—it was then just a place to try to find a way to see a major-league ballgame free; but it is a park that would get earn Landmark status—any changes in it would have to be approved by the City Council!—and Wrigley Field would be known widely as one of the most extraordinary sports stadiums in the world, renowned by architects, landscapers, and laymen alike for its aesthetic design, its graceful symmetry, its pure beauty. ("What I've always loved about Wrigley Field," said the noted Chicago architect Sheldon Schlegman, "is its intimacy. Anywhere you sit in the park—the bleachers, the grandstands, anywhere—you feel you're close to the field, which adheres to when it was built, when ballparks were constructed on a small scale. And it's nestled in a real neighborhood, in the middle of small homes and apartment buildings, not in some suburb with a sea of parking around it. It has retained its century-old charm; it's a magical place."

And while the Cubs, who have played in the ballpark continuously since 1916 (the park was built in 1914 for a Federal League team that became, like the league, defunct), had not been in a World Series in my memory (I was five and no sports fan in 1945, the last time such a cataclysmic event occurred for the Cubs), and had not *won* a World Series since 1908 ("Well," said the ebullient former Cubs broadcaster Jack Brickhouse, "anyone can have a bad century"), I still followed them with unwavering, if often despairing, interest.

In fact, from 1947—the awakening of my baseball consciousness—to 1966, the Cubs established the unenviable record of finishing in the second division (that is, in the bottom four of the then eight-team National League—and in the bottom five of the expanded 10-team league in '66)

for 20 consecutive seasons, and generally finding themselves in the basement for many of those years.

One may wonder what harm following a team that invariably losses
could do to the psyche, but in looking back I'd like to think it provided a
dollop of reality, for as Shakespeare (perhaps a typical Cubs fan if he were
to re-appear after some 400 years) noted, "As flies to wanton boys are we
to the gods; they kill us for their sport."

Of course, the mass of Cub fans had not been done in, as far as I can
tell, but they've had to deal with the incessant vagaries and vicissitudes
of an unpredictable world. Even, in later years, when the Cubs looked
like they were going to triumph in the playoffs, teetering on the verge of
elevating to a World Series, some untoward bolt from the heavens seemed
to ultimately stymie them. And "Wait," cries the ever optimistic Cubbie
follower, "'til next year." "Or," cries the ever pessimistic Cub follower, "the
year after!"

When I was a boy in the 1940s I was aware that the Cubs had won 16
pennants, going back to 1876, their charter year in the National League.
And I was aware of the Yankees making their move to top that record.
When the Yankees won their 15th pennant in 1949, I was hoping that that
would be the end of their string, and maybe the Cubs could add one or
two in the coming years. The latter, of course, didn't happen. And the
Yankees won number 16 in 1949 and 17 in 1950. To add insult to injury,
they went on to win in '51, '52, '53, '55, '56, '57, '58, 60, '61, '62, '63
'64—each of those early succeeding seasons was a twist of the knife in the
Cub fan's heart. After a while, one stopped paying attention. The cold fact
is, however, that after the 2010 season, the number of Yankee pennants
won had risen to 40. And the ruthless—with or without Ruth—Yankees
captured their 27th World Series. The Cubs, meanwhile, were still stuck
at just a pair of World Series championships.

George Will, the inveterate Cub fan, Illinoisan, and conservative political Washington columnist, had written: "Liberals are temperamentally
inclined to see the world as a harmonious carnival of sweetness and light,
where good will prevails...Conservatives (and Cub fans) know better.

Conservatives know that the world is a dark and forbidding place where most knowledge is false, most improvements are for the worse…and that an unscrupulous Providence consigns innocents to suffer."

I read this in the early 1970s, and quoted this, and a Cub fan living on Long Island, disagreed with Will in a letter: "The central tenet of liberalism is the perfectability of man…that society will be improved, that tomorrow will be better, that progress is inevitable…Only if you believe that can you be a Cub fan."

Whichever side one comes down on, it is irrefutable that, win or lose, fans from all over the country travel to "The Friendly Confines," as Ernie Banks, one of the greatest of Cubs ("Mr. Cub" as he came to be known) had called Wrigley Field, to watch and cheer. The now 41,000-plus seating capacity is almost always filled, with added standing-room-only adherents, many of whom from coast to coast had become fans when WGN became the first television super-station, in 1978, and broadcast Cub games via satellite. Until night arc lights were installed in the ballpark in 1988, Cub games were sometimes the only form of sports entertainment on television during weekday afternoons from Maine to California. And since most of the Cub games are still played in daytime, many viewers around the nation remain or become Cub fans.

The adage "No cheering in the press box" is, generally, firmly embraced by the sportswriters. That is, you're a journalist first, a fan far, far distant, if at all. If you're going to write fairly and objectivity, as is the goal of most serious professionals, then you don't allow—or, surely, shouldn't allow—prejudices to cloud your observations. Covering a game should be like covering a fire, or a political event, or a PTA meeting. Write what's there, not what you wish were there. And for all these years, while my heart said "Cubs," my head said, "Everyone gets their proper due." In the end, I tried to remember and hoped it pertained to me what the great essayist E.B. White once wrote: "All writing slants the way a writer leans, and no man is born perpendicular, although many men are born upright." Yet inevitably I kept a sly, if jaundiced, eye on the intrigues of the Cubs. How could I not?

While I was standing behind the batting cage that long-ago morning and with the hitters going through their paces, jumping in and out of the cage to take their hacks, crack of the bat after crack of the bat echoing in the park, a ball that a hitter let pass from the batting practice pitcher rolled under the netting of the cage and at my feet. I picked it up.

The ball was still white but stained in spots brown and green, from the several times it was slugged and bounced in the dirt and hopped in the grass. The red stitching stood out almost sensually to my touch. For some unaccountable reason I smelled it. Pungent to the core. There is a distinct muskiness to the tanned horsehide of a baseball. Smell being one of the greatest mnemonic devices, it was easy to be transported several yards into the milling stands and 20 years away to the moment when I obtained my first big-league baseball.

Strange how tight a grip baseball has on one's boyhood, or perhaps even girlhood, though I feel I can speak with more authority to the former. Even now, with basketball and soccer, particularly, growing in popularity for kids, baseball remains a powerful force of imagery and aspiration for young people. You can see them still flock to the ballparks, and there is no dearth of pitchers and catchers and shortstops in the youth leagues and high school teams. Posters of home-run hitters and strikeout aces still cover the bedroom walls of the starry-eyed.

In recent years, the influx and interest of girls and women in baseball and softball has added millions to this panoply. Among the fans on a given day, or night, at Wrigley Field, the males might even be outnumbered by the females, dressed in bikini tops or furs, depending on the way the desultory wind is blowing to or from nearby Lake Michigan. From an upper-deck seat on a clear day—beyond the three-story apartment buildings with roof seating for games across from the park on Waveland and Sheffield avenues and, farther in the distance, the high-rise buildings along Lake Shore Drive—the great shimmering lake plied by sail boats may come into view.

Baseball fan and insightful humor writer James Thurber had declared that "the majority of American males go to sleep at night dreaming of striking out the Yankee batting order."

That wasn't one of my dreams—altogether. Growing up in Chicago, I had other notions, of hitting a baseball over the ivy-covered walls of Wrigley Field and onto the adjoining Waveland Avenue (or busting one into the right-center-field alley in the South Side Comiskey Park—but the more austere White Sox park never held for me the allure that "Tthe Friendly Confines" did). Of course, I felt certain that if called upon I could perform double duty and stride in from the bullpen and strike out the batting order of the Yankees. (My dream included a Cubs-Yankees World Series, a very far-fetched idea, to be sure, yet the two teams actually played in the World Series in 1932 and again in 1938—the latter was the Cubs' second-to-last appearance in the so-called Fall Classic—with the vexatious Bronx Bombers winning in both in forlorn four-game sweeps.)

I didn't become a major-league ballplayer, though I've spent close to half a century on major-league ballfields—*before* the game. I became a sportswriter and sports columnist, and when the batting cage was rolled away and the game began I repaired to the press box. I had no problem with this, no lingering regrets. Major-league ballplaying was for other people. They had their skills, and I, I'd like to believe, had mine.

Even before the conclusion of my Sullivan High School baseball career, which had its ever-so-brief moments of actually muddling through, I had gone beyond, as the Bard said, "My salad days, when I was green in judgment." My judgment seemed to gradually improve as I advanced in age—trying to hit the darting curveball (as well as endeavoring to throw one) helped considerably in this regard. And it gave me added appreciation and respect for the special skills of those I would cover as a writer.

But on that summer day in 1971, I cradled the ball in my hand and recalled that other summer day, in 1951. The day before, my friends and I had fought in the autograph jungle under the cool stands as our Cub paragons of those days—Andy Pafko, Hank Sauer, Phil Cavarretta, Roy Smalley, Dutch Leonard, Twig Terwilliger, Handsome Ransom Jackson, and the ambidextrous Native American pitcher with the improbable name that we all memorized and loved to roll off our tongues, Calvin Coolidge Julius Caesar Tuskahoma McLish, nicknamed, unaccountably, "Buster." It was a team that would wind up in eighth place, once again, but they were big-leaguers, and our heroes. They emerged like gods from the clubhouse, big and self-assured and leathery-tanned and hair-slicked and redolent of Wildroot cream oil. Last in the National League, but first in our hearts.

Roy Johnson, whom everyone called "Hardrock," appeared. He was a tough-looking, craggy-faced coach, but pigeon-toed, which gave away the humor under his gruff veneer. He was in a hurry, he said, and had no time to sign. I continued in hot pursuit. Maybe he'd change his mind. No, no, he persisted. In desperation he said, "Come to the park tomorrow, kid, and I'll give you a ball," slamming his car door a millimeter from my nose.

I believed him. My friends were much too sophisticated. He was just givin' you the slip, Dope. It was not all that easy to fall asleep that night, hardly able to wait for the first crack of dawn through the window shade.

Armed with my lunch—with the usual soft fruit my mother packed carving a soggy hole in the bottom of the brown paper bag—I was off to Wrigley Field with my friends. They poked little jokes, even up to the time I left them in the grandstands (the stealthy assault on the box seats would come later). I ran down through the shadowy stands as the park began to fill, past vendors hawking peanuts, past the steamy hot dogs broiling succulently on portable grills.

I descended to the short, red-brick barrier along the first-base line. Straight out, maybe 10 yards away, was No. 42, Hardrock Johnson, whacking fungoes into the bright blue sky. I watched a baseball drop through the clouds, down past the Baby Ruth billboard on the building across the street, get lost momentarily in the white shirts in the sun-splashed bleachers, and finally disappear silently into the dark outstretched glove of a fielder in front of the flora on the outfield wall.

"Mr. Hardrock, sir," I called through cupped hands. No answer. I called again: "You promised me a ball yesterday, Mr. Hardrock, sir."

Whack went another soaring fungo. "Just a dirty old ball, Mr. Hardrock," I pleaded. The few adults seated nearby tittered.

I'm not certain how long I kept this up, several minutes, probably. Soon there was the predictable yank at the collar. I was explaining the situation to the grim usher when there arose this great, throaty rumble: "Hey, kid!" I turned, and Hardrock Johnson tossed me a ball in a long, underhand motion. Up the stairs I flew.

My several pals all wanted to see the ball—slightly smudged but who cared!—and I showed my possession to them. One by one—with me holding the ball tightly. That finished, the ball created an uncomfortable but wholly welcome—and secure—bulge in the right front pocket of my jeans. Home, I fondled the hard ball with the bumpy seams. I inspected the dirt and grass stains closely, the Spalding trademark in a small drawn baseball, the stars etched alongside, "Official Ball, National League," and the signature of Ford C. Frick, the league president. I smelled the intoxicating horse-hide aroma of the ball—a scent that had not changed 20 years later, and that has not changed in 100 years.

My friends offered numerous suggestions to get the ball clean as new. The one that sold me was to put it in milk. I immersed the ball in a large bowl of milk for two days, periodically coming by and rolling it around with my finger to make sure no patch was left unmilked.

When I finally removed the ball, it had turned a sickly yellow. I mounted the ball on a shelf in my bedroom, for a while. But eventually I took it to play with in nearby, narrow Independence Park. Soon, one end came unstitched and grew a flappy tongue and, in time, the whole cover came off and the ball was reduced to a sphere of string. I taped it up and we played with a little while longer, then it seemed to just disintegrate into nothingness.

At the batting cage now, I felt the red ridges against the smooth, off-white horsehide. It was a ball that had been pretty well pummeled, a ball that I knew would soon be discarded into a garbage can. But not by me. I slowly tossed the ball in the air a couple of times, smelled it again. Then

I casually squeezed the ball into the pocket of my slacks, and went up to the press box…

There is an addendum to this particular Wrigley Field story:

In early April, 1986, I read a short obituary in the *Sporting News* that Roy (Hardrock) Johnson, at age 90 and living in a nursing home in Scottsdale, Arizona, had died. I admit it—this hard-boiled sportswriter grew emotional as he read the news. And my thoughts inevitably returned to that summer morning when I was 11 years old and begged Hardrock Johnson to make good on his promise to give me a baseball—and he did!

The obituary related that, after his coaching career with the Cubs, Johnson had become a scout for the team in the Southwest. I called around and got the phone number of his wife, Fanetta. She was 86 and her voice sounded clear over the long-distance wires from Scottsdale to Manhattan.

"Some people called him 'Hardrock' because he used to work the pitchers so hard as a coach," she said, "but most people called him 'Grumpy,' including me and our daughter and even our grandchildren. But living with Roy was wonderful. We were always laughing. He had that grumpy look, and sometimes his temper was short, but usually it didn't mean anything."

The couple was from Haileyville, Oklahoma. To avoid becoming a coal miner likes his father, Roy Johnson first became a prizefighter. It wasn't long before he understood that this was as tough a way to earn a living as digging coal, and turned to baseball, and pitching. He was a big-leaguer for one season, with Connie Mack's last-place Philadelphia A's of 1918. The baseball encyclopedia attests that Johnson won one game and lost five.

Fanetta Johnson recalled how Roy would tell about pitching to Babe Ruth, who was then still primarily a pitcher but making a reputation as a slugger with the Boston Red Sox.

"Roy said that Mr. Mack told him, 'This guy can hit,'" recalled Mrs. Johnson. "He said, 'Don't give him anything. Make him bite. Or walk him if you have to.' Roy threw and the Babe hit the ball 400 feet into the last row of the bleachers. Roy said, 'It might have cleared the Bunker Hill monument, but at least I didn't walk him.'"

After 1918, Johnson spent many years in the minor leagues in a classic itinerant baseball life—playing, coaching, and then managing, in towns like Bisbee, Arizona, and Fort Bayard, New Mexico, and Ottumawa, Iowa. In 1935 he was promoted to be a coach with the Cubs.

"Roy loved to work," said Mrs. Johnson. "He was going out with his cane and sitting in a beach chair to scout high school and college games until just a year or so ago. And, you know, when he died he still had his teeth."

"Still had his teeth," I repeated. "That's nice, that's very nice." And I meant it.

Comiskey Park:
On Its Last Pillars

October 1, 1990

CHICAGO, ILLINOIS—The last game in Comiskey Park, the oldest major-league ballpark in America, was played here yesterday afternoon, as the wrecking ball awaits, as it does not just for old ballparks, but for the rest of us, too.

Comiskey Park was the first ballpark in which I saw a big-league game, having been taken there by my father when I was eight years old. It was a Sunday doubleheader at Comiskey Park between the White Sox and the Yankees, and it took place in the summer of 1948, a few months before the *Chicago Tribune* ran a banner headline that declared that Dewey had beaten Truman. I asked my father recently if he remembered taking me to that game. "No," he said, "it was a long time ago."

Absolutely, and yet 42 years seems to have just shot by, as is its wont. And all I can remember about that game, a game Joe DiMaggio probably played in, and Rizzuto and Berra and Henrich, of the powerful Yankees, and, of the last-place hometown White Sox, Luke Appling and Fat Pat Seerey and Taft Wright—all I can remember is this:

The ballplayers kept getting lost on the field. The reason was that my father and I were seated behind one of the many pillars in the park, and the players kept disappearing behind them.

I remember that the green of the field was striking and the peanut vendors were loud but welcome, and as evening came on and the wind blew in from nearby Lake Michigan it grew cold in the grandstands, and even before the first game was over I wanted to go home. Eight-year-old kids aren't as wild about sitting through long ballgames as they're cracked up to be.

In the next couple of years I began spending more time there, traveling with pals by red trolley car from home on the West Side to this old South Side ballpark. We regularly sneaked in through a vendors' gate well before the turnstiles opened, or, if rebuffed, attempted to slip in with a busload of tourists.

Comiskey Park has always seemed a rather scruffy but friendly ballpark. Never scruffier or friendlier, however, than now.

Next season the team will cart its bats and balls and bases across the street to a newly constructed, pinkish facility, bigger than the old one and literally dwarfing it in its shadow.

Maybe this move will be good. After all, the team was going to leave town if city officials didn't help provide for the new ballpark.

Sometimes, though, progress takes a toll in the psyche, and maybe the heart, too.

Sentimentality can be a dangerous luxury, having the property of skewing reality. Yet the ballpark is in fact a Chicago landmark, a landmark with white paint peeling on the exterior and exposing blotches of old brick.

The ballfield—a rough-hewn park for a raffish town—is a city monument of sorts, like the Water Tower on Michigan Avenue, which survived the Fire of 1871, and Al Capone's whisky still on Diversey Avenue.

Comiskey Park, built in 1910, is exactly 80 years old, older even than Fenway Park and Tiger Stadium and its more glamorous, ivy-clad crosstown rival edifice, Wrigley Field, the only other existing major-league parks built before 1920.

"Well, memories won't leave, just the building is going down," said Jerry Reinsdorf, chairman of the White Sox.

He added that there will be a museum in the new park—this park will be torn down to make way for a parking lot for the new one—and that White Sox memorabilia will be encased there.

Maybe there will be a pair of Shoeless Joe Jackson's baseball shoes, or a packet of the chewing tobacco that Nellie Fox, with a cheek the size of a baseball, chewed at second base, and maybe there'll be a photograph of Babe Ruth here hitting the first home run in the first All-Star Game ever played, in 1933.

But it's not quite the same as sitting there and looking out and saying: "There, right there on that upper-deck roof, Hank Greenberg or Jimmie Foxx or Minnie Minoso parked one. And on that mound Bob Feller in 1940 pitched the only Opening Day no-hitter in history."

And unforgettable was that electric moment when Ted Williams was kneeling in the on-deck circle, working the bat with twisting wrists, and watching the pitcher with ferocious intensity.

Through the years, my work had periodically taken me back to Comiskey Park, and I didn't much think about it. But now, with its end in sight, you take another look, as you might at an independent, slightly eccentric old aunt whose charms, the funny hat and cheery circles of rouge on the cheeks, you appreciated only as she began to fail.

The last game at Comiskey Park was played on a crisp, sunshiny fall day. Little was riding on this contest between the second-place White Sox and the fifth-place Seattle Mariners.

Certificates were handed to incoming fans, proof positive of their attendance at this historic game. It was a capacity crowd of 42,849, the game having been sold out for months, and the last of 72,801,381 paying customers over eight decades.

This throng seemed happy to be here, sharing this would-be memory. GOODBYE, OL' FRIENDS, waved a banner on the left-field wall. The mayor, Richard M. Daley, threw out the first ball.

When it was all over, and the White Sox had defeated the Mariners, 2–1, the local players left and then returned to the field and threw some baseballs into the cheering crowd and waved their caps.

Shortly, the fans stood, and to the accompaniment of an organ over the public-address system sang "Auld Lang Syne."

Possibly there were some tears among some of those fans. Then all departed, for the final time here.

For me, I felt a chill as the sun was going down and the lake wind was picking up. Just as I remember it at my first ballgame, 42 years ago, when I was a boy of eight.

The Universe and the
Case of Pete Rose

July 6, 1989

IT WAS NOT A dark and stormy night, it was a dark and somewhat over-cast night, but the rings of Saturn came in remarkably clear anyway through the lens of a large, powerful telescope on Long Island.

The man who owned the telescope, which had been set on a platform on the beach beside his home, had invited friends over to observe close up the latest goings-on in the solar system.

The lights from the house had been turned off, and no lights were on near the telescope, the better, to quote the wolf from Little Red Riding Hood, to see you, my dear. That is, Saturn, and a red giant star, which came in yellowish, and various nebulae.

In the dark, as each person one at a time leaned down and squinted into the viewer and oohed and aahed or said, "I can't quite make it out," someone turned to another and, nearly stepping on his toes in the black night, said, "What do you think is going to happen to Pete Rose?"

Precisely. In cosmic settings come cosmic questions. Thus we attempt to unravel the riddles of the universe.

Still, after nearly four months of virtually daily headlines and news reports, the Rose case remains intriguing to the country.

Could he have been that dumb or that arrogant or that addicted, to gamble on baseball and the Reds?

Will the commissioner be allowed by the courts to make a ruling?

If it were anyone other than a star of this magnitude—a Rose giant, in effect—would he have captured so many headlines, been the cynosure of so many cameras, have dominated so many conversations?

"It's all a tempest in a teapot," said a woman at a July 4th picnic. "I'm tired of it."

"I guess," someone else said, "the problem is that we have so few heroes, that nobody wants to lose another one."

Whether it ought to be or not, we've made heroes of our sports stars, and none more so, and for a longer period, than baseball players.

Baseball, from the turn of the century, was marketed as the National Game. It was the first national sports event that made an impact in the newspapers—before there was any kind of professional football or tennis or basketball or hockey or golf. It was the first to have regularly announced games on radio. It was the first to have cards produced with the likenesses of the ballplayers on them, so that kids could carry around images of their heroes in their pockets.

A paper entitled "An Examination of Professional Baseball Players as Heroes and Role Models" by two University of North Dakota professors, Monty E. Nielsen and George Schubert, was presented at the Baseball Hall of Fame in Cooperstown last month. It quotes Governor Mario M. Cuomo of New York describing the game's significance:

"Baseball, more than any other sport, is a uniquely American tradition that binds generation to generation, unlike any other ritual in society. It's a Little Leaguers' game that major-leaguers play extraordinarily well, a game that excites us throughout adulthood. The crack of the bat and the scent of horsehide on leather bring back our memories that have been washed away with the sweat and tears of summers long gone…even as the setting sun pushes the shadows past home plate."

Elsewhere in the paper, a writer named Richard Crepeau notes some characteristics admired in the American culture that are depicted in professional baseball:

"Morality, truth, justice, opportunity, the self-made man; Horatio Algerism, competition, individualism and team play, initiative, hard work, relentless effort and hustle; instant and automatic action, self-independence, never-give-up-the-ship; respect to proper authority, self-confidence, fair-mindedness, quick judgment and self-control; it is all important that the game be clean; and good sportsmanship."

Pete Rose, who embodied all of these traits; Pete Rose, who played in more winning games than any other major-leaguer dead or alive; Pete Rose, who grew up in an area along the Ohio in which the residents are sometimes called River Rats, and then only a few miles away hit the hit that broke Ty Cobb's hallowed career record; Pete Rose, who only a few years ago reached the absolute apex of national popularity by being on the cover of a Wheaties box, this Pete Rose is now involved in a scandal with charges that he tampered with, or might have jeopardized, this game, this dream, this thing that so many of his countrymen look to as one of the few constants of integrity, of childhood and adulthood, of nationhood, of, well, of universehood, too.

Maybe that's why Rose, like Saturn, remains ever present in our cosmos.

X.

BASEBALL AND WRITING

Painting with Words

SOMETIME IN THE EARLY 1970s while I was in the throes of the young manhood of my career as a sportswriter in New York City, and browsing in a used book store, I happened upon a very slim art volume that would have a significant impact on my life and work. A very slim volume indeed. It consisted of 32 pages of text, followed by color plates of 18 oil paintings and watercolors of landscapes, street scenes, and still lifes (some of which were exhibited in London's Royal Academy) by the author, Sir Winston Churchill. The title of the book was *Painting as a Pastime*.

I was initially attracted to the book more for my interest in Churchill, that canny, paradoxical, invariably fascinating man, than an interest in painting, though I had an involvement in art from the time I was a boy growing up in Chicago. I had occasionally been taken by my parents to the glorious Art Institute there—and introduced to, among other works, the riveting pointillism of Seurat's "A Sunday Afternoon on the Island of the Grand Jatte"—then taking up drawing in grade school, getting a scholarship to the school at the Art Institute, but then casting aside my temperas and brushes to concentrate on the more compelling youthful embrace of chasing ground balls on baseball diamonds and lofting basketballs through hoops on any available courts.

For the used-book bargain—a used-book steal, it turned out—of, as I recall, about five dollars, I bought *Painting as a Pastime*, which was first published as an essay in Churchill's collection of pieces, *Amid These Storms*, in 1932. It tells the story of when Churchill was dismissed from the Admiralty in 1915 and felt lost, "like a sea-beast fished up from the depths." He needed something to occupy his time and mind, and, by happenstance, discovered painting, and took to it, he wrote, "with Berserk fury."

One section of the essay made a particular and stunning impression on me. It concerned enhanced observations of the world around us:

"I was shown a picture by Cezanne of a blank wall of a house, which he had made instinct with the most delicate lights and colours. Now I often amuse myself when I am looking at a wall or a flat surface of any kind by trying to distinguish all the different colours and tints which can be discerned upon it, and considering whether these arise from reflections or natural hues. You would be astonished the first time you tried this to see how many and what beautiful colours there are even in the most commonplace objects, and the more carefully and frequently you look the more variations do you perceive." And Churchill's new view of Nature, such as: "So many colours on the hillside, each different in shadow."

I found this all to be true. I had never before noticed, or absorbed, the drama of, for example, shadows on buildings. In museums and in art books, I keyed in now on what Hopper and Vermeer, for two, did with shadows. Keeping this in mind when I went to cover sports events—and struggling in the never-ending struggle to become a better writer—I would make it a conscious point to look for the variety and the perhaps obvious but generally little-observed particulars of a setting or scene or individual, and to use this, when fitting, in the descriptions of my stories. It was something, also, that the great sportswriter Red Smith would advise young writers: give the reader the sense of "being there." And how better than with vivid detail.

I remember an early and explicit example of this, this aspect, for example, of "noticing shadows." It was baseball spring training, March, 1973, the Mets were playing a game against the Dodgers at Al Lang Field in St. Petersburg, Florida. Willie Mays, the future Hall of Famer then with the Mets, was two months shy of 42 years old, and in his 21st big-league season:

Mays came to bat in the first inning to polite applause from the fans, many of whom were retired and appreciated, I wrote, "an old fellow's efforts." I added that "Mays and his shadow, which was slight in the early afternoon sun, each acknowledged the reception with a characteristically quick wiggle of the bat…He looked lively and light at the plate. His helmet was fastened tight on his head. His knit, concentrating brows, pursed lips, and soft Mets cap stuffed in his left back pocket gave the impression that he was still the ebullient 'Say Hey' kid of Polo Grounds lore.

"The eye deceives. Mays is an aging veteran hanging on…His knees have to be constantly drained, there is gray in his balding head…" In that first time at-bat he managed to crack a double off the left-field wall, but in his second and last time up, on a 3-2 pitch, "he and his shadow took a mighty swing at an outside-corner curveball. 'Whoo,' went the crowd. But Mays' effort was fruitless. He struck out.

"Mays walked back to the bench: his shadow trailed behind. The shadow was longer than before. The sun was lower. It was later in the afternoon."

And that latter shadow, alas, seemed to augur the end: 1973 was Willie Mays' last season as a baseball player.

In reading *The Letters of Van Gogh*, to his brother Theo, I was impressed with Vincent Van Gogh's ability to plumb his heart as well as appreciate his powers of observation. One sentence in particular resonated with me: "You ought to have seen it this week when we had rain, especially in the twilight when the lamps were on and their light reflected in the wet street."

I'm sure I buried some of these views in my subconscious, or even conscious, for when I was in the press box to see a game that would be rained out, I wrote:

"…Rain everywhere. The big black scoreboard is blacker for the wash. The outfield is soaked. Cops stand outside the dugout, their black slickers glistening in the downpour.

"Lights turned on: an ersatz sun which brings no relief from the rain. But the tarpaulin's puddles are now sprinkled with stars. The geometric railings give a glassiness to the stands."

And could I get on my particular paper (later screen) canvas the colors that Churchill sought to get on his, or Van Gogh on his (like the "lemon-yellow lamps" in "The Night Café" that he described in his letters), or on a Gauguin still life? I tried. On a column about the retired Triple Crown winner Citation in a paddock at Calumet Farm in Lexington, I took in the setting: "His handsome bay coat shines in the warm Kentucky sunlight… Pink and white dogwood trees are in blossom. Sycamore, pine, and oak trees are slipping into green coats. Jonquils and tulips and red sage and blue ageratum are blooming in the sweet springtime. Here and there, colts and fillies frolic."

In wishing to see how artists saw, to sharpen my own perceptions, I occasionally interviewed a true-blue artist. One of them was Roy Lichtenstein, in his studio in Manhattan in 1968. I asked how he viewed a sports event.

"Distorted," he said. "My favorite sports viewing is football on color television. And I like to turn the knobs to throw the picture out of focus. You get startling effects. The images are fantastic.

"In fact, the results have sometimes influenced my work. My style is not simply to portray realism, but to parody the style of everyday art and commonplace things. And football sometimes offers elements of brutality and even hostility which may be seen in an artistic or aesthetic way—something tragically beautiful with Baroque entanglements."

In writing about football in October, I took notice of such "entanglements": "The sky can be bright blue or mellow yellow or soft gray with a sharp relief of charcoal clouds…Permit for a suspended moment a nation caught up, eyes raised, mouths agape…at the short flight of a halfback, dangling on a concealed string at the goal line, as a mass of men, waiting for him to descend, crouch with arms wide like the jaws of crocodiles."

I once asked Frank Stella about watching sports:

"I like sitting down on the floor at a basketball game and you're right there when a player puts the ball down on the floor and he goes," he said. "Sometimes you don't know where he's going to go. It looks like he's going to the basket but sometimes he goes into a tangle of arms and legs and bodies and you don't even see the pass, but another player is slamming the ball down into the basket. It's a beautiful mystery. Reminds me of art."

At some point, I began to notice in paintings the look of eyes—like the characters in Munch, with ghoul-like expressions that reveal anxiety, fear, jealousy, inner turmoil; or Renoirs that delineate quiet pleasure, or Rembrandt's self-portraits of an aging man—sometimes, when getting up close to a Rembrandt canvas, you see it's just a simple but deft brush stroke that tells the tale.

"More than 20 years ago," I wrote about Joe DiMaggio, in 1991, a baseball hero who had been retired for 40 years, "Paul Simon wrote a song that included these lyrics: 'Where have you gone, Joe DiMaggio, a nation turns its lonely eyes to you'...A few years ago, in the locker room at Yankee Stadium, before an Old-Timers' Game, a man with thinning white hair, rheumy eyes, in his 70s, was putting on a baseball uniform. He worked his way into the spiked shoes. 'Oh, God,' said Joe DiMaggio, 'these hurt like hell.'"

Or the heart-wrenching story of Ruben (Hurricane) Carter:

"With his one good eye, his left still piercing from behind steel-rim glasses, the black man, the onetime middleweight contender, half-blind because of a botched operation in prison, stood Friday at the lectern in front of an audience of some 400 people in the Austin Hall auditorium here at the Harvard Law School.

"For nearly 19 years he had looked out from behind steel bars until, in 1985, a federal judge in New Jersey determined that he had been unjustly and wrongly convicted and sentenced to imprisonment for a triple murder he did not commit..."

Or a memory of Rich (Goose) Gossage, the fearsome Hall of Fame relief pitcher for the Yankees: "He was built more like a walrus than a goose, big and beefy, wearing a drooping mustache the ends of which were as long as tusks. His ball cap was pulled down so far on his face that hitters saw only the lower parts of his eyes."

Or Michael Jordan, having left basketball to try his hand at professional baseball, and having a tough time of it with the Class AA Birmingham Barons: "'It's been humbling,' he said. And you could see that in his eyes. Gone is that confident sparkle they had at playoff time against Magic's Lakers, or Bird's Celtics, or Ewing's Knicks. 'I just lost confidence at the plate yesterday,' he said, about his three strikeouts on Saturday. 'I didn't feel comfortable. I don't remember the last time I felt that way in an athletic situation…" (Jordan returned to the Chicago Bulls the next year, and led them to three consecutive NBA championships.)

Then there was the felt pool table that I saw when covering a billiards tournament and which was spotlighted by fluorescent lights from the low ceiling. From somewhere in the recesses of my memory, I imagine I was aware of the pool table in Van Gogh's "The Night Café," and I described the pool table in my story as "lushly bathed in green."

Such detail was, I'd like to think, what Ernest Hemingway referred to in his famous interview with George Plimpton in the anthology, *Writers at Work*. Hemingway said he visited museums and was influenced by painters such as Tintoretto, Bosch, Brueghel, Goya, Giotto, Cezanne, Van Gogh, and Gaugin: "I was trying to learn…and was searching for the unnoticed things that made emotions, such as the way an outfielder tossed his glove without looking back to where it fell, the squeak of resin on canvas under a fighter's flat-soled gym shoes…and other things I noted as a painter sketches. These were the things which moved you before you knew the story."

Such, perhaps, is what I took from one of Degas' paintings of a race horse—the thick tail. It was in my story on the three-year-old Secretariat when getting a washing-down in the stable area from his groom, Eddie Sweat, following a good gallop around the track at the Pimlico Race Course in Baltimore in 1973. Secretariat had most recently won the Kentucky Derby and was a favorite for the upcoming Preakness, the second leg in the Triple Crown: "Steam from the warm bath water and the sweat of this beautiful, robust chestnut curled and shimmered in the sun, creating a glow. Don't be misled. This horse may be a great athlete, but he's no angel. He slung his sopping red tail around, devilishly getting Eddie Sweat wet. It was like a kid in a tub splashing water on his mother." (Secretariat went on to triumph in the Preakness and the Belmont Stakes for the Triple Crown.)

Thomas Eakins' "The Wrestlers" perhaps gave rise to my fascination with the ear of the "champeen rassler" Bruno Sammartino: "To peer at an ear of Bruno Sammartino is to look upon an object of awesome and grotesque magnificence. The shape is known as 'cauliflower,' but that renders a sense of the delicate which is altogether what the appendage is not. If the ear were planted, it would be a bulbous potato; if installed, a carburetor. It could also be mistaken for a gnarled fist, a pummeled nose, a mangled toe."

Of hands: a weathered elderly man in top coat and fedora, who was about to pass me and my wife on Second Avenue in Manhattan one morning in 1980, walked with his left hand holding a cane and his right hand in the crook of the arm of his companion, a woman who may have been his wife or daughter. I quietly said to my wife, Dolly, "See him? He was once the toughest man in the world." It was the former heavyweight boxing champion Jack Dempsey, then 85 years old. Upon his death three years later, I recalled those hands in a column:

"They were and were not…the gloved fists that were painted by George Bellows in his famous oil titled 'Dempsey and Firpo.' In that muscular painting…Dempsey, the defending champ, is seen flying backward through the ropes and into the first row of ringside seats from a blow by Luis Firpo… Dempsey, dazed and enraged, would climb back into the ring and knock out Firpo in the second round. They were and were not the hands that, in 1919, some 60 years before, had savagely pounded Jess Willard to win the title.

"'I remember Jack Dempsey's hands,' recalled Theodore Mann, artistic director of the Circle in the Square theater. 'I was a boy of about eight years old, and his hands seemed huge, the biggest hands I had ever seen. My father had taken me to his restaurant on Broadway. This was years after he had retired from boxing. He shook my hand. Funny, I remember that they were not menacing hands. They were kind of comforting."

Myron's sculpture "Discobolus (discus thrower)," Elaine de Kooning's abstract expressionist "Baseball Players" (runner sliding into the plate to avoid the catcher's tag), and Picasso's bull-fighting lithograph, "Jeu de la Cape (matador in a nimble pass with a charging bull)," are among the ideals for me of capturing in a frozen moment of action an athlete's resolve, power, and grace. Perfection in performance, however, will always have a primary association with Nadia Comaneci, who, at the age of 14 in the 1976 Olympics in Montreal, scored the first 10—perfect score—in Olympic gymnastics history, then went on to achieve six more 10s and three gold medals. Five years later the 19-year-old Comaneci was touring the United States in a gymnastics exhibition. I wrote about her in practice at Madison Square Garden, seeking to depict her in such a frozen moment, or, more precisely, moments:

"In a simple, black warmup uniform, her ponytail tied in a shimmery blue ribbon, wearing eye shadow and with red polish on the fingers of her calloused hands, Miss Comaneci elegantly, buoyantly, wingedly whirled through a series of flips, spins, and leaps."

The humor and cubist idiosyncracy in Paul Klee's "Runner at the Goal" made me wonder later if it wasn't an inspiration for a piece on the New York City Marathon in which I concluded with the crowds at the finish line cheering "the pooped and plunging runners home."

A painting at the Museum of the City of New York by John O'Brien Inman caught my attention primarily because of the moon that overlooked ice skaters on an otherwise dark pond. It stayed in memory, surely, when I traveled to interview the Philadelphia Phillies relief pitcher Mitch Williams, who, as he described it, lived, "in the sticks, four miles from paved roads." I began my piece: "A pale moon, like an eavesdropper, had appeared above the modest redwood ranch house here in Hico, in central Texas…"

One of the most unusual artists I've interviewed was former middle-weight world champion, the inimitable Rocky Graziano. After his boxing career ended in 1952, he became a television personality and comedian. But he also became an amateur painter. He was 55 in 1974 when we sat down to talk.

"His face had aged, with that lumpy nose and the eyebrows that were applied, it appeared, with charcoal," I wrote, "and the gentle eyes that one wasn't prepared for in a brawler named Rocky…

"'I like to paint,' he said, ''cause it's very, very—it's sometin' in my life what makes me feel good and it always has since I started wit' it in de reformatory when I was t'irteen. And it was good even for kids, 'cause den you don't have to just be in sports or robbin' or bookmakin' to get along.

"It gives you pride, like you done sometin', like, Ma, look, I made dis pitcher myself…I paint bright. Green and red and white are my favorite colors, believe it or not. Come to t'ink of it, my boxin' robe was green and white. So I always liked dem colors. And red, too. Yeah, t'row red in wit' 'em. Some people who ain't bums and know about art tell me I got good perspective and good coordination. My subjects are anyt'ing I see: a building, a face, a cab passin' by.

"I even done copies of Picasso. He was fantastic. He had guts enough to do stuff people thought was nuttin' but a rag, and he became a champ in his field."

I asked him about Rembrandt. "Oh tree-mendous." Da Vinci? "Un-friggin-belee-vable!"

I asked if he knew Van Gogh. "I don't know the guy," said Graziano. "But I liked his pitchers a lot."

I did a piece about Whitey Ford and Salvador Dali doing a television commercial in an unusual advertising campaign for Braniff Airlines, in which the telling line is, "If you got it—flaunt it." Before the commercial, Ford had never heard of Dali and Dali thought Ford came in two types—automatic and stick shift.

Ford recalled: "Dali had this terrific mustache and kept twirling the tips of it. He called me Vitee. I say to him, 'Now tell the truth, don't you think a knuckleball is muuuuch harder to throw than a screwball?' He mumbles something about how to pitch. Then he says, 'When you got it—flaunt it.' Actually Dali wrote his line on a cheat card. He wrote it just the way he spoke it: 'Ven you god id—flaund it.' Ron Holland, who's one of the heads of the advertising agency who did the commercial, took the card and had Dali sign it. He said he now has an original Dali."

Perhaps it was stories like these that caught the attention of some editors and publishers in areas outside of sports, and who were interested in my doing pieces for them regarding art (including those of *ArtNews*).

In 2006, I was invited to do a piece for *The New York Times'* special Museums section:

"I visited the Museum of Modern Art on a Sunday in early March to see the 'Edvard Munch: The Modern Life of the Soul' exhibition. When the escalator deposited me on the sixth floor, where Munch's paintings and lithographs are hung, I came upon what seemed at first sight like standing room only at Madison Square Garden.

"It was as if half the population of the tri-state area had heard there were free pastrami sandwiches and made a beeline there. I couldn't help recalling what Picasso said was his favorite joke—'Anarchists at drill: When the command is "Left Face," they all turn right. Because they are anarchists.' Well, I could have used a lot of those people I was encountering to do an about-face and leave. But I endeavored. After all, I already had a ticket."

And I was glad I did. It was a ticket into the wondrous and instructive world of art that knowingly or unknowingly I have gratefully possessed for quite some time. I can envision Churchill, with lit cigar, fully understanding.

Red Smith: The Shakespeare of the Press Box

AT THE END OF this millennium, the magazine *Editor & Publisher*, the respected "bible" of print journalism, commissioned a blue-ribbon panel to choose for its special centennial issue the 25 most influential newspaper people of the 20th century. One the final list were publishers like Joseph Pulitzer and Adolph Ochs and Katharine Graham, to be sure, and writers like H.L. Mencken and Walter Lippmann and Ernie Pyle. And one sportswriter: Red Smith.

It was a designation I could not quarrel with. I was an admirer of Red Smith's writing from the time I began reading him in the 1950s as a teenager in Chicago, where I grew up. He appeared in the *Chicago Sun-Times*, one of some 250 newspapers that carried his sports column nationwide, a column that then emanated from his flagship paper, the *New York Herald Tribune*.

Smith could make me laugh out loud from his stories and metaphors (an outfielder leaped for a ball against the outfield wall "and stayed aloft so long he looked like an empty uniform hanging in its locker"), and he could make me contemplative when he composed a kind of legal brief in entertaining prose on a serious subject (when outfielder Curt Flood in 1970 shocked the baseball hierarchy by refusing to accept a trade from the St. Louis Cardinals to the Philadelphia Phillies without being able to seek a team of his choice, even though he was making the then huge salary of $90,000 a year, Smith wrote: "'You mean,' baseball demands incredulously, 'that at these prices they want human rights, too?'")

In time I would learn that he was also called "The Shakespeare of the Press Box," and that his fans included people from Bing Crosby to Bernard Baruch, the brilliant financier and counsel to presidents, from professors who taught him as "literature" in their English classes to truck drivers to housewives to Ernest Hemingway, who, in his novel *Across the River and into the Trees*, write of how one of his characters "was reading Red Smith, and he liked him very much."

And in 1976, at age 70 and now a columnist for *The New York Times*, Smith was awarded the Pulitzer Prize for Commentary, an honor that was widely viewed as long overdue. "In an area heavy with tradition and routine," the Pulitzer citation read, "Mr. Smith is unique in the erudition, the literary quality, the vitality and freshness of viewpoint he brings to his work and in the sustained quality of his columns."

When I went away to college—Miami University in Oxford, Ohio—I had my sights set on becoming a lawyer, for want of something better to do. A quirk of fate sent me in a different direction. It happened this way: a guy living across the dormitory hall from me in my junior year, a fellow named Dave Burgin, the sports editor of the school newspaper, was also a huge fan of Red Smith.

Now, a lot of college boys had *Playboy* centerfolds taped on their walls. Not Burgin. On his wall was a recent cover of *Newsweek* magazine (this was 1959) which featured the face of Red Smith—receding hairline, glasses, small-boned features, and generous, wise, perhaps somewhat skeptical eyes.

The cover headline read: RED SMITH: STAR OF THE PRESS BOX. Burgin and I clearly shared an enthusiasm for Smith. Burgin suggested I take a stab at writing for him on *The Student*. Warily—I had never considered anything like this before—I did. I fell in love with it. And one day I wrote to Red Smith, sent him two of my columns, and, with aplomb, asked for advice. He gave it to me straight, though gently:

"When I was a cub in Milwaukee," he wrote, "I had a city editor who'd stroll over and read across a guy's shoulder when he was writing a lead. Sometimes he'd approve, sometimes he'd say, 'Try again,' and walk away.

"My best advice is, try again. And then again. If you're for this racket, and not many really are, then you've got an eternity of sweat and tears ahead. I don't mean just you: I mean anybody."

I took Smith's best advice and tried again. And again. I sent him a few more of my attempts over the next few years, and, I am pleased to report, he found me improving. So did Dave Burgin, apparently, who elevated me to a columnist on the school paper. When I became a professional, Red Smith and I crossed paths numerous times and developed a friendship. We overlapped at *The New York Times* for nine months, from the time I joined the staff in March 1981 until his death, at age 76, in 1982.

Dave Burgin went on to become one of the distinguished editors in American journalism in the last decades of the century. He was sports editor of the *Washington Daily News*, a city editor of the *Washington Star*, and editor-in-chief of the *Orlando Sentinel*, the *Dallas Times-Herald*, the *Houston Post*, the *San Francisco Examiner*, and the *Oakland Tribune*. He is now editor and publisher of Woodford Press, a book publishing firm in San Francisco, near his home. We have been in touch over the years, and he once told me a story about Red Smith that I still treasure.

"I got a job at the *New York Herald Tribune* just a couple of years after we were in college," Burgin said. "One of my first assignments was with the *Herald Tribune* news service, which was in the middle of the newsroom. The columnists for the paper would send in their pieces by Western Union. I would take them, paste them up in a book, edit them, and then give them to the teletype operator who would punch in the columns, sending them out to the newspapers, like the *Chicago Sun-Times* where you first read Red, and the *Dayton Journal* and the *Cincinnati Enquirer*, where we both read him when we were in school.

"On this day—it was in the summer of 1963—Red was in Philadelphia. He had written a baseball column. He sent it in. It was all very routine. My instructions from the editor, a no-nonsense guy with a quick temper named Tom, were to edit some of the other columnists but leave Red Smith and Art Buchwald alone. I was told, 'They don't need your help.'

"So all I had to do with Red's column was paste it up, put in the dateline, and designate the paragraphs with those copyedited hook-marks. That's it.

"The column comes in four takes. I accidentally transpose the first take with the third take, so that the third paragraph becomes the lead.

"The column is sent out just this way. Red is still in Philadelphia. He gets up the next morning, where the column appears in the *Philadelphia Inquirer*, and, as he routinely does, reads it. Any other columnist would have gotten an uzi and gone looking for me.

"Red just gently waits until he gets back to New York, a couple of days later. He comes into the newsroom, as he does maybe once a week to get his box of mail, to say hello and leave. I see him and I'm standing there with my mouth hanging open. I have no idea what's going to happen to me. Red walks right by me and says hello to Tom, the editor in charge of the news service. Red says, 'Tom, I'm just curious, what was wrong with my column the other day, the one you changed?'

"Tom says, 'What! We didn't change anything, Red.' Then Tom looks right at me. 'What did you do, kid, goddam it? This is Red Smith here.'

"Red says, 'Well, what we have here is transposed paragraphs.' He's low-key, amiable.

"Tom says to me, 'You're on probation! If you ever do anything like this again, you're fired! You're not to edit Red Smith again under any circumstances!'

"And Red says, 'Well, Tom, all I wanted to say was that I thought you made the column better.'

"Then Red turns around and walks out. He doesn't look at me, though he surely knows that I'm standing in fear and about ready to burst into tears. Tom never said another word to me about being fired.

"Red figured out very quickly that I had made a mistake, was sorry about it, and got me off the hook in the most gracious of ways."

I recall this story at some length because it says so much about Red Smith the man and Red Smith the writer. It displays his sensitivity and his ingenious, even poetic way of handling a subject, delicate or otherwise, and getting to the core of a problem rather than flying off the handle. And while he gave Tom a kind of comeuppance, it was not devastating to him ("You made the column better," he said to Tom). Both Tom and young Burgin were left with their dignity—and Dave with his job. It also served Red's self-interest—no small item for a writer—since more care would surely be taken with his column in the future.

While Smith the columnist wrote on subjects from the Olympics to harness racing, from Super Bowls to hoops, from world heavyweight title fights to fishing, it may well be that he loved to write baseball best of all. He became a baseball writer in 1929 for the *St. Louis Star-Times*, covering the St. Louis Browns and later the Cardinals. When he took a job in Philadelphia in 1936, he was also the beat writer for the Phillies and the A's. He did this for 10 years—while also writing columns—until he joined the *Herald Tribune* in September 1945. There he was a sports feature writer for three months before being given the column, and a columnist exclusively he remained for almost 37 years.

He once wrote that the distance of 90 between bases, as devised in 1845 by Alexander Cartwright, is "the nearest to perfection that man has yet achieved. It accurately measures the cunning, speed, and finesse of the base stealer against the velocity of the thrown ball."

And he would think of baseball, as he wrote, "as an evocation of childhood," and recall his playing it in his hometown of Green Bay, Wisconsin: "It was a game played in a pasture lot on hot summer afternoons, leisurely afternoons, and it was great fun, even for nonathletes like me." And "as a boy I never willingly missed seeing a game in the Wisconsin-Illinois League."

He maintained a lifelong enthusiasm for the game. "Baseball is dull only to dull minds," he once wrote. "Today's game is always different from yesterday's game, and tomorrow refreshingly different from today."

Red Smith's view of the people who played these games, his insights into the human condition, or the human comedy, as it were, the stories he weaves and the art of his prose, transcend to a remarkably high degree the timeliness of many of these stories, and they continue to delight. As do the pieces on baseball people away from the ballpark.

Such as when he covered the funeral in Washington, D.C., of the great and gentlemanly fastball pitcher from Kansas, Walter Johnson:

"...Another said, 'Remember the time Ruel and Milan were hurrying to a show with him and some fan spoke to him and held 'em up half an hour? They kept signaling him to break away and when he finally did they gave him hell. He said he was sorry, but the fan was a fellow who grew up in Kansas and knew his sister well and he didn't want to be rude.'

"Milan said, 'I didn't know you had a sister.'

"'I haven't,' Walter said. 'But he was such a nice feller!'"

Or about Jackie Robinson, making a sensational play in an extra inning of a critical, end-of-season game: "the unconquerable doing the impossible."

Or when Reggie Jackson hit three home runs in three consecutive at-bats, and on three straight first pitches, in a World Series game in 1977 against Los Angeles. Red captured the moment with this quote: "I must admit," said Steve Garvey, the Dodgers' first baseman, "when Reggie Jackson hit his third home run and I was sure nobody was listening, I applauded into my glove."

And then there is his widely quoted lead on what is almost universally considered to be the most extraordinary game in baseball history, when on October 3, 1951, Bobby Thomson hit a home run in the last inning of the final playoff game to give the Giants the game, 5–4, and the National League pennant over the archrival crosstown Dodgers:

"Now it is done. Now the story ends. And there is no way to tell it. The art of fiction is dead. Reality has strangled invention. Only the utterly implausible, the inexpressibly fantastic, can ever be plausible again."

Oscar Madison Passes Away

July 6, 2000

IF A SPORTSWRITER PLANS to write his autobiography, and believes he needs a little help, then it would seem natural for him to seek out another sportswriter. That, apparently, was what Walter Matthau did. Oddly enough, Matthau, the Tony Award and Academy Award winning actor, might be the most famous sportswriter of his time, Red Smith, Jimmy Cannon, Jim Murray, and Dave Anderson notwithstanding.

For many, the role of Oscar Madison—"the poker-playing sportswriter and all-around slob," as Matthau described him—created by Matthau in both the Broadway play and the Hollywood film version of *The Odd Couple* in the mid-to-late 1960s, remains by virtue of his acting brilliance the quint-essential sportswriter.

One day some 15 years ago Matthau invited me to lunch at the Beverly Hills Tennis Club. We sat at a table outdoors and under an umbrella. He was, in many ways, the Matthau I had come to know from the screen: intelligent, witty in an understated manner, with sympathetic eyes that took the measure of a man without piercing him, but, unlike Oscar, neatly dressed in a sport jacket, and he knew which fork to use without making a show of it.

We talked generally about sports, about acting, about language—he loved words and recalled reading Shakespeare as a boy and not understanding it fully but being mesmerized by "the rhythm of the language"—and then Matthau, in that familiar gravelly voice, said to me: "Swifty Lazar, the literary agent, tells me that if I write my autobiography, I could make $2 million. If you write it with me, I'll give you half." I was eating a bowl of borscht at that moment and nearly choked on the sour cream.

Though we did work on it, we never completed the book. What we did establish, however, what we shared, was a friendship. We talked often over the years, we met, we corresponded. Then Walter took ill with pneumonia and assorted ailments and was in an induced coma for much of 38 weeks last year. He was released from the hospital and in the last few months rallied, fell back, rallied. Then last Saturday at about 4:00 AM Los Angeles time, I received a heart-wrenching phone call from his wife. I was out of town but she left a message: "It's Carol. It's what you think. Please call." Walter was dead, at age 79.

Matthau once told me that *The Odd Couple* made him a star. "I think without that part," he said, "without doing Oscar, I'd still be doing character roles on Broadway."

Matthau had, by the time the show opened on March 10, 1965, been in more than 30 films, but primarily in supporting roles. He accepted an offer to play Whiplash Willie, the unscrupulous lawyer, in *The Fortune Cookie*, opposite Jack Lemmon, and won an Academy Award.

Matthau was a great sports fan, but, beyond that, he was addicted to gambling on sports. He admitted to being a compulsive gambler. He said that he lost $5 million in his life betting, but he earned more than $40 million. As a young stage actor he lost $185,000 on baseball games to bookies, was threatened by mobsters, and for the next six years paid them back with, he said, "Almost every cent I made."

Matthau would sometimes have 15 television sets going in his home, each with a game on, each with a $5,000 bet on it. He'd scream at the referees, or umpires, when his bet was going south: "You're blind! You're a crook! You're robbing me!"

And then when they called a play his way: "Oh, maybe these guys are honest."

He said that perhaps he worked so hard, and gambled so hard, because he never lost the desperation of trying to overcome poverty from growing up on the Lower East Side. (He recalled conversations with friends at the time: "You think the rats are bad in my house, you should see the rats in that guy's house. You could put a saddle on them.")

Despite gambling, he could enjoy the artistry of an athletic performance, of the drama of the event. He marveled at Kareem Abdul-Jabbar and Willie Mays, among others, but his favorite player, he said, was Chubby Sherman, a classmate of his at Seward Park High School, and the school's basketball ace. "Chubby was a dead shot," Matthau once told me. "And he was blind." Blind? I said. "He could hardly see. He wore glasses, but only off the court. He just got an idea of where the basket was and threw it up and it went in. Uncanny."

Matthau also played sports. He was a center fielder in the Broadway Show League for a play he was in. Henry Fonda, a friend whom he admired and with whom he had spent hours talking about acting, was a spectator at one game. Matthau came running in, as he recalls, "to make a Willie Mays catch," and the ball "hit me right between the legs."

"I went down," Matthau added. "I was writhing in pain, screaming, 'Help me, oh God, help me!' A big crowd gathered and Fonda nudged me with his foot. He said, 'Walter, bring it down a little.'"

Matthau laughed when telling the story. We've all laughed for years with him. Now we shed a tear.

Ode to Marianne Moore

February, 1972

MARIANNE MOORE VIEWED SPORT as it ought to be, and soaringly more. "It is a legitimate triumph as a feat of skill, like writing," she once said.

She valued "self-mastery" and the joy of deep involvement: "I'm foolish about Willie Mays. He is just full of intellectual energy. He kind of lets everything go for the end in view. Quite scientific, and he certainly gets around the bases!"

Marianne Moore, a slight (5-foot-3½), gray-haired woman who favored tricorn hats, died on February 5 at age 84. She was one of America's most celebrated poets. "Her work," T.S. Eliot has said, "is a part of the small body of durable poetry written in our time." She possessed a captivating genius to see and delight in the interweaving of seeming disparities.

In her poem, "Baseball and Writing," she said: "...Writing is exciting/ and baseball is like writing./You can never tell with either/how it will go/ or what you will do."

"Yes," she said in an interview a few years ago, "sport has its counterpart in life, and I can hardly credit a person who thinks sport is mindless. An 'intellectual' who is above sports really isn't an intellectual."

She saw that "sound technique is indispensable to the musician, painter, engineer, mechanic, athlete, fencer, boxer." She could be "carried away" by grace of performance. About the great race horse Tom Fool, she wrote:

"Tom Fool is a 'handy horse,' with a chiseled foot. You've the beat/of a dancer to a measure or harmonious rush/of a porpoise at the prow where the racers all win easily—/like centaurs' legs in tune, as when kettledrums compete;/nose rigid and suede nostrils spread, a light left of hand on the rein, till/well—this is a rhapsody."

"Fortitude," "finesse," "equipoise," "expertness," "the miracle of dexterity," were highly admired by Marianne Moore. She became a solid Dodger fan when watching the "vim" with which Roy Campanella went about his catching chores: "I remember his walking back to the mound to give some earnest advice to the pitcher, Karl Spooner. Then Roy hastened back to the plate. His brisk, confident roll as very prepossessing and I thought, 'I guess I'll have to keep an eye on him.'"

She knew several top athletes personally. The first was Jim Thorpe. In a quirk of fate, Marianne Moore taught typing and shorthand at the Carlisle (Pennsylvania) Indian School. Thorpe was her student in 1912 and 1913.

"James was the most pleasant athlete to watch," she said. "He was so limber and could perform wonderful feats with the grace of a leopard, and then take no credit for his achievements. A very unaffected person. And, you know, he wrote an old-fashioned Spencerian hand, very deliberate and elegant."

She once met Muhammed Ali in a restaurant, and the boxer took her outside and demonstrated his "Ali Shuffle." "Magnificent," she recalled. She developed a friendship with Floyd Patterson, respected his triumph over a troubled youth. Wrote Marianne Moore about Patterson's autobiography, *Victory Over Myself:* "The victory involved 'application and concentration'—age-old formula for results in any kind of work, profession, art, recreation—'powerful feeling and the talent to use it!'"

Perhaps she understood so well the struggles and joys of mind and body in orchestration because she herself had participated in sports.

On learning to ride a bicycle as a teenager: "Riding itself was hard, but I delighted in sweeping down smooth roads and looking at trees in blossom. That was worthwhile." She once played tennis almost every day, and often her face "would become scarlet because I was trying so hard...But I had to—after all, I would perish if I couldn't try hard.

"But in sport you must learn to accept grieving situations, like losing by a slight accident. That was nearly unbearable for me. But you can't cry on someone's shoulder. You can't ask people to give credit for what you don't do. Yet I like something I once read in the *Boston Transcript* about a scull race that Harvard had lost. The paper said, 'Win or lose, their speed is marvelous.' Harvard still was a winner in a sense."

In her eigties, in her small Greenwich Village apartment, Marianne Moore would still exercise by swinging from a bar in the doorway of her bedroom. She also had a photograph of Honus Wagner which she valued: "Whenever I'm despondent I turn to this picture. It puts me in good humor. Honus has a look here of impeccable optimism. Maybe that's too general, but he has no chip on his shoulder, not malicious in any way."

She was both buoyant and dogged, and found these traits inseparable from the pursuit of joy in sport and life. This was well-expressed in her pithy poem, "I May, I Might, I Must":

"If you will tell me why the fen/Appears impassable, I then/Will tell you why I think that I/Can get across it, if I try."

Jerry Holtzman: "They Served Ice Cream on Friday"

August 11, 1990

JERRY HOLTZMAN—JEROME HOLTZMAN TO the readers of his baseball column in the *Chicago Tribune*—grew up, like many of us, in a house with kids. Unlike the homes of many of us, the house contained 300 kids, about 150 boys and 150 girls. It was on the West Side of Chicago, and called the Marks Nathan Jewish Orphan Home.

Jerry went to live there when he was 10 years old, with his younger brother and sister, after his father died, in 1936, and his mother, in those dark Depression days, was unable to properly look after her children.

The mind builds its own castles, and its own dungeons, and an orphanage during the Depression conjures the life of Oliver Twist and gruel and water, and stinging raps on the ear. "I thought it was terrific," Holtzman said recently. "The building was about a half-block square, and there was a ballfield beside it, and we had ice cream every Friday night. My wife, Marilyn, says there has to be something wrong with someone who liked an orphanage."

There was pain, certainly, in separation from his family home, but Jerry Holtzman learned somewhere that you try to make the best of a situation, and you do not look back in anger or sorrow or bitterness.

So Jerry Holtzman, now 64, stocky, with a shock of wavy gray hair, eyebrows furry as caterpillars, wearing suspenders and smoking a cigar not quite

413

as long as his arm, has made his way, one of the brightest, most respected men in his profession. So good, in fact, that last Monday in Cooperstown, New York, he was inducted into the writers' wing of the Baseball Hall of Fame.

Once, Holtzman walked over to a ballplayer with a surly reputation and introduced himself. "I'm not talkin' to the press today," said the ballplayer.

"No problem," said Holtzman, lighting his cigar. "Maybe I'll catch you next year. Or the year after that."

Several years ago, Holtzman discovered a way he hoped he could augment his sportswriter's salary. He bought the rights to 10 of the finest sports books, bound them handsomely, and reissued them in a set. "I took a bath on it," Holtzman recalled. Nonetheless, behind a batting cage in Shea Stadium one evening, he was introduced to Nelson Doubleday, who then owned Doubleday & Company. "It's nice to meet a fellow publisher," Holtzman said.

In his remarks at the induction ceremony in Cooperstown, as the ballplayers Jim Palmer and Joe Morgan sat nearby waiting to receive their induction plaques, Holtzman thanked first his wife for her support, and his family, including his three daughters and his son. One of his children wasn't there, however.

"We lost Catherine Ellen six months ago, to cancer, three days before her 37th birthday," said Holtzman. "A day or two before she died, she said to me, 'I'm sorry I won't be with you in Cooperstown, Dad.' She was a much-loved person and an avid baseball fan. I taught her how to keep score when she was a freshman in high school, and she learned to keep an almost perfect scorecard."

It was with still heavy heart that he recalled that, and yet Jerry Holtzman wished to share with those in the modest-sized but packed Cooperstown Central High School auditorium—the ceremonies had been moved indoors because of the pelting rain—the memories of this much-loved person, and something that she loved.

It is like Holtzman himself, a man who hums when he types, who shares with his readers his love of baseball, and of sportswriting. Holtzman said he grew up not with dreams of becoming a baseball player, as many youngsters did, but of becoming a baseball writer. He worked on his high school paper and, he said, discovered he had "a modest flair for writing." He joined the *Chicago Times* in 1943 as a copy boy, immediately after "graduating" at 17 from the orphanage. "They gave me a suit and $10," he said. He spent two years in the Marines, returned to the newspaper in 1946, covered high school sports for 11 years, and then in 1957 became a local baseball writer for the *Chicago Sun-Times*, and moved, nine years ago, to the *Tribune* as its national baseball columnist.

In 1974, Holtzman recorded and edited the sportswriting classic *No Cheering in the Press Box*, a warm and provocative collection of interviews with veteran sportswriters.

"I remember Jimmy Cannon telling me, 'A sportswriter is entombed in a prolonged boyhood,' because we're always writing about youth, the athletes," said Holtzman. "But I also remember Shirley Povich saying that when he was young, all the players were heroes, but it seemed he matured overnight, and stopped writing about the roar of the crowd. I know what he meant."

Another who is also in the baseball writers' wing at Cooperstown discussed the coming honor with Holtzman. "It'll change your life," the man said.

This concerned Holtzman. "I don't want my life to change," he said. "I like it the way it is."

Some Baseball Is the Fate of Us All

SURELY, CLARENCE DARROW AND Robert Frost, if alive today, would be pleased by the revived interest in their lives and work—especially coming as it does on the heels of spring training.

For both Darrow, the powerful defense lawyer, and Frost, the powerful poet, were proof personified that you can take the boy out of the sandlots, but you can't take the sandlots out of the boy.

"Nothing flatters me more than to have it assumed that I could write prose—unless it be to have it assumed that I once pitched baseball with distinction" wrote Frost, at age 63.

"I have snatched my share of joys from the grudging hand of Fate as I have jogged along, but never has life held for me anything quite so entrancing as baseball," wrote Darrow, in his autobiography, published when he was 74.

There has been a celebration, in newspaper and magazine articles and on television shows, of the 100th anniversary of Robert Frost's birthday, March 29. This might almost be expected, since Frost was one of America's finest poets. More unusual is the Darrow revival. On Broadway now, Henry Fonda is playing the iconoclastic criminal lawyer in a one-man play. Darrow died in 1938. For him to be honored today says as much about Darrow as it does about our times.

Looking back, Darrow's humanity, honesty, and pleas for justice in unpopular causes are reassuring today, when sliminess seems the order among our "leaders."

What does this have to do with baseball? In his plea to save the lives of Loeb and Leopold, the boys who committed the "Crime of the Century," as it was called in those hysterical days in 1924, Darrow said: "I know that every influence, conscious and unconscious, acts and reacts on every living organism…I know that life is a series of infinite chances, which sometimes result one way and sometimes another…Before I would tie a noose around the neck of a boy, I would try to call back into my mind the emotions of youth. I would try to remember what the world looked like to me when I was a child…"

Loeb and Leopold, intellectual teenagers who murdered young Bobby Franks to see if they could get away with it, were influenced by their dark interpretations of Nietsche. Darrow, however, could recall his own boyhood which was so influenced by the brightness of baseball, "the perfect pleasure," as he called it.

Later, he spent one year at Allegheny College. "And I came back a better ballplayer for my higher education," he said. "I don't know just when I gave up the game, but I think that it forsook me when I was no longer valuable to my side." He eventually became a lawyer by one of those "infinite chances," or, as Frost wrote in his poem, "The Road Not Taken":

"I shall be telling this with a sigh
Somewhere ages and ages hence:
Two roads diverged in a wood, and I—
I took the one less travelled by,
And that has made all the difference."

In its most healthy sense, sports may give one the courage to be an individual. One's best batting stance, for instance, must be arrived at naturally. It has to feel right. Which doesn't mean therefore one must always go right. John Dillinger was also a fine ballplayer in his pressures from society. Frost suffered great criticism because of his unusual style of writing poetry, as though the earthy people he wrote about were speaking in verse.

All sports interested Frost. He wrote, "Your heart is fully in it. You excel at tennis, vaulting, tumbling, racing, or any kind of ball game because you have the art to put all you've got into it. You're completely alert. You're hotly competitive and yet a good sport. You're having fun, skillfully taking risks, increasing the hazards...Success is measured by surpassing performance, including the surpassing of your former self."

He related this poetry: "The nearest thing in college to the arts is not the classroom," he wrote. "The nearest thing to the arts is the gymnasium and the athletic field."

He also said, "Some baseball is the fate of us all....And I never feel more at home in America than at a ball game, be it in a park or a sandlot."

XI.

PERSONALLY SPEAKING

Hank Sauer and His Glove
that Disappeared

August 27, 2001

THE THEFT OCCURRED IN the summer of 1952. I knew the story—one of the few who did—and Hank Sauer didn't. And I know it caused Sauer, the great Cub slugger of the time, bewilderment as well as an unsettling sense of loss. I read in a magazine after the season that it had.

From that time, when I was 12, and on into my adulthood, I had wanted to confide to Hank Sauer how his glove had just happened to disappear one late morning during batting practice in Wrigley Field. And then one dramatic day, 37 years after the larceny had occurred, I did.

I was reminded of this tale of guilt and criminality when I learned that Hank Sauer died Friday at 84, having suffered a heart attack on the first hole of a golf course in Burlingame, California, near San Francisco.

There was a moment of silence held before the Cubs-Cardinals game in Chicago on Saturday, and well there should have been. Sauer was the first player to be named most valuable player while on a team that finished in the second division—his Cubs finished fifth of eight teams. That was, yes, 1952. Sauer was co-leader in the major leagues with 37 homers and led the majors with 121 runs batted in. He had a fine 15-year major-league career with four teams, but he was so popular in Chicago, where he played seven seasons, that he was called the Mayor of Wrigley Field.

He was a large man—6-foot-3, 200 pounds—with a long, rugged, lined face but not an unkindly one; in another life he might have been a long-shoreman who stood up to the management thugs.

And that was the face—it was unmistakable even after all these years— that I saw on Tuesday evening, October 17, 1989, in Candlestick Park, at around 5:30. It was shortly after the earthquake hit the Bay Area, and the third game of the San Francisco Giants–Oakland A's World Series had been postponed.

The crowd of some 60,000 was streaming out of the ballpark. As I was heading for an exit, here came Sauer from the opposite direction. He even wore a nametag on his white sweater, since he was then a scout for the Giants. He was with a small party, which turned out to be his wife and daughter and son-in-law.

Now, I had been a professional sportswriter for 24 years at that point, and had never once crossed paths with him, though I had kept an eye out for him. I decided, earthquake or no earthquake, this was, finally, my chance.

"Mr. Sauer," I said.

He stopped. "Yes," he replied, with a quizzical smile. Maybe he thought I wanted his autograph, even while a portion of Northern California was collapsing. I introduced myself and then said, "Mr. Sauer, I've got some-thing I'd like to say to you. In private, if you don't mind." He looked at me strangely, excused himself from his family and moved over a few feet to a railing.

"It's something that happened in Chicago in 1952," I said.

"'52—that was my MVP year," he said.

"I know." Then I told him how two kids from the West Side—one 14, the other 12—had sneaked into Wrigley Field through a vendors' entrance early that day and made their way into the dugout. There were no ushers, since the gates had not opened. Sauer came in from shagging balls in the outfield, tossed his glove on the dugout bench, and, hardly noticing the two kids sitting there, went for batting practice.

The 12-year-old took the glove and tried it on, pounding the pocket, thrilled to be inside a major-leaguer's mitt. He handed it to his friend to check out. His friend took the glove, slipped it under his sweater: "Let's get out of here!" He leaped up and ran up the steep ramp leading from the dugout under the stands.

"You crazy?" shouted the younger boy. "That's Hank Sauer's glove! Come back!" The older kid was flying, and then so did the younger boy.

The older boy was not a bad kid—he grew up to be a solid citizen—but temptation had got the best of him. Hank Sauer listened intently. "I—I was the 12-year-old boy," I confessed. Sauer reached out and placed his large hands around my throat.

"You stole my glove," he said, his eyes narrowing.

"No, Hank, I didn't steal it—and I won't say who did—I just wanted you to know that."

Then he withdrew his hands, and broke into a smile. "Thanks for telling me," he said. "I had always wondered. And I'm happy you got it off your chest."

Everyone I've ever spoken to about Sauer has said he was a gentleman, besides being a good ballplayer and a good scout. I don't know what eventually happened to his glove, and it doesn't matter. I'm glad, though, that I told Hank Sauer the story when I did, for I never saw him again.

Jim Bouton and the Author:
Two Baseball Careers in
Opposite Directions

ONE DAY, WHILE IN Chicago, I had noticed in the newspaper that Sullivan High School was playing a baseball game against Lakeview High School. Forty years earlier I had pitched for Sullivan against Lakeview. In fact, before I ever considered throwing a chunk of my life into baseball, I had first given my heart to baseball, playing it in the sandlots while growing up and then in Little League and the Pony League. I played with modest success as a first baseman and as a pitcher. I could throw better than I could hit. And in late March of my freshman year at Sullivan, in 1954, I saw a posting on the bulletin board in the gym that baseball tryouts were to be held. I oiled my glove but had no idea what to expect.

In the spring baseball broke out at Sullivan High School, "broke" being the operative word because indoor practice was a necessity in the winterlike spring of Chicago, and the baseballs that ricocheted off the walls and plaster of the school gym not infrequently collapsed and fell to the floor.

There was no frosh-soph team, as there were at some larger schools, no B team, just the varsity. So if you made the team, you were in there with all the upperclassmen.

The coach of the high school team was called "Nemo" by the players because of his sunny disposition. He was called Nemo when he wasn't in earshot, since Nemo was the name of the grim sea captain in *20,000 Leagues Under the Sea*. When he was nearby, we called him "Coach."

424

His real name was Alex Nemkoff, and I can remember him entering the small Sullivan gym for the baseball team tryouts. Coach Nemkoff wore a plain black baseball cap with no insignia, the bill pulled low to shade his eyes like a riverboat gambler, and, under the bill, one would find a dark scowl, the stub of a dead cigar, and sweatshirt, and a whistle around his neck.

He also carried a baseball bat that in his hands, looked like a dangerous weapon. The gym was filled with players in sweatshirts and jeans and sneakers and baseball caps, to keep the glare of the ceiling lights from their eyes, I imagine. Several balls were being thrown at once, with balls smashing off the metal coverings of the broad windows and careering off the walls as the players dived out of the way. The place resembled a pinball machine.

Nemo began hitting ground balls, the ball bouncing on the wooden basketball floor with an unnatural thud, thud, thud. "Around the horn," Nemo grumbled. "Show some life!" And to a kid who flubbed a fungo: "Hey, buddy, did you ever play organized ball before?"

I made the team and got a uniform with a shirt that didn't quite match the pants—the underclassmen took what we could get from a pile of old uniforms in a back closet. I told the coach that I was available to pitch or play first base and the outfield.

I remember ballgames on cold days in the spring. The wind came whipping in off the lake, and the lake always seemed to be across the street, even when you were miles from it. There were snow flurries. A fire had been lit in a garbage drum behind the backdrop so we could warm our hands. After an inning in an early season game, Rob Sanders came jogging to the bench from his position alongside another outfielder, Herb Fagen. "Gee, Herb," said Rob, "it's cold in right. Is it cold in center, too?"

Nemo wore his low-lying baseball cap and a long overcoat buttoned at the collar. Sometimes he'd shot encouragement: "C'mon, you jokers, get a hit." He'd give a signal to the base runner to steal, and often the runner had forgotten the signals, if he had ever learned them in the first place—in my first couple of years at Sullivan it was that kind of team—and Coach Nemkoff pulled a handkerchief from his pocket and began to wave it at the runner. "Hey," he'd shout, "Steal!" Such macabre humor led us to believe that Nemo wasn't quite the ogre he seemed to want us to believe.

Barry Stein, the pigeon-toed second baseman, often ignored Nemkoff's tactics. He had another agenda. He invariably had money-making schemes that he would discuss at the pitcher's mound. He once tried to convince me to go in on one while rubbing up the ball for me at the pitcher's mound. "Listen to me," he said, "and we'll be farting in silk underwear."

One of our two catchers was Cal Feirstein, a stocky, streetwise guy who looked about 40 years old for as long as anyone had ever known him. Nemo called him "Wooden Arm," because his throws to second base often ended up in center field, and Feirstein accepted the name as a badge of honor. It was hard to insult Cal.

But for all Nemkoff's bleakness, from my view, he had his adherents, especially my cousin Ian, a rangy, 6-foot-3, red-haired third baseman who was a semester ahead of me. Ian believed that Nemo was a good strategist, that our practices were organized, and that if you had talent, Nemo recognized it. He certainly saw talent in Ian. While some others in the school, including the basketball coach, Art Scher, thought that Ian was less than a serious-minded student-athlete ("They thought I was a screw-off," he said), Nemkoff saw an intelligent, solid citizen with leadership qualities and even named Ian player-coach the few times Nemkoff was unable to be at practice.

Years later, when Ian became one of the most highly respected judges in Chicago, the *Chicago Tribune* endorsed his reelection to the Cook County Circuit Court bench and cited his "integrity," "scholarship," and "hard work." So Coach Nemkoff proved to have a certain farsightedness, too.

I characterized myself primarily as a pitcher, though on a team like ours, with limited resources, one had to be prepared to play any position at any time. But I dreamed of pitching for Sullivan one day. As a freshman, though, and a fairly skinny one, I sat on the bench and watched the juniors and seniors play. But one day, about midway through the season, I got my chance, in the last inning of a game against Waller High School. We were getting soundly beaten. "Hey, you! Warm up!" I looked around to see which you he was speaking to. "Yeah, you!" said Nemo. It was me. "You're pitching the next inning."

When I entered the game, I stood on the mound and peered toward home plate. It seemed about seven miles away. Not only was my heart thumping, but I discovered I had made a grave error in warming up on the sideline. I had mistakenly thrown from about 50 feet away, rather than the requisite 60 feet, six inches. I had also warmed up throwing downhill.

When I pitched, it was the Fourth of July. The Waller hitters boomed and rocketed my pitches all over the field. It was all like a dream, and, in retrospect, memory commingles with fact, and I can see that one ball was miraculously caught by an outfielder in a tree; a line drive was snared by an infielder who threw up his glove just in time to save his life; and someone else made another impossible catch, and thus the inning ended. Three up, three down. Nothing to it.

Nemo didn't acknowledge the performance, and, as one game followed another, I didn't pitch again. A few weeks after the Waller game, however, the coach collared me in school on the morning of the last game of the season.

"You're starting against Von Steuben this afternoon," he snarled.

"Sure, coach," I said. And he was gone.

Starting? Van Steuben? They're meaner than Waller!

After two innings, the Sullivan fielders were dying of exhaustion from chasing base hits, and Nemo, scowling by showing uncustomary humanity toward them, yanked his freshman hurler.

I played three more seasons for Sullivan and Coach Nemkoff. And I had some games that I am fairly proud of. One was in my junior year, when I played first base and hit a solid double down the left-field line off one of the best pitchers in the state, Jim Woods of Lane Tech, who led his team that year to the Illinois state high school baseball championship (and he later played briefly in the major leagues as a third baseman for the Cubs and the Phillies). Lane beat us 9–0 in that game in which I hit a double—oh yes, I also popped up and whiffed my other two times at bat.

It also happened that in a game in which I was pitching in early May of 1956, shortly after the Lane game, I was on first base when the pitcher tried to pick me off. I dived back head first, and avoided the tag by jerking my shoulder away from the ball that was being swiped at me. I heard some sounds in my shoulder, like the ripping of clothes. I went back to the mound the next inning and felt a lot of pain, but I finished the game and won, raising my record to 2–1. In the days to come, the shoulder didn't stop hurting. I tried to warm up to pitch a week later but could hardly lift my arm.

I didn't realize it then, but this was the end of my pitching career, such as it was. I was diagnosed as having torn tendons—today, it would be called a rotator cuff. I started at first base the next season and never threw the ball overhand again. I was concerned that my bad shoulder would affect my basketball shooting, but it didn't, for good or ill, because the shot is more of a push than a throw and I didn't stretch the shoulder when looping the ball to the basket.

I learned years later that while I was beginning and ending my pitching career on the North Side of Chicago, over in a South Side suburb, another kid, also a six-foot-tall, right-handed high school junior, was having better luck. In April 1956 two weeks after I had pitched a game against Lakeview, he had pitched a curiously similar one for Bloom High School against Argo. Each of us gave up three runs on five hits and pitched complete games. The difference was, I lost 3–0, and he won 6–3. Six summers later he would be pitching for the New York Yankees and I would be once again working between college semesters on the garbage truck (where I imagined I would have been regardless of any arm injury). That other pitcher's name was Jim Bouton.

I have gotten to know Bouton over the years, and I was intrigued to learn that at age 57 he was still pitching in semipro leagues. After winning 21 games for the Yankees in 1963 and 18 in 1964 (winning a couple of World Series games and pitching in an All-Star Game as well), Bouton lost his fastball, and his career apparently had come to an end when he was released by the Houston Astros in 1970. But a few years later he became determined once again to make it to the big leagues, this time as a knuckleball pitcher. He played for several minor-league teams and then, by the grace of Ted Turner, who appreciated an unconventional spirit—"This Bouton's no dummy," Turner was heard to say—Bouton found himself on the mound for the Atlanta Braves in 1978, eight years after his last big-league appearance. He was 39 years old and won a game for them at the end of the season while losing three. And then, dream realized, he went home. But he has never stopped pitching.

One day not long ago I went to visit Bouton, who lives with his wife, Paula Kurman, in a house on a hill in western Massachusetts. Bouton is still trim and engaging. I asked him how he had done in his outing the night before while pitching for Mama's Restaurant in the Twilight League in Clifton Park, New York. "Not well," he said. "I lost. It wasn't working. My knuckleball made one of its trips out of town and didn't tell anyone. Not a note, nothing. Sometimes I wonder what the hell it's doing."

I had the impression that this is the way I sound when my shot is not on target. I don't know if there are any more baseball pickup games in America, as there might have been a quarter of a century or more ago, but if there were, I could envision Bouton doing exactly what I do with basketball games. Instead, he plays in these semipro leagues, against players including former college and minor-league players and who are some 25 years younger than he.

"When I'm on my game," Bouton said, "they have trouble hitting me. But when I'm not, I get ripped. I can't just throw my scrapbook onto the mound and expect to win."

Are there times now, I asked him, when he returns home and tells Paula, "This is it, I'm hanging up my spikes"?

"It's never that definite," he replied. "I usually say, 'I think it might be over.'"

"And what does she say?"

"Well, she's heard it before. More than once. And she says, 'There, there. It'll be okay.'"

He laughed.

"But I don't say it much anymore," he said.

"Oh, what changed? More confidence?"

"No," he said. "I think she just got tired hearing it. And I guess I got tired saying it. Now I just think it."

"Yes," I said. "I understand."

"I'm scheduled to throw again next week," Bouton told me. "I'm hoping for the knuckler to come back. I'm thinking it just took a vacation. It's happened more than once."

In *Ball Four* Bouton wrote that beautiful, poignant ending that described for all time a ballplayer's love of a sport: "You see, you spend a good piece of your life gripping a baseball, and in the end it turns out that it was the other way around all the time."

Since I have relatively small hands, I can't palm a basketball. But I can grip one with two hands. And I believe that Bouton's baseball metaphor worked for basketball and me, too.

Jim Woods: At 17, and in the Big Leagues

I HAD BEEN LOOKING for Jim Woods, on and off, for years. Long ago, Woods had done the nearly impossible—going straight from high school graduation at Lane Tech, where he was a baseball sensation, to Wrigley Field and the Chicago Cubs, a distance of two miles by bus, but worlds apart. It was 1957; he was 17 years old.

Growing up in Chicago, I'd played against Woods several times—he was my lone connection to the major leagues, my one degree of separation from the big time. When the trail of his professional career faded away, I tried several avenues to locate him, but came up empty. How could someone who'd enjoyed such early fame—he played briefly with the Phillies, as well—just drop from sight? In August 1986 I wrote about him in my column in *The New York Times*: "Most of us have had some connection, however distant, with someone who reached a particular height," I wrote. "And we followed that person's career, knowing that there but for just a little more talent, a little more speed, a little more power, a little more courage and/or a little more brains, go I."

I concluded: "I think about Woods sometimes, think of the homer he hit off me [in a Pony League game] that may still be going, think of him as my link to the major leagues, and that he realized that boy's dream that so many of us once shared.

"And I wonder: Where have you gone, Jim Woods?"

The last time I'd seen James Jerome "Woody" Woods, as the listing in *The Baseball Encyclopedia* has it, was on a dusty baseball field on a warm late afternoon at Winnemac Park, at Foster and Damen on the North Side of Chicago. It was early June of 1957, and our high school teams were playing against each other in a Chicago Public League game, he pitching brilliantly for Lane Tech, I playing a nominal but sincere first base for Sullivan.

Some three weeks later, both of us were graduated from high school, and I—also 17—went to work, that summer before college, collecting garbage for the Fiftieth Ward office of the Department of Streets and Sanitation. Woods, meanwhile, was headed to another part of the city, as I learned from the newspapers: "Cubs Sign Chi School Phenom," read one headline, in the *Sporting News*. Woods didn't just sign a contract; he was going right to Wrigley Field—No. 48, in the dugout alongside Ernie Banks and Bob Rush and Dale Long and Turk Lown. In the same league with Willie Mays and Stan Musial and Hank Aaron.

This jump from a high school sandlot to the big leagues was virtually unheard of for the Cubs and had happened only a few other times in baseball history. But Woods was extraordinary. In 1956, in his junior year, he led Lane to the Illinois state high school championship, pitching and winning the semifinal game, striking out 18 of 21 Belleville batters and giving up just one hit. Less than 24 hours later he was pitching and winning a complete game against Freeburg, and whacking a triple for good measure. When he wasn't pitching he played third base, knocking down fences as a slugger.

When I was in the batter's box facing him, Woods didn't look much different from any of the rest of the teenage boys on either side of the diamond. In his green-and-gray uniform, he stood about six feet tall, and he appeared to weigh 165 pounds or so. He was a redhead, with high, almost gaunt cheekbones, and, though the bill of his green cap was pulled low, shading his intense eyes, he gave the impression that he'd be as comfortable in a 7-Up ad as he was on the spike-scarred mound at Winnemac Park. A right-hander, he threw hard, to be sure, but he seemed to be standing unfairly closer than the 60-foot, six-inch regulation distance from the rubber to home plate.

Yet, as fine a pitcher as he was, he was perhaps an even better hitter, batting .444 in his senior year, with a bunch of home runs. The tales about him circulated from word of mouth to newspaper stories to major-league front offices. At 16, as a third-year high school student, he walloped a home run at Lane Field that sailed through the crossbars on the adjoining football field. (Jerry Krause, the former Bulls general manager and current special baseball scout for the New York Yankees, was a batting practice catcher for Taft High School then, and he recently recalled seeing that blast. "It must have gone 450 feet," said Krause.) Later that summer, in a Colt League World Series championship game held at Comiskey Park, Woods whacked a 370-foot home run (the newspapers reported) into the left-field bleachers.

I had my own dismal experience pitching against Woods. We were 14, playing in the Pony League at Thillens Stadium, that small, well-appointed ballpark on the North Side. I was with the Giants; he was with the Red Sox. I threw my customary quasi-fastball customarily over the heart of the plate, and he smashed a line drive toward the third baseman, who flung up his glove in self-defense. The ball rose over the poor fellow's head and kept rising as the left fielder retreated to the high chain-link fence behind him. The ball sailed higher, over the fence, over the canal that ran behind the fence, over the trees that lined the canal, as I recall. Maybe the ball cracked against the building a block away. I don't remember.

After high school, I casually followed Woods' baseball career. He played two games for the Cubs in 1957, appearing as a pinch runner in each, and never played for them again. The Cubs, as it turned out, had decided to rest their fortunes on another promising third baseman, a kid from Seattle named Ron Santo.

Woods had signed a nonbonus contract with the Cubs for $3,999.99. One more penny and, under the major-league rules, he would have been a "bonus baby," required to spend two years with the major-league team. Under $4,000, and he could be assigned to the minor leagues and—so the theory went—gain valuable playing experience. (With his signing, the Cubs had quietly informed Woods that they'd give him an immediate but brief taste of the big leagues, which, the team's management reasoned, might help him better understand what it would require to make it with the Cubs. They also thought a little media attention on the signing and elevation of a local prep star couldn't hurt from a publicity standpoint.)

After the 1957 season, the Cubs assigned Woods to the minors, where he did reasonably well in places like Burlington, Iowa; Lancaster, Pennsylvania; and Fort Worth, moving up the professional ladder. Then the Cubs traded him to the Phillies, and he played 34 games for Philadelphia in 1960 and '61. He hit two home runs in the span of five days in May of 1961. His future obviously looked bright. He was 21 years old. But his batting average had suffered in the early season—it was just a little over .200—and the Phillies sent him back to the minors. (Oddly enough, it was right after he had gone 2-for-4 against Milwaukee on May 24 with a single and a home run.) Then James Jerome Woods seemed to fade away. I learned that at age 24, in 1964, he was out of baseball.

Over the years, I thought about the spectacular skill it must take to make the major leagues—and stay there. I wondered how Woods felt about his career: Did he despair that he didn't fulfill his promise? Could this be another of those melancholy tales of the golden boy getting too much too soon?

While I'd never actually talked to him when we competed against each other, he seemed like an easy-going guy, never preening. I knew that his home life hadn't been perfect. In high school, he had lived for a time with his mother and stepfather above Emil's Tavern on the 3400 block of Lincoln Avenue, not far from Wrigley Field. His mother worked as a waitress, and his biological father, Jim Sr., with whom he had only a distant relationship, tended bar in a tavern across the street from the ballpark. I learned later that his stepfather, said to be a difficult man, had been knifed to death in a bar fight.

Over the years, I would occasionally ask about Woods from people who knew him. No one seemed to have an answer. Even after my column on Woods appeared in the *Times*, I heard nothing of his whereabouts. Once, I asked Yosh Kawano, the Cubs' longtime clubhouse man, if he remembered Jim Woods. As everyone else had said, he replied, "Oh, a real nice guy." Then he added, "You know, I saw him a few years ago."

"You did?"

"He was handling luggage at a ticket counter at an airport in Miami," Kawano said.

But the Miami phone books had no listing.

Then, in February of this year, 18 years after the column, I got a call from a former Lane Tech teammate of Woods', Bob "Shotgun" Becker, with whom I had been in casual touch. "I found Jim," said Becker. "I told him you'd like to talk with him, and he said, 'Sure, no problem.'"

So I called Jim Woods, and we made arrangements to meet in Turlock, a small California town south of Modesto. His son lived there, and Woods had just bought a three-bedroom house in nearby Keyes. He was retired from the airlines, having been a ticket agent for National, Pan American, and American, and now he drew a livable pension. He'd also been working weekends at a Wal-Mart selling sporting goods, for medical benefits. "When I was asked about my background at Wal-Mart, and told people I played a little baseball, they got all excited," he said. "It was funny. The assistant manager came over, the stock boys came over—everyone came around."

I also mentioned to Woods (I had pointed it out in my column) that I was sure I'd gotten a hit off him in our junior year, when Sullivan played Lane, and he beat us, 8–0, striking out most of our batters. As years went on, I had begun to wonder if I'd only dreamed that little spot of glory. When I remarked on the purported hit to my cousin and former Sullivan teammate, Ian Levin, now a federal judge in Chicago, he told me that he'd collected a hit off Woods in that game, too. That virtually confirmed I'd been dreaming—apparently, everyone who played against him in those days later imagined they'd gotten a hit.

About two weeks later, I flew to California, and Woods, driving a dark-blue Saturn, picked me up in Turlock in front of my hotel. He was wearing, with intended humor, a retro 1957 Cubs cap, with white stripes against the blue background and the big red "C," the style of cap he'd worn in his brief stint with the Cubs. "Good to see you," he said, pleasantly, though I was sure he didn't remember me. He introduced me to his wife, Stella, and we drove to their son's home, where they were staying, since their new house wouldn't be ready for a few weeks.

I looked for the young man I remembered, but didn't quite see him. Woods, of course, had aged, just like the rest of us. He now wore glasses, sported a mustache that was mostly gray, and had put on some 20 pounds since his professional playing days. When he removed his cap, his hair was still red, though a darker shade than in his boyhood. Medication had pretty much controlled his arthritis. And the hip replacement he'd had a few years earlier aided his gait.

Woods was surprised to learn that he had "disappeared." "I just got involved in my life in Florida, and then the same when I moved to California," he said. "I should have kept in touch more with people. But, well, I had a family, and then my son, Jimmy, was a ballplayer, and we followed him wherever he played. He wound up a good left fielder for California State University at Stanislaus, here. I thought he should have been a third baseman, but I didn't want to interfere with the coach. I let it go."

Woods and Stella have been married for 28 years. "She's my third or fourth wife, depending how you look at it," he said, with an easy laugh. He explained that he had married his first wife a second time, in between divorces.

We talked about his baseball career. "I thought that was a huge amount of money the Cubs signed me for—almost $4,000—like all the money in the world," he said, sitting on a padded chair in the living room, a thoughtful look on his face. "I mean, until then I was getting a dollar a day lunch money from my mother. I went out and bought a '57 Ford Fairlane convertible, and a down payment on a home for my mother.

"I had signed the contract on my own, without anyone advising me, or giving me direction. There were no negotiations with the Cubs. I didn't know about such things. And I didn't consider going to college—maybe that would have been best. But everyone I know says that if they'd been offered to play in the major leagues at 17, they would have taken it too.

"It had been my dream to play big-league ball, sure. And I had a chance to sign with almost every team in the big leagues, but chose the Cubs because I'd always been a Cub fan. Used to go to their games and sit in the bleachers. I'd keep score listening to Cubs games on the radio.

"When I first joined the Cubs, I was amazed, when I walked into the big-league clubhouse. You never had to do anything for yourself. People did everything for you. And I saw the center fielder, Jim Bolger, smoking in the clubhouse. I thought athletes didn't smoke. Unbelievable. And in the dugout, that was amazing too. Bob Scheffing was the manager and he swore at the umpires. I always thought you were supposed to be polite to the umpires."

He remembered during batting practice standing in awe at the power and bat speed of Musial and Aaron and Banks. "Chris," Woods remembered telling his friend Jim Christopher, when they were 17, "it's like a magic show."

As for his new teammate Ernie Banks, Woods recalled: "A great guy. He'd try to build my confidence by telling me that I would get a good shot one day. He'd holler on the bench to Scheffing, 'C'mon, put the kid in.'

"In fact, the one time I played in Wrigley Field, with the Phillies, I got as big a thrill as anything out of hearing the old public address announcer, Pat Peiper, say, 'Now batting for Philadelphia, number 30, Jim Woods.' I'd been to a lot of games there with my friends, and now he was announcing me. And all of my friends were there."

Woods didn't get a hit in his lone appearance there, but he did lay down a successful sacrifice bunt that Santo fielded and threw for an error that allowed in the run that won the game for Philadelphia. "So I contributed," Woods said with a smile. And Woods recalled playing third in a game in which Willie Mays hit two triples. "I was taught when running the bases to never look where the ball went, but to listen to your coaches for direction. Well, Willie watched the ball all the way. When you're great, you can break the rules."

Woods sat on the bench for much of the month of September, in 1960, after he'd been called up from Indianapolis, the Phillies' Triple A club. Then Gene Mauch, the manager, summoned him before a game against the Dodgers. "You should do well against the pitcher; he's a left-hander,"

Mauch told Woods, who batted right. The pitcher was Sandy Koufax. Woods admitted to being nervous. "I was so anxious to do well." He struck out twice, before giving way to a pinch hitter. "I had never seen a ball move the way Koufax's ball moved."

He felt he was learning, however, and when he faced Koufax a second time, the following season, he hit the ball hard. "It was in the Los Angeles Coliseum, and I pinch hit and I crushed one—a real shot—that hit the top of the high screen in left-center, a double," he said. "If the screen hadn't been so high it would've been out of there. I was looking for a fastball, and I got it."

Still, as Billy Williams, who played in Burlington with Woods, said: "You have to hit consistently, and, at third base, you have to hit with power too. I guess Jim didn't do it. But I loved playing with him. I especially remember that he could get down and dirty at third. He'd get everything— diving, sprawling, didn't matter. Had a great arm too. Surprised he didn't go further."

So was Woods. "When I was sent down by the Phillies," he said, "I thought I didn't earn that—I had started to hit, but I guess they had other thoughts."

Gene Mauch, now 78 and living in Rancho Mirage, California, recalled Woods and the reason he didn't stay with the Phillies: "Jim was a young guy with potential, and I thought he needed more instruction. The place for instruction was in the minor leagues."

Wherever he played, Woods seemed to run into bad luck at his position. "There was Santo with the Cubs; there was Richie Allen, who later went to first base, with the Phillies," Woods recalled. "And then I was purchased by the Reds and went to Macon in the Class AA Southern League, and there was a young Cuban, Tony Perez, at third—a future Hall of Famer.

"My mother and sister had moved to Miami, and they'd come up to see me play in Macon. But I was spending most of my time on the bench. I was disgusted. Also, by then, I had got married. I was only making about $6,000 a year—$1,500 less than the major-league minimum with the Phillies—and decided that I'd come to the end of the road as a ballplayer, even though I was only 24. You only get so many opportunities, and I had gotten mine. I just didn't hit as well as I had to. When I was offered a job with National Airlines for more money, I took it."

Why didn't Woods try making it as a pitcher? "I just never thought about it after I went into pro ball," he said. "When I look back, I'm kinda shocked that no one even suggested that I walk to the mound. But baseball was different in those days—less, what, detailed? Less businesslike? A lot of things were overlooked."

Woods said that, yes, he wishes he'd had a longer career, but he sees himself as having realized a dream, of making the major leagues.

"I think Jimmy's content," said Stella.

"My dad did great, and I'm proud of him," said his son, Jim Woods Jr., a grade school teacher. "But his career was cut short."

"It's been fun for me to have a father who made the big leagues," the son continued. "I went to a Cubs game against the Giants a few years ago at Candlestick Park and called over Billy Williams, then a coach for the Cubs. I told him I was Jim Woods' son. He got this big smile on his face. And he invited me back to the clubhouse to meet some of the other players, and gave me an autographed ball."

"Funny how things work out," said Woods. "If I hadn't left baseball when I did, I might not have moved to California, might not have met Stella; we might not have had Jim. Yeah, things worked out okay. I have few regrets."

One other thing. When I came into his son's home, Woods, who had his scrapbooks out to help me with the story, fished in a box and pulled out a yellowed copy of the *Lane Tech Daily*, a four-page, comic-book-size newspaper, dated Friday, May 4, 1956. (Lane Tech, remarkably for a high school, published a daily on its printing press.) "You have to read this," he said, with a grin.

The sports page, on the back, detailed the Lane-Sullivan game played the day before, in which Woods had pitched his third straight shutout. Down in the 11th paragraph of the story, there it was: "In the sixth inning after Woods had retired 12 of 13 batters since the first, Ira Berkow and Ian Levin opened with singles…"

No dream. This alone was worth the trip to California.

When I left Woods to return home, I too thought that he'd done well. He seemed happy with his home life and comfortable with himself. As for his baseball career, well, how many guys make the major leagues at all? How many guys live out that boyhood fantasy? And how many guys can say that they cracked a double off Sandy Koufax?

And I recalled that towering home run Jim Woods hit off me in the Thillens Pony League. So he had crushed a pitch off both Sandy Koufax and me. Yes, I thought, yes. I was in very good company.

Face to Face with Denny McLain

June 17, 1970

I STOOD IN THE batter's box facing the pitcher, who happened to be Denny McLain in Bermuda shorts. As he stooped in that classic pose, gloved hand on left knee to get the sign, I waggled my bat. Not so much to get loose—for that was quite impossible—but mostly for effect. I wanted McLain to know that, while I may not be Mickey Mantle, I am certainly not George Plimpton, by God.

This improbable scene took place recently in an early evening on the Lakeland (Florida) High School baseball diamond. McLain is here during his suspension from baseball and works out every day preparing for his return to the Detroit Tigers on July 1.

Every evening around suppertime, with the warm sun down, but still a couple hours left before nightfall, McLain pitches a nine-inning "Piggy Move-Up" game to a ragtag of local high school and college players. His catcher is Jim Handley, the local high school baseball coach who until recently caught in the New York Mets and Tigers farm systems.

The seven fielding positions are taken by the kids, who feel honored as heroes. Handley is permanently behind the plate, fingering signals and calling balls and strikes. McLain stays on the mound, throwing about three-quarters speed, as the rotation continues.

That afternoon, when I learned of the games, I had asked McLain if I might play. "Why not?" he said with a shrug.

441

I confess I was rather excited about the prospect because I hadn't faced a big-league pitcher since I was about 11 years old. It had been something like the 1951 World Series, Yankees versus Giants, played against the wall of the Bryant Elementary School on the West Side of Chicago. Jerry was Vic Raschi, and Allie Reynolds, too. And I, crouched with a bat and the rectangle of strike zone chalked on the dark wall behind me, waiting for Raschi to serve up that Spalding rubber ball, I was Willie Mays.

Now I stood, batting helmet and gym shoes and soft knees, facing the real McLain. I gripped the bat tightly. McLain appears chunky, from 60 feet, six inches away, but becomes formidable as he kicks and whirls and comes around in that graceful, smooth, grooved delivery and the ball popped into Handley's mitt. Strike one.

A breaking ball broke low and outside. I tried to watch the ball all the way, as I had read to do years before in *The Way to Better Baseball*, by Tommy Henrich, the "Old Reliable" of the Yanks. But how magnificently McLain hid the ball. You never saw the white of it until it was traveling plateward.

I fouled off a ball to the right that bounced down and almost into the hazy lake, which was fringed by pine trees dripping moss. The count went to 3-2 and then, staring and frozen, I struck out on an outside fastball. I trotted head down to right field.

Next time up, on the second pitch, I hit it up the middle, past McLain's right, and I ran like hell. I knew I shouldn't watch where the ball was going, but I had to. The shortstop charged over but threw late. I had beaten out a hit!

The inning ended with me stranded on first. But I had another turn at bat. I was up second in the ninth inning. And I was concerned. McLain's pride might be hurt. He told me once that he wants to win at everything, that he'd even whip his mother at Monopoly. (Later, he said with a smile when I bragged a bit, "That *hit*? It took 13 bounces.") His competitive fires burn bright.

At bat again in the growing evening, the fielders seemed far away, while McLain loomed close. His tanned face and arms were dark with sweat, and so was his gray T-shirt with DETROIT TIGERS lettered across the chest.

Quickly, the count came to 2-2. A high, medium fastball push me back. "Oh, gee," said McLain, with feigned anxiety, "I wouldn't want to hit *him*." Meaning a sportswriter. Handley echoed a laugh from behind his mask. I swallowed. (At the time, I did not realize that I had just experienced an authentic brush-back pitch.)

3-2 count. McLain wound up and—my God!—he was coming in *side-arm*. "Where you goin'?" asked Handley, as I strode into the bucket.

The ball came in and, as I swung awkwardly, creakingly, the ball kept coming in. A changeup! By the time it had reached the plate, I had crumpled to one knee.

McLain's smiling white teeth looked very bright against the dark of his face. Yes, I had struck out ignobly, but as I trotted out to right field in the warm haze of the Florida evening, I was absorbed in the already fading details of my hit. I was batting .333 against Denny McLain. I still am, and will be, forever.

Final Countdown: The Fatalism
of the Baseball Writer

February 20, 2005

IT IS ONE OF the rites of early spring, for better or for worse. Many people envy journalists like me who receive an annual card each February from the Baseball Writers' Association of America that entitles the bearer, who, as it states on the front, "is a duly qualified member," to "press courtesies of the clubs of the National and American Leagues of professional baseball clubs." That is, with this wallet-size plastic card, you can get free admission to any major-league baseball game in the world. Of course, you actually have to work once inside the ballpark, but that's another matter.

Sportswriters, though, approach the card's arrival with a certain amount of dread, if not trembling. For they know it's a living symbol of the end of another game—that game being life. Few people in any profession have a clearer indication of where they stand in relation to the eventual embrace of the maker. For printed on the top right-hand corner of my blue-and-white card this year is the number 20. The number is related to seniority. In other words, of the now nearly 800 active members in the association, only 19 writers have been in it longer than I have. Each year, the number gets lower, as in the mind's eye the jaws of eternity widen. I know some writers who refuse to tell their numbers, fearing they would seem old, never mind the bald pate and slowed stride.

Last year I was No. 22. That meager decline may mean—in my imagination, anyway—that time is slowing for me. The drops in the last three years have been the smallest I've experienced in my journey through the dugouts and clubhouses of the nation. I began as a 25-year-old baseball writer for the *Minneapolis Tribune* in 1965, when, according to Jack Lang, the retired longtime secretary-treasurer of the B.B.W.A.A., there were about 800 members. There is no record of the exact number I started at, and I have been saving the cards since only 1983. But in the last 40 years, some 780 newspaper baseball writers or columnists who cover baseball have either retired or died.

Here follows my march to cliff's end—from 1983 the numbers go thusly: 142, 130, 121, 105, 100, 91 (double digits beginning in 1988), 86, 78, 71, 62, 56, 49 (broke the half-century mark in 1994), 45, 40, 36, 32, 31, 29 (broke 30 in 2000), 28, 24, 23, 22, and now 20.

I once asked a writer who had attained card No. 1 what that was like. "Better than the alternative," he replied.

Roger Angell, truthfully but mystically, has written in *The New Yorker*: "Since baseball time is measured only in outs, all you have to do is succeed utterly; keep hitting, keep the rally alive, and you have defeated time. You remain forever young." There has never been a game, of course, that went on forever (the major-league record is 26 innings), although some, even those that go nine innings, feel as if they are going on forever—with all the posturing and scratching of the pitcher and the diggings-in of the batter seemingly searching for buried treasure. But the baseball writer eschews this for a focus on the drama, the beauty, the ambience, the strategies of the contest, and the people in the game.

I've seen the inevitable diminishing of skills, the careers gradually drawing to termination. Even the "immortals," as those enshrined in Cooperstown are known, have not been spared mortality, including those I covered as players, including Mickey Mantle, Catfish Hunter, and Hoyt Wilhelm, and those I covered as managers or coaches, like Ted Williams, Joe DiMaggio, and Casey Stengel. And so, at some point, for the superstars as well as the journeymen, the writer must consider baseball players and his card not morbidly but objectively: there must be a conclusion.

A few years ago, there was an old sandlot player, an 87-year-old baseball fan named Harold, who lay in a Chicago hospital bed with severe heart congestion. The doctor took Harold's son aside and told him that his father had maybe a month or so to live. Should he tell the father? The son said yes, his dad could take the truth, and also, the son could never lie to his father or deal in subterfuge. His father would see right through it. With Harold propped up on a pillow, the doctor related the news to him as gently as he could and then departed.

The son, now sitting alone at bedside, looked at the man who had just been given a literal death sentence. "How do you feel, Dad?" he asked.

There was a brief silence. "Like I told Ma," my father said to me, "nobody lives forever. I'm not scared, and I'm not depressed. I've tried to live a full and good life, tried to do the right thing. I hope I have."

I told him, yes, he had, and then grew emotional. I believe, or want to believe, that Babe Ruth and Red Smith may have felt the same way as my father. As I hope I feel when the number on my baseball card is about to reach 0.

Acknowledgments

TO MY FRIENDS AT Triumph Books, including and especially Mitch Rogatz, Tom Bast, and Adam Motin, with appreciation and admiration for your considerable care with the books you publish, and with the writers who write them.

To the sports editors and the book and magazine editors I've worked with who were particularly instrumental with the pieces in this book: Neil Amdur, Richard Babcock, Sandy Bailey, Bill Brink, Ivan R. Dee, Larry Freundlich, Paul Golob, Lee Gutkind, Sunil Joshi, Jay Lovinger, Laurie Mifflin, Murray Olderman, Sandy Padwe, Arthur Pincus, Rich Rosenbush, Joe Vecchione, and John Walsh.

About the Author

IRA BERKOW, A SPORTS columnist and feature writer for *The New York Times* for 26 years, shared the Pulitzer Prize for national reporting in 2001 and was a finalist for the Pulitzer for commentary in 1988. He also was a reporter for the *Minneapolis Tribune* and a columnist for Newspaper Enterprise Association. He is the author of 25 books, including the bestsellers *Red: A Biography of Red Smith* and *Maxwell Street: Survival in a Bazaar*, and, most recently, *Giants Among Men: Y.A., L.T., Big Tuna &*  *Other New York Giants Stories*. His work has frequently been cited in the prestigious anthology series, Best American Sports Writing, as well as the 1999 anthology Best American Sports Writing of the Century. He holds a bachelor's degree from Miami University (Ohio) and a master's degree from Northwestern University's Medill School of Journalism, and has been honored with distinguished professional achievement awards from both schools. In 2009 he received an Honorary Doctorate of Humane Letters from Roosevelt University in Chicago. Mr. Berkow lives in New York City with his wife, Dolly.